MY TIBETAN CHILDHOOD

TRANSLATION PROVIDED BY

ANGUS CARGILL *and*

SONAM LHAMO

EDITED AND ABRIDGED BY

ANGUS CARGILL

WITH A FOREWORD BY

THE 14TH DALAI LAMA,

TENZIN GYATSO

A FOREWORD BY

RALPH LITZINGER

AND AN INTRODUCTION BY

ROBERT BARNETT

My
Tibetan Childhood

WHEN ICE SHATTERED STONE

Naktsang Nulo

DUKE UNIVERSITY PRESS   *Durham and London*   2014

DESIGNED BY *Natalie F. Smith*
TYPESET IN *Minion Pro* BY *Copperline*

LIBRARY OF CONGRESS CATALOGING-IN-PUBLICATION DATA
Naktsang Nulo.
My Tibetan childhood : when ice shattered stone / Naktsang Nulo;
translation provided by Angus Cargill and Sonam Lhamo;
edited and abridged by Angus Cargill ;
with a foreword by the 14th Dalai Lama, Tenzin Gyatso,
a foreword by Ralph Litzinger,
and an introduction by Robert Barnett
pages cm   Includes index.
ISBN 978-0-8223-5712-4 (cloth : alk. paper)
ISBN 978-0-8223-5726-1 (pbk. : alk. paper)
1. Naktsang Nulo. 2. Children—China—Tibet Autonomous
Region—Biography. 3. Tibet Autonomous Region
(China)—History—1951– I. Cargill, Angus. II. Title.
DS786.N327 2014   951'.5055092—dc23   [B]   2014009913

ON THE COVER: The author and his brother in Chinese clothing
at their first government school. Courtesy of the C. V. Starr East
Asian Library, Columbia University in the City of New York.

CONTENTS

FOREWORD

The 14th Dalai Lama, Tenzin Gyatso

My Tibetan Childhood is the autobiography of a young Tibetan that vividly describes the brutal repression of Tibet by Chinese forces in the 1950s. The author personally witnessed the events he describes in this book, and he records them convincingly and straightforwardly. Today, only a few elderly people remain who can recount these sad events from personal experience. Candid recollections such as these are of great value not only to new generations of Tibetans who want to understand the recent history of their own people but also to readers abroad who are interested in what actually happened in Tibet.

This book, originally written in Tibetan, was earlier translated into Chinese. Now, it has been translated into English. Readers of both Chinese and English who are already familiar with what took place in Tibet after 1950 will recognize what is described here; for others it may be a revelation. Either way, I am sure the candor of these recollections will convince readers of the justice of the cause of Tibet and lead them to lend us their support.

FOREWORD

Ralph Litzinger

In the summer of 2011, I spent a month traveling through the Amdo region, making my way through the present-day provinces of Gansu and Qinghai in the northwest of China. This was about the time that Naktsang Nulo's book, which records in vivid and striking detail memories of his childhood in the 1950s, appeared in Chinese translation in Taiwan. I knew nothing then of this remarkable tale, nor did I know that Tibetans by the thousands had been reading the book, first written and published in a local Amdo dialect in 2007. The purpose of my journey was to visit the families of Tibetan friends in the south of Gansu. We traveled as well to the Labrang Monastery in Xiahe and then made our way overland to the Repkong valley in Qinghai Province. With my twelve-year-old son by my side, and always in the company of Tibetan friends, we traveled by bus and car across some of the very terrain recorded in Naktsang Nulo's book.

The 1950s were not much on my mind. I was making this trip to get a sense of what life was like in Amdo since March 14, 2008, when violent attacks on Han and Muslim shops and antigovernment protests ripped through the Aba region of Sichuan and the Amdo regions of Qinghai and Gansu. For so many in China outside of these regions, the protests and riots of 2008 are slowly being erased from memory. I recall meeting one young man from Beijing, making his way from Lanzhou in Gansu to Lhasa by bicycle, who told me: "I have never understood why the Tibetans were so angry and violent that March. In any case, it doesn't matter. Everything is back to normal. And besides, what we all remember now is the massive earthquake [in May 2008] that leveled towns and schools in Sichuan, and the many thousands who perished. We remember how all of the country wanted to help. It was a terribly sad time, but also a great moment for China." I encountered this sentiment again and again during my travels in 2011.

Within months of that summer trip, a new form of protest began to appear: the self-immolation. To this day, most people in China do not know that since late 2011 more than 120 Tibetans have self-immolated. These "criminal acts," as the Chinese state labels them, are purged from the press within China and forbidden to be discussed at academic conferences in China. It was impossible for me to not come away from my travels with a sense that memories of violence, in almost any period, are forbidden territory. Everything now must be about the future: the new towns built for resettled and displaced nomads, the endless miles of newly paved roads and new railways, the growth of the tourist industry, and the mines that allow minerals and other resources to be stripped from the ground. Harmonious Development and the Chinese Dream, it seems, have little use for certain kinds of troubled history, and certainly no use for Tibetan memories of struggle, protest, violence, forced relocation, and incarceration.

By focusing on the tumultuous decade of the 1950s, Naktsang Nulo beseeches us to remember the past, to resist a half century of enforced forgetfulness, as Robert Barnett puts it in his masterful introduction. As Naktsang tells it, the 1950s were a time of tremendous change: violence, war, exile, survival, and life and death defined so much of the everyday in Amdo and indeed across much of the Tibetan plateau. Told from the perspective of a child, his tale takes us into the complex and at times violent world of Tibetan clans and chiefs. We travel with him and experience the dangers faced on the road: bandits, soldiers, ferocious storms and cold fronts, and hungry wolves. We learn of a child's pain at losing a mother much too early, just as we are invited into the joy a child experiences when aunts and uncles tell him endless stories of the Naktsang family, or when meat or a coat of thick wool is shared to keep a small child from freezing. We learn of Tibetans' love for their domesticated animals, just as we encounter vivid descriptions of a Tibet once populated by wild yaks, antelopes, donkeys, bears, and wolves. We experience what it means for a child to learn the names of sacred mountain passes and peaks; why, for a family on pilgrimage, the places and the events that surround them must be committed to memory. Finally, we learn much of the violence that accompanied the "peaceful liberation" of Amdo and the subsequent "reforms" in the late 1950s, as the ten-year-old Naktsang unsuccessfully flees with his family on yet another dangerous journey across grasslands and perilous mountain passes.

With this powerful memoir of his childhood, Naktsang Nulo's book is a gift to us all. It reminds us that Amdo is alive with memories, especially those that do not fit comfortably into official state historiography. To be sure, his tale will challenge a lot of people in different locations and with different political sensibilities—the exile community, Han scholars of Tibet, the Free Tibet movement, the Western and Chinese media, and Western and Chinese tourists who too easily cling to colonial and neo-Orientalist images of an unchanging spiritual Tibet, the Shangri-la on the roof of the world. However one digests this work, it will force us to return to the forgotten 1950s. This return will stir debate. Most important, it puts Amdo where it properly belongs: at the center of the remarkable, and at times painful, history of China's ethnic borderlands.

INTRODUCTION

A Note on Context and Significance

Robert Barnett

Naktsang Nulo's *My Tibetan Childhood* is both a project of recovery and an act of record keeping. It reinserts long-erased memories into the knowledge bank of younger generations in his community, who until now have had severely limited access to information about their past. And it gives an account, in all senses, of the costs of China's initial state-building project in Tibetan areas a half century ago: with little comment or condemnation, it records the price paid in lives and lifestyles by the author's family and community for their incorporation into modern China. It also serves for outsiders as a vivid reminder that events, even those involving widespread atrocities and occurring at pivotal moments in a nation's history, can be removed from the record in the aftermath of nation-building, lost in the waves of deliberate erasure, ideological preference, and state-driven selectivity that take place at such times.

The author was not a likely candidate for such a project. Born in 1949, he served most of his life as an official in the Chinese government, with successive positions as a schoolteacher, a police officer, a judge, a prison official, and a county leader in relatively remote counties in the eastern Tibetan grasslands until his retirement in 1993. His first and so far only work of literature is an autobiographical account that appears at first glance to be a simple recitation of his experience as a child (Nags tshang 2007). It has so much precision in its details that one scholarly publication categorized it as a "semi-autobiographical novel," on the grounds that no writer could remember his or her youth with such specificity (Latse Library 2008); Naktsang states in his preface and reasserted later that his recollection of these events was clear and that nothing extra had been added to the text.

The work begins with a description of the author's upbringing in a nomad community in the early 1950s and then recounts a six-month, 1,500-mile pilgrimage by the family to and from the Tibetan capital, Lhasa. In the second half, it describes another attempt by the family to make that same journey on horseback across the grasslands to Lhasa, but for a very different reason—to flee from advancing Chinese troops in the autumn of 1958, when the author was ten years old. In the final section of the book, we learn of the consequences of that failed flight, as experienced by Naktsang over the following twelve months as he and those around him were integrated into the new and forceful Chinese state.

The text was written in a plain style without literary pretension, using a colloquial dialect found only in the author's birthplace in eastern Tibet, making this the first book known to have been published in that form of Tibetan. The author described the book as a recollection of a child's experience, and the original cover showed a cartoonlike sketch of a smiling infant with braided hair running down a snow-clad mountainside, as if to emphasize the innocence of the work. And in many senses, it is a naive story, the chronicle of a world seen through a child's eyes. But to readers within Tibet, it was a revelation. It told of epochal events that had rarely if ever been described before in print, and it used a style and approach that ignored the conventions and requirements of history writing in China, let alone in its Tibetan regions.

The book was written in 2005 and 2006 and published a year later by the author at his own expense in Xining, the capital of Qinghai, with a legal publication number indicating that it had official approval. It was limited to internal distribution only (Nags tshang 2011b), meaning that it was not supposed to be made available to foreigners or to Chinese citizens other than officials. This was probably the main reason it was allowed to appear without redaction.[1] The first print run consisted of three thousand copies, but research by Xénia de Heering has indicated that some forty thousand copies were produced in the first two years, almost all of them pirated—about twenty times the normal print run for a book in Tibet, let alone one in a local dialect (personal communication, 2012). This made it a unique phenomenon in modern Tibetan publishing. A version in standard Tibetan was published by Tibetan exiles in India in 2008 (Nags tshang 2008), and a Chinese translation appeared in Taiwan three years later (Nacang Nuluo 2011).

The book appeared in the sunset moments of a relatively relaxed period in the Amdo region, another reason it might have escaped close attention from the censors (Andric 2011; Sulek 2014). But in the spring of 2008, within a year of its publication, many of the towns and villages in the region where Naktsang lived and worked erupted in protest against Chinese rule, leading to dozens of deaths from police shootings and, from 2011 to the end of 2013, to more than one hundred self-immolations, carried out as protests against Chinese rule. The scale of unrest was unprecedented in this area of the Tibetan plateau, which had been largely calm for thirty years. There was no direct link between the book and these waves of protest, but it had emerged just as a sea change was taking place in public opinion among Tibetans. As the first uncensored recollection published within Tibet of events erased by a half century of enforced forgetfulness, it epitomized the process of collective remembering that appears to have transformed and energized Tibetan cultural life at this time, fueling a reemergent and potent sense of nationhood.

— THREE CONCEPTIONS OF TIBET —

The word "Tibet" is used in different ways to describe very different places and societies, and its meaning shifts over time as well as place. Naktsang Nulo's book provides a sketch map of these changes, and at the same time contributes to them and their impact. The Tibetan plateau is a vast area of pastureland, snowcapped mountains, some cultivable valleys, and uninhabitable tundra at an average altitude of some 12,500 feet above sea level, about the size of Western Europe minus Scandinavia, or three and a half times the size of Texas. It has included a number of political entities at different times. From 1642 until 1951, the central part of that plateau and most of its western areas were ruled by the Dalai Lamas, their government, and an aristocracy based in the city of Lhasa, with a rigid social system later defined, somewhat controversially, by the Chinese Communist Party (CCP) as a form of "feudal serfdom." This Tibet had its own army and administration and a long history of effective self-rule over a large part of the plateau. It is this area that Chinese writers and officials refer to as Tibet, and in Chinese the word used these days for Tibet—*Xizang*, literally "Western Tibet"—can refer only to that western half of the plateau ruled by the Lhasa government. In the past Tibetans who lived in the eastern half of the plateau for the most part followed a similar linguistic practice: they generally used the Tibetan word for Tibet, *Bod*, to refer only to the area ruled by the Dalai Lamas to their west, and in many cases still do so.

The eastern part of the Tibetan plateau, an area about three times the size of France, consisted until the 1950s of a plethora of localities and microsocieties differentiated by custom as much as by distinctive governments. They were sometimes seen as principalities, chiefdoms, or tribal areas and were ruled by semi-independent chiefs, local kings or princes, lamas, occasional Chinese armies, and sometimes Chinese Muslim warlords. These areas were known by local names, and there was no single term to describe them as a collectivity. The Chinese language likewise has no term meaning "eastern Tibet" or "eastern Tibetan areas." British officials in the early twentieth century referred to the eastern area as "Inner Tibet," but the Tibetans referred to it mainly by local toponyms or in broad terms as "the upper" or "the lower" areas. Today, in the era of nation-states, single terms for the whole area are much more in vogue, and the northeastern part of the Tibetan plateau is now referred to by Tibetans most frequently as Amdo, while the name Kham is used for the eastern and southeastern areas. Amdo and much of Kham were not consistently ruled by Lhasa after about 1700, although in brief periods up until the 1930s the Tibetan army was able to regain control of one or other border zone in Kham. In this period most of the numerous localities, chiefdoms, and so on within Amdo and Kham fell under the administration of the western Chinese provinces of Sichuan, Qinghai, Gansu, and Yunnan. But Chinese rule in these Tibetan areas was largely nominal until sometime in the late 1950s, as Naktsang demonstrates in his book.

The eastern Tibetan areas are far from Lhasa but are by no means insignificant. Fifty-five percent of the 6.2 million Tibetans currently residing in the People's Republic of China (PRC) live in that half of the plateau. It is of seminal importance in Tibetan religion and economy, and in Tibetan history generally, since much of Tibetan literature was written by scholars from those areas. Many of the most famous monasteries, hermitages, and sacred mountains were located there, and these places produced a succession of leading religious teachers—lamas, as the more senior teachers in Tibetan Buddhism are called—and scholars in Tibetan history. Among them were Tsongkhapa, the founder in the fifteenth century of what is now known as the Gelukpa school, the dominant branch of Tibetan Buddhism, and the current Dalai Lama, the fourteenth in his lineage. In modern times, these eastern areas have continued to dominate Tibetan cultural history, with the most famous modern Tibetan writers since the 1950s, as well as leading Tibetan poets, essayists, and filmmakers, coming from Amdo, the northeastern part of the Tibetan plateau.

Prior to 1950 the histories and politics of these areas were very different from those of Lhasa-ruled Tibet. Naktsang's memoir provides graphic evidence that Tibetans from his area, probably like many eastern Tibetans at that time, regarded the Lhasa government, its aristocrats, and its officials with contempt; their respect and reverence for Lhasa were reserved for its high lamas and its sacred sites. The Tibetan army and its troops were seen as natural enemies, and in one extraordinary episode, hardly imaginable from the many accounts given by Lhasans of their history, Naktsang tells how his group of fellow Amdowans took it for granted while in Lhasa that no official of the Dalai Lama's government had the right to lay a hand on an eastern Tibetan, even if he had committed murder in the capital (chapter 33). There is no suggestion that the accused man in that incident might have been innocent, only that the troops of the Tibetan government had no authority to touch him. This reflects a political reality at the time, demonstrated by the fact that easterners often used the term *Bod* to describe the region or country ruled by the Tibetan government, not to refer to their own areas.

But there were terms used by Tibetans for centuries that referred to the entire Tibetan plateau. They were probably a statement of identity rather than of political organization, a reference to the shared cultural heritage of the Tibetan peoples, and to their common links with the high plateau and its mountains. These were the phrases *Gang ljongs*, *Gangs can*, or *Kha ba can*, all meaning roughly "the Land of Snows." These referred primarily to the shared religion, geography, and customs of the Tibetans on the plateau rather than to a political entity, leading Western scholars to describe this usage of the word "Tibet" as "ethnographic" or "cultural" (Richardson 1962). Today, exiles and their supporters almost uniformly use the word "Tibet" in a third sense: to refer to the entire Tibetan snow-land as a political unit, one that was ruled in the past by a single administration. During its long-running talks with China, the exile Tibetan leadership has formally requested several times that this area should be allowed to have a single Tibetan administration (Central Tibetan Administration 2008); Beijing has vigorously rejected this proposal. There were Tibetans who had argued on pragmatic grounds for such an institution to be set up in the 1940s too, though at that time it was Lhasa that, for pragmatic reasons, had rejected the proposition (see Goldstein, Dawei Sherap, and Siebenschuh 2004). This broader and more controversial usage of the term "Tibet" is not without some historical basis, since from the seventh to the ninth centuries and for a period in the mid-seventeenth century as well, much of the plateau had been unified under the rule of Lhasa. But Naktsang's account of Amdowan attitudes toward the Tibetan army suggests that this idea of a single Tibetan polity was remote from the lives of eastern Tibetans when he was a child: he was unaware of any political linkage between the Tibet ruled by Lhasa and his area of Amdo.

The final sections of his book indicate that such views may have begun to change even during his childhood. The drive of the People's Liberation Army (PLA) to enforce Chinese rule in eastern Tibet in the late 1950s seems to have led to the opposite of its intended effect: facing the experience of invasion, many eastern Tibetans reverted to a probably half-forgotten or perhaps half-invented memory of political unity. When a rebel army was formed by eastern Tibetans in Kham in 1956 in an effort to oppose attacks by Chinese forces on their monasteries and lifestyles, it soon moved westward to join forces with Tibetans in Lhasa and to defend the Dalai Lama; resistance became a national, not a regional, project, one that was political as well as cultural or religious. Similarly, Naktsang describes Tibetans in Amdo attempting to flee to Lhasa in 1958 as resistance spread there too. It was largely the flood of eastern Tibetan refugees in Lhasa as they fled from conflict with the Chinese forces in eastern areas that led to the famous uprising of March 1959 in the Tibetan capital. The failure of that rebellion culminated in the Dalai Lama and about eighty thousand followers seeking refuge in India, where they remain today.

There are thus at least three Tibets—one recognized by China as the administrative area ruled by the Dalai Lamas until 1950 and limited to the western and central parts of the plateau, another referring to the common cultural and historic heritage found throughout the plateau, and a third implying a single political entity covering all the Tibetan areas. It would be unwise for any writer within China today to speak of the third Tibet, and only faint echoes of that notion can be found in Naktsang's book. Nevertheless, whether intended or not, the moral logic of his memoir implies a sense of common purpose among Tibetans, irrespective of their location on the plateau, fueled by their similar experience of Chinese policies in the 1950s. The rapid reemergence of this third idea of Tibet among eastern Tibetans, which became commonplace after the Chinese military and political responses to the protests of 2008, may thus be due not just to exile or foreign propaganda, as Chinese officials have claimed, but to memories of some of the earliest policies imposed by the PRC after their arrival in the 1950s. Naktsang's memoir is the first description of those policies to appear in Tibet that has been widely available, and it is part of, and an inspiration for, the growing recollection of a shared Tibetan past that has reshaped Tibetan thought and politics.

— THE NAKTSANG FAMILY —

Naktsang Nulo, or in full, Naktsang Nuden Lobsang—the name, if rendered literally, means something roughly like "Daring-Good-Mind" or "Capable-Good-Mind" of "the Forest Family"—came from an area about 750 miles northeast of Lhasa. His birthplace was just to the east of a locality known as Golok, which was feared for its ferociously independent nomads, ruled by local chieftains and often associated with banditry and violence, and in the book he is referred to as a Golok by other Tibetans. Throughout recorded history, the Golok area and Naktsang's own birthplace saw little penetration by outside forces, Tibetan or Chinese, apart from occasional military raids, until the PLA finally established its authority there in the 1950s (Horlemann 2002; Sulek 2010). The impact of the PLA's arrival in this area, certainly the first time that Tibetans there had experienced administration by outsiders at the grassroots level, is the most striking and important topic of this book.

Naktsang Nulo's birthplace, Madey Chugama, is a village that today is within a county called Machu, part of the prefecture known in Chinese as Gannan (Southern Gansu) in Gansu Province. His childhood imprisonment and schooling, which are described in the final part of the book, took place in

Chumarleb, a county within Yushu Prefecture, in the neighboring province of Qinghai. It was in Chumarleb that Naktsang was to spend most of his adult life. Between Chugama and Chumarleb lie some three hundred miles of grassland and high mountains, with almost no roads even today. This is the distance that Naktsang and his father and older brother managed to cover on horseback in their desperate forty-eight-day flight from Chugama in 1958 before being captured and imprisoned.

For most Tibetans from these areas, there would have been little or no contact with China or Chinese people before the founding of the PRC. The Chinese were encountered only on rare occasions, such as at times of punitive raids by imperial troops or when visiting a garrison town; Naktsang describes seeing some Chinese soldiers when he was taken as a child on a pilgrimage to see the Panchen Lama (chapter 36). When Tibetans from these nomadic areas traveled to a major town, as we can see from the memoir, they went not to nearby Chinese cities but to Lhasa, even though it was much farther away. That city remained the center of their cultural, religious, and geographic world: we find no mention in the memoir of any city or society to the east. Before the arrival of the PLA, the most important events in the lives of nomads such as Naktsang were not the occasional incursions by Chinese Muslim warlords and their armies but the visits to Buddhist monasteries, which were for them the focal points of their religious life, education, learning, and trade. Many of those monasteries—most famously those of Labrang and Kumbum—belonged to the Gelukpa school of Tibetan Buddhism, and devotees of that school would have revered first the chief lama of the local monastery or tradition and second the Dalai Lama, since he was the most famous and important lama of the Gelukpa school. It was his religious standing that was of significance for these easterners at that time, not his position as the head of the pre-1950 Tibetan state far to their west.

To summarize, the Naktsang family was from the northeastern part of the Tibetan plateau, living within an area currently known to Tibetans as Amdo, and to Chinese as Gannan, part of Gansu Province. While they spoke a dialect similar to that found in other Amdo areas, and thus unintelligible at first encounter to Tibetans from central Tibet, they shared the same literary heritage as other Tibetans, since written Tibetan, the language of the scriptures, was the same in all Tibetan areas. They described themselves according to their clan name or their place of origin, generally using the Tibetan word *Bod pa*, now translated as "Tibetans," only to describe Tibetans from central Tibet. They were followers of the Gelukpa school of Tibetan Buddhism and were devotees in particular of a famous lama, Alak Gungthangtsang, at nearby Labrang Monastery, and thus were indirectly followers of the Dalai Lama too. Like probably one-third or so of the two to three million Tibetans at that time, they were nomads who lived in tents on the grasslands, moving two or so times a year, tending flocks of yaks and sheep, and eating mainly meat and dairy products. They bartered these products with farmers and townspeople in return for salt and barley flour, which they ground and roasted to make *tsampa*, the staple food of all Tibetans. They also lived by hunting, despite their Buddhist faith, which formally forbids killing, and, as Naktsang notes in chapter 13 of this translation (and again in chapter 23 of the original text), despite the serious moral problems that this practice entailed.

After the death of the author's mother and grandparents, his father abandoned nomadism. Instead, he moved with his children, when the author was two years old, from the grasslands to a small house attached to a local monastery in Chugama, where the boy's uncle was a monk. The father then relied on trading, spending lengthy periods traveling and probably using his skills as a hunter and a marksman to obtain rare and ethically questionable products such as deer antlers. These skills seem to have caused him as much trouble as they did local fame, and he is described as running into serious conflict with an official in the monastery at Chugama, apparently because he had carried a gun while on monastic property (chapters 34 and 35).

The Naktsang family had little contact with towns or the outside world except when they went on pilgrimage, and like most nomads felt an extraordinary commitment to their birthplace and to other members of their clan. As the author states repeatedly, the entire book is driven by his overwhelming feeling of attachment to his natal place. The author recollects or restates several times his father's words: "Wherever you go, do not forget your native land and language," and it is the distance between Chumarleb, where the author is to spend his working life, and his birthplace that forms the emotional core of the narrative. In the new China, the book makes clear, that distance was not just a geographic one: after 1958 it was policies, not topography, that had to be crossed in order to traverse it. Once the Maoist administration was finally able to impose itself on the Amdo Tibetans in the autumn of that year, Naktsang, like most citizens of the new China, was no longer allowed to travel freely. We learn from a solitary mention in the text that, after he was sent to school in Chumarleb as a ten-year-old, it was twenty years before he was able or allowed to return to his birthplace in Chugama. In formal terms, the memoir is thus a lament for the author's lengthy separation from his birthplace and his kinsfolk. Whether this is to be considered a personal anguish or to be understood as standing for a feeling of separation from their lost homeland felt by all Tibetans is left for the reader to imagine.

In 1882 the French philologist and scholar of religion Ernest Renan famously pointed out that the formation of new nations and nation-states depends essentially on writing and rewriting history. A nation or a people could not exist, he wrote, without stories of "common glories in the past." His words have been followed by more than a century of academic discussion about the nature of nations and their methods of construction, whether military, political, or epistemic. But his more important insight was not about what was created in the nation-building process, but about what was destroyed. With utter disregard for the romantic sentiment of his time, he identified, perhaps for the first time, the role of forced oblivion in the formation of nations and nation-states:

> Forgetting, and I would even go so far as to say historical error, is a crucial factor in the creation of a nation, which is why progress in historical studies often constitutes a danger for [the principle of] nationality. Indeed, historical enquiry brings to light deeds of violence which took place at the origin of all political formations, even of those whose consequences have been altogether beneficial. Unity is always effected by means of brutality: the union of northern France with the Midi was the result of massacres and terror lasting nearly a century. (Renan 1990 [1882], 11)

Within a few years of Renan's observation, the formation of the Soviet Union demonstrated a modern, efficient form of enforced forgetfulness by creating a society in which a single version of history was written and distributed by the state and a univocal media. It was this model that was put into practice thirty-two years later by the People's Republic of China. "Even more so than the emperors," wrote the sinologist Jonathan Unger, "the Party leaders who entered the former imperial capital in 1949 were determined to control the messages imparted in the works of history—and to bend those messages in ways favorable to official policy lines and to extirpate any manifestation of dissent or opposition that might be hidden within historical allegory" (1993, 2).

For the Chinese leaders who seized power in Beijing in 1949, the priority was to create a historical narrative that showed their enemies (the Nationalists, or Guomindang, led by Chiang Kai-shek) to be irredeemably evil; that showed themselves (the CCP under Mao Zedong) to be the only rightful leaders of China; and that demonstrated socialism as the only correct political and intellectual system. For much of the ensuing sixty years, any versions of history that risked unsettling these tenets were excised by force. After the death of Mao in 1976, the "main melodies" or themes of state propaganda and official history shifted slightly: paeans to the glories of socialism were replaced by accounts of the glories of China as a great nation, and one could read more often of the atrocities of Western imperialists than of cruel landlords or the Guomindang. Since the late 1990s, there have been further shifts; recently, for example, the historical enemy of choice has become Japan rather than the Western powers (Mitter 2000; Unger 1993; Wagner 1990). The amount of leeway allowed to writers and intellectuals increased in 1981 when the post-Mao Party leadership finally declared that the Cultural Revolution, the period of ultraleftist violence and cultural destruction between 1966 and 1976, had been a "comprehensive, long-drawn-out and grave blunder" (Central Committee of the Chinese Communist Party 1981). This allowed Chinese historians and authors to criticize the excesses of that period and led to the emergence of a vibrant form of writing known as "scar literature," in which Chinese intellectuals and former students used short stories, novels, and films to describe the deprivations they had experienced during those ten years, when their schools and colleges had been shut down and they had been sent to spend a decade or more working with the peasants in remote rural areas.

Since this time, other liberalizations have occasionally taken place in Chinese historiography. Official newspapers in China have, for example, recently carried articles noting that the most disastrous of all Mao's policies—the Great Leap Forward of 1958–1961, in which peasants were encouraged to abandon farming in favor of local smelting, leading to millions of deaths from famine—resulted from human error, not inclement weather or Soviet demands for repayments of its debts, as had been claimed at the time (see Becker 1996; Dikkötter 2010; Yang 2012; Zhang 2012). Some Chinese historians and writers have been able to explore the past in ways that offer some complexity or sometimes even challenge certain aspects of official history (see Barmé 1993; Müller 2007). The larger picture, however, remains the same: the history of China is determined by the Party and the state, and the key elements of its narrative cannot be changed except by them.

The work of Naktsang Nulo is of primary importance because this relative relaxation in history writing after the 1980s applied to Tibetans and their history only in extremely limited ways. Most Tibetans, especially in towns, experienced major changes and improvement in their material lives and physical environment as a result of the rapid modernization and economic growth that swept across China from the early 1980s, much like their fellow citizens in the rest of China. But the improvements in public discourse and expression allowed to the ethnic Chinese citizens were much more limited in the Tibetan areas. Relaxation of discussion and resumption of religious life was allowed to some extent in the early 1980s, especially in the eastern parts of the plateau, but writing about recent Tibetan history remained largely confined to endless assertions of socialist glory and national achievement, much as it had been since the 1950s. Even scar literature, commonplace among Chinese, was rarely published by Tibetans, although the depredations of the Cultural Revolution, with its collective smashing of the monasteries and its public violence toward scholars, lamas, and intellectuals of any kind, appear to have been as vicious in Tibetan areas as anywhere in the rest of China.

The restrictions on Tibetan historiography are similar for writers and scholars who are ethnically Chinese, even if they live in the relatively relaxed milieus of Beijing or Shanghai: writing in China about Tibetan history must support the claim that Tibet has been an inalienable part of Chinese territory since the thirteenth century. Books on recent Tibetan history, like novels, films, and other types of art, are expected to depict social conditions in Tibet before the 1950s as a form of living hell for all Tibetans except the elite, with only rare exceptions, and the arrival of the Party and the PLA in the 1950s is always shown as having brought extraordinary benefit to ordinary people in Tibetan areas. As far as I know, no writer within China has ever questioned those benefits in public. In particular, nothing had ever been published there that suggested any wrongdoing by Chinese troops in Tibet in the 1950s or at any other time: the record of the PLA seems to have been considered above debate. Nothing like Naktsang's memoir had ever been seen in print in Chinese within China, let alone in the Tibetan language (de Heering 2013), and even outside China most of its revelations were unprecedented and unforeseen.

— EMPIRE VERSUS NATION —

The histories that have been written both by exile Tibetans and by the CCP have presented relatively simple narratives about the Tibetan past. The exile story was one in which Tibet is seen as an independent country throughout its history until invaded by China in or around 1950 and as languishing under military occupation ever since. The current version maintained by the CCP describes Tibet as having become a part of China in the thirteenth century, although there were earlier CCP versions that dated the incorporation of Tibet into China to the seventh century or even the seventeenth century (Sperling 2009). All the Chinese accounts presented the arrival of the PLA in Tibet in 1950 as a liberation from oppression and as a reunification of the Han Chinese with long-lost fellow nationals, all of whom, apart from die-hard reactionaries and the feudal elite, welcomed their arrival.

The Tibetan version involved much eliding of their complex relations with China in the past, as well as of stark inequities in their social system, while the Chinese narrative involved overlooking Tibet's history of separate governance, its largely autochthonous cultural and social evolution, and earlier forms of obvious national spirit and belief. These forms of forgetfulness were not equivalent: the Tibetan exiles promoted their version through pro-paganda and persuasion, often with endorsement from the work of foreign scholars, while the Chinese version of history was implemented more or less coercively. Even slight divergence from it by people within China could lead to sanctions and imprisonment, and a number of Tibetan writers are cur-rently serving prison sentences for producing histories or essays that suggest Tibet was independent in the past.

Naktsang Nulo's memoir provided an account of history that undermined to some extent the versions told by both sides. It did this not by making any statements about Tibet's political status in the past but by telling that story with some degree of nuance and complexity.

The lack of clarity in the Tibetan situation arises in large part because international relations in pre-twentieth-century Inner Asia were so different from those in Europe at the time, with forms of statehood that were peculiar to imperial systems and not found among nation-states. Relations between nations were articulated through semireligious rituals rather than through written texts or declarations, at least in the Tibetan case. Tibet had become a part of the Yuan Empire, which included China, in the mid-thirteenth cen-tury, an arrangement that lasted for just over a hundred years. At some point in the early eighteenth century, or possibly earlier, it had been incorporated into the Qing Empire, which took over China in 1644. The current claims by Beijing to sovereignty over Tibet are therefore not at all without any ba-sis, though it is hard to say exactly when those claims began or what mod-ern model of interstate relations they resemble. But, even once it was clearly within the Qing domains, Tibet retained the functions of a separate nation in most respects and largely ruled itself, and in modern terms it might be considered something like a protectorate. Because the Qing never established direct rule over Tibet (despite an abortive attempt by their military to do so in 1910), it never became what is now described as an "integral part" of China or the various Chinese empires. The Tibetan government argued in the 1940s and before that Tibet's relations were not with China but between the Dalai Lamas and individual emperors in Beijing. The exile leadership makes the same case now, adding that, according to modern legal standards, Tibet never lost its identity as a separate state while it was within the Qing Empire.

The Qing emperors and the commissioners whom they sent as their rep-resentatives to Lhasa between 1720 and 1911 (who were until the last decade always Manchus or Mongols rather than Chinese) had an important if limited role in the running of government or society there at times of leadership change, crisis, or invasion. But they had a much lesser role at other times, and most Tibetans would never have set eyes on a Chinese or a Manchu, since very few ever lived in Tibet or even visited, other than in border areas.

In Tibetan literature and political documents there are numerous references to the Chinese emperor, who was often said to be ruling over all, yet these same texts always referred to China as a separate country. Tibetan people may have thought of themselves as in some sense under the emperor, if they even knew that he existed, but did not consider themselves a part of China, let alone Chinese.

This premodern form of political relations (the British termed it "suzerainty," later describing this as meaning that Tibet was "autonomous" and that China had only "a special position" there) ended with the collapse of the Qing empire in 1911, when China declared itself a republic. Two years later, following the example of his counterpart in Mongolia, the Thirteenth Dalai Lama, whose forerunners had ruled Tibet since 1642, declared that his country was no longer a Qing colony and was therefore independent. For the next thirty-seven years, Tibet functioned as a separate state in all practical ways. Unlike the Mongolians, however, the Tibetan leaders failed to establish their claim in the international community (Shakya 2012), and once the CCP sent the PLA to take over Tibet in October 1950, the Tibetan army was quickly defeated and the government in Lhasa was unable to get substantive support from any foreign power, leaving it with no choice but to surrender. In May 1951, for the first time in history, it declared in writing that Tibet was a part of China.

Like the majority of Tibetans, Naktsang Nulo was born in an area that was outside the territory ruled by the Dalai Lamas. Since around 1700 or so his area had become a part of a Chinese province and so was in theory under the direct rule of the Qing emperors or their appointees. Imperial administration was, as we have seen, largely nominal in rural areas, and most residents of these vast eastern Tibetan borderlands would have encountered it only rarely, living as they did in largely self-ruling chiefdoms and principalities within a thinly administered frontier zone, with societies and politics that were very different from those of inland China, and in some ways from those of Lhasa too. The histories of these areas and the account given by Naktsang do not fit comfortably with exilic narratives of a plateau-wide independent Tibetan state under foreign occupation or with claims by Beijing that eastern Tibetans had been under effective Chinese administration for centuries.

— HISTORIES OF TIBET IN THE 1950S —

Naktsang Nulo's memoir is one of the first accounts of events in Amdo in the 1950s to appear in English,[2] and the first detailed account of political or military operations there at that time. Most modern biographies of or by Tibetans published in a Western language have been written by Tibetans from Lhasa or elsewhere in central Tibet, usually aristocrats or lamas who fled into exile in 1959 (see Andric 2011; McMillin 2001), and Chinese historians have also focused on events in Lhasa, generally treating events in the eastern Tibetan areas as footnotes to the histories of the western Chinese provinces they are part of, which are majority Chinese. For such reasons, most writing on modern Tibetan history and politics has been about events in Lhasa or the areas around it; in addition, foreign writing has tended to reflect the views of the traditional elite based there. The voices of ordinary Tibetans have been little heard, especially those from the east.

The details of China's annexation of the central Tibetan areas, those then ruled by the Dalai Lama, are thus relatively well known. After the Tibetan army was defeated in October 1950, the Chinese authorities allowed the Dalai Lama and his officials to continue running day-to-day affairs in Lhasa. Beijing also promised to delay indefinitely the implementation of radical social reforms in Tibet, such as redistribution of land to the peasants and the practice of "class struggle." Chinese officials argued that the PLA had been sent to Tibet to "liberate" Tibetans from the threat of domination by Western imperialists, though there were only six foreigners in the country at the time and the nature of the threat they posed was never specified. Once the Tibetan government formally surrendered in May 1951, it was referred to as "the local government of the Tibetan region," and Tibetans were no longer allowed to describe China as a separate country but henceforth had to refer to it as *neidi*, or "the inland area." However, the vast majority of Tibetans, living and working in villages or pasturelands, saw little sign at that time of Chinese soldiers or officials, and their lives barely changed after the arrival of the Chinese troops in 1950.

Beijing's agreement not to impose reforms on Tibetans applied only to the area it considered to be Tibet. The Chinese authorities were thus not breaching any agreement when, in 1955, they first began to impose land distribution and "religious system reform" in those parts of Kham that were within Sichuan Province. These reforms met with resistance from many Tibetans, and this rapidly escalated to major battles between Chinese troops and Tibetans trying to defend their most important monasteries, some of which were bombed by the Chinese air force. As the rebellion spread, a number of Khampa traders formed an army of resistance, which was partly supplied after July 1958 by weapons air-dropped by the Central Intelligence Agency (CIA). Gradually the fighting spread to central Tibet, leading to the armed uprising of March 1959 in Lhasa. Once that had been suppressed by the PLA, China ended the concessions it had promised to the Tibetans in central Tibet as well: radical social reforms were imposed there immediately, and all members of the lay or religious elite who had not escaped, of whatever social level, were dispossessed of any property, "struggled against" (the political practice in China of publicly beating and humiliating a class enemy), imprisoned, or executed.

For the next twenty years, Tibetans were organized into collectives and eventually into communes; gradually, all monasteries were closed down, and almost all monks and nuns forced to resume lay life. From 1966, when the Cultural Revolution began, any remaining monasteries were torn down or dynamited. Former landlords, scholars, teachers, monks, and any others connected to traditional culture were paraded in public and abused, often for days or weeks on end, sometimes leading to their deaths. This continued until around 1976 (some accounts say 1979), when Deng Xiaoping introduced liberalizations that allowed the return of the household economy along with a measure of cultural and religious expression. Tibetans who remained in prisons were gradually released, Tibetan language and religion could again be studied, and over the next twenty years the greater proportion of the destroyed monasteries were rebuilt, largely by local communities.

This history has been elaborated in numerous accounts, including those written by the Dalai Lama and other officials of the former government after they arrived in exile, notably that of Tubten Khétsun (2007). These accounts have focused on events as seen from Lhasa, but some also included information about the fighting that took place in Kham. After 1979, extensive documentation appeared about the three thousand or so Tibetan guerrillas backed by the CIA who staged sorties into Tibet from secret bases in Nepal until 1974. But few of these histories made any mention of events in Amdo. It was generally assumed that the area had been taken over by the PLA after 1949 with little fighting, and that it had been subjected to land reforms and social leveling some seven or eight years later without major conflict. There was little information about opposition or resistance there, and sometimes there were even hints of a vague sense among some exiles that Amdowan Tibetans in general might not have actively resisted absorption into the new regime. Most of the refugees who escaped to India in 1959 were from the central Tibetan areas or from Kham, and it was only when controls on movement were relaxed within China in the 1980s that Tibetans from Amdo began to join the 130,000 or so exiles then living in South Asia.

In 1994, one of those recent arrivals in exile, a senior lama known as Alak Tsayu Tenzin Palbar, produced a history in Tibetan of extensive battles that he said had taken place in Amdo in the late 1950s (Tenzin Palbar 1994). It was, however, a largely technical list of military maneuvers and exile recollections that were at that time hard to verify. It was published only by an exile press in India, with no version appearing in English, and I remember treating it with some puzzlement and even skepticism at the time, since I had heard of nothing like it before and had no other materials with which to compare it. By the late 1990s, however, historians and scholars had begun to realize that major unrest had taken place in Amdo after the PLA advanced into the region. But they had no written materials or images to work with, and most foreign scholars spoke only Lhasa dialect and so could not converse directly with the Amdowan informants arriving in India at that time.

Since then, historians and scholars have been able to bring much more information to light. Although the Amdo region had been largely brought under Chinese control by the end of 1949, a series of uprisings continued until 1953, of which the largest was led by Wangchen Dondrup, the Tibetan *dpon tshang* or headman of the Nangra region, together with Chinese followers of Ma Bufang, the former Muslim warlord of Qinghai.[3] Once these uprisings had been suppressed, there were relatively few conflicts in Amdo for about five years, apart from some smaller incidents in the southern areas neighboring Sichuan, triggered by the fighting that raged in Kham in 1956. This was in large part because the Party officials and the troops who accompanied them to Amdo in those first years had initially been under orders, like their counterparts in Lhasa but unlike those in Sichuan after 1956, not to impose reforms on rural Tibetan communities.

This reticence was a carefully considered strategy of gradualism that Mao and the Party leadership had insisted on in the early 1950s, which one could say reflected a recognition of Renan's insight that you cannot form a nation until a certain kind of story has been instilled in people. In Communist terms, this meant that Party officials needed to wait until the masses had come to see their situation in terms of, first, national liberation and, subsequently, class oppression. But from the earliest days of the CCP there had been fierce debate within its ranks about how long to wait before demanding that radical reforms be enacted. Leftists argued that, since reactionaries and the elite are never really won over anyway, there was no point in delaying radical reforms such as land redistribution and class struggle, and in late 1955 Mao had decided to shift in that direction. He ended the gradualist approach and started a nationwide push for partial collectivization known as the "High Tide"; it was this that set off the reforms in Sichuan and triggered the uprising in Kham that later spread to Lhasa. But Mao's "High Tide" reforms seem not to have been aggressively enforced in Qinghai, and by the summer of 1956 Mao had ordered that the pace of reforms should be slowed or halted across China because of signs that they had failed. There are reports of considerable anxiety among Tibetans and other communities in Qinghai about the initial attempts at collectivization there in 1955, but they did not lead to armed resistance. This seems to be the origin of the perception that Tibetan resistance took place in Kham and Lhasa, rather than in Amdo.

We know now that, just as Alak Tsayu had explained, major fighting took place in Amdo in 1958 (Li and Akester 2013b; Robin 2012). By January of that year Mao had succeeded in outmaneuvering more pragmatic leaders in the CCP and had launched a move to push China decisively on the path of rapid collectivization, under the policy known as the Great Leap Forward. But conflict in Amdo seems to have broken out even before officials had had time to introduce the Great Leap policies there. Fighting began in the Tibetan areas of Gansu Province; by March 5 it had spread to Repkong, an important center in Qinghai. A few weeks later, fighting broke out in Xunhua, where it involved the Salar Muslim community as well as Tibetans and, later, Mongols. By the autumn, fighting was widespread throughout Amdo. According to one official document, out of a population of nineteen thousand in one Tibetan area, several thousand took part in armed resistance. Another reported that fifty-five thousand people in Qinghai were detained for involvement in resistance in this period, with many of them released or posthumously rehabilitated only twenty years later.

In his memoir, Naktsang recalls being told by his father that a number of Chinese land surveyors had been driven out and the troops escorting them killed by Tibetan fighters in a neighboring area (chapter 38), suggesting that land reforms had been attempted there. This supports evidence that in many areas of Amdo, the immediate cause of the uprisings may have been not the radical collectivization policies of the Great Leap but one of the other leftist campaigns being waged around that time. In the areas of Gansu where the Amdo uprising began in the spring of 1958, the trigger was probably a *suku*, or "speaking bitterness" drive, that Beijing had ordered cadres to implement nationwide in August 1957. Such drives required cadres to organize spectacles of public "struggle" or humiliation in which the masses would denounce rich peasants, landlords, and other "bad" elements (Anagnost 1997). In other parts of Amdo, speaking bitterness drives seem to have been first implemented only after fighting had broken out (see Makley 2005; Weiner 2012, 382–390). For the villagers of Chugama, their first encounter with Chinese reform policies and Chinese officials was a drive in 1958 requiring monks to close down their local monastery and destroy the contents, described in chapters 39 and 40 of Naktsang's work. He makes no mention of any earlier visits or reforms by Chinese officials in his home area before that date, an indication that extreme leftist measures were introduced there without any kind of consultation, with little or no explanation, and by force.

Whenever an uprising was quashed, the authorities responded by immediately ending all attempts at gradualism, imposing military reprisals, class struggle, "democratic reforms," and other leftist policies. Naktsang's description of the massacre of the lamas Ganden Wula and Sera Lama with four of their followers in chapters 56 and 57, one of the most gruesome episodes in his book, may read to foreign audiences as a description of mass murder by a wild mob. But it is in fact a rare and important firsthand description of an organized, required "speaking bitterness" event in Tibet, arranged by Party officials as a reprisal for resistance in that community.

The fighting in Amdo continued in many parts of the region until at least 1961, a hidden war that came to represent at times a serious challenge to the Chinese authorities. These events were given due attention by scholars and others only decades later, paradoxically because conditions in the Amdo area after the Cultural Revolution and the death of Mao were far more relaxed than in Lhasa. The eastern Tibetan areas were not greatly affected by the surge of pro-independence feeling in Lhasa after the protests of 1987, with the result that policies in Kham and Amdo remained relatively liberal. Tibetan schools in the Amdo area were allowed to teach in Tibetan language all the way up to the university level; cultural life—poetry magazines, short-story writing, religious publishing, popular music, thangka painting, and filmmaking—flourished to an unprecedented degree; and monastic study and public teachings by lamas were frequent and hugely popular. None of these practices was allowed to any significant degree in central Tibet after the late 1980s.

In the 1990s Western scholars began to flock to Amdo, since controls on movement were less strict there than in central Tibet. Few chose to research politically sensitive issues, since to do so might have jeopardized their visas and would certainly have placed their contacts at risk. But one who did, despite the dangers, was the American scholar Charlene Makley, who lived in Labrang in 1995 (Makley 2005). She found most Tibetans still reluctant to speak openly about the 1950s. As an anthropologist she focused on the social implications of that reticence rather than on piecing together the histories that they had experienced. But her work showed that some people were beginning to talk about what had happened in the area forty years earlier (Makley 2005, 47–50) and provided outline confirmation of the reports published by Alak Tsayu in exile in 1994.

More detailed information came from an exile Chinese writer and essayist living in the United States, Li Jianglin, who, working with the scholar and translator Matthew Akester, collected a trove of previously unpublished official documents that described in detail the battles waged in Amdo from 1958 until 1961 (Li 2012; Li and Akester 2013b). In 2012, the historian Benno Weiner was able to give the first detailed description in English of events in the 1950s in Zekog, a nomadic area adjoining Naktsang's homeland, based on official reports circulated in the 1950s among Party cadres working in the area. These studies describe a major rebellion in Amdo at this time, as well as the reprisals taken against the population and remnants of the traditional local leadership. It is these events, which until recently had been largely overlooked both by exiles and by foreign scholars, that are described in detail in the latter half of Naktsang's memoir.

Nags tshang zhi lu'i skyid sdug—literally, "The Joys and Sorrows of the Naktsang Child"—is in part a detailed description of nomad life in the region before the PLA arrived. Although it is suffused with nostalgia for the pastoral life, it also shows the frequency with which theft, banditry, and killing were encountered, as well as the high risk of death from wild animals and extremes of climate, especially when traveling cross-country. It offers an unusually frank impression of life in Lhasa and central Tibet, where the Golok pilgrims are shocked by scenes of utter destitution and by forms of corporal punishment that even they, no strangers to punitive violence, appear to consider extraordinarily brutal (chapter 29). The nomads operate, even within Lhasa, as an armed militia of their own, subject to no other authority unless they are outgunned, as we have seen, and at one point they kidnap ten soldiers from the Tibetan army, with relatively little concern about the threat of Tibetan troops being sent to pursue them (chapter 33). Yet, back in their home area, we read of the unquestioned power exercised by one official in the local monastery, who sentences Nulo's father to 1,500 lashes for what seems to have been a breach of etiquette. The monk official is able to impose what for most people would be a death sentence without meeting any resistance, even though the father remains armed, other monks openly oppose the punishment, and the father's crime seems to have been extremely minor (chapter 35).

Other insights are given into political conditions at the time. There was clearly little if any presence of Chinese or Hui forces in the author's area before 1958, even though the PLA had taken over Qinghai nine years earlier, and in most ways people in the nomad areas still ruled themselves. Soldiers of the Liberation Army were considered relatively benign, and when the child Nulo is taken to see the Panchen Lama in a nearby monastery, it is a PLA soldier who helps him to receive a blessing (chapter 36). When PLA troops first take up arms against their neighbors, the Tibetans of Chugama, having heard only good accounts of Communist soldiers before they finally meet them in 1958, assume that the attackers must belong to some other Chinese force (chapter 38).

Besides overturning assumptions that Amdo had been relatively untouched by violence and revolt in the 1950s, the book describes measures taken by the PLA against Tibetans at this time, apparently witnessed by the author, that were until now more or less unknown to historians. In some cases, these measures seem to have been a response to armed resistance and so would fit with official Chinese descriptions of PLA troops "suppressing rebellion" and "eliminating reactionaries." But in other cases the violence must have been arbitrary or intimidatory: the author describes on several occasions seeing the bodies of women and children who had been shot dead by Chinese troops, with no indications of conflict from the Tibetan side and the bodies left abandoned on the grassland. This may thus be the first known eyewitness account of atrocities carried out by the PLA in Tibet or elsewhere in China to have appeared in print within the PRC. The description of the underground prison holes with 3,900 occupants in Chumarleb is similarly unprecedented, not because there is any shortage of accounts of abusive prison conditions in China after 1949, but because in this case the mass deaths of prisoners appear to have been more or less an intended feature of the prison design. Much has been written from outside China, but little has appeared within the PRC that has hinted at such phenomena.

Some of these atrocities in Amdo had been referred to in the famous seventy-thousand-character petition written in 1962 by the Tenth Panchen Lama (1938–1989; see Barnett 1997), the highest-ranking lama to have remained in China after the Dalai Lama fled in 1959 and the same person that Nulo had been taken to see as a child at Labrang Monastery. The Panchen Lama, who was himself from Amdo, had been appointed to a very high position in the Chinese government as a reward for not joining the Dalai Lama in exile, and had been allowed to travel back to Amdo to inspect conditions there in late 1961. He had thus been able to see the effects of the reforms and of the Great Leap Forward in that area. Despite his loyalty to the Party, he was shocked by what he found, so much so that his petition remains the most incisive, frank, and strongly worded criticism of the CCP ever written by a leading official while still serving. He spent the next fourteen years in prison or under house arrest as a result. But that petition was an internal memorandum sent directly to China's then premier Zhou Enlai, and through him to Mao, and it remains a top secret document. Until I obtained a single copy in 1996, no one besides very senior officials in China had seen what the Panchen Lama had written, and even now few people in Tibet will have been able to obtain copies from abroad. But even the Panchen Lama had not been able to provide detailed, firsthand accounts of atrocities such as we find in *My Tibetan Childhood*.[4]

The scale of the famine during the Great Leap Forward, when by some accounts between eighteen and forty million people across China starved to death, is relatively well known, and as we have seen, its causes and extent have been gradually acknowledged in the state media. Naktsang's book is the first widely circulated account to give a firsthand account of the famine's impact in a Tibetan area, which apparently included people being forced to resort to cannibalism (chapter 69).[5] In the camp to which the author and his brother were sent, all but 63 people out of a group of 1,600 died from starvation within a three-month period (chapter 61). The author and his brother survived only because of their skill at trapping animals and scavenging. At the same time, we learn that the boys later discovered a large, state-owned herd of sheep nearby, its animals apparently largely untouched throughout the famine. It is representative of the careful tone maintained throughout the book that no comment is made about the terrible irony of this discovery.

Some episodes in the book describe not armed conflict or large-scale disaster but apparently routine political practices at the time. For that reason these represent even more serious criticisms of the Party. The first of these is the destruction of the interior of the monastery at Chugama, which local villagers and monks appear to have been forced to carry out by Chinese cadres and troops within a day of their arrival (chapter 40). At least as the author remembers these events, no reason was given for the destruction of the monastery's statues and ornaments, except that the local masses were said to have demanded that it be done, a demand that we are shown was fabricated by the cadres. This episode rewrites the standard periodization of Chinese historiography, followed in most Western history writing too, which attributes the destruction and closure of monasteries to the ultraleftist era of the Cultural Revolution. But it is clear from this account that this process had begun in Amdo at least seven years before the Cultural Revolution, as the Panchen Lama in his 1962 petition had noted was the case in central Tibet as well (Arjia 2010; Li and Akester 2013a).

My Tibetan Childhood raises other questions about assumptions in exile and Western history writing. It shows that class violence was carried out by some Tibetan nomads to a degree that is almost unimaginable. The killers of Ganden Wula and Sera Lama, with four of their attendants, are described as having carried out the massacre with relish, tearing the bodies to pieces and smashing them on the rocks, presumably because of resentment at having been exploited. The officials who supervised the event intervened only to the extent that they required the mob to first state that their reason for the killings was to avenge former class abuses (chapters 56 and 57). Extreme violence by individual Tibetans toward Tibetans who resisted Chinese rule is also described repeatedly. Conventional exile accounts have in recent years accepted that there were Tibetans involved in such abuses, though not with the degree of violence described here, but incidents of mass Tibetan involvement in class struggle have usually been attributed to the Cultural Revolution, when Chinese Red Guards are said to have traveled to Tibetan areas and created a kind of mass frenzy or psychosis that infected Tibetans too. Those versions depict Tibetan radicals as having acted against their better judgment, or under pressure, or in a kind of mass hysteria. That argument is hard to sustain about events in 1958 in areas where the presence of Chinese troops or officials was irregular or rare, and at a time when there were no Red Guards. Naktsang's story, which probably understates the extent of Tibetan support for China's violent overthrow of the ruling system, therefore raises troubling questions for those who view Tibetans as having been uniformly opposed to Chinese rule, while at the same time raising grave questions about the complicity of the Party and the PLA in these killings.

— THE BEGINNINGS OF REMEMBERING —

It is unclear when knowledge of these events became widespread among younger Tibetans in Amdo. Françoise Robin has argued that memories of this history circulated widely in oral form in Amdo but were overlooked by writers in exile or in other Tibetan areas and by foreign scholars because they were focused on a story that said fighting began in Kham and then spread to Lhasa (personal communication, 2013). Others believe that discussion of these events may only have become commonplace among Tibetans in the 1990s or even later; many of the letters written by younger readers to Naktsang said that they had never known of these events before they read his book (Latse Library 2008, 57). Both explanations are possible. During the twenty years up to 1979, at the height of Maoist rule, it would have been very dangerous for Tibetans to speak about any experiences challenging the state narrative, and it seems that many people who survived that period internalized the fear and self-censorship acquired in those decades and found it natural to keep silent. When the ultraleftist policies were replaced in the late 1970s by the dissolution of the communes and signs that cultural traditions could be practiced again, there was a spectacular resurgence of religious faith and cultural pride among Tibetans: thousands decided to join monasteries or to study Tibetan, and countless numbers revived religious practice in their homes. But the legacy of Maoist control remained evident in the extreme caution shown by some older Tibetans, and no doubt others too, concerning the disclosure of the past, with many survivors in Tibet—especially those who had been involved in the perpetration of violence—retaining an ingrained distrust of others and a lifelong avoidance of personal revelations.

For some Tibetans, this seems to have been because the liberalizations of the late 1970s were understood as conditional, as moves that could be reversed at any time in a given area if certain political lines were crossed. Where these lines might be changed over time had largely to be guessed at, though they certainly included not challenging the Party's right to rule or China's claim over Tibetan territory. Such concerns turned out to be well-founded: key liberalizations allowed in other parts of China were withdrawn in central Tibet after protests erupted in Lhasa calling for independence in the late 1980s. In 1996, officials canceled the tacit permission that had existed for some fifteen years allowing Tibetans there privately to worship the Dalai Lama, and that same year required Tibetan students and government employees to halt any form of Buddhist practice. From 1998, similar bans on worship of the Dalai Lama were beginning to be gradually applied in some monasteries in Kham too, and later in Amdo, even though up until that time those regions had seen few protests in the post-Mao era. Older Tibetans had reason to be cautious and to keep to themselves their personal recollections and opinions. And there was a clearer sign that events of the 1950s were not safe to discuss: official accounts published within China did not refer to any misdeeds by Chinese soldiers or officials in Tibet at any time, an indication that these subjects remained taboo. Survivors may also have assumed their experiences to have been of little interest to outsiders, since history telling by exiles and foreigners had remained largely silent about those events.

Naktsang's book was thus in many ways a revelation, but it was not entirely an isolated phenomenon. By 2007, when the book appeared, the events of the late 1950s were being talked about within Amdo. There was much less reticence among older people about these episodes than when Charlene Makley had tried to interview survivors ten years earlier, and in the summer of 2007 I remember an elderly Tibetan in Yushu telling me, without any prompting, about an incident in 1957 when Chinese troops had opened fire on a group of pilgrims, including him, as they returned to their homes in Yushu from a pilgrimage to Lhasa. In 2006, the Amdo writer Tsering Dondrup had finished writing *Rlung dmar 'ur 'ur* (The howl of the red wind), the first novel to describe the Cultural Revolution in Tibet, based on eyewitness accounts that he had gathered, though it only began to be distributed three years later (Tshe ring Don grub 2009). In 2008, the essayist Chamdo Rinzang produced two book-length collections of similarly frank interviews with survivors of the 1950s (Bya mdo Rin bzang n.d.). These books were published in Amdo without official permission: none of them had ISBN numbers, which each book requires in China, and which can only be obtained after official approval for the book has been received. Unlike Naktsang, whose book was authorized and who so far is not known to have faced repercussions, Tsering Dondrup was removed from his position as the local archivist, and Chamdo Rinzang is said to have been arrested and tortured. The books of both writers reportedly were banned shortly after publication, and there are unconfirmed claims that Naktsang's book was banned after 2011 (Robin 2011, 4, 5).

The impact of Naktsang's work rested not just on the events it described but on his stylistic and intellectual choices as a writer, and it may be these that helped make his book a publishing sensation while at the same time helping to shield him from punishment. Those choices relate to the language used and the moral framework invoked. The book, as we have seen, was written in a colloquial language rarely if ever used before in print, one that can only be understood by fellow Amdowans (hence the version published in standard Tibetan by exiles in India [Nags tshang 2008], so that it can be read by those from the wider Tibetan area). This choice of language gives the book a sense of intense simplicity and an absence of pretension, as if devoid of any intellectual claim. But the primary device that allows the author to diminish the appearance of political purpose is the use of a child as the narrator. As Naktsang put it in his preface, "When I finished the book, I examined it carefully from beginning to end. It seemed to me that the narrative was simply the unvarnished evidence of a young child—what he saw, what he heard, and what he thought. There was no grand description in it or purpose behind it, or even deep analysis of individual character." As in the work of the Iranian filmmaker Kiarostami, the persona of a child is used to describe experiences without contextualizing them.[6] There are judgments, but they are moral, not political. Events are assessed as cruel or kind, good or bad, according to the child's immediate response. We find no ethnic preference—often, Chinese soldiers are described as kind, and Tibetan ones as brutal—and no political justifications: killing a person is wrong whatever the circumstances, except when one has been attacked or when it is done to spare a person from intolerable suffering (chapter 26). In the child's world, political rationalizations for destructive actions do not make sense; only moral values about human relations apply.

In the body of the text, the narrator claims no lofty purpose for his writing. He says only that the book's purpose is to extol the value of respecting the place of one's birth. "Oh native land, my adored home," he writes, "why did I not want to stay with you when I was a child? . . . I am a little boy who has wandered far from home, but in the end I would like to return to you" (chapter 1). The book is thus presented as a story about a boy's wish to return to his home, and the final words reprise the same theme: "'How wonderful that the two Naktsang boys have been able to return to their native land alive,' they will say. My dearest hope is that this day will come." This is the child's voice speaking, with unaffected innocence. The longing for return to one's birthplace is similarly eulogized in other examples of modern Amdo writing, such as the television drama *Su ru'i me tog* (Liu Ren 1984) and the film

'Khren zhen (Phag mo Bkra shis 1993), which are both about Tibetans who are grief-struck because of long separation from their natal homes in Amdo.[7] But Naktsang's decision to depict this theme through the eyes of a child refreshed and renewed this form of nostalgic literature, embedding it within an unstated discussion about nationhood and history, while making his work seem less sensitive politically.

That broader discussion is touched upon in the preface: "If the history of the fathers and uncles is not passed on to the nephews and sons, then the history of the family and even the nationality will be lost before it is heard. This is the importance of writing this book. Now we are getting old, so we must write our history and that of our chiefdom, native land, and nationality before we pass away." This project of national history telling is set in a moral rather than a political context, as if to defuse any provocative implications it might have: the purpose of this national remembering is, he adds, to help avoid war and conflict in the future. "Peace is clearly preferable to war, disease, and hunger for any nation," the author wrote. "Can the next generation keep our country free from these evils?" Even these thoughts are put in the mouth of an imaginary commentator responding to this work. In the foreword to the original Tibetan publication, the author is even more cautious, writing as if the book's primary objective is ethical—to promote understanding of the inevitability of suffering in men's lives. But in the final lines, he again refers very briefly to the importance of providing historical knowledge to the next generation. The book also aims, he says, to teach younger people about "the time of great changes" when "the earth and the sky were turned upside down," since "no detailed account of it can be found in any history book."

Four years later, when the political climate in Amdo and Tibetan areas in general had become more acute, Naktsang wrote an online commentary about the book in which he discussed the importance of knowing the history of one's nationality. There he went much further than before, arguing that such knowledge is essential to create awareness of the need for development, without which, he noted in his most telling statement, a smaller people can be swallowed up by a more powerful one (Nags tshang 2011a; Robin 2011, 5–6). In the main body of the memoir, however, issues of this kind are rarely invoked explicitly. The memoir itself is confined to the perspective of the child, focused on his feeling of loss at his separation from his family and his home. The reader is left to work out any wider purposes and implications for himself or herself.

This narratorial restraint is found not just in the absence of broader commentary but also in the avoidance of specific words and terms. The child's voice allowed the author to quietly set aside conventions about the style and lexicon expected of historians and chroniclers in China, but for any reader there, the absence of these terms is in itself expressive. Works of history and public statements in China typically begin and end each text or chapter with some sort of praise for the Party's policies or with affirmation of a current slogan or opinion. In many cases, a work of history might be relatively free of political or ideological content except for such paragraphs at key points in the text. These would remind the reader, for example, that Tibet has always been part of China, or that life for the masses has improved greatly since liberation. Instead, the book opens with lengthy praise for the pastoral life, with no mention of what in Marxist parlance in China is known as "analysis": the fact that the Tibetan areas belong to China, that society needed liberation, that life improved under Chinese rule, or that the old society was oppressive. It is as if Naktsang's work had been written in a different age and place, a place untouched by the rituals and requirements of socialist writing practices.

This is also true at the level of individual words and phrases. The words "China," "the Party," "Communism," and "policy" are not found in the text. Even the place-names Gansu and Qinghai do not appear, although the action takes place within those provinces; it is as if they have no meaning or significance for the author. There is no reference to class, local lords are not described as feudal, the Tibetan administration in Lhasa is not referred to as a "local government," exploitation and abuse are criticized in moral terms but not politically, and the concepts of oppression and liberation are not invoked. There are some five references to Chairman Mao, but they are within statements by speakers who appear obstreperous and naive, as when the teacher in charge of the "Joyful Home" tells the author, "'Thanks to our leader, Mao Zedong, we have enough to eat and drink,'" just before the famine starts (chapter 63), and again, after the famine has concluded, when the same teacher announces to those who have survived, "'Thanks to Chairman Mao Zedong, we will have rice soup to drink, starting tomorrow'" (chapter 74). There is no hint as to whether these profoundly grotesque statements should be considered ironic, innocent, forced, or tragic, or even if they should be judged at all. Political terminology has been removed from the text along with judgment, separating it from the body of public writing about history in China. This is thus a book in which what is not said about the past is as important as what is declared.

Editorializing is absent from the book in part because it presents itself initially as literature rather than history. It conforms to a model found in modern Amdo writing, particularly short stories and dramas, in which rural life is praised, with lavish attention to details of local landscape, natural features, climate, and customs, often as the background to a story of nomad life or romance. In Tibetan literature of this genre, the text is interspersed with frequent proverbs and maxims that refer to nature and to rural knowledge. This is a major feature of Naktsang's work, with its celebration of the richness of Tibetan nomad culture and its descriptions of the intricacies of tented life, types of grass, details of climatic change, and ways of avoiding wolf attacks. Though many such passages have not been included in the translation published here, it is still clear that the memoir starts as a more or less traditional literary exercise about the recollection of rural life and shifts only in its later sections to an account of historical events.

Conversely, certain words appear in the memoir that are found infrequently in officially permitted histories. Naktsang uses the word *Bod*, "Tibet," as a place-name only some eight times in his book, but his usage is rich with significance. In six of those occurrences it is combined with one or another of the epithets found in traditional Tibetan literature that link the place-name to its geography—*Bod gangs ljongs, Bod gangs can*, or *Bod kha ba can*, "Tibet the snow region" or "Tibet the land of snows." As we have seen, this invokes a larger, cultural Tibet that consists of the entire plateau and that includes all Tibetan people, without necessarily suggesting any political conception. The author thus seems to avoid following the current Chinese practice of classifying citizens according to their ethnicity, a practice that emphasizes a people's cultural identity rather than their connections to a certain place or history.[8] "My actual homeland is in the eastern part of *Bod gangs can*, Tibet the land of snow," the child says of his home in the original, unabridged version (chapter 1, my translation), clearly using the phrase to describe a geographic space as well as a cultural domain. "May the whole world be at peace, especially our *Bod gangs ljongs*, our Tibetan snow region," the author says in the preface (my translation). By such usage, Naktsang identifies himself not just as a person who has Tibetan ethnicity but also as a person who lives in a place he calls Tibet. This is a statement he can make in Tibetan language un-self-consciously, drawing on past literary conventions, but which could not easily be said in Chinese, since, as we have seen, the word used in that language for Tibet refers only to the western part of the plateau.

Once, Naktsang refers to his birthplace as "the happiest part of the *khams gsum*, the three areas" (chapter 2 of the original text), hinting at the traditional notion of a greater Tibet consisting of three provinces—Kham, Amdo, and the central western areas. The author's memory may be incorrect, but at least twice he says he or his father used the word *Bod* on its own to refer to the whole plateau without literary embellishment, such as when he predicts that "Tibet will have to live through bad times" (chapter 38).[9] This could be read as a suggestion that in the 1950s the Golok people saw themselves as part of a Tibetan nation and of a single place known as Bod that included the Lhasa area. Perhaps these were cultural rather than political assertions, or were misremembered, or are points the writer wished to underline for his readers, but in any case they present a perception of Tibet that is strikingly at variance with official Chinese views and terminology. Equally, they unsettle arguments by some Western scholars that eastern Tibetans, because they use the word *Bod* only for the central area, did not consider themselves at that time to be living in Tibet. Such details raise the question as to what extent the concept of a single Tibetan region, at least in a cultural sense, existed in the 1950s among the eastern Tibetans. Clearly, the evidence of protests, self-immolations, flag-waving, photographs of the Dalai Lama, thinly veiled blog postings, and allusive pop songs eulogizing unity since 2008 shows that the idea of a single Tibetan nation is now widespread in Amdo and other Tibetan areas, and only further research will show how prevalent this notion was among eastern Tibetans in the past.

— CONCLUSION —

A surge of Tibetan national feeling, both in intensity and in spread, has taken place in the thirty years since Deng Xiaoping renounced the Maoist legacy and allowed some space for cultural and religious expression in China once again. The leftist view of the return of "local nationalism" in China, now as in the 1950s, attributes the spread of pro-Tibetan feeling to excessive leniency by China's leaders and to their overtolerance of mystifying social practices such as religious devotion and bourgeois culture among the local "nation-alities." According to that view, the problem is still seen as the failure of the Party to introduce radical social change immediately after taking power in the years after 1949, which allowed the ruling classes and the bourgeoisie to linger within society and to poison the hope of revolutionary change with their re-actionary instigation of separate identity, cultural essence, otherworldliness, and class privilege sanctioned by tradition. A more mainstream view within contemporary China attributes the abrupt rise in national feeling among east-ern Tibetans in the last ten years or so to the influence of the exile Tibetans from across the southern borders in India and Nepal, spread through the secret distribution of videos and DVDs, the words of returning exiles, and, af-ter 1990, the shortwave and satellite transmissions of Tibetan-language radio stations based in Washington, DC.

A third view, voiced only rarely within the PRC, sees resurgent Tibetan identity as a more or less reasoned response to the abrupt increase in re-strictive Chinese policies in eastern Tibetan areas after 1998, particularly the somewhat arbitrary decision by Beijing to ban the worship of the Dalai Lama, along with a raft of other restrictions and policies that included much tighter control of many monasteries, encouragement of migration by non-Tibetans into Tibetan areas, the required settlement of nomads, and a significant diminution of Tibetan-language education in the region's schools (Barnett 2009). Such policies had a more divisive impact on Tibetans in Amdo and Kham than when introduced in Lhasa some five or ten years earlier because the eastern areas had not seen significant protests since the 1970s, and indeed had prospered culturally as well as economically: there therefore seemed no reason for such measures to be imposed. Tibetans in Lhasa had long become accustomed to living under a veil of silence, with almost no practice of public expression even among friends, apart from brief, erratic street protests. But by the late 1990s younger Tibetans in the eastern areas did not see themselves as needing to comply without objection with official policies that they could not explain.

My Tibetan Childhood thus represents a moment of coalition between two generations. The older Tibetans, schooled in the necessary arts of silence by their witnessing of numerous state-inflicted deaths and punishments in earlier years, looked across Naktsang's narrative toward the younger generation, already energized by a growing awareness of a distinctive cultural and religious heritage that seemed to them endangered. The story that it told seemed to say, though not in so many words, that there was a substantive historical basis for the sense of loss and deprivation, and for the feeling that a future had been denied, implicit in the dissatisfactions expressed among Tibetans in the Amdo area, as in Lhasa too, after the turn of the millennium. Before Naktsang's book appeared, the only knowledge that could have given substantial basis for such ideas would probably have been largely limited to private conversations, smuggled exile propaganda, and ambiguous pop songs about unity, long-lost friends, and separation from one's homeland. With its patient, detailed, uneditorialized accounting of historical atrocities, seemingly inflicted without reason or explanation by an outside force fifty years earlier, Naktsang's book provided an intellectual foundation for thoughts and emotions already circulating within his community, a story of the past that made sense of those emotions.

Naktsang's initial purpose may have been no more than to make younger Tibetans proud of their identity, their culture, and their past, without any larger political objective. At that time every Tibetan in Amdo and every publication there talked of pride in past Tibetan cultural achievements above all else, such that when I gave a lecture at the main university for Tibetans in Xining in 2007, I was vigorously criticized by the Tibetan students for having failed to speak about how rich Tibetan culture is, and for not having told them of one or another achievement by their forebears. That was the zeitgeist at the time, a yearning for what Renan had described as accounts of great deeds performed together and stories of "common glories in the past." It was also the only form of national pride and expression that people then imagined would be allowed them by the state.

But shortly after the book was published, the situation in Tibet, and especially in Amdo, changed dramatically, first with the outbreak of protests in 2008, then the uncompromising response of the authorities, and finally the devastating impact on Tibetans of the self-immolations, almost all of which took place in Kham or Amdo. At this time, Naktsang changed too: he came out of retirement and became a vice-director of a highly regarded local organization supporting Tibetan culture, the Qinghai Tibetan Research Institute, one of the very few approved nongovernmental organizations in the Tibetan areas. In 2010 he became the editor of the institute's website, Bodrigs.com (the title means "Tibetan nationality.com"). He thus went from government service to civil society, from being an unknown author to an online commentator, from a literary memoirist to a public intellectual. As a member of the older generation using the medium of the young, he became an important voice in a new, cross-generational discussion that he had helped start with his book.

In 2013, five years after his book was published, he wrote a column that spoke out for the first time about the wave of immolations that had swept across Tibet. It was unprecedented in its explicitness. It began by discussing the varying limits on action and speech for Tibetans, an indication that his famous book may have meant much more than it said, and that in the face of the immolations crisis the time had come to speak out:

> Whether one expresses one's views, whether one is allowed to say what he feels or thinks or whether one has the courage to articulate one's opinion depends upon various factors. Hence one cannot expect everyone to respond in a uniform way. Take my case as an example. My livelihood depends on my salary. For someone like me who has even lost the power over his life and death to an external authority, I do not have the freedom to express any critical opinions on an issue which is linked to the one who pays me my salary. Nor do I have the courage to hurt the feelings of my patron. . . .
>
> But I do not have the habit to tell lies and smile over a cup of tea to fool myself and others. Moreover, I do not have to stretch my hands to measure the size of a golden image of the Buddha. (Nags tshang 2013)

He then states without equivocation that the immolations are nonviolent and well-intentioned. Their objective is, he says, "the return of His Holiness the Dalai Lama to Tibet. There is no disagreement on this. This is the wish not only of the self-immolators but the unwavering hope of all Tibetans." By the time Naktsang wrote this, the Chinese authorities had declared that the

Dalai Lama was a political enemy, that all immolations had been organized by him and his exile operatives, and that Tibetans expressing support for the immolations in private, let alone online, were liable to be arrested, as indeed many were. His statement was remarkably bold given that any public expression of support in Tibet for the Dalai Lama risks being treated as a threat to state security.

Naktsang's purpose in his online commentary was not primarily to challenge China. He wanted to persuade immolators to choose methods that would not involve the sacrifice of their lives, and his main point was a plea to the Dalai Lama to request Tibetans not to immolate—something the Dalai Lama has consistently refused to do. But in order to show his sincerity and respect for those considering self-immolation, Naktsang put himself at serious risk, openly endorsing their right "to fight for freedom, to fulfill one's aspirations and to struggle against the government": "But what I want to request again is that no matter what savage and brutal rule you may have to endure, please do not set yourself on fire. Whatever methods of struggle and resistance one must adopt, do not resort to self-immolation. No matter how pure and incomparable your hopes and faiths are, please do not set yourself on fire."

This remains probably the most explicit statement made in Tibet by a public figure, and certainly by any former official, about the current political situation. But it is one in which Naktsang still does not criticize the state or its history; instead, on largely humanist grounds, he defends the right of others to do so in certain situations. His method is to concede to the emotions and values of those he seeks to reach out to, whether immolators or the government, while asking them to consider changing their views.

In his book, Naktsang led public discussion among Tibetans beyond a tired focus on the "common glories" of their culture to contemplation of a darker aspect of the past—in Renan's words, "the deeds of violence which took place at the origin" of the state-building project in Tibetan areas. But his achievement was not just revealing long-erased national memories: it was that he enabled these to be distributed legally despite the strict confines of the current system in Tibet. Tibetans acquired a record that they could openly consult that told of the human costs of the Party's effort in 1958 to impose its own version of Tibetan identity and nationhood in Amdo. Similarly, in his more recent writings, he is exploring the potential of new media to serve as a vehicle for an older figure to subtly shape opinion and express fundamental truths without, so far, antagonizing either the state or its opponents. We can now see him not as an autobiographer who dared to speak about the past or an intellectual who speaks truth to power but as a strategic communicator and conciliator, an ex-official who pioneered unique pathways by which to negotiate the contours and crevices of the state system in the quest to widen public debate and understanding on topics never previously allowed. Where he had used the convention of childish innocence to enable the act of public recollection, he now uses concession to others' values to plead for moderation in policy. A project that began as a handing down of the past to coming generations has become a quiet search for ways to nurture a thinking Tibetan public, rich with knowledge of its history as well as of its responsibilities and limitations.

— NOTES —

I would like to acknowledge the invaluable work on Naktsang Nulo's writings by several younger scholars and the help that they have provided, in particular Xénia de Heering, Emilia Rosa Sulek, Françoise Robin, Franz Xaver Erhard, and Lauran Hartley.

1. Two years after Naktsang's book was published, another important document by a retired official from Qinghai appeared that gave detailed information about events in the 1950s (Dajie 2009). Written by Dargye, a former county leader in Golok who died in 2013, it was distributed after heavy redaction as an "internal reference document," a more restrictive form of circulation than that allowed for Naktsang's book.

2. Four memoirs by Tibetans from Amdo have appeared in English, all written after the authors came into exile: Hortsang Jigme 1998; Diki Tsering and Khedroob Thondup 2000; Pema Bhum 2001; and Arjia Rinpoche 2010. Of these, only Arjia Rinpoche writes in detail about events in Amdo in the 1950s.

3. The account given here of uprisings in Amdo is based largely on Weiner 2012.

4. According to an exile publication, citing an internal document, the Panchen Lama told an internal meeting in Beijing in 1987 that during the detentions in Qinghai in 1959–1962, "almost half of the prison population [in Qinghai] perished. Last year [1986], we discovered that only a handful of people had participated in the rebellion. Most of these people were completely innocent. In my 70,000 character petition [of 1962], I mentioned that about 5% of the population had been imprisoned. According to my information at that time, it was between 10 to 15%. But I did not have the courage to state such a huge figure. I would have died under *thamzing* [struggle session] if I had stated the real figure" (see Panchen Lama 1991 [1987]).

5. See Becker 1996, 162–186, for a collection of accounts collected by the author in Qinghai in the 1990s; and Kolas and Thowsen 2005.

6. The leading Amdowan short-story writer and film director Padma Tseden (Wanma-caidan) used the same device, drawn from Kiarostami's work, for his award-winning feature film *Lhing 'jags kyi ma Ni rdo 'bum* (The silent holy stones; 2005).

7. The television series *Su ru'i Me tog* (Suru flower) begins with the narrator reciting in an impassioned voice:

An old Tibetan proverb goes, "Birds reach for their nests as they get old, and people reach for their homes as they get old; / The grief of a long-distance separation from home is like turbulent ocean waves that rise high; / Though high in the blue sky is where he hovers, the place where he lands is the rungs of the red cliff. . . ." The craving for his own home place and motherland makes him lose appetite during the day and keeps him awake at night. Just like the disappearance of a fine horse on the grassland, or little birds from their flock, the grief that comes from wandering alone turns the lungs upside down. (Liu Ren 1984, episode 1)

8. Before 1995, official English-language publications in China used the term "nationality" to refer to the distinctive peoples in China (*minzu* in Chinese), drawing on the Leninist and Stalinist notions of nationality. Since 1995, officials in China have been required to translate this word in English as "ethnicity," presumably to emphasize cultural rather than political distinctions and to avoid associations of the term "nationality" with nationhood.

9. "Rgya dmag gis btsan gyis bod kyi dus 'di bskyur ba yin na / bod 'di las ngan pa'i dus ngan mgo la lhung ba yin"—literally, "If the Chinese troops by force were to change this era of Tibet, then Tibet will fall headlong into an even worse time than this" (Nags tshang 2007, 255). The version in standard Tibetan published in Dharamsala replaces *mgo la* with *mgor* (Nags tshang 2008, 229).

— REFERENCES —

Anagnost, Ann. 1997. *National Past-Times: Narrative, Representation, and Power in Modern China*. Durham, NC: Duke University Press.

Andric, Niko. 2011. "Nagtsang Boy's Joy and Sorrows or How China Liberated the Tibetan Grasslands." *Newsletter*, no. 57 (Summer): 12–13. Leiden: Institute of Asian Studies. http://www.iias.nl/sites/default/files/IIAS_NL57_1213.pdf.

Arjia Rinpoche. 2010. *Surviving the Dragon*. New York: Rodale.

Barmé, Geremie. 1993. "History for the Masses." In *Using the Past to Serve the Present: Historiography and Politics in Contemporary China*, edited by Jonathan Unger, 260–286. Armonk, NY: Sharpe.

Barnett, Robert, ed. 1997. *A Poisoned Arrow: The Secret Petition of the Tenth Panchen Lama*. TIN Background Briefing Papers, No. 29. London: Tibet Information Network.

———. 2009. "The Tibet Protests of Spring, 2008: Conflict between the Nation and the State." *China Perspectives* 3 (July): 6–23.

Becker, Jasper. 1996. *Hungry Ghosts: Mao's Secret Famine*. New York: Henry Holt.

Bya mdo Rin bzang [Chamdo Rinzang]. n.d. [2008a]. *Nga'i pha yul dang gzab nyan* [My homeland: Listening carefully]. N.p., n.p.

———. n.d. [2008b]. *Nga'i pha yul dang zhi ba'i bcings grol* [My homeland and peaceful liberation]. N.p., n.p.

Central Committee of the Chinese Communist Party. 1981. "Resolution on Certain Questions in the History of Our Party since the Founding of the People's Republic of China." Adopted by the Sixth Plenary Session of the Eleventh Central Committee of the Communist Party of China, June 27.

Central Tibetan Administration [Tibetan Government in Exile]. 2008. "Memoran-

dum on Genuine Autonomy for the Tibetan People." November. http://tibet.net
/important-issues/sino-tibetan-dialogue/memorandum-on-geniune-autonomy-for
-the-tibetan-people/.

Da jie [Dargye]. 2009. *Guo luo jianwen yu huiyi* [Golok: Seen, heard and remembered]. Internal reference document, Xining.

de Heering, Xénia. 2013. "Une visite à Chukhama, au pays natal de l'auteur tibétain Nagtsang Nülo." *Carnets du Centre Chine*, April 16. http://cecmc.hypotheses.org /10770.

Diki Tsering and Khedroob Thondup. 2000. *Dalai Lama, My Son: A Mother's Story*. New York: Viking.

Dikkötter, Frank. 2010. *Mao's Great Famine: The History of China's Most Devastating Catastrophe, 1958–1962*. London: Bloomsbury.

Goldstein, Melvyn, Dawei Sherap, and William R. Siebenschuh. 2004. *A Tibetan Revolutionary: The Political Life and Times of Bapa Phuntso Wangye*. Berkeley: University of California Press.

Hartley, Lauran, and Pema Bhum, trans. 2008. "Excerpt from *The Joys and Sorrows of a Boy from Naktsang*, a Semi-autobiographical Novel by Naktsang Nülo." *Latse* 5 (2007–2008): 60–61.

Horlemann, Bianca. 2002. "Modernization Efforts in Mgo Log: A Chronicle, 1970–2000." In *Amdo Tibetans in Transition: Society and Culture in the Post-Mao Era: PIATS 2000: Tibetan Studies: Proceedings of the Ninth Seminar of the International Association for Tibetan Studies, Leiden 2000*, edited by Toni Huber, 241–269. Leiden: Brill.

Hortsang Jigme. 1998 [1989]. *Under the Blue Sky: An Invisible Small Corner of the World*. Translated by Lobsang Dawa and Gussje de Schot, with Elia Sinaiko. Dharamsala, India: privately printed by author.

Kolas, Ashild, and M. P. Thowsen. 2005. *On the Margins of Tibet: Cultural Survival on the Sino-Tibetan Frontier*. Seattle: University of Washington Press.

Latse Library (Pema Bhum). 2008. "An Introduction to *The Joys and Sorrows of a Boy from Nagtsang* (Nagtsang Shilu Kyiduk)." *Latse* 5 (2007–2008): 54–60.

Li Jianglin. 2012. *Dang tie niao zai tiankong feixiang: 1956–1962 Qingzang gaoyuan shang de mimi zhanzheng* [When the iron bird flies: The secret war on Tibet Plateau, 1956–1962]. Taipei: Lianjing (Linking) Publishing.

Li Jianglin and Matthew Akester. 2013a. "Destruction of Tibetan Buddhism—Introduction," "Destruction of Tibetan Buddhism—Tibetan Sources," and "Destruction of Tibetan Buddhism—Chinese Sources." Posted on "War on Tibet" website, May 1. See http://historicaldocs.blogspot.hk/2013/05/when-did-destruction-of-tibets.html; http://historicaldocs.blogspot.hk/2013/05/destruction-of-tibetan-buddhism-tibetan.html; and http://historicaldocs.blogspot.hk/2013/05/destruction-of-tibetan -buddhism-chinese.html.

———. 2013b. "War on Tibet—Chinese and Tibetan Documents on the History of the Communist Occupation in English Translation." May 14. http://historicaldocs .blogspot.hk/. For a summary, see Matthew Akester, "When the Iron Bird Flies: A

Summary of Findings." http://historicaldocs.blogspot.hk/2013/05/when-iron-bird
-flies-summary-of-findings.html.

Liu Ren (director). 1984. *Su ru'i me tog* [Suru flower]. Television drama series, 3 episodes. In Chinese, with dubbed Tibetan version, for Gansu TV.

Makley, Charlene. 2005. "'Speaking Bitterness': Autobiography, History, and Mne-
monic Politics on the Sino-Tibetan Frontier." *Comparative Studies in Society and
History* 47 (January): 40–78.

McMillin, Laurie Hovell. 2001. *English in Tibet, Tibet in English: Self-Presentation in
Tibet and the Diaspora*. Basingstoke: Palgrave.

Mitter, Rana. 2000. "Behind the Scenes at the Museum: Nationalism, History and
Memory in the Beijing War of Resistance Museum, 1987–1997." *China Quarterly*
161: 279–293.

Müller, Gotelind. 2007. *Representing History in Chinese Media: The TV Drama* Zou
Xiang Gonghe *(Towards the Republic)*. Berlin: Lit Verlag. http://www.sino.uni
-heidelberg.de/representations/gonghe/gonghe.html.

Nacang Nuluo. 2011. *Na nian, shi shi fanzhuan: Yige Xizangren de tongnian huiyi* [The
year the world turned upside down: Recollections of a Tibetan childhood]. Taipei:
Xueyu chubanshe [Snowland Publishing].

Nags tshang Nus blo [Naktsang Nulo]. 2007. *Nags tshang zhi lu'i skyid sdug* [Joys and
sorrows of the Naktsang boy]. Xining: Qinghai Xining yinshuachang.

———. 2008. *Nags tshang zhi lu'i skyid sdug* [Joys and sorrows of the Naktsang boy].
Rewritten in standard Tibetan by Gser rta Tshul Khrims. Dharamsala, India:
Khawa Karpo Tibet Cultural Centre.

———. 2011a. "Lo rgyus shes dgos pa'i skor nas slob phrug rnams kyi dri bar lan 'debs pa"
[Response to questions from some students about the need to know history]. Bodrigs
.com (Xining), June 8. http://www.bodrigs.com/special/nagtsang/2011-12-30/31.html.

———. 2011b. "'Nags tshang zhi lu'i skyid sdug' dang 'brel nas mgo log bsam rtshe la
springs pa'i yi ge" [A letter sent to Golok Samtse about "Joys and Sorrows of the
Naktsang Boy"]. Bodrigs.com (Xining), April 8. http://www.bodrigs.com/special
/nagtsang/2011-12-30/23.html.

———. 2013. "Hre hor Blo bzang Chos 'phel sogs kyi dri bar lan 'debs ba" [Response
to questions by Trehor Lobsang Choephel and others]. Bodrigs.com, January 15.
http://www.bodrigs.com/literature/prose/2013-01-15/530.html. Published in translation as "A Tibetan Intellectual, Nagtsang Nulo, Shares His Thoughts on Self-
Immolations in Tibet." High Peaks Pure Earth. http://highpeakspureearth.com/2013
/a-tibetan-intellectual-Nagtsang-nulo-shares-his-thoughts-on-self-immolations
-in-tibet/.

Panchen Lama, 10th. 1991 [1987]. "The Panchen Lama's Address to the TAR Standing
Committee Meeting of the National People's Congress, 28th March 1987." In *The
Panchen Lama Speaks*. Dharamsala, India: Department of Information and Inter-
national Relations.

Pema Bhum. 2001. *Six Stars with a Crooked Neck: Memoirs of the Cultural Revolution*.
Dharamsala, India: Tibet Times. In Tibetan with English translation by Lauran Hartley.

Phag mo Bkra shis (Phamo Tashi). 1993. *'Khren zhen* [Longing], also known as *Rtswa thang gi 'khren zhen* [Longing for the grasslands] and as *Nyi ma tshe ring dang Zla ba sgrol ma* [Nyima Tsering and Dawa Drolma]. Television drama for Qinghai TV, Xining. In Tibetan.

Renan, Ernest. 1990 [1882]. "What Is a Nation?" Lecture, Sorbonne, Paris, March 11, 1882. Translation by Martin Thom. In *Nation and Narration*, edited by Homi Bhabha, 8–22. London: Routledge.

Richardson, Hugh. 1962. *A Short History of Tibet*. New York: Dutton.

Robin, Françoise. 2011. *L'histoire au miroir de l'art: (D)écrire la catastrophe au Tibet* [Literary creation and history: Writing/describing the Tibetan catastrophe]. Fourth Congress of the Asia and Pacific Network, September 14–16, École nationale supérieure d'architecture de Paris-Belleville and Centre de conférences du Ministère des Affaires étrangères et européennes, Paris, France. http://www.reseau-asie.com/userfiles/file/D01_robin_creation_litteraire_histoire_tibet.pdf (accessed January 3, 2013).

———. 2012. "La révolte en Amdo en 1958" [The revolt in Amdo in 1958]. In *L'histoire du Tibet du XVIIᵉ au XXIᵉ siècle: Compte rendu de la journée de conférences au Sénat le 3 mars 2012, Rapport de groupe interparlementaire d'amitié n°104*. June 18. http://www.senat.fr/ga/ga104/ga104.html.

Sde rong Tshe ring Don grub [Derong Tsering Dondrup]. 1995. *Wode Xinyuan* (Tibetan: *Bdag gi res mon*). Ganzi baoshe yinshuachang [Ganzi Newspaper Office Printing Press], n.d. [November]. Internal publication.

Shakya, Tsering. 2012. "Mongolia and Tibet: The Search for Nationhood. A Comparative Study of State Formation in the Early 20th Century." Manuscript.

Sperling, Eliot. 2009. "Tibet and China: The Interpretation of History since 1950." *China Perspectives* 3: 25–37.

Sulek, Emilia Róża. 2010. "The Wranahs: A Story of Discovering, and Forgetting the Tibetan Tribes of Amnye Machen." In *Altaica et Tibetica: A Volume in Honour of Prof. S. Godzinski on his 70th Birthday*, edited by A. Bareja-Starzynska, 237–252. Warsaw: Elipsa.

———. 2014. "Like an Old Tent at Night: Nagtsang Boy's Joys and Sorrows or a Personal History of the Years 1948–1959 in Tibet." In "Trade, Travel and the Tibetan Border Worlds: Essays in Honour of Wim van Spengen (1949–2013)," edited by Emilia Roza Sulek, John Bray, and Alex McKay, special issue, *Tibet Journal* 39, no. 1: 109–131.

Tenzin Palbar (Alags Tsa yis Bstan 'dzin dpal 'bar [Alak Tsayu]). 1994. *Nga'i pha yul gyi ya nga ba'i lo rgyus* [The tragic history of my fatherland]. Dharamsala, India: Narthang Publications.

Tshe ring Don grub [Tsering Dondrup]. 2009 [2006]. *Rlung dmar 'ur 'ur* [The howl of the red wind]. N.p., n.p.

Tubten Khétsun. 2007. *Memories of Life in Lhasa under Chinese Rule*. Translated by Matthew Akester. New York: Columbia.

Unger, Jonathan, ed. 1993. *Using the Past to Serve the Present: Historiography and Politics in Contemporary China*. Armonk, NY: Sharpe.

Wagner, Rudolf. 1990. *The Contemporary Chinese History Drama: Four Studies.* Berkeley: University of California Press.

Weiner, Benno Ryan. 2012. "The Chinese Revolution on the Tibetan Frontier: State Building, National Integration and Socialist Transformation, Zeku (Tsékhok) County, 1953–1958." PhD diss., Columbia University.

Yang Jisheng. 2012. *Tombstone: The Great Chinese Famine, 1958–1962.* New York: Farrar, Straus and Giroux.

Zhang Zhilong. 2012. "Starved of Memories—Great Leap Forward." *Global Times*, September 6. http://www.globaltimes.cn/content/731589.shtml.

TRANSLATORS' NOTE

We hope that you enjoy our translation. We have at times altered the phraseology to make the text more accessible to readers of English, but we believe that in doing so we have clarified the meaning of the author's words. The primary cultural problem was how to denominate the social structure of pre-Communist Amdo. The word "tribe," with its associations of prehistoric simplicity wholly inappropriate for the highly sophisticated and literate society of nomadic Amdo, we have avoided entirely, preferring to use "family" for a social unit based on a single home, and "clan" (a word introduced into the English language nearly six hundred years ago precisely for this purpose) for a wider kinship group. The word "sept" (again with a specialist meaning appropriate in this context) denotes those groups of "tent" families with a shared family name (e.g., Naktsang or Lang) who may or may not share the name of their clan but who are constituent parts of it. In Amdo, clans always formed larger or smaller associations, structured in a variety of ways, under "high chiefs," and to these we have given the name "chiefdoms," as the Tibetan language makes it clear that these should not be called "kingdoms." *Phayul*, literally "father home," has been translated as "native land" rather than "fatherland," which lacks a precise English meaning, or "home," which is ambiguous. However, although truthful, neither the text nor our translation of it should be considered as a textbook for a study of nomadic society. Naktsang Nulo wrote his book for an audience familiar with it and is fairly free in his description of its institutions and practices. We have merely tried to make things a bit clearer for the general reader.

Some of the original text has been omitted for reasons of length and coherence. The original text contained very lengthy descriptions and stories of nomadic life that all readers agreed were suitable only for a specialist readership. Some of the lengthier eulogies of life on the grassland may have been included to lessen the possibility that the publication would fall foul of the censor; if so, that strategy was successful. Whatever the reason, the text as it has been presented here is more balanced between information about the author's background and upbringing on the one hand, and the core drama of the author's life on the other.

The text was translated from a dialect that is very remote from modern Standard Tibetan. This led to some difficulties in translation, as standard English-Tibetan dictionaries did not contain many of the necessary words, let alone phrases. The translators therefore had to effectively translate twice in many cases, once from dialect into Standard Tibetan, and then from Standard Tibetan into English, with reference to the context of the original dialect version. It was a difficult and slow process, but fortunately familiarity with the culture and lifestyle of the area and its history helped achieve an accuracy that would otherwise not have been possible, and we are confident that we have been faithful to this very impressive work of Tibetan literature.

We have included photographs from the C. V. Starr East Asian Library at Columbia University, from the collection of the Arnold Arboretum at Harvard University (photographer, Joseph Rock), and from the archives of the Federal Republic of Germany. The ss Ahnenerbe, or Ancestral Heritage Research and Teaching Society, sent a German expedition to Tibet from 1938 to 1939, largely for bona fide scientific purposes, of which these photographs from the archives of the Federal Republic of Germany are a record. While disassociating ourselves entirely from the organization and some of its pseudoscientific concerns, we have made use of its images, which show extremely rare scenes not only immediately relevant to the text but also contemporary with the events described in it.

The text has been abridged, and in places chapters have been amalgamated or moved; the appendix shows the correspondence between the original Amdo Tibetan chapters and the ones numbered in the published text, as an aid to scholars and students who wish to compare the original with the translated work.

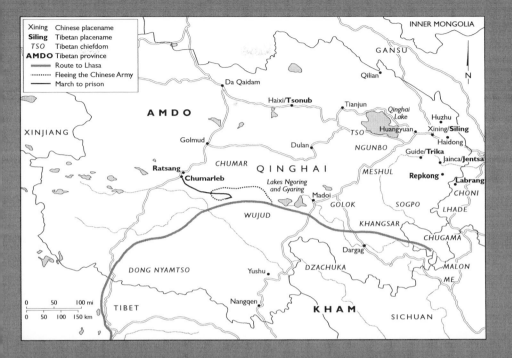

Northeastern Tibet, showing places and territories
mentioned in the text, with routes taken by the author
on pilgrimage and on his final journey.

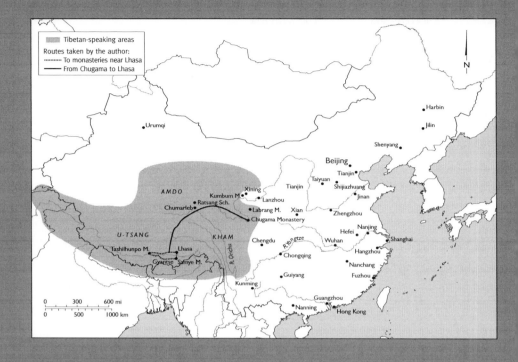

Tibetan-speaking areas in Asia
and Naktsang Nulo's pilgrimage to Lhasa.

MY TIBETAN CHILDHOOD

AUTHOR'S PREFACE

My dear readers, I am delighted to have written this small book and to have been able to place it in your hands. I would be honored if you read it carefully when you have the time.

In preparing this book, I wrote freely whatever I wanted to, said whatever I wanted to say, and explained the entire story and the circumstances in which it took place. I feel more relaxed now that I have finished writing. When I finished the book, I examined it carefully from beginning to end. It seemed to me that the narrative was simply the unvarnished evidence of a young child—what he saw, what he heard, and what he thought. There was no grand description in it or purpose behind it, or even deep analysis of individual character. But subsequently I reflected that I was born during an exceptional historical period. Perhaps because of my karma, or the changing times, I experienced and witnessed much suffering, and not only I but many thousands of other people did too. Each person's mind contains his or her own account of these events, and each chiefdom and family will have its own long story or legend of its ups and downs. Writing these stories in the form of a book has its disadvantages, but if they are not preserved in print, no one in the future will know what happened. The stories will only remain true in the mind of one individual. If they want the next generation to know about what happened in their lifetime, the previous generation must write down the history of that period carefully and hand it on to the next one. This is especially important if you want your own children to pass on your story. So, I decided that my story could only be preserved by writing it in the form of a book; otherwise it would not survive. These things are true for a nationality and a family, just as they are for an individual.

If the history of the fathers and uncles is not passed on to the nephews and sons, then the history of the family and even the nation will be lost before it is heard. This is the importance of writing this book. Now we are getting old, so we must write our history and that of our chiefdom, native land, and nationality before we pass away. This would be an invaluable gift to bestow upon the next generation. However we look at it, our life span is only sixty or seventy years, and at the end of our life everything will stop, but a book written by a man or a woman will give great benefit to many of the next generation. So my conclusion is that knowledgeable people of the older generation should write their account of the great events of our history without fear for their own descendants or nationality, and place it in the hands of their nephews and sons. This is a courageous and important task in my opinion.

I am not an educated man, and have seen and heard little, so I have written only about the joys and sorrows of my own childhood. Although I have recorded these events in detail, I am not able to educate anyone by them, but believe that my small book can be a drop of water in the ocean of Tibetan history. Some will drink this water to slake their thirst, but I know that those who are already nauseous may not wish to drink this dark and malodorous liquid.

Even those who have studied the great Kanjur and Tenjur[1] may not feel satisfied by the knowledge they have acquired, and such people will not value highly the autobiography of a young child, but perhaps a few interested youngsters, or old people with time on their hands, may wish to pass their time with it, accompanied by a delicious pot of tea. My friend Thubten Gendun told me this: "However fine your writing, hundreds of people will choose to read it after it is published, while thousands will not, and if your writing is poor it will suffer the same fate." It was these words that stimulated me to preserve this history in the form of a book, because without publication it would lose its value. Readers will find it—first ten, then fifty, then one hundred—and I will have fulfilled my goal in writing this book. Who knows how many people will read this small book as years go by, into what languages it may be translated, and what nationalities may come to know it? What tears, happiness, and sorrow may not be aroused in Mongolian and Tibetan readers? Each reader will have a different outlook—some may find in it something related to their own life, others may find stories that they recognize from their own knowledge of written history, and still others may simply feel sorrow or pity for the little Naktsang boy with his joys and sorrows. Readers read the same words, but their understanding differs, depending on their desire and

1. Canonical scriptures of Tibetan Buddhism.

inclinations. A proverb states, "If thirty people think differently, they will have thirty different opinions about the same thing." One reader might think, "I'm not interested in what one silly child saw," another, "This is contemporary Tibetan history, so we should know about it," a third, "Peace is clearly preferable to war, disease, and hunger for any nation. Can the next generation keep our country free from these evils?" Then more readers will join them. When young people read this book, it will become clearer to them that "life's joys and sorrows have as many ups and downs as a gazelle's horns." We should all be aware that, even though life has its ups and downs, we should not fear suffering, but work to make the best of it and to preserve our humanity.

Well, everyone in the world has their own history of happiness and tragedy, but though many are similar, each one is different. One person may say, "Oh, yes, this is true—I had many experiences like that," while another of the same nation may say, "This is just a crazy old man telling lies." I write from the point of view of Tibetans of my generation, many of whom had similar experiences to mine. It seems to me that a lot of people have had similar experiences of these negative events in our history, and that this provides evidence that these negative events actually occurred. I faithfully recorded all the problems that I saw exactly as I saw and heard them. I never excluded or included anything because it suited my prejudices. These stories are an exact reflection of what happened at the time, recorded fifty years after the events took place. Despite the passage of fifty years, I have not granted myself the authority to change anything in the story to suit my personal point of view. I thought that the story would lose its meaning if I changed it, and it would certainly not deceive future generations.

The essence of my justification is this. I wrote only the reality of what happened to the people, chiefs, and chiefdoms. Half a century has passed, and no doubt some unintentional mistakes will have crept into my narrative for that reason. Old men's memories are not exact. There are many still alive who were affected by the events described here. As they will recognize the mistakes that I have made, I beg their forgiveness from the bottom of my heart, and I welcome their corrections and complaints!

A proverb says, "As raising a long stick makes dogs shy away, so talking too much makes people shy away." As my small book has no more than a hand's length of meaning, it is not necessary to give it an arm's span of talking. Readers can decide its merits, and history will pronounce on its truthfulness. My goal is to produce a complete picture of this history from start to finish.

May our native land and our country be free from disease, hunger, and war. May our Tibetan nationality preserve its integrity, and may the whole world be at peace, especially our Tibetan "land of snows." May the whole world be increasingly friendly, peaceful, and free from disease, famine, and conflict!

It is difficult to write history, and even more difficult to write one's own history, especially if it incorporates the joys and sorrows of one's own lifetime.

Some human beings experience inconceivable suffering in their lives, and as I was born during times of great change, I experienced inconceivable suffering. Sometimes I think that of all people of my age I have suffered the most, but then again I reflect that in fact I was only one of hundreds of thousands who suffered in this way.

It is natural to wish to be happy and to resent suffering, and there are people who say that good and ill fortune are the result of our own actions. This may be so, but suffering is inevitable in all our lives and must be borne whether we like it or not.

Do we prefer to tell happy stories or those that deal with suffering? From the stories that most people tell, it would seem that people prefer to speak about sad things. Men worry about journeys and women worry about food, and all humans suffer in the same way. The difference is in the way we feel about our happiness and sadness.

Speaking about happiness in our lives makes us happy, just as speaking about sadness makes us sad, even if in our lives the circumstances are the opposite.

Among humans, lamas, chiefs, and leaders eat yogurt, meat, butter, and honey without needing to do any work at all. They wear silk brocade and lambskin robes without having to do any work. They sit on carpets and have horses to ride on their journey. There is food on the table whenever they want to eat, and they consider themselves very happy. A nomad family living in a black or a white tent may be fortunate in sheep, yaks, and horses. They ride a horse as swift as a bird, and their gun fires like lightning when they go to rob weaker chiefdoms. They hunt wild animals on the high mountains and think they are very happy. Even a beggar with a few goats considers himself happy when he has a bowl of *tsampa* with fresh butter to eat and manages to scrounge some food for his family from other households.

Considering my own life, I have experienced many joys. Since I was a small child I have had the opportunity to study, clothes on my back, and food to eat. Wherever I went I had a horse to ride, and both pistol and rifle to carry on my back. I have held high position and completed my work successfully. I thought that my life was the happiest of all people in my position, and that this happiness was enough for me.

What does it mean to say that one's life is a happy one, whether it is mine or anyone else's? If one's life is too full of joy, one does not recognize whether it is happy or not. The proverb says, "If a person is too happy, he will even sigh when he is riding his horse." Naturally, this is true. This proverb means that a person's happiness is not dependent upon his worldly success but on his mind. If the mind is right, even someone whose only possession is a bowl of tsampa can be happy. If not, nothing can make him happy.

Life is unpredictable. While some experience happiness after great sadness, others experience the opposite. The old proverb says, "Our happiness is inside our robes—it is in our minds." Every soul can tell of many joys and sorrows.

I will tell of the hardship I have experienced. In life the highest positions are held by the lama and the chief on their thrones. In the middle come the family men and women, and at the bottom the lowest beggars. None of them can escape old age, sickness, and death. Of course, we all have our sadness. Leaders suffer because of the responsibility of their position, rich people from the instability of wealth, and poor people from lack of wealth. Beggars suffer from not having enough food to eat. Rich people suffer from a surfeit of possessions, and poor people from a lack of them. Whatever the reason, we all have sorrows to tell of until our life is ended as a lamp is blown out. Looking back, my life has been a mixture of happiness and sadness, of joyful and sorrowful experiences. I have passed half a hundred years of life span, and if I thought again and again of all the happiness and sadness in my life, it would make me cry and make my heart sick.

While I was still too young to know her, my mother left for the peaceful place and left me behind her. From the age of two my father led me with him, and we passed our lives wandering from home to home. When I was ten my father left for the peaceful place, regretful that he had left me behind in a distant place. My brother was left there too, and when I think of the suffering of our pitiful orphan lives, that is the worst part of it.

On reflection, however, it was not only us two who suffered such things. During that time of great changes the entire land of snows experienced inconceivable suffering and misfortune. Many people died from war, disease, and famine, and compared with them my sufferings were small, and I have embarked on a happy path now. I do not regret my suffering now. A person or nation is a happy one if it does not forget its own joys and sorrows and can preserve them in the form of a book to pass on to the next generation. This is a way to encourage them and give them confidence.

When I was a small child my father used to tell me, "Son of a great father, do not let small hardships dismay you. In life you will experience as many ups and downs as a gazelle's horns. As you grow older you will see that your suffering will be the same as everyone else's." I have never been able to forget his words, and although I have experienced much suffering, my dear father's words have taken root inside me.

Joys and sorrows in life are the result of karma, and are how our life is formed. Our life is not what we wish for as children, and every year that passes brings more hardship. It is pointless to hold out unrealistic hopes for our lives when we are younger.

When I was a small child, I heard people say, "If I eat *droma* with butter I don't want any more, but if I drink watery cheese soup I want more." Human life is as unpredictable as this—happiness and sadness follow each other as the years go by. Each person's happiness and sadness are different from another's. When I was young, my uncle Jakho said, "We cannot know the course of human life. Even though one person desires happiness, joy and sorrow are stronger, and will come whether he desires it or not." I have always remembered this, and thought that it must be true, because I have experienced this in my own lifetime.

It makes no difference whether your status in life is high or low, rich or poor, male or female, young or old. From youth until old age, sickness, famine, misfortune, and many other things influence our happiness and unhappiness. Life has to be lived whatever our feelings may be. We must work for our food and clothes. We are never free until we die and leave our lives behind, and even then the lord of death places the yoke on our neck and drags us away, leaving us to wander in search of our next life without being able to control our destiny.

Everyone's life is different, and mine is not the same as that of anyone else. The proverb says that everyone is happy or sad in a different way, and when I was young I experienced the life of a wandering orphan, and suffering that scarcely anyone else of my age can possibly have experienced.

I have emerged from my trials without losing the ability to feel, and my life was saved from among the many who died. I have recorded exactly what happened to me in my childhood in the hope that young people can learn that a human life can experience such great ups and downs, and that they should not make useless wishes for their lives. They will meet many difficulties on their way through life, and cope with them through personal ability and hard work. The proverb says, "Without hard work you cannot eat good food," and this teaches us that a happy life does not come free. They will experience danger and misfortune, but they must not be afraid because this will not kill them. They should try their best to find a way though their problems, and know that no one will make you happy but yourself. The most important thing is to walk forward with one's own personal ability. If this brief history can make people think in this way, then it will have been successful.

History is a factual record of the past, the exact circumstances of the time. It is not something that can be fabricated in accordance with contemporary desires, preferences, or policy. Everything that I wrote in this small book was as my eyes saw it or my hands touched it, and I wrote nothing that did not exist or that did not happen.

These things happened fifty years ago. Anyone of my age knows clearly what happened at that time. Undoubtedly they have stories of their own to tell, things they saw with their own eyes and touched with their own hands. We are the people of the "time of great changes." Will young people believe that the stories in this book are true? They will have heard stories like this from their family and relatives but never have seen what happened. They know nothing of this era in history because no detailed account of it can be found in any history book. At that time of revolution the earth and the sky were turned upside down. Nowadays young people living comfortable lives cannot believe that these things took place.

If the next generation considers that I am an old man, near to death, who has no reason to tell stupid or untruthful things, and no reason to deceive the generations that follow me, then they will find my history credible.

— MY BIOGRAPHY —

I was born on the fifteenth day of the eighth Tibetan month in the Earth Marmot year of the sixteenth *rabshung*[2] into Naktsang Dradel's family in Madey Chugama chiefdom, Machu County, Ganlho Prefecture, Gansu Province. When I was a child, I visited many great monasteries on pilgrimage such as Sera, Drepung, and Ganden in Lhasa with my father. In November 1959 I entered Chumarleb Nationalities Middle School, Chumarleb, Jyekundo (Yushu) Prefecture, Tsongun (Qinghai) Province, graduating in 1964 from Jyekundo Normal School. In 1965 I entered Tsongun Nationalities University, and in October 1965 I became a teacher in Chumarleb County Primary School in Jyekundo Prefecture. In 1967 I moved to Wargon Primary School, also in Jyekundo Prefecture. In 1971 I became a police officer in Wargon town. In 1979 I became the deputy chief judge in Chumarleb County prison. In 1984 I became deputy leader of the county court office and studied in the Communist Party school at the prefectural and provincial level before and after this appointment. I achieved distinction in the study of political science and law for cadres at provincial and central Party schools and in 1987 became deputy leader of Chumarleb County. In 1990 I was transferred to the Central People's Prison in Jyekundo Prefecture. In 1993 I retired and a few years later contacted both reincarnate and ordinary lamas, foreign well-wishers, and others, and with the particular help of Gungtang Denpi Wangchuk of Labrang Monastery, Gansu Province, I collected enough money to build a Buddhist institute in Chumarleb County. I also constructed buildings for four large prayer wheels and five small prayer wheels containing transcriptions of the Kanjur, Tenjur, Mani, the Tibetan Book of the Dead, the

2. The sixty-year cycle of the Tibetan calendar.

One Hundred Sanskrit Scriptures, and other works. They stand to promote the fulfillment of devotees' wishes. I frequently assisted the prefectural high school, Tibetan county middle school, and Chugama primary school financially.

Now I am the director of the Qinghai nationalities folk culture research team. I am a son of the Tibetan people. If something is for the benefit of the Tibetan people, I will do it to the best of my ability, and continue to work to the best of my abilities.

PRELUDE

The Charnel Ground

It was hot at noon that day. We were making our way wearily across a river when we heard guns firing repeatedly from up ahead. We had no idea what was going on, but we were all frightened. Everyone dismounted except for me. Some Tibetan gazelles, startled when they saw us, sprinted to the top of a mountain. I rode over and looked down to the road beneath. It was a Chinese military column, so long that you couldn't see the beginning or end of it. They were on horseback.

"Father, it's the Chinese army!" I called. "Over there!"

"Here we'll be face-to-face with them," Father said. "There's no way out. Quickly—into that ravine!" Everybody rushed into a small ravine near the road, leading their horses. Maybe the Three Precious Jewels protected us. We were in a bend of the ravine, and even though we could see the road, they couldn't see us. The gazelles that had run away looked down at us from the mountainside above. Father, Tenzin, and Lochu squatted closest to the road with guns at the ready, watching the troops moving past. We hid behind them, holding our horses. We could hear the Chinese talking and hear the hoofbeats of their horses as clearly as if they were beside us. We just sat still, so silently that we could hear the sound of our own hearts beating. The Chinese had some Tibetan yak drovers with them, and we could overhear their conversation clearly, too. Suddenly, two of our monastery horses broke free and cantered out of the ravine and up the mountain. We tried to grab them, but there was nothing to hold them back with. Father waved his hand to tell us to keep still and leave them be.

Then one of the Tibetans in the military column spoke.

"What beautiful horses," he said, "I wonder where they came from?" They kept talking about it, but nobody came out of the column to drive the horses away. We had no idea what they would do, and stayed frozen where we were. We heard troops continue to march past, and more Chinese speech that we did not understand. Father and the others moved back toward the road, signaling us to stay where we were. Suddenly we heard two gunshots, "Pag-shar, pag-shar!" Our horses shied, afraid, but we held on to them tightly. Some of the monks began praying. "The Protector bear witness," they muttered, and "Gungtang Jampeyang bear witness," and many other prayers.

Then I remembered the gazelles on the mountain above us and realized that the troops had been shooting at them. They missed, but if they had hit one, it would have gone badly for us. No wonder the monks were scared. They thought the Chinese were firing at us.

"There were five hundred soldiers in that column," my father said.

"The Three Precious Jewels protected us today and prevented them from seeing us," someone said.

"The deities of this place protected us," others said. Our terror at meeting the Chinese army for the first time had subsided.

We continued along the road, but now no one spoke. We weren't ready to talk about the fear and sadness we all felt after seeing so many civilians and monasteries destroyed in the past few days.

"If we meet the Chinese troops," I asked my brother, Jabey, "will they murder us like they did the people on the grassland?"

"We can flee to the mountains," he replied. "They can't destroy us so easily there."

"If they are going to kill us, there's no reason to travel so far every day," I said. But the monk Monlam snapped at me: "Don't say such unlucky things!"

"Stop talking—we've got to catch up," Jabey said. I still felt I was right, though.

We crossed a river. A large flock of vultures was circling in the sky ahead of us.

"Hey, Lochu," Father said, "why are there so many vultures over there? It's not a good sign. We should go and have a look. You others follow us slowly." They went ahead to check it out. As we rode along the river, we began to smell something rotten. It got worse and worse, and then we saw the cause. Dogs were wandering around, eating the corpses of dead sheep and yaks, and the bodies of dead men lay scattered on both sides of the river. They were naked and dark blue. When we rode away from the river toward a cliff, we kept finding more dead people, young and old, lying on the ground.

"Om mani padme hum,"[1] we all prayed and chanted.

---

1. This prayer is often referred to in shorthand as *mani*.

I prayed from my heart because I was unable to speak—I could not chant with my mouth. By this time I had lost my fear of dead bodies. Farther on there were many dead children lying alone, and mothers and children still holding each other in death. In that area I counted twenty-six or twenty-seven corpses. One could see, by looking at their hair and size, that most of them were women and children. I thought, "I am not afraid. Even if I am killed, I won't have fear or regret."

We climbed higher up the side of the mountain, which had an upper and a lower ledge. On the lower was a group of tents, many of which had fallen over. Several had bullet holes through the cloth. Father and Lochu were sitting on the higher shelf.

"Oh, the Protector bear witness!" we all said when we reached them, so great was our shock. Here, the ground was completely covered by the corpses of men, women, monks, yaks, and horses. Some horses had been hobbled close to the tent door and shot. Riding yaks and *dzo* had also been tied up with ropes and killed. Wherever I looked, there was death. Then, I couldn't look any more and turned my gaze away, up the mountain. I tried to block it out of my mind because my heart was getting more and more anxious, and my feelings were so strong. I got on the horse and rode away without looking back.

"By the look of their clothes and hats," my father said, "they were pilgrims from our chiefdom who were on their way back from Lhasa, and the Chinese troops massacred them all." Lochu and I found a lot of machine gun bullet cases higher up the mountain.

"I wish it was the Chinese who were dead," Lochu burst out. "Why did they do this? Is there any way these people could have fought back?"

"According to their clothes they came from Lhade or Modma chiefdoms," Tenzin said. "It's a tragedy that they ran into these Chinese devils."

"I want to beat them," Molam said. "How did they have the heart to kill children? They are absolutely evil."

"It happened this morning," Father said. "The Chinese soldiers killed people and animals together, young and old together. They didn't make any distinction between them. From the way they are lying, most of these people were probably killed while washing their faces in the river. None of them had a chance."

"If I meet the Chinese troops again," Tenzin said, "I will take revenge on them, even if they kill me."

"It's easy to kill or be killed at a time like this," Father said. "The time is not right yet for revenge. It's more important to get these children safely to Lhasa. First the monks will say prayers for all the fallen people, but then we must leave quickly." The monks chanted their rituals, while Lochu and I went up the mountain on lookout. I looked down from the ridge. The bodies of people and animals were strewn everywhere among the tents, a few of which were still standing. Stray dogs fed from the corpses, and vultures circled overhead. I had no desire to look, but I did look, and many strange feelings came into my heart. I thought, "The Three Precious Jewels bear witness! Where can we escape to? When I am free, I will never move from that spot again."

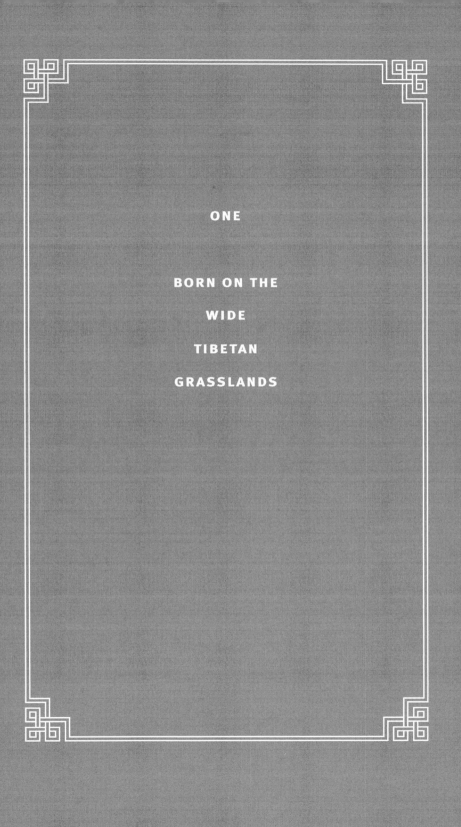

ONE

BORN ON THE

WIDE

TIBETAN

GRASSLANDS

1

Madey Chugama, My Native Land.

The first day I went to Ratsang school a teacher from Golok named Tserang Dorje asked me, "Hello, Golok boy, where are you really from?"

"Madey Chugama," I replied.

"I know that region," he said. "Ngora Village, Chokho Chugama. . . . Sure, sure, I visited there as a child. It's a great place with strong families and brave men." Even though I was young then, still I felt happy to hear someone speak well of my home.

"My homeland is in the eastern part of Tibet," I say if I am asked. "It is south of Amnye Machen, to the east of Dugre Mountain and in the first of the eighteen sheltered plains of the Machu River, near the chiefdoms of Madey Chugama and Chokho Chugama. That's my native land."

Madey Chugama was rich in grass, water, mountains, valleys, and soil. It was a lovely place with good plants and flowers, and it was a moral place, too. On the highest mountains there were Tibetan gazelles, various types of deer, and many other wild animals. There were bears, wolves, foxes, and many other predatory animals among the forests and juniper bushes near the Machu River. The mountain area where the families lived had broad grassland with deep soil. A place rich in grass and plants is a good place to raise livestock. When I was young I often heard Uncle Shotse arguing with other people.

"Yes, boys," he would say. "Our Madey Chugama is not like other chiefdoms.[1]

1. In this part of Tibet, the social structure as described in this narrative consisted of tent-dwelling families, clans, smaller chiefdoms, and larger chiefdoms, which sometimes, though not always, correspond to contemporary administrative divisions, and whose territories fluctuated along with the fortunes of their chiefs. Larger chiefdoms would contain one or more monasteries that shared in the administration of the chiefdom, as in contemporary Bhutan, a culturally Tibetan country.

Because all our valleys and mountains have rich grass and watering places. this is a fortunate place for yaks, horses, and sheep. It is good for female yaks and cows who are milking and it breeds fast horses. The bravery of young men abounds here, and this land makes the girls beautiful. Religion prospers, and chiefs and lamas are authoritative here." He said many other things like that, but no one tired of listening to him. Madey Chugama really was a fine place. As the temperature rose and fell throughout the year, the old people described the changing seasons like this:

"The Bird month[2] is called the 'month of darkened paths and rivers,' because when ice melts on the paths and rivers they get darker. The second month is called the 'Dog month of colorful turf,' the third month is called the 'Pig month when grass grows green on the plain,' the fourth month is called the 'Marmot month of green mountain pasture,' the fifth month is the 'Ox month of overflowing grass and rivers,' the sixth is the 'Tiger month' and the 'month of hot sunshine,' the seventh is the 'Rabbit month when we eat barley,' the eighth is the 'Dragon month of leaves blown off by the wind,' ninth is the 'Snake month which ends by freezing,' tenth is the 'Horse month when ice fringes the river,' the eleventh is the 'Sheep month frozen face,' and the twelfth is the 'Monkey month when earth and stone explode' [as ice swells to shatter rock]."

There were about seven hundred families in Madey Chugama. Most of them lived on either side of the Machu River, and a few lived across the Guchu River. The clans were called Gotsa, Gochen, Warshi, Gulag, and other names. The Tashi Chulong Monastery used to number five hundred monks. The front of the mountain where it was located is known as "Padmasambhava's Hat." It used to be an exemplary monastery where morals and religion prospered. In Madey Chugama man and woman, young and old were all treated well. Everyone was very good-hearted and well-behaved. They followed the laws of karma modestly. The chiefdom and its families enhanced their wealth and that of others. Both the leaders and their followers had enough food to eat and clothes to wear. We were the happiest part of all the provinces of Tibet. That was the Madey Chokgo Chugama chiefdom.

I thought that my good luck in being born there was due to my meritorious previous life and because I'd taken refuge in the Three Precious Jewels: the Buddha, the Dharma, and the Sangha. After twenty years of absence, when I revisited and saw the mountains and rivers of my native land, it was just as beautiful, enchanting, and pleasurable as I remembered it. When I looked up, there was the vulture—I heard its cry, and the scream of the Lhachen Dorje lynx, the magnificent deities of my birth. When I looked down from the mountain, there was Padmasambhava's Hat, with the Guchu River on the

2. The first month of the Tibetan calendar.

right, and the Machu River on the left. In front was the wide pasture next to Tashi Chulong Monastery. I was joyful and at peace. Now I was back in the arms of my native land, and my dream to return had become a reality.

"You boys are all grown!" Uncle Norta said to me and my brother. "You must have missed the native land that you knew as children. Your birth deities must have been watching over you, or else you would have died far away."

"That's right," Aunt Damkho said. "The Three Precious Jewels bear witness! It was as if you were dead, but now the dead and the living have met face-to-face. I never thought I would see your faces again. Surely you were spared from death because of your desire to return here. So now you must stay—I swear you must not leave us again." But I did leave.

Oh native land, my adored home—why did I not stay with you when I was a child? I left, unintentionally and against my will, because of the great changes and dangers wrought by time. I am a little boy who has wandered far from home, but in the end I would like to return to you. If my life were free I would definitely not stay in this distant place.

Karma cannot be changed, and sooner or later I will die far from Madey Chugama. At that time may my mind be released as a small bee with the help of my native land's birth deities, its lamas and monks.

2

A Wealthy Place, a Happy Family.

When I was young I often asked my father and my aunts Rigdron and Damkho how I was born and what my mother was like, but they wouldn't tell me. My interest grew, and I asked them more and more often. One day I asked Aunt Damkho again.

"The boy is crazy," she said. "Why are you always asking about this?"

"You shouldn't say that," Uncle Norta countered. "He wants to know, and one day you should tell him everything. Just because he's young doesn't mean he can't think for himself."

"I can't tell him," Aunt said, "because I would have to speak the names of many dead people." From the way they were talking it sounded as though telling these stories would involve saying the names of *many* dead people, risking *a lot* of bad luck. Maybe it was hopeless. But a few days later, at bedtime, Aunt Damkho told me the whole story of my birth.

"Many years ago, before fighting had broken out between the chiefs of Madey Chugama and Malon Me, Madey Chugama was on a wide and open grassland beside the blue waters of the Machu River. On the pastureland that autumn, the Gotsa clan was living close together like a patch of mushrooms sprung from the grass. Above them was a black, cube-shaped yak hair tent with colorful prayer flags behind it shaking in the wind. On either side of the tent entrance, two dogs were tied up. We called them 'four-eyed,' because above each eye they had patches of fur like extra eyes. When anyone came close to the tents, they jumped up and threw themselves fiercely against their ropes, threatening to pull their tethers out of the ground. At the end of the day, many yaks, sheep, and horses filled the pens. Even if you hadn't known, you could tell with your own eyes that this was a united family, and a rich one too. If you asked, they would have told you that this family was called Naktsang Damkho. The family was always at work outside or inside the tent. Everyone—guests from both near or far—was welcomed with warm laughter.

"So, the most beautiful girl in the Naktsang family wore coral decorations on her head. She was the youngest of four daughters from Warje Meshe Wagen, a wealthy family among their clan, and was called Tserangkyid. She married the eldest son of the Naktsang family, whose name was Durkho.

"In our clan they used to say that after Tserangkyid came to the Naktsang family, their fortunes improved and their livestock prospered. Wealth, clothes, and food flowed to the family. They called her an auspicious wife. She had a son, and when he was four years old the monks of Alak Drak Monastery named him Jamyang Badma.

"Then, on the night of the fourteenth day of the eighth Mongolian month, rain clouds gathered. You could scarcely see the fingers of your own hand in front of your face, it was so dark. The rain grew heavier and heavier. In the red lightning you could see the prayer flags flapping in the rain behind the Naktsang family's tent. You could catch glimpses of the yaks, horses, and sheep sleeping quietly beside the black yak hair tent. Inside the tent the altar was alight with butter lamps whose flames shifted in the wind. Inside, the stove smoked, and fire flickered to the left and right of the gleaming copper pot on the stovetop. Beside the stove an old woman with white hair took beads in her hand and said, 'The Three Precious Jewels bear witness and Gungtang Danba Jamyang bear witness. I pray for the safety and long life of this mother and baby.' She chanted many other prayers too, coughing a little as she did so.

"Lightning flared and thunder blasted at almost the same moment.

"'Jamyang bear witness! What's going on tonight?' the old woman said nervously. Grandpa Naktsang Tame was dozing near the side of the tent.

"'Stop barking into the night,' he ordered. 'You'll come to no harm. Just take care of the girl and make sure she's safe.'

"'Don't talk like that,' the old woman chided. 'She is in great pain, but it seems to be getting better. And people give birth every day.'

"'Hey, Durkho my son,' the Naktsang grandfather called out a little later. 'Go outside and see whether the yaks and sheep are safe.'

"'I'll check, father.' The young man with long black hair left the tent, holding his gun.

"The young woman yelled, panicky. 'Ayo, Mother, the pain, the pain!' she screamed. 'Please help me!'

"'It's all right, my dear,' the old lady told her. 'A great mother's daughter will be patient. Have courage, the dawn is near and you will give birth. The Three Precious Jewels bear witness and and Gungtang Jamyang bear witness . . . !' Near dawn heavy rain fell, lightning flashed, and thunder roared behind the tent. The Naktsang tent filled with smoke. The old man raised his head.

"'What's happening to the weather tonight?' he asked. 'That lightning almost struck us.' Right then, a tiny cry came from the direction of the young woman.

"'The Three Precious Jewels bear witness!' the old woman shouted. 'She's given birth, she's given birth!'

"'That's great,' Old Naktam said happily, 'but it's a shame that the baby has been frightened by all this lightning.'

"The old woman was still excited: 'Thanks to the Three Precious Jewels the Naktsang family has got another son! How wonderful to have another son!'

"'That's absolutely right!' Old Naktam said. 'I dreamed many days ago that it would be a son.'

"'Stop exaggerating,' the old woman said. 'I know you didn't really dream that.' He retorted, 'I promise that's exactly what I dreamed. Now, where has Durkho wandered off to? It'll be daybreak soon, so we'd better hurry and burn incense for the offering.' He said this and many other happy things.

"Dawn broke. Behind the Naktsang family's tent, a large heap of incense sent smoke rising into the sky. In the tent a tiny baby's cry, 'A-wa, a-wa,' could be heard over and over as the light grew."

Aunt Damkho stopped talking, without any hint that there was more to her story. Everything happened as my grandfather dreamed and my grandmother prayed. Perhaps it was the consequence of my parents' merit in a previous life that I was a baby experiencing my first day in this world. Before my head was dry, all my family members wanted to hold me as if I was a jewel. If I hadn't received the consciousness of a human being, I would have continued to wander in the gloom and fear of the "intermediate state,"[3] and nobody had any idea how long my soul might have roamed with nowhere to live. Today I had arrived in the bright light of human life. My grandparents

---

3. *Bardo.* In Tibetan Buddhism, a period of limbo between the death and reincarnation of the consciousness.

had taken beads and chanted *manis*. I was born in this Tibetan land of snows, a religious land and country. This would give me an excellent opportunity to perform religious deeds and avoid karmic retribution. Because of the Three Precious Jewels, or perhaps because of deeds I had done in a previous life, I was beginning my life in the world of humans.

"Whose consciousness does he have?" my parents often asked. "What was he in his previous life?" I overheard many things that I did not understand. I could not answer their questions and had no reason to think much about where I came from or whose consciousness I had entered. Whether life is short or long, with good or bad luck, wealth or poverty, low or high status, life will provide as many ups and downs as the antlers of a deer. From the day of my birth, I started to take single steps on this variable path of life. It's hard for anyone to predict the joys and sorrows of destiny.

"The destiny we call karma cannot be changed," our father often told us. "Our joys and sorrows are written within our own foreheads." That is true.

In my early childhood I could already read the six syllables of the mani, "Om mane padme hum." In my heart my wish was always this, "To seek refuge in the Three Precious Jewels. In these bad times, without my protectors, please show me the way through the sea of sadness and beyond the world of *samsara*. Since my life is as impermanent as this butter lamp, protect me always with gentle winds."

3

Experiencing Buddhism, Monks, and the Monastery for the First Time.

After Aunt Damkho had spoken for a long time about the story of my birth, I fell asleep. The following evening, while I was going to bed, she came to me.

"My dear," she said, "tonight I am going to tell you of some things that happened after your birth." I settled into her arms and listened carefully.

My brother Japey had been staying in Aunt Damkho's home for many days. One morning he heard that the Naktsang had produced another son. Aunt Damkho took Japey by the hand and led him toward the Naktsang tent. When they arrived at the animal pen, the Naktsang daughter-in-law, Meshel Tserangkyid—she who had just given birth to me—came out of the home to restrain the dog and welcome them.

"Are you crazy?" Aunt exclaimed when she saw my mother. "You can't get up today! I swear you'll hurt yourself."

Chugama Monastery, the author's home monastery, where he spent much of his childhood.
Courtesy of the C. V. Starr East Asian Library, Columbia University in the City of New York.

"It's fine, Aunty," she replied, "I'm fine now." She led my aunt into the tent. Grandmother was holding me in her arms.

"This one just can't stop crying. He's been crying all morning." She gave me to my mother, and I stopped crying as soon as I began suckling.

"Why do you keep going on and on about this?" my grandpa said. "You should hurry up and get ready to leave. You need to meet Alak in the monastery and ask his protection for our grandson and for him to be given a name." I cried and cried. My mother held me, and rocked me, but whatever she did I couldn't stop crying.

"It's a good time to go to the monastery and ask Alak's advice," Grandpa Naktam said. "This is such a pity. Maybe he was frightened by the storm and the lightning last night?" I continued crying, no matter what anyone did.

"Dear Mommy," my brother Japey said, "give me the baby. Let me put him in my robe."

My mother finally put me in his arms, and Japey said, "Sweet brother, dear brother. Don't cry now. Your brother is holding you. Please don't cry. Do you understand?" After listening to his voice a little while, I stopped crying.

"How lovely!" my mother said.

"Children do prefer other children," Grandpa Naktam said. "Maybe if the two brothers stay together he won't cry."

"Anyway, we're going to the monastery now," Grandmother said. "Damkho, take our elder son and a little butter and yogurt for Alak. Daughter-in-law, it's not good for you to go out today. I will carry the baby boy." She put me in her robe and we set off for the monastery. After the torrential rain of the night before, the grass was covered in drops of water. Many flowers had opened, and the air smelled sweet in the sunshine. The monastery was far away, and it was hard going because of the muddy road and the soaking grass.

"Grandmother," Damkho said, "do you need help carrying the baby? Can you walk all right, holding him?"

"Of course I can walk," she answered. "And if he cries, just let him cry. We're near the monastery now, Jamyang bear witness!" We walked on. As we neared the monastery, we looked toward the Chulong Valley grassland where the golden roofs of Madey Chugama Tashi Chulong Monastery glinted in the sunshine. The incense smoke of the monastery smelled sweet as it drifted toward us. We could hear the voices of the monks chanting rituals, and the music of the drums and brass trumpets. When we saw the monastery, it gave us a deep sense of happiness, and as soon as we arrived we began to pray.

Then my mother rushed up to join us.

"What's going on?" Aunt Damkho said. "Girl, are you mad? You shouldn't have walked all the way here. If you get sick it would be terrible."

"No problem," Grandmother said. "When we were young we'd do the milking and housework the night after giving birth. We never had any problem. It will be OK! Here, take your crying boy and let him suckle. Then, we need to go and see Alak Tagrang."

First we circumambulated the monastery, stopping at each temple and the monks' assembly hall to see the deities, butter lamps, and other treasures. After that, we headed toward Alak Tagrang's chambers. When we reached the entrance, a monk spoke to us.

"First, go to Alak's kitchen and have something to eat. He will receive you afterward." When we got to the kitchen we met other families from Gochen and Julag clans, who had come with their three babies. These babies had all been born the night before or that morning, and were also there to be put under the protection of Alak. A little later we were all allowed into the teacher's presence. Everyone had brought *khatags*, butter, yogurt, silver coins, and other items to give him.

In Alak's audience chamber one of the senior monks of the *nangchen* took our things and led us into audience.

Alak Tagrang was sitting on his bed with a white cloth draped over his bare arm.

"Come and sit down," he said. "You needn't have brought so many things. Well, well, what a day! So many babies born in a single day and night? I haven't seen so many babies all together for many years!" Then he asked what each family wanted and carefully noted the parents' names.

"How about each of you speak to me in turn?" he offered. My mother sat with the others, holding me. Try as she might to comfort me, I wouldn't stop crying, and she didn't know what to do. Alak suggested, "If you put him to your breast he won't cry." My mother held me to her breast, stood up, walked around, but I didn't stop crying.

"OK, come and sit down now," Alak said. "He really does cry a lot!"

"Alak, last night there was very strong lightning near our tent. Is he still frightened of the lightning and the storm?" my grandpa asked.

"Maybe," he replied. "There are usually one or two babies who cry a great deal, but few as forcefully as this one." Then Alak blessed all the guests with holy water. He also told each family which prayer they should say to benefit the life of their baby. Later, he gave a name to each newborn. "To the daughter from the *dewa*[4] give the name Chujid, to the boy from Julag give the name Gonbo Dondrup, to the daughter from Kochen give the name Shukyid." Then it was my turn. He looked at me again and again and said, "Yes, yes, crying so loudly. Who knows what's in his mind?" He gave me the name Gonpo Tashi and said, "I'm not sure about it, but I'm going to give him this name anyway. Call him this for now. Generally babies born today will suffer misfortune because of the planetary influences. In a very prosperous family or a lama's family they would be all right, but in ordinary families like yours, their lives may be in danger. If parents wish to prevent these influences, they should take their baby on a pilgrimage before the age of one, or let the child become a monk or nun. Doing this will help your children's lives and keep them safe; it will prevent them from being struck by misfortune before they are thirteen years old." At these words the parents' tears fell like beads from a broken necklace.

"Alak have mercy!" they wept. "Please keep our babies in your thoughts and protect them."

"Yes," Alak replied. "You should go to the monastery and ask for their protection, and I will ask for protection too. May the Three Precious Jewels protect you!" My mother was the last to present herself to Alak.

"Alak," she said, "please breathe on him to prevent his crying."

"Yes," Alak said, "it's especially meaningful and sad that he is crying. He is in the sea of the world's suffering, which is why he can't stop. Some children can sense this when they are small, but as they grow they forget, and cease crying. Some children have a premonition of a tragedy that will strike their lives in the future, and they become frightened and cry. This boy's life will

4. The generic name for a small settlement around a monastery.

probably be hard whatever you do. If you have time, take him on pilgrimage to Labrang Tashikyil Monastery and take refuge in Gungtang Jamyang. Here we are a small monastery with less exalted lamas, so it will take longer to have an effect." He said many things that left my family members uncomfortable and worried.

"Alak, there is nothing you don't know," my grandma said. "There are four hundred monks in Tashi Chulong Monastery, and please: all of you remember to protect my son." Wiping at her runny nose and tears, she pleaded for advice and comfort.

Finally, Alak gave protective threads blessed by lamas to the four babies. He gave red ones to the boys and green ones to the girls.

"Don't worry too much," he told everyone. "I am not one of those who can foretell how long someone will live and I cannot control the influence of karma on a person's life, but I promise that I and the monks in the monastery will pray to the Three Precious Jewels and make offering for these babies. Is that all right?" After these words the families calmed down.

The audience had taken a long time, and we arrived home at dusk. That day I had traveled far and cried a lot. When I was finally home again, my mother gave me her breast and I fell fast asleep. My grandma told the other family members all about our visit and what Alak had said.

"It's so sad!" she said. "If he were crying for his past life then it wouldn't be a problem. But if he is crying for this life there's nothing we can do about it!" Everyone in the family felt uneasy.

"Don't worry too much," Grandpa Naktam said. "When he is older let's allow him to become a monk. That will make it better!" He tried hard to comfort his family.

4

A Friend from a Previous Life Stops My Crying.

My crying got worse.

"He doesn't even sleep!" Grandma said. "Japey, come here and hold him. That might help again." Japey put me in his robe and walked outside.

"Darling, don't cry, don't cry," he said. "Your brother is holding you." After that I stopped crying, which was wonderful for my family. They learned that it was always true: when they handed me to my brother the crying stopped.

"It's a pity," Grandma said. "Why does he only stop crying in Japey's arms?"

"Don't worry about him. I'll take care of it," brother Japey said. "Sweet baby, don't cry—I'll put you in my robe."

"That's right," Grandpa said. "Since neither parent can control his crying, when Japey is here he can do his parents' job."

One day, when I was three months old, a hermit called Aku Manrang came to our home. My parents and aunts told him about all the crying.

"What did Alak say?" the hermit asked. Grandma relayed what Alak had said: that I felt submerged in deep waters of the world's sadness and could not stop crying from despair. "Really? It looks as if his crying portends much sadness in this life." He held me in his arms and whispered in my ear, "If that's right, you can cry, because nothing we can do will help." My family also heard him say, "Don't cry, sadness is only fate," but no one heard anything else that he whispered to me. Strangely I stopped crying soon afterward. "You didn't know," the hermit said to the others, "that this boy was my friend in a previous life. Starting today, he is like my nephew, and you can see that he isn't crying anymore. When he grows up he will be a monk. Don't worry. It's good that when Japey carries him he doesn't cry. These two brothers can't live apart for long in this life. They are heroic sons of the Naktsang clan. That's how I know they'll do well in the end." This and many other words like that made my family very happy.

As the old proverb says, "There's a doctor suitable for every patient and a lama for every soul."

"This child will meet with much sadness." This worried everyone, although each person had their own interpretation of his words. Grandpa Naktam said, "Everyone has their own road through life and can do nothing to change its course. In my Naktsang family, even when an uncle or father is as fine as a sandalwood tree, their nephew or son may be like a piece of rotten driftwood. However good or bad it is, our karma cannot be changed. Each of us has his own way of living with hardship. We are not going to worry from now on, even if we cannot help." Everyone accepted this as truth.

When I was older, my father spoke to my brother Japey and me.

"You are from a good family, both sons of a loving father," he told us. "A boy who grows up exploring his world will learn to take care of himself. A little suffering when young does a person good." I never forgot these words. They gave me mental strength and prepared me to overcome problems.

I had no idea that I would encounter so much suffering in life. However, I was able to survive it because of my dear father. Had he not made us self-reliant, we could not have survived.

A Wealthy Family's Karma.

Spinning her prayer wheel clockwise, Aunt Damkho told me more stories of my upbringing. I listened to her wide-eyed.

"It was nearly winter, and the late autumn brought snow and rain. My dear mother carried me every morning and afternoon to the monastery and temple. At noon she milked the yaks, while my brother put me in his robe and roamed around in the pen where she was working."

Brother Japey was four, she told me, with a big head and even bigger eyes. He was a kind and clever boy whom all our neighbors loved. Normally children would have their hair cut for the first time when they were three, but Japey's hair had not yet been cut. He carried me everywhere, so that my face became weatherbeaten and dark.

"Hey Big Head! Bring our black boy!" my parents and grandparents used to tease. One day Japey took me with him while he tethered the yaks and watched our mother do the milking.

"Mother Japey!" my mother teased him. "Don't tie the yaks too short, they'll kick you," she said. "Sit over near the tent rope." She always sang while she milked. "Oh, oh, dear female yaks, give your good milk and yogurt. Oh, oh good female yaks, may your goodness protect you in this lifetime," she used to sing.

Here is some history. When my mother was sixteen she married my father. When she was eighteen she gave birth to my brother, Japey, and when she was twenty-two gave birth to me. She was the youngest of nine brothers and sisters in the Meshel Wachen family. She was young, beautiful, kind, hardworking, and many families from our clan and others inquired about marriage to her. However, she preferred to remain at home with her parents, doing housework. Then one day her mother spoke to her.

"Daughter," she said, "you are old enough to leave the family now. Would you like that? I swear I'll be embarrassed if you stay at home much longer!" She told my mother many things about the blessings of marriage.

"I don't have to do anything I don't want to," my mother told my grandmother. "If I can't stay at home with you, I will become a nun." She didn't marry for a few years after that. Around that time the Naktsang family fought the chief of the Wachen but were defeated. They sought the protection of their close friend Rinchen's clan. However, while they were taking refuge, war broke out with the Malon Me chiefdom. Grandpa Naktam was shot and

Mother and child from Golok, northern Tibet.
Bild 135 S 15 48 23. From the collection of the Federal Archives of Germany, Koblenz.
Photographer, Bruno Beger. Ahnenerbe Expedition, 1938–1939.

wounded. Then my family, led by Deputy Chief Gondag, moved to Chugama chiefdom. Naktam took his elder son Dadul (my father) and his younger son Norjab and moved in with the Gotsa clan.

By good fortune my mother and father met then, and a year afterward my father took her as his bride to the Naktsang family. Even though she was happy with her own family, she came to ours. She lived with my father through many ups and downs, until the end of her life. Our family was large and wealthy and owned a lot of livestock. All her fellow clansmen said how lucky her family, the Meshel, was that its daughter was going to the Naktsang family. They were right. For the three or four years after she came, our family had thirty or forty horses, about one hundred bulls, a hundred cows, a hundred black yaks, and five hundred sheep. Every month our family invited lamas and monks to burn incense and pray to deities on their behalf. Visitors and friends came from near and far to see them. As the proverb says, "The wealthy walk proudly, speak loudly, and have many guests. Their deities are brave, brides generous, and guard dogs fierce."

The Naktsang family's fame had spread far and wide. The old people said, "These days the Naktsang family is flourishing and prospering. They never stop eating meat, even in the summer months. They never stop eating yogurt, even in the winter. They ride horses wherever they go, and carry guns on their backs. Their sons stay at home. Now this happiness has been extended to Meshel Tserangkyid (my mother's name)." The people who said this were right. Maybe the Naktsang family was lucky, or perhaps my mother's family was lucky that she went to us. And from the day she arrived the Naktsang became even more numerous and wealthy, happier and more prosperous!

One year, the New Year celebrations were over, and spring was in its first month.

"My heart is a little disturbed these days," my dear mother told my father. "Sometimes when I wake up at night I'm so frightened I feel sick."

"Maybe it's not an illness," Father said. "Did you ask Alak Tagrang when you went to the monastery?"

"I did, but he didn't say anything," my mother answered, weeping. "How terrible! If something happened to me while the boys are so young, it would be very hard for you."

"Don't worry so much," my father reassured her. "I swear it's only a headache or a stomachache," and he wiped away my mother's tears.

"I'd like to go to Labrang Monastery to meet Alak Gungtang there," my mother said. "Let me take the two boys with me, so they can have his protection."

"You must have a good companion," Father said, "or you can't go, especially because you will have to carry our youngest."

"There's no problem finding a companion," my mother said, "but I didn't tell my parents. They might not let me go. They will tell me to go with them during the Monlam festival during the winter, but I can't wait until then."

At that time no one really knew what my mother sensed in her heart or whether she had real cause for her sadness. Four or five days later she set off before dawn with one of her sisters and a neighbor's daughter. The three of them walked to Labrang with nothing but some food.

"Aunt, where did my mother go? When will she be back?" Japey kept saying.

"Your mother and aunt went on pilgrimage to Labrang Monastery," Aunt Damkho said. "They'll be back tomorrow or the day after." But it was half a month later before my mother and her companions made it home.

"Did you meet Alak Gungtang?" my father asked. "What did he tell you?"

"Yes, I met him," my mother said, "and he put the two boys under his protection and said he wouldn't forget them. He told me to go home as soon as my pilgrimage was over, but apart from that he didn't say anything." She took the red ribbons Alak Gungtang had given her and knotted them around my neck and my brother Japey's. In the afternoon she told the whole family about her pilgrimage.

"You were very brave," Grandpa Naktam said, "and now your wish has come true. Our crying boy is protected by Alak Gungtang, so there will be no problem." The whole family ate a delicious meal together with lots of meat and fat, and talked until midnight. The next day Aunt Rigdron, Aunt Damkho, the Meshel family grandmother, and many other relatives visited my mother.

"Yes, daughter-in-law, cook them some delicious meat," Grandpa Naktam said. "Today you should eat and drink like thirsty deer at the stream and take time to chat with each other. Take your time. We've got nothing important to do, have we?"

"We'll do that, Grandpa," my mother replied. She cooked meat and large and small intestines and put milk in the pot for everyone to drink. Later, she brought out fresh yogurt for my aunts.

"I hope you're not attached to the Naktsang family wealth—we're going to eat and drink plenty of it today," Aunt Damkho said.

"Wealth is impermanent," Grandpa told her. "Today we have it, but tomorrow it might be gone. I wouldn't be upset if you came and ate here every day. I'm a Naktsang man who can't be shocked in his body or in a single hair." They expressed their loyalty to each other, and they talked and ate and drank until the afternoon was over.

Vultures gathering for a "sky burial," Lhasa.
Bild 135 S 12 50 22. From the collection of the Federal Archives of Germany, Koblenz.
Photographer, Bruno Beger. Ahnenerbe Expedition, 1938–1939.

6

Misery and Disaster. My Mother Passes Away.

Two or three days later my dear mother couldn't get up in the morning. She complained of pains in her entire head and neck. At first, she told us she had a cold. Then scrofula began, and the disease became more serious day by day. The Naktsang family invited many lamas and monks to perform rituals and chant prayers for her. They invited many doctors to bring medicine, and invited many exorcists as well. Whatever they did, my mother's illness didn't improve. It was like pouring water on stone.

"Darling Durkho," she said, "it seems there is no hope that I will live. I am causing you sadness by leaving you with these two boys, who are so young and will cause you much hardship. At least I placed the two boys under the protection of Alak Gungtang. If I die it would be best for you to remarry, so the boys have a stepmother."

"Don't talk about such pitiful things—you aren't dying," my father said, and burst into tears.

"Yes, great father," my mother said, "your sons have no reason to cry now. Human beings have their life span, and it's natural that my life should end.

I went to Labrang and met with Alak Gungtang, so now I have no reason to worry. You must remarry, and make certain the two boys become worthy human beings. Alak said before that the boys would suffer, and now they have encountered hardship through the Law of Karma. It's a pity they are too young to understand. Nulo has been told he will be a monk and has got Alak's ribbon, so you shouldn't worry about him. You will just do your best—I don't fear that you will have an unhappy life." While she spoke, tears trickled down her face, expressing the tragic separation of death and the end of life together with my father.

Afternoon shadows covered the valleys. My mother lay in the bed, while my father held her. From time to time she opened her eyes. She gazed intently at my father and brother Japey, who wrapped me in his robe and stayed close to them. She stopped speaking. Tears ran down her face. Then in one moment she passed away as though she had fallen asleep in my father's arms, without pain or suffering. She never returned—just traveled to the west where the Buddha Amitabha's paradise awaits, oblivious now of any family: of father, Japey, or me. She left us behind her.

There were many butter lamps on the altar near the Naktsang family's *do*. Ten monks came to chant rituals every day, and the sound of their bells and horns could be heard from far away. Relatives, neighbors, and friends from other clans came to the Naktsang family to mourn and give comfort. The flow of guests coming to see the Naktsang never stopped. On the third day twenty horsemen came and put my mother's body on horseback. They took it to Tashi Chulong Monastery. Our women neighbors collected a lot of ashes and poured them on my mother's bed. When my mother's corpse arrived at the monastery, four hundred monks chanted and performed a ritual of ablution on the stairs in front of the monks' assembly hall. Then they put my mother's body on horseback again and took it to the monastery's sky burial site. This is on the grassland at the end of the Chulong Valley—a beautiful place. There were thousands of mani prayer stones all around the cemetery. Above the piles of mani stones hung thousands of *lungta* prayer flags—white, red, and yellow. Sometimes they made sounds in the wind, "Shog, shog," "Ar, ar." It was a little frightening. After the corpse reached the cemetery, the old man in charge of the funeral let down his long hair and rolled up the sleeves of his robe. Then he removed my mother's clothes and lay her down on her front. He put a white rope around my mother's neck and tied it to a stake. Ten monks, stationed above the cemetery, blew horns and chanted. Not far to the west, white vultures, brown vultures, and black vultures were flying in the sky above the cemetery. For a moment they just circled, and then one by one they landed near my mother's body. The monk used a knife to cut many crosses in my mother's back and bottom, and also cut some pieces of flesh from my mother's back and legs, and he threw them on the ground. However, the vultures just walked around the body and didn't eat. Then the old man cut some pieces of flesh from my mother's body, put them in his mouth and chewed them.

"Yes, my little white one and my little black one, you should come here and eat a little for yourself," he said to the vultures and gave a piece of meat to each one. Still the vultures did not eat. The old man knew all the vultures personally and called them by name, putting flesh mixed with *tsampa* in front of them. Usually, he gave blood to the ones who liked blood, then collected the pieces of bone and gave them to a *segoyur* bird. But that day, whatever he tried, they would not eat. Then a white vulture shaped like a conch shell, a *dungya kyi*, flew in from the west and settled on the ground above my mother's body. It pecked at my mother's back three or four times. After the white vulture flew in, all the other vultures immediately ran to my mother's body and tore and ate the flesh and skin until it was gone.

Some people were cooking near the cemetery. The man in charge of the funeral wiped the blood off his hands onto his robe and came and sat down to eat his meal. He didn't seem to feel unclean. After eating the remains and tsampa, most of the vultures were full and flew to perches on a mountain near the cemetery to rest. Some were still eating. The man had smashed my mother's head into pieces, leaving hair and bone together, and had given it to the vultures. He smashed the leg bones and other large bones and gave them to the vultures and segoyur. Later the monks finished their chanting rituals and left. The man in charge of the funeral finished giving my mother's body to the vultures, leaving everything very tidy and clean. He returned home with his companions. All that was left in the cemetery was a tiny scrap of meat and blood that was being eaten by crows. So my mother left her poor family behind in the world. Who knew how long her mind, like a small bee, would wander in the darkness of the intermediate state, waiting for rebirth?

The Naktsang family performed rituals for my mother for forty-nine days. The family gave generously of yaks, horses, and sheep to the monastery. They gave a great quantity of meat and other food to stray dogs and beggars. Alak Medo told us that my mother had been reborn as the son of a wealthy family in Lhade chiefdom. However, dead people are dead, and you cannot meet them again to see whether their rebirth in this world is a happy one or not. Still, on hearing Alak's message the family and relatives said, "Oh happiness," "Oh love," "She was a good-hearted girl, so she had a good rebirth." Everyone expressed many happy thoughts. Alak's speech calmed them all.

7

The Naktsang Family Experiences One Calamity after Another.

My older brother Japey was young, and he experienced the full sadness of my mother's death. Every afternoon, while he was carrying me around, he lingered near the tent rope where she used to milk.

"Mommy, mommy, where are you?" he cried. My father's sadness could be read on his face every day, too. Starting then, the Naktsang family became weaker. While the family was busy at home one day, ten horses were stolen by thieves. After my dear mother's funeral day, my uncle Norjab left our sheep on the mountain while he joined a posse of armed men to recover the horses. During the night the sheep suffered a serious attack by wolves—they killed fifteen sheep and injured eight or nine others. All our neighbors were sated with that meat.

"Now my Naktsang family is like the Horgurkar family," Grandpa Naktam said. "This year is an unlucky one, and from now on things will get worse. It's a pity that the wrong person died—it should have been me that died. Yama, god of hell, was blind, and took the wrong person to death." He wept and beat his breast.

Several days after my mother passed away, my aunt Rigdron took me to her home so that she could look after me. At that time I was seven months and fifteen days old. Aunt Damkho and Grandma Tsolo helped the Naktsang family by doing housework and some of the outside work. At that time an especially unfortunate thing happened to my family on their way back from Labrang Monastery, where they had gone to perform religious duties for my mother. On the road home they met robbers from Ngora Lhade chiefdom. Shooting broke out, and Norjab, Grandpa's youngest son, was shot dead. Misfortunes were falling from the sky one by one for the Naktsang family. Eventually the killer was identified, and it was one of Norjab's companions, a close friend of his. However, as the shooting had taken place at night, they hadn't known each other. Two of the Lhade people had been killed during their ambush. At daybreak everyone recognized each other, and Norjab's friends helped take his body to the monastery. They asked the monks to look after his dead body well.

The monasteries and chiefs of the two chiefdoms discussed the matter with Lhade, but there must be a blood payment to recompense for the murder of a single human being. Money cannot settle it, and the loss of a son is beyond price.

"Who will satisfy the Naktsang family's hunger for revenge?" Grandpa

Naktam said when he heard about it. "May their dead heads turn into blood! I am finished—my beloved son is lost! How deep is my anguish that I can't leave this house. In the past, if I had gone after them, not one of them would have been left to make themselves a fire! I swear that we will be revenged—I swear it a hundred times by *seryim.*" He lay on his bed crying and writhing. At that time my grandpa Naktam was over seventy-seven. The wound he had received the year before from the Malon Me army's bullet still had not healed. After that he was confined to bed and could not get up because he was so oppressed by sadness and anger. He could only move his head, and everyone said that he would die. The astrologers calculated and the diviners prophesied. The monastery performed prayer rituals. Then Alak announced that Grandpa's illness would go on longer, but that he would come through. He would not lose his life.

The sun rose and fell as it always did. From each sunrise to each sunset, the Naktsang family, like all other families, had to look after themselves as carefully and peacefully as possible. Then, in the summer of the following year, the Madey Chugama and Malon Me chiefdoms made war on each other over land. Chugama lost, and we fled to the Lhade chiefdom to live. After that, the Lhade fought among themselves, and our family left that chiefdom to cross the Machu River into Sogpo. Other clans—the Tolag and Gojara—settled there permanently.

When Aunt Damkho told me these stories, my mind filled with sadness, and whose would not? My mother had a short life, and I was fated to misfortune. I did not remember my mother taking care of me or looking at me with love in her eyes. Most of the time I wasn't conscious of my longing, but again and again when I heard the other children in the village calling their mothers, I would fall down and cry.

"Why don't I have a mother?" I asked myself. When I was a child I used to call "Aunt!" "Grandma!" "Father!" but I never called "Mother!" When I heard about someone else's mother dying, or heard that their babies were crying, my tears fell as freely as theirs. Now I understand that it was not her fault that she did not look after me—it was the black Lord of Death that forced her into the next life. I still had my dear father, and if he was safe, I was happy.

I had no opportunity to express my gratitude to my dear mother personally. I did chant some mani prayers for her when I was young, and went to many monasteries and asked many lamas for prayers on her behalf. I wished that if I chanted prayers for my dear mother with full concentration in my heart, that they could revive her body like rain. I never understood why the old people chanted all morning and afternoon, but when I chanted prayers as a child I wanted them to benefit my mother's soul as it wandered somewhere in the intermediate realms.

It was hot at noon that day. Aunt Damkho was sitting in the sunshine, rubbing marrow into her shin and knees. I lay in front of her, naked, eating tsampa with my fingers. Uncle Norta came out of the tent.

"Are you telling stories about the past today?" Norta asked.

"I don't have the patience to tell stories every day," Aunt replied.

"You should tell him some of the Naktsang family's history now, so it's clear in his mind. Durkho would feel uncomfortable doing it," Uncle said.

"Last time, when I talked about the death of the boys' mother, something happened in my heart and I found I was still angry. I swear I can't do it. Can you tell the stories, please?" Aunt asked.

So, my uncle told me many tales about the Naktsang family.

After the fighting between the Madey Chugama and Malon Me chiefdoms was over, Chugama lost their land and lived in Sogpo for two years. At that time the Naktsang clan lived at Kousen Dolog. The Meshel clan and many other relatives tried to persuade my father to marry again.

"No, I won't get married," my father told them. "I want to let my sons grow up first. Nothing can replace their mother."

"My son," Grandpa Naktam told him, "behind death is life. In spite of all these things you've been saying, it would be good for you to have an uncomplicated, whole family."

At that time I was still living at Aunt Rigdron's home. Sometimes my brother, Jabey, came to the tent door and cried, telling me he missed me.

"Don't cry," Grandpa Naktam told him. "After the New Year your father will take him back. If he doesn't, Grandma and I will bring him to our home. Understand?"

Originally Grandpa Naktsang Tame's family was from Zorge. When he was a child he was known as Tame Mdanglo. He was a brave boy who became a great bandit.

Later Naktam got married and lived in Wayan chiefdom with the Lang sept. He had two sons, Durkho and Norjab. After a while my father wanted to start a family and became engaged to a girl called Chujid. But then Grandpa Naktam and the high chief of Wayan had a bitter argument. Also, one day, a close and sworn friend of my father's, Rinchen Taso, heard that the Wagen clan was preparing to attack the Naktsang family. Rinchen Taso left that same night on horseback, carrying two guns and leading an extra horse, to warn our family and raise a force against the Wagen clan. The entire Naktsang family escaped, with the help of Rinchen Taso. After that my family moved to Madey Chugama, and my father married into the Meshel family. Chujid of Wayan chiefdom was soon engaged to someone else.

The autumn that my mother and my uncle died, Grandpa Naktam fell and broke his arm while he was out walking. His wound had still not healed, and now his arm was broken, too. From that day on he became progressively sicker and could not eat, drink, walk, or even sit without assistance. But many people helped us. Uncle Gontag and his cousins found a female servant from the Gangchen clan to care for Grandpa Naktam, and with Norjab gone, neighbors looked after the Naktsang family's livestock.

Also, we had plenty of food. My father was famous throughout the chiefdom as a good shot. He loved guns (and horses), and owned a gun of the type known as "Bira Gongtong." Friends and neighbors were always happy to go hunting in the mountains with him. When I was a child my father often killed deer, and he brought home their antlers and meat. I also remember him killing foxes, wolves, male musk deer, and other animals.

8

I Return to My Own Home.
My Grandfather Departs for the Peaceful Realm.

Not long afterward, my father came to Aunt Rigdron's and brought me home. Japey and I walked into our tent hand in hand and went to where Grandpa was lying in bed.

"Hey, my big-headed, dark-skinned son," Grandpa said, "come here so Grandpa can have a look at you. Oh, good, my grandson is growing up." Tears fell from his eyes as he looked at me, his face filled with kindness. He took some red fruits from under his pillow and gave them to Japey and me. At that time I was four years old, but my birth hair had still never been cut. My family dressed me in a small calfskin robe patched with felt. I had no shoes to wear.

"What a shame our family has no nice *dzagpa* for my son," Grandpa said. "Tomorrow Grandpa will make you a warm little robe." The next day Grandpa cut off the sleeves of his sheepskin robe. With these he made me a small sheepskin robe. Even though it was old, the sheepskin was very warm. He also made winter boots for me out of the same robe. The boots had sheep fur inside and sheepskin outside. It was the first time, since I was born, that I had worn a good skin robe and boots on my feet. When Uncle Norta told me this tale, I could remember it slightly.

As New Year came closer, Grandpa's illness became worse. Prayers were said for him, rituals performed, and monks and lamas took him under their protection. Although this eased people's minds, Grandpa's illness became even more serious. He was not getting better. One day Grandpa called my father to him.

A nomadic family with their flocks and herds on the grassland of northeastern Tibet.
121999-243191. Photographer, Joseph Rock, 1924.
© President and Fellows of Harvard College, Arnold Arboretum Archives.

"Gracious son," he said, "I know that I am going to die. Don't call any more doctors or put me under the protection of any more lamas or monks. This is the end of my life. Tomorrow ask Deputy Chief Mgotag and Uncle Jakho to come here. I have something to tell them. Oh, and please also ask Alak Ganden to come here if he is available."

"The monk-doctor's coming tomorrow," my father said. "Maybe he'll give you some medicine that will make you better."

The next morning Mgotag, Jakho, and Alak Ganden all came to see Naktam.

"I'm a sinful man," Grandpa said to them. "Only prayers and rituals can help keep me from going to hell. But my life was drawn by my own hands. Now I have to bear the burden on my own shoulders. When I was young I had no regrets for what I did, and now, when the time comes to die, it's too late for regret. All that's left is my son Durkho, who has two young sons, and no brother to help him when he needs it. In the future, please look out for him and help him. I'm an old man now, and have nothing more to tell you."

"Before New Year I'm going to finish the prayers asking for you to have protection," Alak Ganden said. "For now, you should pray to the Three Pre-

A chieftain in traditional dress, Amdo, northeastern Tibet.
123444-245417. Photographer, Joseph Rock, 1924.
© President and Fellows of Harvard College, Arnold Arboretum Archives.

cious Jewels for help during the intermediate state of the next life. If you have committed a great sin that might be punished in your next life, and you regret it in your heart, you can confess it before your death. That would be of great benefit to you, in this life and the next." Then he spoke a lot about religion.

"Yes, greatest of Alaks," Grandpa said, "but I'm not sure whether sudden regret and confession only at the time of death is helpful. I am not frightened to die now. My fear is less than a tiny hair. From now on, only the Three Precious Jewels know what is good or bad in me." Later in the afternoon, as they were leaving, Uncle Mgotag spoke to my father.

"From the way he was talking, it doesn't seem as though he can last long. Make your preparations, and I will make arrangements with the monastery," he told him.

Two days later, Grandpa could no longer speak—he could only move his hands. Deep in the night he turned his eyes up, and took long breaths in and out. His left hand trembled. At daybreak he coughed a little and then breathed no more. He had gone to the peaceful place.

Aunt Damkho, Uncle Norta, and others came to our home to help my dear father. Someone brought millet oil, and others lit butter lamps. Aunt Damkho, my father, and the others did not make any sound as tears rolled down their faces. At noon Uncle Mgotag led ten monks to the house to perform rituals for the dead. Relatives, friends, and well-wishers from near and far came to mourn with the Naktsang family, and my father welcomed the guests to our home. On the day of Grandpa's funeral, horsemen came to put my grandpa's body on horseback and take it to the monastery.

Now only my dear father, my brother Japey, and I were left in the family. The Naktsang family was still somewhat wealthy in livestock and money, and all the members were still gathered in one area. However, from the time my dear mother left us, the family members had scattered farther apart and become poorer. Our black yak hair tent measured eighteen cloth breadths[5] on each side and needed three wooden posts inside to pitch it properly. When the entire family was still together, it had seemed small for all of us, but now that the family was separated it seemed too big and empty inside.

After many days, Deputy Chief[6] Mgotag, Meshel uncle Mgontse, monk-uncle Jakho, and others came to our home. Japey and I played outside while they talked all day. At the end of the afternoon they left.

"It's up to you," Uncle Mgotag said to my father. "It doesn't seem like a bad

5. Twenty-four to thirty inches, or the width a woman can straddle during hand weaving.
6. Madey Chugama chiefdom was ruled by one "high" and three "deputy" chiefs, who had different constitutional roles, some of which still operate informally today.

idea. You should leave some yaks and sheep with your cousin's family, and I'll go to the monastery to make preparations for your stay there."

"Yes, yes, thank you," my father said. "There's nothing else I can see to do, so I will do this. To join a new family now would not be good for the boys. It's better for them both to grow up with our own monastery and clansmen." Then he sent them on their way. The next day, our neighbors helped us strike our tent. They took down all the prayer flags around it and offered them to Lhachen Dorje Yidra, our mountain deity. Then they gathered ten large and small horses, thirty large and small yaks, and seventy sheep and gave them to Chugama Monastery. Apart from some furniture, the family gave away almost everything, even our tent. Two female yaks, four or five horses, and about thirty sheep were taken to the Meshel family and to Uncle Norta's family. Nothing was left with us, except two stallions, three cows, and three female yaks.

Then we folded our tent and went to the monastery, where Grandpa's body had been taken.

On the day that we folded our tent, the Naktsang family came to an end. From that day on there was a Naktsang father and Naktsang sons, but no Naktsang family with a tent pitched in Madey Chugama. There is a saying that human life is always changing, and that wealth is unpredictable, too. A few years ago there was a family called Naktsang with many people. It was a prosperous family, fortunate in its flocks of sheep, its horses and yaks. Now only a single man and his orphan sons were left.

9

Fetching Charity Soup from the Circuit Path around the Monastery for the First Time.

"Right," Uncle Jakho said cheerfully, "with these two boys to stay with me and help me, I'm happy. Durkho, you can go wherever you like. I'll look after them."

"That's good, dear Uncle," father said, "but I worry that I'm giving you trouble. If you'd like me to cook food or fetch firewood for you before I leave, I'll do it. Now that the boys are safe with you, I will feel relaxed as I go from place to place, visiting other families." Four or five days later, my father left to visit Uncle Tsode's home in Ngawa. Japey joined the monastery classes with Uncle Jakho. They both rose before daybreak and went to study, souring the day I was in the house alone. After sunrise I got up and lit a fire in the stove. I made a little tea, drank it, and ate some tsampa. At noon Japey brought me a bowl of charity soup. Even though he was so young, he cared for me like a parent.

"What a wonderful child this is," our relatives and the monks said. "Without his help the two children would not be all right, as their father is always away on business, wandering from family to family." Japey was still a young child, but after our mother died he cooked for the family, collected firewood, cleaned ash from the stove, fed the dog, and did much other work with my late grandfather. Now he was eight or nine, and he knew how to do all of the inside and outside work very thoroughly and well. If he went to find firewood, he put a rope and a small bag in my hand and took me with him. When he fetched water, he put a small kettle in my hand and took me with him then, too.

"I am a monk and don't have enough free time away from my classes to collect all the firewood and fetch water," he would tell me. "These are jobs you should learn at an early age." When we cooked noodle soup for dinner, he showed me how to make the flour for the noodle dough. Sometimes we made dumplings together. He kneaded the dough, and I cut the meat and put it in the dough. Before this I had known how to make a fire in the stove and cook a little, but I had no idea how to do these other things. Japey walked hand in hand with me and showed me where to go and what to do. I collected firewood from the mountain behind the monastery or beside the Machu River. I would fetch water from the spring near the circuit path around the monastery, then cut up the meat for our dinner and make flour. At night, after Japey and Uncle Jakho got home, I made the tea and finished cooking dinner.

"Well now," Uncle Jakho said, "Nukho really is very good—he's just like our mother. But don't go too far away to collect firewood, otherwise the dogs from the dewa will bite you." He was very happy and proud when he said all of this. A few days later Jakho went to perform religious services in some other villages, leaving Japey and me alone in his home. I missed my father.

"Why hasn't our father come back yet, brother?" I asked Jabey.

"Father went to Ngawa on business. He'll be back soon," he told me. "When he returns, he'll be impressed that you can cook and collect firewood and fetch water." I was happy to hear that, and every day while Jabey was in class I cleaned inside or outside, emptying the ashes, fetching water, collecting firewood, and other things.

One day Uncle Jakho returned with two very big pieces of meat.

"Hey, Nukho, I've brought meat for the two of you."

"Where did it come from, Uncle?" I asked.

"A family gave it to me as the fee for my chanting. Let's cook it now. It will be delicious when Jabey gets here." The meat was too large for me to cut very well, but Uncle finished cutting it into pieces and put it in the pot to cook. Jabey came home before the meat was cooked, carrying two small pats of butter, another big piece of meat, and three silver coins.

"Who gave you the silver money?" Jakho asked.

"One of Alak Tag's cousins died, and there's even more coming in a few days. There was as much tsampa as you could eat, and I filled myself with noodle soup. They say that there's one yak for every four monks," Jabey told us. However you look at it, if a monk living in a monastery can feed himself and two others at home, then that monastery is rich.

"Tomorrow morning take the small aluminum pot," Jabey told me a few days later, "and go to the place opposite the kitchen where they give out soup every day. There will be many dewa families there. Go and get some soup. You are a child, so there's no reason to be shy about asking."

The next day I went to the door of the kitchen. An old man, an old woman, and many children were sitting there chanting manis.

"How lovely," said the old woman when I got there. "It's Durkho's younger son. Come here and sit with me while we wait for the soup to be poured." I sat and waited with them, also chanting manis. Soon after, a group of monks brought the soup and gave some to each of us.

"Yes, chant your prayers, chant your prayers," the monks told us. "It's hard to get religious food flowing. Chant a lot of manis." When they got to me they exclaimed, "Here's a new one!"

"That's the Naktsang family's younger son," the old woman explained.

"Oh, poor thing!" the monk said. "This is the Meshel dead daughter's son then. Well, my boy, as you are a new guest you'll get extra meat!" He added soup to my pot until it spilled over the brim. It was too hot to carry, so I waited for it to cool. Everyone else took their soup home, and I watched the monks give leftovers to the dogs. When the pot had cooled, I took it home. So, when Jabey got home that evening there was no need to cook, as we had the monastery soup to eat.

"Don't go for soup tomorrow," Jabey said. "If you get it every day we won't be able to finish it." From then on, I went for soup every other day.

10

A Lonely Life. My Gratitude toward Uncle Jakho.

A few days later my father returned. "You often leave the boys alone like this. It's hard on them," all of our cousins told my father.

"My boys can feed themselves, even though they are little, and it will get easier for them every year, as they grow. There's no need to worry," my father said. He stayed for about ten days in the monastery and then went off on his travels again. Japey and I were all right whether my father was there or not,

A lama with his monastic attendant, Lhasa.
Bild 135 S 10 09 39. From the collection of the Federal Archives of Germany, Koblenz.
Photographer, Bruno Beger. Ahnenerbe Expedition, 1938–1939.

but sometimes I asked him, "Dear father, please will you come back soon this time?"

"All right my darling," he would reply. "I will come home quickly. You must do what your brother Japey says, understand? Your father will be back soon this time." Then he would leave, but even though he had said it would be a short time, he wouldn't come back for one or two months. Uncle Jakho was always with us, and he took care of us, and worried very deeply about us in his heart. I loved Uncle Jakho more than any of my other relatives.

Despite this, sometimes I gave him trouble. One day Uncle Jakho said he was in a "retreat" and needed to practice fasting and keeping silent. I took it into my head to try to interrupt Uncle Jakho's meditation. At first, I stood in front of him.

"Would you like something to eat?" I asked. I tried everything I could think of to make him laugh and then went behind him.

"Uncle!" I yelled, but he didn't respond. A little while later I went behind him again.

"A . . . na . . . na . . . !" I cried out, as if in pain, and pretended to cry.

"Right then, what's wrong now?" he said and broke off his meditation. I laughed, and then he knew that I had tricked him.

"What a pity!" he said. "What a bad boy—you should be sorry. I swear I'll never try to do my hermit meditation near you again. You will have to bear the sin and punishment for that. All right, go and get us some food. It's too late now; I have lost my meditation."

One day I went to get soup as usual and on the way back met Zodpa, the monastery's water carrier. One of his eyes wasn't right, so behind his back people called him "Blind Zodpa."

"Nukho, where have you been?" he asked.

"I've been to fetch soup," I told him.

"Right," he said. "Starting tomorrow, don't wait outside the monastery, but come directly into the kitchen, and I'll give you soup. We're relatives, didn't you know that?" The next day I went straight to the monastery kitchen, and Akhu Zodpa and his partners filled a pot full of rice for me and poured soup into my wooden bowl.

"Boy, eat as much as you like," one of the monk-cooks said to me, "and then take your pot home." After that, I always went into the monastery kitchen, and after they fed me I brought more food home. I never went by way of the path around the monastery again. As thanks for their soup, I helped the monk-cooks carry firewood, clean the ashes from the great furnace, and empty the tea leaves.

"How wonderful that such a young boy can work as well as this," the monk-cooks said. They were very kind to me. They helped me wash my face and hands, and when they poured my soup, they always gave me an extra piece of meat. Sometimes they also gave me a little butter or a bone with meat on it. Whatever else was happening, I still had enough to eat and drink every day, and some to bring home as well. Japey and Uncle Jakho were both very pleased.

11

Working for the Monastery as a Little Water Carrier, and Feeding the Orphan Puppy.

One day I brought home some of the discarded monastery tea leaves and dried them. Then I put them in the churn and made tea with them. I had made a delicious kind of tea soup!

"Nukho," Uncle Jakho asked me, "where did you get that delicious tea?"

"It's not real tea," I answered. "It's made from the monastery's old tea leaves."

"What a good experiment!" he said. "Even if we can't afford real tea, we can make this soup!"

One morning, Akhu Zodpa came to our door.

"Nukho, son of a great father," he said, "please help me fetch water today." I went out and helped him lead his horse. The previous day the horse had kicked him in the shin, and he couldn't walk well. When we got to the spring, I held the horse while he poured water into two big water buckets on the horse's back. When they were full he said, "Right, my brave boy, now lead the horse slowly back to the monastery kitchen, and when the monks have finished taking the water out lead it back here again." I walked the horse to the kitchen, and when the monks had poured out the water, they put its lead rein in my hands, and I took it back to the spring. After refilling the buckets, we walked back to the monastery together, with me leading the horse. In the kitchen Akhu Zodpa told his fellow monks, "Without this dear boy's help, I couldn't have brought you water today. Akhu Dragpa, please give him extra meat in his soup."

"Well, you little water carrier boy, I'm going to give you your reward," Akhu Dragpa said as he poured my soup. He added a lot of meat to it. From that time on I sometimes helped Akhu Zodpa fetch water from the spring.

Then, one day a brown bitch that had given birth to a litter of puppies was found dead among the monastery firewood. No one knew what had happened. Akhu Zodpa dragged the dead dog to the monastery path and threw it over a cliff. Only two of the puppies were left alive—their eyes had just opened. They walked around crying. I was so sad to see them suffer and thought, "Their mother is dead, just like mine," and wept freely.

I made a round bed for them. "Now, don't be afraid to sleep here," I told them. "Even though your mother is dead I will look after you, understand?" I gave them soup from my own bowl. They did not know how to eat yet, but I fed them one by one with my mouth, first chewing the food myself. Five or six days later, when I put the soup bowl near their mouths, they understood how to eat. After they had finished the soup they gnawed the top of the bowl, scraping and gouging it with their small teeth.

One day, for some unknown reason, the larger puppy died, leaving only the little black one. I couldn't control my heart's sadness that only one puppy was left.

"My poor little thing," I told the remaining one, "don't be sad that your brother is dead. We'll stick together." I tucked him into my robe and went home. Japey was happy to see him too. The puppy never slept in his own bed but climbed into mine. Then he would lick my nose, mouth, and face all over and keep me awake.

Every day I led the puppy to the monastery kitchen. If I helped the monk-cooks fetch water, I left him in the firewood pile outside the kitchen. He never wandered off but just waited for me to return. Whenever the monks gave me soup, we ate together from my bowl.

When we were out walking, I told him "You should stay close behind me so you don't get lost." He ran behind me and sometimes fell over. One day Japey gave me a small bell. "Tie this onto the puppy's neck," he said. So I tied it around the puppy's neck and it rang, "Ting, ting, ting." The monks recognized the sound and said, "There goes Nukho's tail!" The little dog really helped me. He lived with me, played games with me, and gave me someone to talk to.

— THE BULLIES —

During the winter the days were dark. The monks had to take their afternoon religious classes in the sunshine of the monastery courtyard. Japey attended these classes. Afraid to stay alone in the house, I went with him. The class took place on the mountain, and there was a tall rock in front of the court-yard. I waited there because I wasn't allowed to sit with the students. The class was long, and I often fell asleep while I was waiting.

One unforgettable night, I fell asleep on the stone outside the grove. I half awoke to feel tepid liquid trickling down my head. I put my head up to look. A young monk was urinating on me.

"All right, boy?" he said. "Now you can have some warm tea." Although the moon was shining brightly, I didn't recognize him. Two other monks were with him, and he said to them, "We woke him up" and laughed at me.

Japey ran over and said to the young monk, "May your dead head turn into blood" and beat him on the head with the handle of his *chabri*. The monk fell over on the rock, and Japey pulled the hair of the other two monks. One of our cousins, an older monk named Tawu, grabbed the young monk's ear.

"You've had it!" he shouted. "I swear I'll kill you here and now if you don't lick your urine off of him with your tongue." The young monk started crying, and he licked my head and robe. Blood trickled down his head. Then the monk responsible for discipline appeared.

"You have behaved badly," he said. "Why are you acting like thoughtless babies?" He helped me wipe off my head and face with his robe, and then Japey and I walked home hand in hand.

That night Uncle Jakho stayed at home to comfort me. I told him about how the young monk had urinated on me.

"What did you do? Did you cry?" he asked.

"Brother Japey and Tawo hurt his head and made him lick the urine with his tongue. I didn't cry," I replied.

"Well done, my brave boy," he told me. "A grown man will meet many good and bad things, so he shouldn't cry whenever something goes wrong." Uncle Jakho left after staying with us for five or six days. After that, when Japey went to his night class, the black puppy and I followed him and waited on the stone by the monastery entrance, as always.

— WANDERERS IN THE GRASSLAND —

Before New Year my father returned and took me to the grassland. First we went to Uncle Mgotag and Aunt Rigdron's home, where we stayed for ten days. Brother Getag, sister Shukyid, and sister Tigbajid were there and played games with me. Getag also took me shepherding with him. By then, everyone called me "Nukho." Aunt Damkho, Rigdron, and the others called me "Aunty Nukho, Aunty Nukho." Nukho had become my normal name, and nobody called me by my lama-given name, Gonpo Tashi.

"You should call my grandson by the proper name that the lama gave him," my grandpa often said while he was alive. "If you don't call him Gonpo Tashi he'll forget his real name," he'd complain, but no one listened to him. The name given to me by the lama was forgotten, and nobody called me that anymore.

One day Uncle Norta came to take us to his home.

Uncle Norta was the husband of my father's sister and had two boys called Gonjab and Tsephel. Their mother had died many years ago, and after her death Norta married Aunt Damkho. The brothers Gonjab and Tsephel were so kind to me while my father and I stayed in their home, and they played with me every day.

"Now, Nukho," Aunt Damkho said, "promise you won't go back to the monastery. You must stay here with us."

"If I don't go back," I replied, "brother Japey won't have anyone to help him cook, and I really need to look after my puppy."

"So you really can cook, can you?" my aunt said.

"Yes, I can," I said. "I cook and clean, collect firewood and fetch water." They hardly seemed to believe it.

"It could be true, because he learned everything when he was a very small child," Uncle Norta said.

So, now that there was no Naktsang family, how did the father and his sons live? Actually, we didn't need to worry about much during our wandering life. There was no plan about where we should go and where we should stay. We lived wherever we wanted and didn't worry about anything, apart from clothes to keep our bodies warm and food to fill our bellies.

However, it would be wrong to call this a happy life. Looking up, we had no tent, and outside we had no livestock. There was no wealth to keep us safe. How could we be happy? But just think for a moment. Nobody would agree with that! My father did not need to worry about his family and wandered from home to home as he wished. His two boys had whatever they needed courtesy of the monastery. Despite their youth they were able to look after themselves. However you look at it, it wasn't too bad.

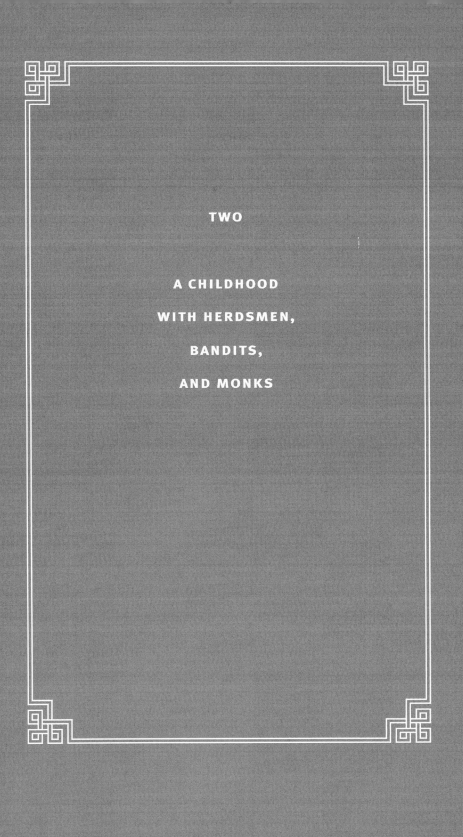

TWO

A CHILDHOOD
WITH HERDSMEN,
BANDITS,
AND MONKS

12

My Mind Full of Life's Hardships.

Fighting with My Playmates about the Little Nestlings.

After the New Year was far behind, green grass grew beside the Machu and Guchu Rivers and right up to the wall of the monastery. I went to the monastery kitchen as usual and came back home with food and drink. The black puppy brought me joy every day. When I got home he ran to me, licked my face, and bounded around the room happily. I normally gave him soup and sometimes a bone or some meat to eat. My father came back to the monastery and stayed for two months, but he often stayed at friends' houses inside the monastery and around its grounds, or in monks' quarters, and seldom stayed at home with us.

"Nukho, my son," my father said one day, "today we are going back to Uncle Mgontse and Uncle Norta's families in Chugama chiefdom."

"If we go, who will cook for Japey?" I asked.

"That will be all right," he said. "Uncle Jakho is here with him." When Japey got home that night my father spoke to him.

"Japey, if I take Nukho with me to Chugama, can you stay here alone?"

"During the day I go to class," Japey replied, "and I get all my meals and drink from the monastery, so that's no problem. It would be nice if Nukho could bring back some yogurt and milk from the families he visits, though."

"I'll do that," I promised.

"It might be too heavy for you," Japey said, worried. We debated that for a while.

A few days later my father and I rode a stallion to the Machu River ferry, the wooden ferry in front of the monastery. The ferryman, Lochu, took us across the Machu River, and we rode all day until we reached the Lhade chiefdom. We crossed the Machu River again at a place called Sang Getong, where there was no ferry and no ford. My father tied an oar to his body and carried me on his back over the river with the horse swimming in front of us. That afternoon we reached Uncle Norta's family, and they were so happy to see us.

"Look how my dear son Nukho has grown up!" Aunt Damkho said. "I swear you musn't go anywhere, but stay here with your aunt."

Ten days later, my father announced: "Tomorrow we are going to stay with the Memgon family."

"If you go you really mustn't take Nukho with you," Aunt Damkho said. "Let him stay with us!" And she wouldn't allow me to go with my father. The next day father went to stay with Uncle Mgontse's family, accompanied by Uncle Norta.

So, I stayed with Uncle Norta's family. My cousin Tsephel and many of the local children played with me, including two girls called Gunne and Chongjid and two boys named Dorba and Sodba. We often played on the mountain or went down to the river naked. While we were laughing and arguing, the days flew by. Sometimes in the evenings I missed my father and Japey, or the black puppy, but the next day I would go happily to play with the other children again, especially the girl Gunne, who was the same age as I was and called me "Brother Nukho." Wherever I sat and wherever I went, she followed me. Some days we played alone by the river, and then when it got dark she was afraid to go home on her own, so I would walk her home.

"Naktsang boy, my daughter cannot leave your side," her mother told me one day, "so when you are older I will give her to you for your bride." I was young at the time, so I felt shy!

"Nukho, when you are older will you marry me?" Gunne asked me one day while we were playing by the river.

"When I grow up I'm going to be a monk. Can I take you to Lhasa?" I asked her.

"When you are a monk are you allowed to take a woman to Lhasa?" she asked.

"When we are grown up we can go together," I replied. I told her many foolish things like that.

In the final month of spring, green grass grew from the mountains and the earth. The flowers competed to see who would open their mouth first and smile. One day we six children were playing together. One group said they were going to catch pikas on top of the hill. Gunne, Chongjid, and I picked flowers and played on the lower slopes. Soon Brother Tsephel and the others came back from catching pikas.

"Come here! There are baby birds," they called from where Chongjid was sitting. We ran over to see. It was true. On the turf was the nest of a *chamo dosh* bird with three eggs inside.

"We must look carefully and not kill them," Brother Tsephel said. We took the birds' eggs carefully out of the nest, touched them to our cheeks, and put them back carefully.

"I'm going to take a baby bird home," Dorba said.

"If you do that the baby bird will die," I said. "And if you kill it, after you die you'll be reborn as a baby bird yourself. You should put it back into the nest so its mother can look after it." Dorba put the tiny bird back into the nest, and we walked down the hill.

"Here's another bird's nest," the boys said when we reached the bottom, and they went to look at it. The girls and I walked down to the river. Later we realized that the two boys were fighting.

"May your mouth turn into blood!" Tsephel was pulling Dorba's hair and shouting. "I told you not to kill it. Now you're going to eat it!" He pushed an egg into Dorba's mouth. When we got close enough, we could see that there had been four bird's eggs, but now two of them were squashed on the ground. Dorba's face was stained with egg yolk.

"You hell-man," Sodba was saying. "You should have listened when you were told not to kill." They kept arguing while we walked back to the river.

Later, the boys began trying to catch fish.

"We're going to catch fish today," Tsephel said, "but if anyone *kills* a fish they will have to eat it raw." We caught many fish and frogs and used them to play games.

"Nukho, is it a great sin to kill a fish?" Gunne asked.

"If you kill a fish it is a double sin," I told her. "The monks say that if you kill a fish, you will not be able to confess your sins, and also if you kill a fish, its mind will enter your eyes at night." I told her that and many other things I didn't really know.

Suddenly a huge storm broke and we had to go home. "I swear they must have killed a fish in the river today because of the way the sky is disturbed," Aunt Damkho said. We told her that we had caught fish but not killed them, and pledged this to her many times. "Boys, if you go to the river and kill fish I swear there will be dangerous lightning." I believed what my aunt said and have never forgotten it.

"Nukho," my father told me often, "if you want to be a real man, do not kill fish, frogs, birds, insects, and other weak animals but have compassion for them. When you grow up you will kill deer and wild yaks, and bears like a brave man." His words stayed in my mind. Even small animals felt joy, sadness, and tears, and each of them had parents and children. I believed I shouldn't kill them needlessly.

Nomadic family from Amdo in traditional dress with their horse.
123442-245415. Photographer, Joseph Rock, 1924.
© President and Fellows of Harvard College, Arnold Arboretum Archives.

13

The Brown Dog Bites Me. Eating *Atarwatar*.

Norta's family had a dog that roamed freely. All the neighbors called him "Old Brown Dog." I often played with him and climbed onto his back. He used to lean his mouth against me, without ever biting. Sometimes I led him while the other children rode him like a horse.

"Boys, don't do that!" Damkho told us. "I swear that old dog's going to bite you one day."

"All right, Aunt," I said, and then put my fingers in his mouth to look at his teeth. There were only two blunt ones—nothing to be afraid of. Later I rode him with Gunne behind me. The dog wouldn't move, so I took a stick in my hand and hit him a little, calling out his name and shouting, "Cho . . . cho . . ." The old dog got angry and turned around and bit my hand, my shin, and Gunne's shoulder after she fell off. Gunne ran away crying, and Damkho led the dog away.

"That was a good lesson for both of you," Aunt said. "I told you not to bother him. How are those bites?" She took some skin from her robe to put on my broken skin. Gunne cried, still afraid. My wound was small, and I didn't cry and wasn't frightened. Aunt said, "Well, say 'thank you' to that dog. It didn't bite you very much, after you wouldn't leave it alone. Why wouldn't you leave it alone?" Gunne and I just looked at each other's injuries and didn't say anything. A little later, Aunt made some tsampa and touched it against the blood seeping from my leg and hand. She said, "Go now and give the dog this tsampa or else the wound will get worse." I walked over and gave the dog the bloodstained tsampa. The dog loved me, then, wagging his tail and licking me all over my face. I let him lick the wounds. He licked off all the blood.

"You dog from hell," I told him. "You bit me today—I'll never do anything for you again," and I shoved his head. Then I put my fingers in his mouth to count his teeth again.

"Son, leave the old dog alone, or I swear he'll bite you more," Aunt called out.

"Nukho, come here," Uncle Norta said. I went and sat by him where he was drinking something that looked like water.

"Hey, boy!" he said. "Today I'm going to test your courage. If you are brave, you'll drink a mouthful of this." I didn't think anything of drinking some water from his bowl. But after one swallow, my tongue went numb, and my throat strung. "What a brave boy. You are a good one," he told me.

"What are you doing, letting him drink alcohol?" Aunt exclaimed.

"It's no problem for young men to drink a mouthful or two!" said Uncle.

That night I had a headache and was drunk, running around with no clothes on. Aunt was drinking tea in the doorway, and I ran into her, upsetting the tea.

"Stop pretending to be crazy," she snapped. I grabbed onto the tent door cloth, which tore with a loud sound because it was old. Aunt Damkho said, "I'm really going to beat you this time," and chased after me with a leather rope. I tripped over a tent peg as I fled, and she beat me on my back and bottom a few times with the rope. Uncle Norta came over and picked me up.

"Why did you beat him?" he asked. "My boy got drunk. It doesn't matter! Nukho, let's go into the tent." There was a red line on my skin where my aunt had beaten me. I didn't cry but went to tell my grievance to Brother Tsephel.

"My aunt is crazy."

"She should know not to beat people. But it's OK, you're young. It's nothing."

"Nukho, come here," Damkho said. "Let aunt have a look at it."

"Don't go," Tsephel said. "She might hit you again." I went over to her.

"What a pity," she said. "I beat you a lot," and she gave me two candies and a bowl of yogurt. I sat in the doorway and ate my yogurt.

Another day while I was eating yogurt again, a person named Gontab brought a newborn calf's dead body to the tent entrance.

"Hey, Nukho!" Aunt called, "if you've finished eating go and find some garlic. Today we are going to eat *atarwatar*." When I got back with the garlic, aunt had finished cutting up the calf's meat. She made the meat into a small ball, added garlic and salt, then covered it with a piece of the cow's placenta and tied it up with string. There were around ten balls tied like this, and after they were cooked, each person ate two of them. It was the first time I had eaten atarwatar. This day I had learned how to make and eat atarwatar, and it was really delicious.

"If you put some calf's blood in the atarwatar it's even more delicious," Aunt Damkho said.

"The next time we kill a calf I'll make atarwatar," I replied.

"I don't call it 'kill the calf'; we should say 'get the calf,'" Damkho told me. But I knew what had really happened to the calf. Immediately after the *dri* had given birth, the calf was dragged away from its mother, and it suffocated. The saying was, "Calves cannot see the white light." This kind of killing was not called "killing" but "getting." If many cows calved, there would be many atarwatar meals.

These calves are very pitiable animals. It is called "getting," not "killing," because the killers of the calves don't wish to suffer the karmic punishment reserved for killing. In this region there is a habit of saying one thing and doing another. When a woman who kills a calf describes it as "getting," not "killing," she hopes to avoid the sin and punishment for killing, and to feel happy as a result. If there is such a thing as karma and a next life, the crucial question is, "Is there any way of avoiding the taking of life?" The normal rule is that you will be punished nine times over for the death of a single living creature. My thinking is that even if "nine times over" isn't true, your punishment will definitely be multiplied. If not, and the killing of a calf does not count as a sin, my opinion is that the Lord of the Dead is not a good judge of karma and its consequences.

14

Stolen *Torma*. Leading a Pika by Its Nose.

That day, as usual, we herded lambs by the river and played together. Gunne brought meat for our picnic, and Dorba brought a yak's horn full of yogurt. I brought a bowl of tsampa ready-made with butter and cheese. We shared our food, and one of us played the part of cook, another, the head of the family, and another, the guest, while we ate our picnic. At noon, Tsephel, Soba, and a few more children came with firewood and a small pot.

"I am going to cook tea here while you pick some wild strawberries," Brother Tsephel said. The rest of us went into the undergrowth and picked berries. A little later we returned with lots of them. Tsephel said, "Now I'm going to find out who has the most courage. Divide the strawberries into equal amounts, then each person eat your share." So we ate the strawberries we had picked and counted out. After a while, the girls could not eat any more, but the boys were still eating. Brother Tsephel said, "Stop eating. Now, everyone has to drink a bowl of warm water." We drank a bowl of warm water each. "Right, now I'm going to test your courage. If you are a brave boy who never complains of pain, come here." A little while later none of us could sit up because of our terrible stomachaches.

"Tsephel, you black blood-headed boy," Dorba groaned, "I swear you are destroying us. I can't stand this terrible pain in my stomach!" Tsephel said nothing but just watched us, smiling. My stomach was so painful I could hardly control myself, but I never showed how much it hurt.

"Look at this!" Tsephel said. "Nukho's head is damp with sweat because his stomachache is so bad, but he is not complaining. What a brave boy he is. The rest of you really have no courage." He laughed at the others. From then on I knew that eating strawberries was not bad for your stomach on its own, but if you drink hot water after eating strawberries, you think you will die from the stomachache.

"Tsephel made us suffer," Gunne said. "I'm going to tell Aunt Damkho when I get home."

"Dear Gunne, if you don't tell her, I'll help you cook tea tomorrow," Tsephel said. We went on like that as we drove the lambs home. When I entered the tent I saw the *amchod* Mgontse was there. He had already been in our home chanting the day before. I didn't know what he was going to chant today, but he was making tsampa and shaping it into *torma*. After making these little shapes, he lined them up on a wooden board and attached decorations made out of butter. He lay the board down near a pile of our possessions that were arranged along the edge of the tent. There was still some tsampa and butter left on the board. I thought that the torma and butter decorations would be delicious together but didn't know if I was allowed to take any. I went up to the amchod.

"Can I have a torma?" I said in a little voice.

"What did you say, you little devil? No, you can't have a torma. Go away!" Akhu said. I went out and crept around the side of the tent and watched him from under the tent cloth. I could see everything he was doing through some saddles that held up the pile in front of me. He finished one torma and put it on the board near me. Then he turned around to make another. "You called me a little devil," I thought to myself. "Today the little devil is going to steal your torma." I crawled underneath the tent cloth and reached my hand through the saddles to grab a torma. I kept watching Akhu. When he turned around to put another torma on the wooden plate, he noticed one of them was missing. His jaw dropped in surprise, and he searched all around near the saddles.

"The Three Precious Jewels!" he said thoughtfully, and then went out of the tent. I stole two more tormas and left. The torma was very delicious mixed with its butter decoration. I found where my playmates were playing and gave them some to eat.

"Nukho! You're not supposed to eat tormas!" Gunne said. "You shouldn't do something so dangerous. I won't eat any!" All the boys ate some, though.

"I swear the girl is lying," Dorba said. "I've eaten a lot of tormas in the monastery and it's not dangerous. You'll probably be fine."

"Let's not argue about it," I said. "If we eat them then that's our own karma. If you want to eat, then eat, and if not, don't. It's up to you." Amchod kept making torma for days, and I stole them three times but it seemed as if he didn't notice. One day, however, he caught me grabbing one.

"Hey, you bold one!" he yelled. I ran away with a torma in my hand. When I got home that night he told Aunt Damkho and Uncle Norta about me: "What a pity that our own son is the thief that stole the torma!" Both of them laughed until tears rolled down their cheeks. "When two of the torma went missing in one day," the amchod Mgontse said, "I wondered if they had been taken by your protector god. And when I saw the hand grabbing the torma today it terrified me as though I'd seen a ghost. I thought, 'What could that be?' Then I saw that it was your son. What a pity this big-headed boy has no fear. Boy, don't you know that there are two kinds of torma—those you can eat and those you can't? My torma is the kind you must never eat. Haven't you heard that in karma you are punished twenty-nine times for eating torma?" He said all kinds of things to try and make us feel afraid. I had eaten many tormas already, so I didn't feel frightened. Still, I never stole tormas again.

One day Dorba and I returned from herding the lambs with two baby pikas. Their eyes had just opened. We decided that we would each take care of one pika. When we got home, we dug a hole near the entrance to the tent and made a small bed there to put our baby pikas. Every day we fed them grass and vegetables.

We had one argument about the pikas. One day Dorba put a string through his pika's nose and led it to where I was. "You ugly boy!" I said. "Do you want to have a dead body instead of a pika?"

"But, Brother Nukho," he said, "if you lead it by the nose it's easier to control."

"You can't lead such a small animal by his nose," I told him. "What a pity for you to cause him pain like this!"

After a month we took the pikas back to where we had found them. A few days later we went looking for them and saw them running around with their parents. That made me happy. There was no reason why we should remove them from their family.

Birds and insects fly through the sky. Animals, wild and tame, walk on the ground. All kinds of fish swim in the river. All of these have different strengths and weaknesses. Some of them can speak, and some cannot. Many kinds of creatures experience the love between mother and child. We all want our family to stay together and be comfortable. No one wants their family to be divided and to experience suffering. Therefore, we say that all sentient beings need a mother, and a peaceful and pleasant life. It is true when they say that the greatest compassion is to be found in deeds. Whatever I do, I cannot forget the suffering I experienced when I lost my mother as a small child. I send my good wishes and blessings to all sentient beings, so that they may not be separated from their mothers as I was.

15

A Mad Dog Disturbs the Inhabitants of an Entire Mountain.

One noon we heard whistles from our neighboring camp. People were running up and down, yelling and bustling about over there. My aunt and I stood with a crowd of our neighbors, watching. I saw that some families in the other camp had lifted their children up onto the roofs of their tents. I was very curious about what was happening.

"Why are children sitting on top of those tents?" I asked my aunt.

"Oh, no, this is not good," Aunt said, peering at the other camp. "There's a mad dog over there," and she ran shouting to tell our neighbors. "Hey, there's a mad dog loose, look after the children!" While she was yelling, she lifted me and Tsephel onto the tent roof. Then she tied up the tent entrance and stood near our tethered dog with a long pole in her hands. All our neighbors, men and women, had armed themselves with tent poles and were guarding their own tents with the children sitting on top. Everyone was very frightened and in a hurry. Most of the men were away herding sheep or yaks, leaving just the old men and the women at our camp. The man defending the Labe family's tent was about eighty years old, and his eyes were dim. He took a long tent pole and stood near the entrance of their tent.

"Right, where's the mad dog coming from?" he shouted. "Hey, girls, where's that mad dog?"

"Take Grandpa into the tent!" Aunt Tsekho shouted. "There's nothing he can do."

"Hey, don't say that," the old man said. "If he comes near me I might be able to knock him over by accident!" But he went into his tent. Then I saw a dog approaching from higher up the mountain.

"Over there! It's coming down the mountain!" everyone yelled. It was a large dog running with its tail between its legs. It was between the two camps. Gonjab arrived with a gun, but Aunt Damkho took the gun away from him.

"You can't shoot a mad dog or kill it with a knife," she told him. "If you kill it with weapons you will catch its disease yourself." She put a long tent pole in Gonjab's hands and told him to stay put. The mad dog ran toward our neighbor's tent with blood dripping from its mouth and its tongue hanging out. Then it charged toward our neighbor's dog. Gonjab and a few of the women rushed at it with their tent poles, and all of our neighbors tried to help, but the mad dog was very strong. The more they beat it, the wilder and stronger it became. Many people hit it, the tent poles thudding loudly against its body, and it still jumped around with blood pouring from its mouth.

"Don't get too close," Gonjab warned, "or you will be infected by the steam from its breath." He broke his tent pole against the mad dog and ran to fetch another one. People tried to drive it away from our tent, while our dog strained against his tether, barking furiously. Damkho ran inside to grab a sheepskin robe, wrapped it around our dog, and lay on him. Then Gonjab struck the mad dog with a stone, and it fell down.

"Now let's kill it!" he shouted. Everyone ran toward the mad dog swinging their poles. It got up and lunged at them again. Women were running all over the mountain, screaming. A group of boys from another encampment arrived brandishing stones, which they threw at the mad dog. It staggered down to the mountain road and escaped.

That evening, after the livestock had been penned for the night, Norta came up the mountain from the lower encampment.

"The mad dog came to their camp," he let us know, "and they killed it." Then we calmed down. But that day I had seen a mad dog for the first time, and for a few days it filled my mind and I was terrified. I was really afraid that time.

"Nukho," Aunt Damkho said, "the next time a mad dog chases you, just run in a circle. Mad dogs can only run in a straight line, so it won't be able to follow you." Her words fixed themselves in my mind, and I comforted myself by saying, "If I meet a mad dog I'll just run in a circle."

Yaks grazing near the shore of a lake, Amdo, northern Tibet.
123222-243844. Photographer, Joseph Rock, 1924.
© President and Fellows of Harvard College, Arnold Arboretum Archives.

16

A Mountain Fire among the Sheep. Pricking the Amchod's Drum.

By autumn, the mountain and the plain were brown. I had about ten calves to herd. Calves are easier to herd than lambs, although sometimes, if I was careless, the calves would drink their mothers' milk when they met in the evening.

"Nukho," Aunt told me, "if you let the calves drink their mothers' milk, you won't have any milk to drink." Actually, the calves frequently drank the cows' milk, but aunt gave me my milk and yogurt as usual.

The hardest job when herding calves was tying them up. There were two very bad calves that I found it extremely hard to tie up, even when I was able to catch them, which was also very difficult to do.

"Nukho," Gunne's mother Tsojid said one day, "when you can't catch the calves, giving them a little salt will help."

"Would you give me some salt for the calves?" I asked Aunt Damkho.

"No, I swear I won't," Aunt said. "Don't let them eat salt, because if they do, when they are grown up they will get out of control, stampede, and eat the tent ropes." So she wouldn't give me any salt, but the next day Uncle Norta gave me some balls of Mongolian salt without letting my aunt see. I touched the mouths of both difficult calves with the salt. In two or three days they came to me whenever I showed them my hand. The female of the two particularly loved salt and would not leave my side all day. I couldn't make her go away. I'd give her a little salt, but when I didn't have any for her, she would lick the snot from my upper lip. My aunt called her "calf of the snot-eating lineage."

One day I was with Gonjab, Tseten, and Merab herding calves, yaks, and sheep at a bend of the Machu River, and there were also some herdsmen with us. Some of us were in the river splashing water around. An old Chinese man came up to us with a young boy of around ten. We didn't know where they came from, and they spoke only broken Tibetan. The man raised his thumb to Gonjab and the others and said he needed help crossing the Machu River. He seemed to be a beggar.

Some of the herdsmen said, "Let's take pity on him and help him get across," but others said, "His Chinese body is going to die in the river," and things like that. Again, the old man showed us his thumb and said something to us. The little boy had tears in his eyes, and he seemed about to really cry.

"You know a place to ford the Machu River, don't you?" I appealed to Mgontse and Merab. "If you take pity on these beggars it will be a good deed for you. Don't let them try crossing on their own or that little boy will drown. Please help them, dear brother."

I showed the man my thumb, too. Then my brother and others took the Chinese man and the boy to a ford and led them across the Machu River. When I saw the man and boy had crossed the river safely, I felt so happy. After they climbed out of the river, they walked for a while and then turned around and waved to us. The others told me that it was a sign that they liked us a lot.

Then one of the herdsmen called out, "A fire has broken out!" We looked up to see a huge fire on the grassland mountain of the Meshe Gejo clan. From time to time we heard a gunshot. We climbed up the mountain and watched. All the Gejo's sheep were on the mountain where the fire was raging. People were running toward the center of the fire to try to drive them away from it. They fired guns and managed to separate the sheep into two groups. Some of the animals were driven away toward the river, but most panicked and ran back into the fire. It was impossible to see clearly because of all the smoke. The fire was climbing toward the top of the mountain, and behind the flames, all over the mountain and the blackened pasture, were sheep that had jumped into the blaze. Many of them were on fire, still burning. We heard that five hundred sheep had leaped into the flames. The fire continued to spread. People from other encampments came to try and help control it but then had no idea what to do and finally just watched from a distance. The fire continued up the mountain during the night, giving the sky a bright red glow. Early next morning the Gejo clan sent out a message saying, "If anyone catches one of the burned sheep they may kill and eat it." After sheep jumped into the fire, their eyes were scorched and they became blind. Their wool was all burned away, and only the meat and skin was left. Sometimes the skin fell down in strips from their bodies or their horns and hoofs had fallen off. They were wandering around dazed, all across the mountain and by the river. Many people from the encampments hunted down the blind sheep and lassoed them. Uncle Norta and Gonjab both went out to lasso sheep for us. The sheepskin was burned and useless, but the meat was delicious. During those days everyone from the encampments was sated with meat. Even ten days after the fire, there were some burned sheep wandering around the mountain. And for a long time people were talking about how the fire started and how sad it was that these crazy animals didn't run away from the fire.

One day an old amchod came to my family. During the hours of darkness he chanted and performed rituals. Sometimes he brought a dead person's skin with him and used it to beat everyone who was watching him. Many people were chanting the ritual with him. His eyes were red and white, and he made sounds on his small drum. When I was very young I was afraid of the sound of big drums, although I didn't know why. When our family was chanting prayers and a drum was necessary, I would run outside or go and stay in our neighbor's tent. This day that he was beating the small drum it didn't scare me the way the big drum did, but the sound of the small drum hurt my ears. I didn't run away.

"There will be more chanting tomorrow," the amchod announced, finally, and put his drum down on our pile of possessions at the side of the tent. I thought, "If I prick the drum it won't be so loud." After sunset I took a sharp piece of shinbone and pricked the little drum twice. The next day many people came to chant rituals with the amchod. Before he began, he noticed that the drum had been pierced.

"Fill your mouths with ash!" the old amchod said. "Who did this?" He scolded us a lot. Uncle Norta and my aunt said nothing. I was sitting outside, and Aunt gave me a lot of sidelong glances, but I pretended not to know anything. The little drum made a strange sound like "gok, gok," but the amchod continued chanting the same as before, beating everyone with a dead person's skin and chanting, "Om pad." That day I didn't go anywhere near the ritual. The next day the amchod left.

"I swear, Nukho might have pricked the amchod's drum," Aunt Damkho said, eying me. Uncle Norta just laughed. I kept quiet, not admitting that I had done it and not denying it either. My gracious aunt was clear in her mind about what had happened but said nothing else. The suffering was borne by the amchod. The money and food that he earned from his small drum had been sabotaged by a thoughtless child.

17

Feeding and Caring for the Foal.

"Nukho, do you miss your father?" Damkho asked me one morning.

"Yes, I miss him a little," I said.

"My dear, I think it's more than a little. Last night you cried out for your father in your sleep."

"Last night I dreamed that my father came back."

"Why is this?" she asked Uncle Norta. "Normally he misses his brother Japey, not his father. Should we worry? Has something happened to his father?"

"Really, you are talking nonsense," Uncle Norta said. "This is a very young boy. It's natural for him to miss his father sometimes. Anyway, we just can't know what his father is doing. Only the Three Precious Jewels know that." A little later Uncle Norta asked, "Nukho, would you like to herd the foals tomorrow? The orange mare died today, and its foal is alone. You could look after it." I felt so happy when he said this.

The next day, after she had given the foal milk, Damkho tied a rope around its neck and let me lead it.

"Now, Nukho, take it down to the river," Aunt told me. I sat on the grass in a bend of the river with the foal. The foal went to sleep, and when he woke up he brushed my face with his mouth. It seemed as though he was looking for his mother's breast, so I gave him my little finger to suck. He sucked my finger and swished his tail, pushing my finger as he did so. I thought he must be hungry so I took him home. My aunt poured milk into a horn with a leather teat made to resemble a breast, and put it in my hand. I gave it to him to suck and led him back to the river. By the time we got there he had drunk all of it. His stomach was full, and he lay down beside me to sleep. After two or three days there was no need for the rope around his neck. When he saw the horn breast in my hand, he ran to me, swishing his tail happily.

"Oh, lolo, my baby, drink milk and grow quickly!" I told him. "Our mothers are dead, so we are alike. I have my father and brother to look after me, and you have me to look after you. Understand?" He listened to me with his ears held up straight, and I guessed that he understood what I said.

When he got home that night he didn't sleep alone. I laid a carpet by my knees and let him sleep on it. I put half of my second blanket on him and I slept under half of it. After that, I couldn't leave his side. Wherever I went, and wherever I sat, he followed me.

"Nukho is becoming the foal's mother," Damkho and the neighbors used to say.

One afternoon the foal and I were coming back from the river, and a bad dog that belonged to our neighbors lower down the mountain rushed at us. While I was picking up a stone to throw at it, the dog nipped the foal's legs. It made a small wound. The foal was frightened, and shook, tears falling from his eyes. I felt sad for him, and I cried too. I stroked him and said, "Oh, my baby, there's no problem! Don't cry. I'll deal with that wicked dog tomorrow." He licked me with his tongue and put his head inside the front fold of my robe. I felt such compassion for him then. I thought, "What a pity he can't speak. His thoughts are just like human thoughts." Two years after I slept with him that one time he still recognized me. If I spoke he would come to me, neighing.

"What a pity that animals don't have minds when they can love so much," Aunt Damkho said. "It's so strange," and she started crying.

"Even after ten years horses and yaks can recognize their mothers," Norta said. "Nukho is like his mother, so of course he remembers Nukho." In my heart I thought, "It's wrong to say that animals don't have minds. They are like any living being, but they just have no human language. In their hearts they feel love for their dear mothers and for their children. If they had no minds, a foal like this could not recognize me and love me."

18

Horse Thieves. Looking After My Own Lamb.

One day Tsephel, Gunne, and I were herding calves and playing at the river. Most of our village's horses were grazing nearby in a bend of the river. A man on horseback rode up to us.

"Hey, which clan are you from?" he said.

"We're from Mgontse's clan," Tsephel answered. "Why?"

"Do these horses belong to your clan?" he asked.

"Yes, why?" But the man rode off. We kept playing, and a little while later we heard dogs barking and shouting from the direction of our camp. We also heard gunshots and had no idea what was happening. Then Gonjab arrived on horseback carrying a gun.

"You idiotic children! What were you doing while the robbers were stealing our horses? Didn't you think to call us? Just get yourselves home." Then he crossed the river, firing two shots. In the far distance we could see riders racing away with about ten of our clan's horses. Horsemen were forging across the water toward them. We drove our calves home. After sunset Gonjab and the others returned, driving most of the horses before them and leading two saddled horses. One of the saddles had blood on it.

"So, who were the robbers?" Uncle Norta asked them.

"They said they were from the Lhade chiefdom. There were five of them, but we killed two and wounded one," Gonjab told him. The Chugama chiefdom often raided horses from other chiefdoms, but this time another chiefdom had stolen Chugama horses. It seemed as if nothing could stop banditry: stealing or being stolen from. But that day, the robbers found out how much suffering could come from stealing horses.

A few days later I was herding Uncle Mgontse's family lambs. Among them was a small black and white ewe lamb. Her mother had been killed by a wolf, and she was an orphan. I used to give her salt and cheese and tsampa, and she often stayed by my side. During the afternoon the other lambs bleated happily when their mothers gave them milk, but she cried because she missed her mother and came baaing up to me. I felt sad for her. I didn't know what to do, other than to hold her and stroke her and give her a little food to eat. I was especially kind to her because she had no mother. Sometimes she crept into the tent and drank milk secretly from the white copper pot. Whenever I called, "Lamb, lamb," she leaped toward me, wagging her tail. When I took a picnic to the grassland, I tied tsampa and yogurt on her back, and she would follow me. When we got to the picnic place we would eat the food together.

"Nukho, the lamb you often feed, that you call Nagdeb, is now yours," Uncle Mgontse said one night. "You can keep her as your own, and any sheep that she gives birth to as well." This made me so happy! I stroked the lamb on the head.

"Well, then, do you understand?" I asked the lamb. "From now on you are my lamb. Unless you die of disease, no one is going to kill you." I told the lamb many things.

"I have told my lamb that her life is spared, and no one can kill her," I said to Uncle Mgontse. The entire family was pleased for me, and I was joyful to have a lamb of my own. But, as it turned out, I never saw my lamb again after I returned to the monastery. I heard later from Rabten that she lived until she was twelve years old and bred about twenty descendants.

Summer was shearing time. If a youth went shearing, the family would give him two sheep's worth of wool a day as payment. If a child helped round up sheep for the shearing, they would give him lamb's wool to make a hat from. That year I helped four or five families catch their sheep and lambs for shearing. Each family gave me meat and yogurt and, if they thought I had done a good job, some candy and dried fruit. A generous family would give you extra meat and a little sausage to eat on the way home. I carried the food and lamb's wool home very happily. Because it was my first salary for working outside our encampment, I was even more satisfied.

"We have a lot of lamb's wool this year," Aunt Damkho said. "I want to make a *hera* for my dear Nukho."

"He will be OK without a hera," Uncle Norta said, "but if you don't make him a sheep skin robe this year he will definitely die of cold." I was very pleased and thought, "They are surely going to make me a new robe this year." In the afternoon I drove some horses from the river toward home, and I saw a rider dressed in gray coming toward the camp. I thought his horse looked a lot like one of our horses that we called "Jolu." I stared, wondering if it could be my father. As the man came closer, I realized that it *was* my father. He had returned! I ran toward the road to meet him. I saw he had a dead deer tied to the horse's back. When I reached him, he dismounted and put me on the horse with his gun on my back.

"Father, I have missed you every day," I told him, then began to cry.

"Father's here now. Don't cry," he said. "I'll give you the deer's head to play with." I hadn't seen him for two months. That night I slept beside my father whom I had missed every night he was away, but I didn't feel very happy. Was he going to go away again? However, when I remembered that the following day I would have a deer's head to pull around by the nose and play with, I felt much more cheerful. For the next few days I traveled from home to home with my father.

"Durkho, is this your son?" one woman questioned. "I thought that he was a son of the Norta family. But he has such a big head—I can see, now, he must be yours!"

"This is my younger son," Father told her. "He is a brave boy and can stay with whatever family I leave him with." While we were traveling around, I told him about my lamb, the mad dog, the horse thieves, and many other things.

"My son, you are five years old now," my father said. "Whatever a grown-up can do, a brave boy like you can do, too. If you have many troubles as a child, it will give you an advantage when you grow up."

A nomad encampment with flocks, tents, and walls of stone and dried yak dung
reinforced with sticks. 123059-243751. Photographer, Joseph Rock, 1924.
© President and Fellows of Harvard College, Arnold Arboretum Archives.

19

The Horse Jolu Is Stolen. Forced to Walk.

"We're leaving in two or three days," Father told Uncle Norta and Aunt Damkho
after we returned from our travels. "We will stay a little while with the Meshel
clan and then go on to the monastery."

"Of course you must go, because poor Japey is on his own at the monastery," Aunt replied, "but I swear you won't take Nukho. I want to look after
him here," and she burst into tears.

"He can come back," Father promised, "but I'd better let the two boys meet
each other again, at least. Of course, if they stay together very long they'll miss
each other too much when they're split up again, so I'll bring him back soon."

Uncle Norta said, "If in the future you want to bring us both sons to look
after, we are happy to do that." Then Aunt also agreed that we could leave.

The next day, after they drove the horses back to the pen, they found
that father's horse Jolu had been stolen. Father and I still wanted to visit the
Meshel clan. "Nobody from this clan knows where my horse has been taken,"
Father said, "and, anyway, I'm sure nobody here would steal it. I suspect that

the horse thieves are from the Mongolian Datsen chiefdom, near the Meshel. I have a close friend in Datsen chiefdom who will get my horse back." The following morning my father and I left for the Meshel camp.

"Do you really think Nukho can walk the whole way?" Uncle Norta asked. "It's not far," Father said "We don't need a horse, and we can stop and visit a family on the way." We set off carrying the horse's saddle. On the way we visited the Shotse family. Shotse's wife made a big *droma*, and butter with tsampa, and put it in my robe. Then Shotse saw us off onto the road toward Uncle Mgontse's clan. When we arrived at their tent, the whole family was excited to see us. Father and Uncle Mgontse talked about the stolen horse.

"You'll get it back," Uncle said. "You have a friend in the Mongolian chiefdom, don't you?"

"Yes," Father confirmed. "I will go to see Norgay and find out what happened."

That afternoon, when the sheep were back in their pen, Rabten appeared with the bodies of two sheep. "The wolf knew that Uncle and Nukho were coming today," he said. "It has killed two sheep for us." The next day my father and Uncle Mgontse rode to the Mongolian Datsen chiefdom to investigate the situation with Jolu. After three or four days they returned, leading the horse.

"When we got to the Mongolian clan," Father said, "I spoke secretly to some of my friends. One day one of them came to me with an old Mongolian man who said he knew where Jolu was. My friend invited him inside and gave him a sheep. . . ." We talked for a long time about this story of victory: how the horse was recaptured.

Ten days later we set off for Chugama Monastery. We borrowed an extra horse from Uncle's family and loaded it with butter, cheese, and meat that were gifts from my father's friends and family. Then I climbed up behind the load, and Father led my horse to Chugama Monastery.

I was impatient to see my brother, Japey, and the black puppy. When we got to the river at Drongda, Father put me on his back and we swam across behind the horses. That night we arrived at the monastery ferry. My father called the old boatman Lochu, who took us across the Machu River. We had a meal with his family and then went directly to the monastery. When I opened the gate to Jakho's home, a big black dog ran at me. I thought he was going to bite me and backed out of the gate again, but the dog jumped up and licked my face. Then I recognized him. It was the black puppy. He had grown so big! Then Japey and Uncle Jakho arrived. I hugged Japey around the neck and cried. Japey had tears of happiness in his eyes. That night we cooked a delicious dinner. We ate good meat, drank tea, and were elated. Jakho and my father sat by the stove talking, and Japey and I curled up together in the small space behind the stove. We probably stayed up until midnight, drinking, eating, and talking. The night flew by. The black puppy lay between Japey and me with his nose on my foot.

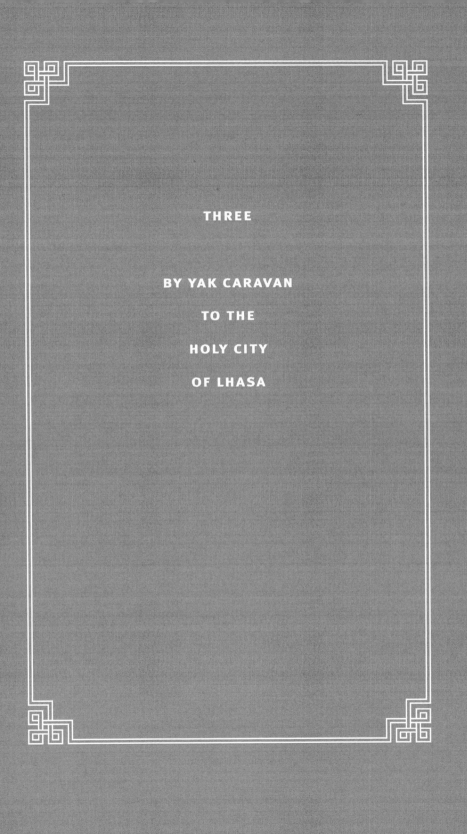

THREE

BY YAK CARAVAN

TO THE

HOLY CITY

OF LHASA

20

Pilgrimage to Lhasa in Gratitude to the Dead.

A few weeks later, in our own house close to Chugama Monastery, my father, Japey, and I were sitting on the grass in our courtyard after lunch. The black puppy was next to me gnawing on a bone.

"Japey, Nukho!" my father said. "Your mother, your uncle, and your grandfather have been dead for a number of years, now. Because you were too little when they died, we didn't take a pilgrimage to honor their memory. Now you are old enough, so this year we are going to Lhasa." Japey and I were overjoyed. Ever since I first began to understand words, I had heard people say "Lhasa, Lhasa." I knew that it was called "the Sun of Tsang" and frequently dreamed of going there. Going to the Jokhang Temple had been my steady desire. Now I was six years old and could walk long distances and ride a horse. If we didn't go now, when would we go? Following my father's decision to bring us to Lhasa, I couldn't sleep for many nights because I was so excited.

"My family is going to Lhasa!" I would tell everyone I met, every single day. My dreams were full of our pilgrimage. For days, cousins, neighbors, and friends dropped by to give us butter, cheese, and other supplies for the journey, as well as silver coins.

Before we left, Father made me a robe out of one of Uncle Jakho's sheepskin shirts, and he went to Labrang and bought a box of one hundred small bowls. He also bought two boxes of long, thick needles called *jazema*. My father had been to Lhasa twice before as a guide on the journey.

"These small bowls and needles fetch a very good price in Lhasa," he told me. He also had eight pairs of dried antlers with bone attached. He said that when he got to Lhasa he would exchange them for a gun. Japey had saved twenty silver coins from his monastic allowance and gave these to my father. I heard that my father had about fifty silver coins. Now our preparations for

Nomad tents on the grassland. 121987-243147. Photographer, Joseph Rock, 1924.
© President and Fellows of Harvard College, Arnold Arboretum Archives.

the journey were complete. For food we bought half a sack of bean flour from Ngawa, a small bag of cheese, about fifty pounds of butter, some flour, and dried noodles. For sleeping, we had a small white tent with a black yak hair roof. Uncle Mgontab lent us a horse and a riding yak. Altogether we had three riding yaks, father's horse Jolu, and the extra one from Uncle Mgontab. Everything was ready, but we had heard nothing from the grassland about whether it was safe to travel, so my father went to check with some friends.

Five or six days later my father returned with a young woman.

"How lovely!" she said when she got to our home. "This one must be Nukho." She stroked my head and kissed me.

"Japey, Nukho," Father said, "this is your aunt—she will help us on our journey to Lhasa." I was happy to see her. She was about twenty years old, very talkative, with a round smiling face. She wore an old sheepskin robe. Her name was Neney. She was from the Wayan chiefdom and a member of the Lang sept. From that day on she shared the joys and sorrows of a father and two brothers until, after almost a whole year, we returned from the Sun of Lhasa.

Several days later we set out from the monastery toward the nomad chiefdoms. We camped on a grassland in a bend of the Machu River with other pilgrims on their way to the Ü region (Central Tibet). There were eighty families from Chugama and thirty families from other chiefdoms. Uncle Mgontse's family was making the pilgrimage. Mingling with the family groups were a lot of horsemen with guns. Fragrant incense smoke and flames rose into the sky from an altar.

"Everybody listen!" said the high chief of Madey Chaguma. "Tomorrow we will begin our journey to Lhasa. Altogether, there will be about one hundred families from our chiefdom and other chiefdoms. Starting today we must no longer say 'your chiefdom' and 'our chiefdom' or 'your people' and 'our people.' We must speak with one mouth and have one chief. We will experience joy and sorrow together. From tomorrow my family will lead, and everyone else will follow in an assigned order. While we're traveling you may exchange places, but if any family does so without authorization they will be fined thirty silver coins. Each family must provide an armed man with a gun and a horse. The Ü-pa pilgrims must be distributed at the front, the center, and at the rear. If we meet any enemies we will drive them away, and if there are any robbers we will capture them. It is very important to pray and do good deeds on the way to Lhasa. You must not kill sheep and yaks when we pass through the mountain pastures, and you must not kill wildlife on the Changtang. If anyone breaks these rules he must pay a fine of fifty silver coins. The guides on this journey are Naktsang Durkho, Golok Wyiga, and Lojam. These three will decide where we will go, where we will stay, and when we start and stop." He delivered many other rules about the journey.

"Yes, we understand, we understand," everyone said. That night my father returned with a new gun that had a horn stand, and a bandana full of bullets. Father was pleased, saying, "The high chief has made me the lead guide on this journey. Uncle Mgontse brought my gun. He still has a lot more bullets, so he gave me these."

"We are leaving tomorrow morning, right?" Aunt Neney asked.

"Starting tomorrow I will have no spare time," Father told her. "Dear Neney, you must do your best to look after everything, and Japey can help you a little. I will carry Nukho on my horse. The high chief agreed that we do not need to keep in the prescribed order but can leave when we want to."

"You really shouldn't put Nukho on your horse," Neney told him. "I will take care of the boy. If we don't need to keep in line, I am free to do what I want. I can leave at dawn and take Nukho with me." The next day before daybreak my father went ahead to guide the caravan, and at sunrise we started on our journey.

Yaks grazing near the shore of a large lake, probably Gyaring
or Ngoring (the sources of the Yellow River), Amdo, northern Tibet.
123441-245414. Photographer, Joseph Rock, 1924.
© President and Fellows of Harvard College, Arnold Arboretum Archives.

21

Amnye Machen Pomra, Lakes Jyaring and Ngoring.

That day Aunt Neney rode the horse, and Japey and I rode behind the packs on the yaks' backs. At noon we reached a mountain pass where there was a large pile of incense burning.

"Aunt Neney, Brother Jabey, there's incense burning over there. Do we need to burn incense?" I said.

"Yes, we do!" Aunt replied. "A real man has to burn incense when he reaches the top of a mountain pass. Both of you need to do it."[1] When we arrived at the top of the pass, there were many Ü-pas burning incense there. Looking up and to the right, we could see a tall, snowy mountain reaching into the sky.

"I think that's the blessed Amnye Machen Pomra! Is that really it?" Japey

1. A propitiation to the mountain gods forbidden to women.

shouted. It was the sacred mountain Amnye Machen, and it made me feel inexpressibly happy.

"Oh oh oh, Amnye Machen Pomra!" I yelled. When I was younger, I had heard older people praying to Amnye Machen Pomra when they burned incense. The top of the snow mountain glowed in the sunshine, and the snowy peak shone like a glass stupa. People told me that Amnye Machen Pomra was the mountain deity for the southern continent of the world: the Rose Apple Tree, called Zambuling. All the other Ü-pas prostrated toward Amnye Machen Pomra, and we did too. The air was full of the piercing sounds of prayers, with invocations and incense smoke. It was hard to hear who was chanting what.

"*Kyiso* Amnye Machen Pomra!" Japey chanted. "The mountain of Ma surrounds nine rocky mountains, the Ma grass mountain contains eighteen big grass mountains, Ma has one thousand five hundred heads . . . ," and he threw incense on the flames. My personal mountain deity, Machen Golu, dedicated to me at birth, was from the Machen range. I did not know any incense-burning rituals or prayers and just threw paper lungta in the air, shouting: "May the gods be victorious!" I collected some stones from the top of the pass and put them onto the cairn above the pass. After the incense had turned to ash, we continued our journey toward the mountain.

— THE GUNFIGHT —

At noon the next day we reached a narrow valley, through which ran a river and a rocky road. We heard many gunshots from up ahead, and as time went on, the sound got closer. Our horsemen took position in the rocks on either side of the road, ready to fight, and fifty more rushed to the front of the caravan. I could see my father among them.

"Aunt, Japey, look at Father up there!" I shouted.

"The Three Precious Jewels bear witness!" Neney burst out, and she began to pray. As my father reached the front, we heard gunshots from all sides. I thought, "We're under attack. What's going to happen to Father?" Neney rushed over and took me in her arms. She had tears in her eyes. I thought to myself, "Neney and I are thinking the same thing." A little while later the noise stopped, and a message came that the caravan could go ahead. After we had moved forward a little way, I saw my father sitting on the ground with some others. I rushed up and hugged him. There was blood on his hand.

"Have you been hurt?" Neney asked him. "How terrible!"

"No, I'm not hurt—I was just tending someone else's wound," Father replied. "Around twenty Golok horsemen attacked us, but then they ran away.

They killed three people and six horses, and another three of our people were hurt but can still get up and walk. We're going to cook here, and after we've eaten we'll move on carefully. Before we leave we can give food to some of the Golok wounded."

The pilgrims stopped and cooked a meal. Father took food to two of the wounded Golok men who were lying at the base of a cliff not far away.

"Thank you, good man," one of the wounded said. "You are truly a human and will be reborn as one. What is your name?"

"You don't need to know my name," my father said. "Stay here. After the Ü-pas have gone, your people will come back for you." I looked down the hill where three dead bodies had been dragged away from the road. The man who spoke had been injured in the leg by a bullet. The other was injured in the neck. Father did all he could to heal their wounds, although they were likely to die. We left them and followed the Ü-pas.

"Father, were you at the front?" I asked.

"Today I was in the middle," Father answered. "When the enemy came I stood aside to let the soldiers come to the front." However, I noticed that my father's cartridge belt was nearly empty.

"How far is it to Lhasa?" I said.

"When we catch up to the sun, we'll be in Lhasa," Japey replied. I knew that I didn't know how to catch the sun, so I understood that Lhasa was far away.

Every morning Neney gave me tsampa and poured tea. After we had finished our meal, Aunt Neney and I dismantled our black and white tent, folded it tidily, and put it on the yak's back. I led Jolu to a rock and climbed up to put the saddle on his back. Without a rock I couldn't get the saddle on him. Then I returned to where they were tying bundles onto the yaks.

We kept traveling for about a month. By that time it was autumn, and the snow had started. One day we came over a mountain pass and saw a huge lake to our right.

"This is one of the twin lakes, Jyaring and Ngoring," Neney told me. We traveled beside the lake all day, and as we rounded a hill in the afternoon saw an even bigger lake.

"Wow," I said, "what an enormous lake!" We camped there that night.

"This lake, and the one you saw this morning," Father told me, "are the source of the Machu River."

The Ü-pas decided to stay by the lake for a few days. A large incense offering fire was lit in the middle of our camp, and then the soldiers held a meeting. When my father returned from the meeting that evening, his bullet belt was full.

"From here onward," Father said, "the countryside is full of robbers, so the chief gave us all more bullets today."

"You have to be careful," Neney said. "If anything happens to you we will all die."

"There isn't going to be a problem, kind lady," Father said. "Just take care of the boys and don't worry about me." During the day, Father and I went to the shore of Lake Ngoring. There was a huge fish skeleton there, with bones big enough for me to crawl inside.

We walked on to where a family was living. Aunt Neney and I went to beg a little yogurt. When we got closer three dogs ran up to us. I picked up a stone to throw at them, but Neney stopped me.

"Don't attack their dogs or we won't get any yogurt," she said. I walked closer to the tent.

"Kind family!" I said. "Could you please give us some yogurt?" Several children, who had been watching from the tent entrance, came up to me and laughed.

"Mother, it's a pilgrim asking for yogurt," they shouted into the tent. The mother came out.

"Bring him into the tent and give him some food," she told them.

"No, I don't want to come into your home. Just give me some yogurt, please," I said. The woman brought us some yogurt in a wooden scoop.

"Did you bring a bowl?" she asked.

I asked her to pour it into my woolen hat. A girl fetched another scoop of yogurt and put some *jachur* on top. While I was licking the yogurt some of it fell out of the hat. The children put some on their fingers, and decorated my face and ears and forehead with yogurt. They thought that was funny, but the woman pulled them away and told them to stop it. I took out a long, thick Labrang needle and gave it to her.

"Thank you for the yogurt. Here is a Labrang jazema needle for you," I said. The woman was glad to have a needle. She took the girl into the tent and sent her out with a little butter.

"Are there needles like this for sale?" she asked me.

"None for sale," I said. She beckoned to Neney, who was sitting nearby.

"You should come inside with your son and drink tea."

"Oh, thank you," Neney called back. "May your conciousness dwell in Ganden for giving yogurt to my son." Then we returned to Father and Japey bearing our food, and we all ate yogurt on the shore of Lake Ngoring and were blissfully happy.

"The first time we went to Lhasa your Aunt Nyolo was killed in this chiefdom by one of the pilgrims," my father mused. "Our high chief fined the killer three hundred coins as a punishment and left them in the Jokhang Temple."

We got back to camp just as it got dark.

22

Eating Yogurt at a Sworn Friend's Home.
Saving the Sheep from the Wolves.

The Ü-pas continued as before.

"I heard that we're in Wujud territory now," Aunt Neney told my father. "They are a dangerous people. Remember to be careful."

"It will be fine," Father said. "I have friends in Wujud." When the caravan paused at noon, my father came over to us with a man who had no fingers on either hand. The man had a whip tied to his wrist and carried a gun with a silver inlaid handle. When he smoked, he held the cigarette between his fingerless hands. After they had eaten, they left together on horseback. That night, my father returned with butter and cheese.

"That man you met earlier was one of my best friends, Hordug Laglo," he told us. "You two should remember him."

"Of course we will remember him," Japey said. "He's the 'touching hands' man."

"He is chief of the bandits around here. If you are his friend, you never need fear bandits in Wujud."

That day at noon the weather was very warm. A little way ahead we could see a few families living on the mountain.

"Nukho," Aunt said, "you have needles, don't you? Could you go to those families and trade them for yogurt?"

"All right," I said.

"Brother, will you come with me?" I asked Japey. "I'm worried the dogs will bite me."

"Don't worry," Japey replied. "Neney and I will watch you from here." I went up the road and waved my hand to the families. The children watched me from inside their tent, and a woman came out to see me.

"Aunt! I'm going to Lhasa," I said. "I want to eat yogurt. Could you give me a drop?" Her daughter went into the tent and came out with a bowl of yogurt. I poured it into my hat, then licked the bowl clean with my tongue.

"Why did you pour it into your hat without eating it?" the girl asked.

"I am not going to eat the rest myself," I replied. "I'm going to share it with my brother and aunt."

"You can eat this yourself," she told me. "I'll bring you more." She fetched another brass ladle of yogurt. I ate half a bowl, and poured the rest into my hat. Then I took a thick needle and gave it to the girl.

"Sister, thanks for the yogurt," I said. "I am a pilgrim and have nothing to give you apart from this Labrang jazema needle. It's a real one." I turned to leave, but after the girl had given the needle to her mother, she brought a big slab of butter from the tent.

"Here, little boy," she said. "You can eat half of this, and put half into the butter lamps in the Lhasa Jokhang."

"I will, aunt," I said, and gave another needle to the girl. I returned to where my aunt and brother were sitting. The children and mother called good-bye and good wishes after me: "Hey, little boy, long life, one hundred years."[2] So once again I had yogurt to eat. We walked back to the campsite.

"Now, we are going to visit a close family friend," my father said, and put me on the rump of his horse. After a short ride we reached a family at the bottom of the mountain with a black yak hair tent and another white tent.

"Nukho," Father said, "this is one of my family's best friends. His name is Geba Chusem. Remember that name." In the tent, my father and the man talked for a long time. He poured tea for me. There were two children there, a son and daughter. They sat beside me, and we tried to talk. Although we could not understand every word of each other's dialect, they had many things to say. The mother gave me a bowl overflowing with tsampa. It was too full to mix, so I licked the tsampa with my tongue. The children laughed at me, rolling on the ground giggling. Then the woman helped me to mix it and gave me a bowl of yogurt. I ate a little and then poured the rest into my own bowl and put the bowl in my robe.

"You're not going to eat it?" the woman asked. "What are you going to do with it?"

"I will take it back for my aunt and brother," I replied.

"Eat this, my dear," she said. "I will give you another one to take back with you." When it was time to go, the woman poured yogurt into a sheep's stomach and gave us the forequarters of a sheep, some butter and cheese, and many other things. I gave her two or three thick needles.

"What nice needles. Do you have another?" she asked.

"Nukho, do you have any more?" my father asked me. "If you have, give them to her." I took the other needles from my robe and gave them to her.

"What a pity—now your son is empty-handed," the man said, and he gave me two white silver coins.

"Thank you," I replied.

"Your father and I are sworn friends," the man told me. "When my son is older, you and he must take an oath of friendship." The light was failing as my father and I returned home to our black-roofed tent. Neney and Japey were waiting for us at the entrance.

2. *Tserang lobga*, a farewell.

"I was so afraid. Why did you not come back earlier?" Neney asked.

"Father was talking a lot, so we were late," I said, and I told them everything about our visit to the family.

A few days later we reached Mkhar Valley, where the Ü-pas intended to get salt. We crossed a wide grassland with a long yellow mountain range on the right. The pilgrims said it was Khare Jagen Ragba. In the morning there was a little snow, and then the sky cleared to a beautiful blue. Our father was waiting for us on the road. He handed some red salt to Neney, and we pushed on. On two low hills up ahead we saw a group of wolves chasing and killing a herd of about a thousand sheep. Father took seven soldiers and ran toward them.

"Don't kill the wolves," he said. "Just fire your guns to scare them away and separate them from the sheep." Brother Japey rode over on the horse Jolu. Aunt and I waited for them while our yaks grazed beside the road. Father and the soldiers fired in the air many times, and the wolves ran away. They rounded up the sheep. Later a man rode up who said he was one of the shepherds. Everyone in our group, including Jabey, received a sheep's carcass, which each person tied to the back of their horse. We stayed there and butchered the sheep, removing the sheepskin, blood, and intestines.

"The shepherds told us," Japey said, "that last night when it snowed, those thousand sheep were driven off by the wolves. They didn't know until the morning. This morning, when they followed the tracks, they found that around 300 sheep had been killed and 170 injured. When we rounded up the sheep and handed them over, the shepherds were extremely grateful and offered each person two dead sheep, but Father said that one sheep per person was enough." In the afternoon we stopped to cook and then sat in the entrance of the tent to eat our meal.

"Both of you look," Father said. "There is a sharp black peak over to the right. It's called Khare Ngulkra Dolma. It's not a big mountain, but it's famous." As we journeyed on, Father pointed out every mountain, pass, lake, river, and valley to Japey and me and made us learn about them. Japey memorized many names.

"While we are on the road, look around at all the mountains and parts of the landscape," Father told us. "You should remember the mountains, in particular. When we go over a pass, look back and memorize the way we have come, and then you will know where to stay and where to go in the future."

"Father, did you kill anything today?" I asked.

"When you make pilgrimage to Lhasa, you shouldn't kill wild animals," he told us. "I heard that if you kill one, you will bear the sin of a thousand deaths. If this was a normal journey, we could have killed the wolves without worrying."

"How many wolves were there?" I asked.

"Maybe around thirty." Even *I* had heard that if Ü-pas kill one animal or person on their way to Lhasa the sin is punished as if it were a thousand.

One morning the Ü-pas entered a chiefdom full of foxes, bears, wolves, deer, Tibetan gazelles, and other animals. It was so nice to see the animals running without anyone trying to kill them. However, when we came across bandits, our soldiers killed or wounded many people and horses. When people's own life or wealth was risked, they forgot the thousand sins, or perhaps they remembered, but they had to kill because of their pride. Otherwise, nobody would have generated many thousands of sins before getting to Lhasa.

23

Killing a Tibetan Wild Ass. A Pack of Wolves on Achen Tang.

Our caravan was passing through the Ma, Yug, and Kar Valleys. In the distance we saw colorful wild animals, which I was told were Tibetan wild asses, but I had not seen them close up. In those days we often heard the saying "Even when thirsty the white-mouthed ass will not drink muddy water." Later that day we passed near a wild ass. It had a short body and a big head, with a white line of fur running along its belly. The asses moved in line one by one, but when they stopped walking they drank or grazed in a group. From far away they looked like donkeys. Herds contained at least fifty and more often one or two hundred asses. Male asses walked separately from females. Hundreds of mothers and foals followed them. In that area they had little fear of humans or yaks. Sometimes they would even cross through our caravan. But if the Ü-pas' yaks and horses came close, the asses would get frightened and gallop away. The ground of the plain was thick with their dung. At that time our fires mostly consisted of ass dung, although there was a bush called *wudora* that we could use for kindling.

At midday we saw a herd of asses walking in line across a valley, perhaps five hundred or more.

Some of our armed escort came down the column and told everyone not to let their horses mingle with the asses, otherwise they would not be able to get them back again. "This is a real wild animal's place," I thought to myself. "There are as many Tibetan gazelles as there are sheep around here, and as many asses as both. In the last few days we have seen deer and wild yaks, and no domesticated animals at all." But at that moment, I looked up and saw a herd of sheep grazing at the top of a sandy valley.

"Japey," I called out, "there are sheep on that mountain."

A caravan setting out on a journey across the grassland.
122002-243194. Photographer, Joseph Rock, 1924.
© President and Fellows of Harvard College, Arnold Arboretum Archives.

"Those aren't sheep," he corrected me. "They are some kind of wild animal." A little later the caravan reached the top of the pass. The animals I'd seen got up and walked away up the mountain. They weren't sheep—they were wolves. They had killed about ten asses, whose bodies lay on the mountainside, and had been feeding from the dead bodies. Some of the pilgrims thought it had been a hallucination. Father came to us.

"That was no hallucination," he said. "It was a pack of wolves. You sometimes see five or six hundred together on this road."

"Do the wolves ever eat people?" I asked.

"Wolf packs very rarely eat people," Father said. "If we don't trouble them, they probably won't trouble us. But some wolf packs do eat humans." I had never heard about packs of wolves before, but that day I saw it myself—a pack as big as a herd of sheep.

"There were at least six hundred wolves on that mountain," Japey said, and we hadn't even seen how many wolves lived behind the mountain.

"The Three Precious Jewels bear witness!" Aunt said. "If they attack us they will eat all the people, yaks, and everything."

"Be quiet!" my father said. "They won't attack us, and even if they do, we don't even need to fire our guns. They can be driven away with a *chaggor*."

"Father," I asked, "have you ever seen a pack of wolves attack people?"

"Not only have I seen it," Father said, "but a pack of wolves attacked our caravan the last time I went on pilgrimage to Lhasa." By then most of the wolves had moved to higher ground, howling and beating their tails on the ground. When one wolf started howling, another ten would join in, pointing their mouths at the sky. It filled us with fear. My father loaded me onto his horse and rode over to the armed guards.

"Take the wolves seriously," he told them. "The noise they're making means they might attack us. Don't fire at them." The caravan walked silently onward. The pilgrims had some dogs that they led, ready for defense, next to them. When we reached the top of the pass, about a hundred wolves were sitting waiting for us. It looked as if they had no fear of humans and were not aware that we were walking toward them. We were truly frightened. Nobody spoke from the time we crossed the pass to the time we reached the river on the far side of the mountain. Then everyone relaxed. Even though I had seen wolves, I had never been so close to a pack before. For the next few days nobody spoke about anything but the wolves.

After dinner at that night's campsite, my father told Neney, Japey, and me a story about a pack of wolves that had attacked the caravan of pilgrims on his second journey as a guide to Lhasa: "There were forty families of pilgrims and about seventy armed horsemen. One day the caravan arrived at Chumarkado and camped there. The sun was about to go down. Wolves were howling and snarling all around us. The pilgrims were frightened and pitched their tents with guns in their hands. We heard that the first family group had fired on the wolves, killing two of them, but later more wolves arrived. By then, the caravan was totally surrounded, and we opened fire. Before we fired, the wolves had only run around us and hadn't attacked livestock or people. But after we killed two of them, they attacked us and wounded some people and killed some yaks and horses. There appeared to be at least one hundred, maybe two hundred wolves. When darkness fell, they became fiercer. People kept doing the same things: the men firing guns and the women beating wolves away with tent poles.

"'Don't fire! Hit them with the chaggor,' one man called out. 'Set cloth on fire and throw it at them.' Then we put down our guns and attacked the wolves with poles, chaggor, and burning cloth. Some people set fire to their clothes and threw them. After that the wolves slowly retreated, although they still harassed our encampment. We did not sleep all night. The next morning at daybreak there were still wolves around, but they didn't come near the families. About ten of our pilgrims had wounds of various sizes. The back of my sheepskin robe was torn, but my back was unharmed. Seven yaks and horses had been killed, and seven injured. When dawn broke, we found that we had killed eighteen wolves. Later that day some of the pilgrims' dogs killed two wolf cubs and brought them to the camp. Their owner skinned the cubs and kept the pelts. The cubs' mother followed them and howled, pointing her nose at the sky and beating the ground with her tail. The wolves surrounded us again. Some people said that as long as we didn't shoot it was unlikely that the wolves would attack us. I wasn't certain about that and fired my gun into the wolf pack." He told us many stories like that. I did not sleep well that night, even though I was in my aunt's bed.

"There's no need to be afraid, my dear," she told me. But I hardly slept at all.

I dreamed of wolves charging us and red blood flowing from the yaks and horses they attacked. I called out "Wolves!" in my sleep.

"You shouldn't tell such frightening stories—I swear Nukho is very scared," said Neney.

Father said, "It's OK! My son is a brave boy who doesn't get scared by stories. Here, Nukho, come sleep in father's bed." I got out of Neney's bed and went inside my father's robe. In a short time I fell asleep.

24

Sewo Jyachen Sumdo (a Place Where Three Roads Intersect) and Feeling Sorrow for the Blind Bear.

The pilgrims pushed on. It was hard to walk that day because of a red dust storm. A little later we came to a big river in a sandy valley and pushed through the sand down to the bank. We forded the river and saw a mountain with a jagged peak rising into the sky on our right.

"That's Ngamrey Chongshog Gomgo," Father told us. A little farther on there was another mountain with three black pillars of rock pointing into the sky. Father said, "That's Rabrey Chen Sum." Then the caravan came to a place where two rivers and two roads met. Above it there was a very long stone wall, where every stone was etched with the mani mantra, and thirty statues of Ling Gesar. The pilgrims dismounted and prostrated in front of the mani wall. Nearby we saw some monks living in yak hair tents. Many of them were carving stones. When we approached them, a small boy carrying a long knife at his waist invited us to his home for a meal. We followed him home. His household lived simply. We sat on the bare floor. His mother brought us tea and food.

"We are called the stone-carving family. This is my son Phurbu," she said.

"Golok pilgrims! What do you have for sale?" Phurbu asked.

"We're going to Lhasa," Japey said. "And we have nothing to sell. Do you need to buy something?"

"No," the boy said, "but can I do anything for you while you are here? My name is Phurbu of the stone-carving family. Everyone knows us."

"Whose chiefdom is this?" Neney asked.

"These are the lands of our Wujud chiefdom," Phurbu explained. "Tonight you will reach the Chinese camp at Sewo Jyachen Sumdo."

That night the pilgrims stayed at Sewo Jyachen Sumdo opposite the Chinese camp. At that time pilgrims to Lhasa needed travel authorization from both the Wujud chief and the Chinese soldiers, so we stayed there for three days—that way, all the pilgrims could go to the Chinese camp to get their papers.

— FIRST SKIRMISH WITH THE CHINESE ARMY —

"The Chinese soldiers and the Wujud took our guns," many of our pilgrims complained. Father sent them to the high chief with this news, then led ten armed horsemen to the Chinese camp. At that point, six Chinese soldiers and three armed Tibetans stopped them.

"Hand over your guns and ammunition," the soldiers ordered. Everyone loaded their guns, and my father dismounted. Those without guns drew their swords.

Father spoke: "Our chiefdom is called Madey Chugama, as sure as a name is called and a handle is held. Until you return the guns you took from our people, I promise we will put on a good show for you today." Then fifteen of our horsemen arrived. The Chinese and the Wujud were in a hurry to get away, then, but our people surrounded them. The crowd was shouting.

"Dear man, don't fight," Neney said to my father. "The chief will be here soon."

"These shit Chinese people don't want to fight," Father said. Another hundred more of our horsemen came up from the river, yelling. Some of them fired their weapons into the sky. When I looked back, I saw that my father had already taken away the guns of the Wujud and the Chinese, and our horsemen had crossed the river and surrounded the Chinese camp. "We're going to destroy this camp!" our people shouted. They destroyed two of the tents with their swords. All together there were about ten Chinese tents, and fifty workers and soldiers. But then the high chief ordered our people to stop fighting and move back.

Later on, some Chinese soldiers, the Wujud chief Migmar "Red Eyes" Shegzod, and his clerk Samba Dondrub came to see our high chief. They gave back the guns they had taken that morning, and we returned the guns and hostages we had taken.

Then our chief and some others went to the Wujud high chief's tent to discuss things further. The Chinese soldiers and workers followed and closed the tent flap behind them. Nearby there was a big tent that served as a shop. We went in and bought candy and tea, and on the way back we met Phurbu from the stone-carving family.

"Boy, does your family have a young male yak?" Father asked him.

"Many," he said. "Why?"

"One of our old yaks has pain in his feet and can't walk properly," Father told him, "so we'd like to exchange him for a younger yak."

"I'll help you with that," offered the little boy.

"Can you bring that yak tonight?" Father asked. "Although we don't need to rush off—I think the Wujud who threatened us have more sense than to come back here." Phurbu appeared that night with a young yak and exchanged it for Uncle Mgontse's elderly one.

"We are business partners now, Golok boy. Come to my home the next time you go on a journey," he said to me.

"Sure, we'll come on the way back," I agreed, and he left with the yak.

The next day the Chinese and the Wujud chief completed our papers, and the pilgrims continued on toward Lhasa. It snowed, and we passed by a tall, rocky mountain with another hill behind it.

"My sons, look over there," Father said. "That gray rock is called Sewo Horda Zaya. Behind that mountain is Tawo Drala Tagtse. That is the Dong Nyamtso chiefdom's mountain deity." At noon we reached a valley called "Camel Neck Bend." Ahead of us, we could hear a dog barking. Looking forward, we saw a group of horsemen on top of a rock. I thought, "What's going on?" but when we got there most of the horsemen had already left. We went over to take a look, and to our surprise, there were two big and two small brown bears next to the rock. One of the large bears was standing on its hind legs eating a *markog*, and a little one was resting on its haunches eating a bone. Beyond them we could see a mother and cub. They were surrounded by the remnants of food, like dried meat, markog, and cheese.

"Nukho, don't go near, it will attack you," Neney said.

"The mother bear is blind," one of the people told us. "She's not afraid of people and eats whatever we throw over." There were dogs close by the bears, barking at them, but the bears took no notice and kept eating as if the dogs didn't exist.

"Do brown bears kill people?" I asked Japey.

"These bears don't," he reassured me. "The blind one definitely wouldn't."

"Should we feed them?" I asked.

"Let's give them some cheese," he said. Neney and Japey threw cheese to the bears, and then we left. I looked back to watch the bears standing up to eat the markog. Other pilgrims turned to look, too. I thought, "This is very strange! If we weren't on the way to Lhasa, our people would have killed both the mother and the baby. Instead, today everyone has been thoughtful and done good deeds to save the bears' lives, treating them with love. But the mother is blind, so they will die of hunger sooner or later anyway." I thought a lot about that.

When we got to the campsite, my father put me on the back of his horse.

"We are going away for a while," he announced.

"Where are you going so close to sunset?" Neney asked. "You might put your son in danger."

"We're only going to Uncle's place. We won't be long."

"Come back soon. Don't wait until after dark," Neney said. We rode stealthily into a small valley and across a river, looking around to make sure the other Ü-pas didn't see us.

"We're going to kill some Tibetan antelopes," Father explained.

"Father, pilgrims aren't allowed to kill animals, are they?" I asked.

"It's just the two of us," he told me. "Nobody can see us." It didn't take long. There were about fifty Tibetan antelopes eating grass on a mountainside. I held the horse and sat down to watch. Father walked very slowly toward one of the antelopes. It trotted behind another antelope and looked over at us. A shot rang out. I led the horse toward my father. He had already finished skinning the antelope and was butchering the meat. We returned home with the saddlebags full. Aunt and Brother were waiting for us beside the entrance to the tent, and we all cooked and ate heartily.

"It's not a sin if it keeps us from going hungry," Aunt said.

"I won't kill any more. This one's enough," Father told us. "You boys must chant manis, all right?" But after that Father killed antelopes or gazelles whenever we were hungry—we filled the saddlebags with meat many more times. We ate well on our journey and chanted a lot of manis.

25

Timid Tibetan Antelopes. Ferocious Wild Yaks.

Every day we traveled through empty valleys and bare places, with no sign of human beings. The land was full of wild animals such as Tibetan wild asses, Tibetan gazelles, deer, Tibetan antelopes, argali, foxes, brown bears, wolves, and more. One day we reached the top of a hill and saw two herds of wild yaks below. Each herd contained about one hundred yaks, one grazing halfway up the mountain and the other at the foot. They were close enough that we could hear the sound of their hooves on the rocks. Their heads were strong and wide between their horns, and they had long legs and fetlocks. Most of them were a dark reddish brown. I looked very carefully at the herds and saw that some of them had tethering ropes around their necks.

"Aunt Neney, Japey, there are normal yaks down there with them," I said.

"Maybe some domesticated yaks ran away and mixed into this herd. If a horse tried to join a herd of wild asses, they wouldn't let it stay, but an ordinary yak can blend into a herd of wild yaks," Jabey said.

"Ge ho ho!" Jabey and I shouted at the yaks. They ran a little farther away and then stopped before slowly climbing up the slope again. Before this, I had never seen wild yaks close up. I had only seen the skulls of wild yaks on the pilgrimage route, or sometimes a few yaks far away.

Soon we arrived at the watershed of the Khar River. On a flat-topped mountain we placed many wild yaks' skulls and prayer flags like a mountain deity altar. Japey and I could both sit cross-legged between the horns of a wild yak's skull, and there was still room for two more children!

In that area many families used the skulls of wild yaks as pails for water and milk.

"If we kill a male wild yak for meat," the stone-carving boy Phurbu had told us, "we need eight or nine normal yaks to carry it home. Also, wild yak leather is really thick. The thickest leather on their backs is about three or four fingers thick. If you use it to make the soles of boots, they don't wear out for at least a year. And if a wild yak licks you with its tongue, it can tear your sheepskin robe. Also, if a wild yak is injured, don't try to stop it. It won't trample you, but it will toss you on its horns. If you look closely at the horns of wild yaks you will sometimes see dried human flesh. You can face down many things, but you can't stand up against an injured wild yak." This made me shiver in fear. I looked carefully at the wild yaks, but I never saw any human flesh. That night when Father got home, we told him about seeing the wild yaks.

"Father, would injured wild yaks kill humans?" I asked him.

"I haven't ever shot one of them," Father reported, "but I have heard that if you injure a wild yak, it isn't afraid to charge humans and horses and is very difficult to kill. Some time ago the Amchog chiefdom went to Lhasa, and on the way eight young boys shot and wounded a wild yak. The wild yak charged them, and they could not stop it. They shot the yak many times, but it still managed to kill two people and three horses. One of the boys was carried away on its horns, and his body never found. The following year they returned from Lhasa, and while out hunting they found the head of a wild yak. Stuck on one of its horns was the upper part of a dried body, which still had its cartridge belt." That made me even more frightened.

"Dear son, come here to your aunt," Neney called. I ran over to her.

"Why do you want to make him so scared?" Neney asked my father.

"When my son is older," responded Father, "he will kill wild yaks himself. He has no reason to be afraid."

"Father, what should you do if a wild yak is injured?" I asked.

"You must shoot the wild yak in the forehead at close range," he told me. "If you shoot over its foreleg into the center of its heart, it will also die. But if you only injure it, you must flee. Humans and horses should move as far away as possible and watch from a safe distance. If the wild yak cannot see the horses and people, it will not get angry, and if it does not die of its wounds, it will keep moving and walk a long way toward the horizon. The Dong Nyamtso chiefdom's people say, 'Keep your distance from two things—an ass that's been shot in the stomach and the lice when you're picking them off a sheepskin robe.' If you approach injured animals, even a wild ass will attack a person."

The pilgrims walked all day until we reached a wide desert. There were many animals, such as Tibetan wild asses and gazelles, but mostly Tibetan antelopes. We saw one herd after another, with hundreds of mothers and their calves eating grass close to the road. There were also herds high on the hills and in the valleys below. They seemed not to be afraid of pilgrims. Wild Tibetan antelopes look similar to deer, but their fur is pinkish. Male antelopes have dark faces, and their horns are sharp and thin like a Tibetan gun rest, while the horns of females are blunt and short. Normally the males would graze separately from the mothers and calves, but sometimes when we passed by they would mill around and get mixed together. There were five or six herds in that place, and each herd had about three or four hundred antelopes. People had told us that antelopes run away very fast when they are scared, and especially fast in a herd. Jabey and I yelled at them, but we couldn't make them run—they just raised their heads and then resumed grazing.

"Antelopes have a bag under their front legs," my father said, "and when they run fast the bag fills with air and they almost fly."

"There are so many of them," Neney said. "They really have no owners?"

"This isn't that many," Father said. "If you go up to a place called Luchu Lumar, that's real antelope country. There you will see a hundred mothers and a thousand foals in one herd. The 'chief of the antelopes' is the deity of that area." Thirty or forty antelopes were running around the main herd playing, and wild asses were walking through the mass of antelopes. They took no notice of the pilgrims walking past them. They didn't show any fear. When the young armed men of the chiefdom saw those herds, they got itchy trigger fingers and wanted to fire their guns, but no one dared, maybe because killing one would have counted for a thousand sins, although the main reason was probably that they would have incurred a fine of silver coins from the chief, who had ordered them not to kill any. Anyway, only my father and I had seen or heard anyone killing an antelope. And no one knew about that apart from Neney and Japey. The four of us bore the same sin. Actually, there was another way to get meat. Along the pilgrimage route you could see the dead bodies of many gazelles and deer. The antelopes in particular were vulnerable to wolves, and male antelopes sometimes killed each other fighting. If a family found a dead antelope or yak, they had to bring it to the altar and burn incense that evening at camp. Whatever meat you scavenged on the way you had to put near the altar in the center of camp and share the meat with others. That was the rule of the pilgrimage. And if you found anything another family had lost, you had to put it near the incense altar in the evening so the owner could find it. I lost my wooden bowl three times on the way but always found it in the evening near the altar. After I had lost it once, everybody knew my bowl and said, "Nukho, here's your bowl."

26

She Didn't Give Up Her Baby to the Wolves, and Lost Her Life.

The weather was snowy in that place. In the morning it snowed again.

"Today we can ride together," Father told me and let me sit behind his saddle. When we reached the end of a rocky chasm, we looked back and saw the line of pilgrims moving along the valley floor. Then we heard gunfire from up ahead. About ten wolves emerged from the bushes on the mountain above us. "Maybe the leaders of the caravan scared the wolves out of our way," Father mused.

"Yes, but maybe they are still there," Neney suggested.

"It's true that if they are hunting successfully they won't leave the area, especially if it's a large pack," Father agreed.

"You shouldn't fire guns into a pack of wolves, should you?" Neney asked.

"It's not a big problem during the day." More shots rang out. Around twenty wolves broke cover above us.

"Father, it's another wolf pack," Japey said.

"Yes, it's another pack, all right," Father replied. We rode on. When we got to the junction of two valleys, we saw a large group of horsemen and two monks looking at something under a cliff. One of the pilgrims, Golog Wyiga, called to my father, beckoning him over.

"Hey, Durkho, come here!" Father and I went over, while Japey and Neney followed the other pilgrims. Ten wolves were squatting on their haunches higher up the mountain. When we reached the group at the cliff, I saw the snow was bloody all around. Someone must have died down below. Father got off his horse to approach the dead body. No one in that large group had dismounted except for my father. He led our horse forward so I could see the body. "A ka ka!" I thought I was seeing things! They weren't gathered around a dead body but a living woman with a one-year-old baby. Part of her scalp was missing, and her body was covered with blood. She wore a sheepskin robe with a blue and red hem, of which only a little was left at the waist where her sash held it. Flesh had been torn from her back and thighs, and from both arms, by the wolves. Her muscles and tendons were clearly visible, as were her rib and shoulder bones where the wolves had attacked her. Her lungs were punctured, and her breathing was noisy. Red liquid oozed from her mouth. Blood and pieces of her robe were spread across the grass. Her left arm held the baby close to her chest, and in her right was a belt with silver chased roundels. She stared wide-eyed toward my father. The most astonishing thing was that the baby, even though it was covered in blood, was silent, gazing at my father alertly.

"When we saw her, the wolf pack was pulling at her from both sides and she was hitting them with her belt," said one of the bystanders. "We fired our guns and came up to her, but no one was able to get off their horse safely, and we watched from a distance." When Father went up to her, she could not speak but pointed to the baby at her chest. She showed her thumb to us and waved her hand, signaling that she wanted us to take the child. Father lifted the baby and cleaned the blood from it. It was a little boy, thankfully uninjured.

"If necessary I will take the baby," Golok Wyiga said. "The high chief will look after it." Father gave Wyiga the little boy. He put it into his robe and left with the monks. The woman smiled and held out her thumb to my father as they left, but tears were running down her cheeks. There was still a group of horsemen with us.

"It's sad," one of them said. "The wolves will come back and eat her."

"But we can't just wait for her to die," another said. "We'll have to leave her." They all joined in this discussion. Even though the woman could not raise her head, she kept on holding out her thumb to my father and pointing to his gun. Everyone there, even me, realized that she wanted him to shoot her.

"We can't shoot her. But if we leave her she'll die slowly," onlookers said.

"It would be better if we shot her," another said. Still she held up her thumb to my father, weeping.

"Words are useless—it's better to end her life quickly," Uncle Mgontse said. My father took out his gun and loaded it. All the horsemen moved back. The woman watched him, thumb outstretched. Father put down his gun.

"I really can't do it." He went closer and covered her with the torn robe. I thought, "The Three Precious Jewels! It's not easy for people to die, even if they're in this state. Maybe thinking of the baby is stopping her from dying. It's terrible!" Father spoke to the woman.

"Don't worry about the boy. And after you die I will take your hair to the Ganden Monastery sky burial site." She smiled at my father and raised her thumb again.

"Man, now it is time to cut off her breath," Uncle muttered. "Om mani padme hum! It is better that way than to die a bad death by the wolves." Uncle had not finished speaking when I heard a gunshot. I looked over and saw her forehead had been smashed by a bullet. While everyone chanted, "Om mani padme hum!" Father took out his dagger, cut off her hair, and put it into his robe. Then we rode away. I did not know what he was thinking, but I saw tears falling from his eyes as he rode. After we had ridden a little farther down the mountain, I looked back to where the woman's body lay and saw the wolf pack crowding around. I thought, "That's right. It was better to shoot her and save her from pain and suffering than to let her suffer a terrible death from the wolves. There was barely enough flesh on her body to cover the palm of a hand. Her upper and lower body were destroyed by the wolves. Her lungs and intestines had been dragged along the ground. Despite that, the little boy held against her chest hadn't even been touched. If I had not seen it myself, even if my mother and father had told me this, I wouldn't have believed it. But no one needed to tell me about it—I had seen it with my own eyes. I saw that even though the wolves had eaten her body and blood, she had held her baby to her chest. Even though she had been pulled and torn apart, the baby had not been bitten once. And then she had signaled my father with her eyes to take the baby. How had she found the strength to fight off wolves and defend her baby? It is impossible to say anything except, 'She was a mother.' Hers was a true mother's compassion and power, a mother's deep strength. My father had killed people and horses and had never before shed tears, but today he wept because of the woman's courage, not because he was afraid of the sin he had incurred by killing her." I thought many things like that.

27

Passing the Red River with Seven Fords. Encountering Evil Bandits.

As the pilgrim caravan climbed, the weather got even colder.

"From now on we will be in *tsagdom*," Father said one night. "You must think about that."

"What's tsagdom?" Neney asked.

"Tsagdom is an extra-cold spell. During the cold weather sometimes a fog comes over like a wave. It is a fine snow, like mist. During that time we cannot travel but must just put on more clothes and wait. After a time it will disperse. Then everything will be all right." That morning the weather was unbearably cold. We traveled after sunrise, but the sun had no heat.

"Aunt, is this tsagdom today?" I asked.

"No, it isn't," Aunt replied. "They say that tsagdom is a gray wind. If you see a gray windy fog coming, Nukho, tell me." I rode a yak, keeping a lookout for tsagdom, but after a while I fell asleep. Suddenly Japey called out.

"Aunt! I see the tsagdom!" That woke me up! It looked as though a gray dust storm was coming.

"Is that tsagdom?" Aunt mused. "Anyway, we'll stop here." Aunt lifted Japey and me down from the yak and wrapped us in our father's big sheepskin robe. The other pilgrims continued on their way. They had to stay in line and were not allowed to stop by order of the chief. When the tsagdom arrived, it really was astonishingly cold. The pack animals stopped grazing and stood with their backs to the wind.

"Is your father's robe warm enough?" Aunt asked. "I'm afraid we'll die of cold." A little while later the tsagdom passed. We ate a meal and then started walking. Two young male yaks were being skinned. "When the cold came, these yaks died suddenly," the butchers said.

The pilgrims had reached a big river. It was reddish and salty. The caravan passed over in a line, but when we got to it we halted, and Aunt Neney tied Japey and me to the yaks' backs with ropes. Then she rode over. Since our home was close to the Machu River, we had no fear of the water. The river was not wide, but it was deep. When we got to the far bank, the first pilgrims were camped there.

"Those young yaks and five or six foals that were following the mares died because of the tsagdom," the high chief, Uncle Mgontse, and other families reported. That afternoon Father came home.

"Did you get very cold today?" Aunt asked.

"Not too bad," Father answered.

"Tomorrow you must wear your thick sheepskin robe," Aunt said. "If there is more weather like today, I swear you'll die."

But the sun rose on a beautiful day. At noon, the caravan came to another big blue river. We walked beside the river on a rocky road. Behind us on the mountain was a vast herd of deer: there must have been four or five hundred of them lying on the ground, or eating grass and watching the caravan pass by. We came to a big sandy plain where the river divided into many fords. The first pilgrims had already reached the far bank.

"This place on the river is called Drichu seven fords.[3] It is the same river that yesterday was red, but here it is green." When we got to the ford, Neney and my father tied Japey and me back onto the yaks with ropes.

"Are you afraid?" Father asked us.

"We're not afraid," Japey and I said. Then we crossed the fords one by one. We crossed seven rivers, but the pack animals could only walk across three or four of them. They had to swim over the larger streams. We finally caught up to the pilgrims already camped on the far side.

That afternoon, there was another meat share at the incense altar. When Japey and I went to get our part of the meat, they were skinning a yak nearby.

"Boys, chant manis," an old man said to us. "Today a pair of my male yaks drowned in the river." That night we drank meat soup. Father turned down the bottom of the tent, and we went to sleep. I slept on Neney's bed. At around midnight, we heard the sound of gunfire. My father ran outside yelling, and when I peered out of the tent, I saw him lying on the ground. I was scared that he had been shot.

"Father!" I shouted. Father fired his gun, then got up and ran. Many armed men burst out of our neighbors' tents to join him. In the torchlight we could see someone half submerged in a small lake near our family tent and another person lying wounded beside the lake. Father lifted the wounded man in his arms.

"A man is lying dead in that lake," the wounded man said, "and two of my friends are injured."

"What a pity he fell into a corner of the Naktsang mouth and got caught in our teeth," an old man from our chiefdom said.

They asked him to call his friends.

He shouted, "Orgyen! Dukhar!" His two companions rose up from their hiding place in the pack animals' tethering area and came over. Our people seized their guns and led them off. They pulled the dead body out of the water and took the wounded man away.

I noticed that the thieves all wore boots with white decorations.

"That means the robbers are from the Nyamtso Shagshe chiefdom," Father informed us. He had been wounded—the flesh of his left wrist had been grazed by a bullet. Neney tore off a piece of woolen cloth and laid it on the wound.

She cried, "Look! You were almost killed! What would we do without you?"

"My dear, there's no need to cry," Father said. "The Nyamtso robbers aren't

---

3. On the Yangtze River, the principal crossing point on the pilgrimage route from the east of the Tibetan plateau to Lhasa.

as dangerous as the Wujud ones. And it is not my time to die yet." Five days after we passed the Drichu River, we were traveling between two mountains. It was so cold that morning. The faces of the yaks and horses were covered in frost. Their white faces made me want to laugh. At noon the vanguard told us to stop walking. A few minutes later we saw a sleuth of brown bears on the mountain above us. Beyond them were another twenty bears. Everyone felt very afraid.

"Those bears are evil!" somebody screamed.

All the pack animals in the caravan were running around, terrified, and people were shouting and banging pots and other pieces of metal together. The bears took no notice. Later, some of them were gathered on the mountain, growling. I sat on my yak's back, scared, and thought, "The protector bear witness! Are all those bears coming up from underground?" Frightened yaks from the front of the column had fled toward us, getting mixed up with other families' yaks in the confusion. The pilgrims nearest the bears started a fire made of old clothes, which made the bears stand up and look around. Later the bears began to dig.

"The bears at the front are digging droma," my father showed up suddenly to tell us, "and they are still in our way. We yelled at them and fired our guns, but that didn't work, so we are trying to drive them away with smoke. They are retreating up the mountain, but slowly. We will be able to pass them soon. It won't be long."

Right then, ten bears were climbing away up the mountain opposite us, but some were still in our path. I don't know how many there were altogether. Some mothers had two or three cubs. If you looked up the mountain, you could see tan-colored bears as big as a young male yak with faces that were over a yard long. It intimidated us to see them up ahead. Finally, most of the mothers and cubs moved away. We passed the black earth where they had been searching for droma. Some of the bears were still digging, and we didn't dare to look directly at what they were doing as we went by. At last we drew clear of them. I thought, "It's such a long way to Lhasa—so many rivers and so many mountains, and such hard weather to endure. There are dangerous thieves and bandits. We have been cold and hungry, already. It is a very strange, frightening, difficult journey—will we ever get to that place they call Lhasa?"

28

Snow and Red Dust Storms Day and Night.

There was more snow the next morning as we trudged on toward Lhasa. We passed through narrow rocky roads and deep rivers. There were ghostly gray rocks everywhere, which made the going hard. By noon we had crested a mountain pass and entered a wide plain. It was windy, and if we followed too far behind the others, the wind would erase any sign of their tracks, and we would have to send messengers to find them. When the snow began to fall heavily, the first pilgrim stopped. We waited in line and then continued on. A little later we passed the high chief's monks who were beside the road with my father, standing over something and chanting.

"Father, we're here," I called out.

"Boys, are you cold?" he asked, coming over to us.

"We're warm enough," Japey said.

"What are you all doing?" I asked.

"Some pilgrims walking to Lhasa died near the road," Father replied. "The monks are chanting prayers for them." I looked beyond and saw the bodies of two monks and a layman lying back-to-back. Their legs were almost covered by snow. After a few moments, we left. Father put me on the front of his horse.

"Father," Japey said, "it would be better to put Nukho on one of the pack yaks, behind the baggage. If you hold him, your hands will get cold."

"I'll be fine," he said.

"Durkho," Aunt pressed him, "aren't you going to wear your big sheepskin robe?"

"It's fine," he reassured her. "The weather's not at its coldest yet."

That afternoon the snow became heavier. "This is called 'the place where gray snow falls day and night,'" father said. The pilgrims continued their journey silently. Father told the armed men to make an announcement to the entire caravan,

"No pilgrim, not even one person, must leave the road. If anyone walks off the road, let us know by shouting or firing a gun in the air." In the middle of the day the caravan stopped at the top of a mountain. All that day the yaks hadn't been able to find grass to eat, and the people hadn't eaten either. But none of the pilgrims had strayed from the road, and nobody had died of cold.

"Father, who were those dead pilgrims we found this morning?" I asked him that night while we were eating.

"Nobody knows," father said, "but they were young. Many years ago the Bubas clan went to Lhasa for the first time. When they got to this place, they

Religious reliefs depicting Buddhas and senior lamas.
Bild 135 S 13 12 36. From the collection of the Federal Archives of Germany, Koblenz.
Photographer, Bruno Beger. Ahnenerbe Expedition, 1938–1939.

found fifty dead pilgrims who had lost their way and died of cold. The Bubas travelers had no idea who these pilgrims were or where they had come from, but there were also about two hundred animal corpses lying around: yaks and horses that had been eaten by wolves. They lost sight of the road that afternoon, and the day became dark in the heavy snow. They had no idea where to go. It snowed all night, and they couldn't find anywhere to pitch their tents. Some of the older men said, 'We must stop. If we're not on the road we might fall through a hole in the ice of a lake.' When day broke they sent a scout up a mountain to try to find their way—he could see a herd of wild asses far off, and they decided to follow them. At noon they found the road again, but by that afternoon three children had died of cold. Many families have died from missing the road in that remote area." This story frightened us. Father spoke again: "Today we did not lose the road even in the snow. That was good. If we pass this mountain tomorrow, we are going to enter a windy zone. That place is called 'the country of red winds day and night.' Go to bed quickly; we must move on early in the morning."

That day we departed before daybreak. Father was leading the caravan. After we reached the top of the pass, the wind began to increase steadily. There was so much red dust that we couldn't open our eyes. Aunt wrapped me in father's robe and tied me on the yak's back behind the baggage. The red wind, mixed with sand, lashed the outside of the robe and chilled me, even inside it. Later Neney bundled Japey in the robe and tied him behind the baggage. She put me in the back of her own robe and rode on our horse Jolu. I was still shivering. Later, the force of the red dust increased, and the yaks and horses turned their backs to the wind and lay down. They could not walk forward at all. The pilgrims were all suffering. Each followed the footsteps of the one in front of them. In the middle of the day Father and some others collected dried yak and ass dung and made a fire. We saw his smoke and then him waiting for us up ahead.

"I thought you had been blown away by the wind," he joked when we reached him.

"I swear I could hardly follow the road, it was so windy," Neney said. A pilgrim came up as we ate our meal.

"Hello, Durkho, what about this terrible wind?" he said.

"It is 'the country of red winds day and night.' We won't be through it today," Father said.

"Fill your mouth with ash!" the pilgrim cursed. "I swear I won't survive it," and he left. Then we started our journey again. After we came out from the shelter of the hill where we'd had our meal, the red sand lashed us fiercely as though it would smother us. A notice came from the front that the pilgrims should take cover. We took our animals over to where a little grass was growing at the bottom of a cliff. The wind was ferocious all over the earth and sky, but in that corner of the cliff it was pretty gentle.

"Father, tell us another story about when you went to Lhasa before," Japey said.

"The second time I went to Lhasa," Father said, "was when I was guiding the Waven chiefdom's pilgrimage. There were forty families. We were attacked relentlessly by bandits from the Wujud and Namtso chiefdoms. From the beginning of the journey to the end, two people were killed, five wounded, and four horses died. I myself got a bullet in the shin. For our part, we killed and wounded twelve of them, and killed around ten of their horses. When we had reached the same place we are now, ten of us went out before daybreak to lead the way. We came across a pack of wolves who were eating the carcass of a wild ass. The wolves charged us. We had eight armed men, and two more without guns. The pack had about a hundred wolves, and at first fifty attacked us. Two of my friends' horses had their stomachs torn open. We dismounted and made a circle with the horses in the center. Those who had guns fired them. I told them not to shoot, and to use their chaggor instead, but still some of the men fired their guns, and the number of wolves increased. A few wolves broke into the center of our group and attacked the horses. A horseman was injured, and his horse dragged away by the wolves and killed. There was nothing we could do to save it.

"There were four black wolves that seemed to be the most aggressive. 'Let's make a line of armed men and try shooting straight into them,' I said to the others. We lined up and managed to kill two black wolves. The wolf pack backed off a little, and we left our dead and injured horses and retreated up the side of the valley. The wolf pack attacked again and pulled one of us to the ground by his shoulder. We lined up again and shot the last few black wolves. Now, most of the pack had surrounded the dead horses, tearing the meat apart. We walked back slowly across the river. That day the wolf pack had wounded two of our people, killed four horses, and injured two others. We killed around thirty wolves. After the first black wolves died, they calmed down, but we used up almost all of our bullets." This story made me afraid.

For three days the pilgrims endured the red wind day and night. Then we reached a comfortable place where we rested for several days. Father took us into a big cave behind our encampment.

"Few people know about this cave," Father said. We walked a hundred paces in, past many carved statues. In front of the statues, pilgrims had left butter and cheese and other offerings. Pilgrims from our caravan followed us into the cave until it was very full, so we left.

"You boys," Father said, "leave a marker at this place so the next time you travel to Lhasa, you may visit it." I thought, "Who carved these statues in this deserted, freezing land? It's very strange to find a place as nice as this cave here."

29

Through the Red Rocky Vulture's Nest and into the Sun of Lhasa.

The days passed. We came to a small monastery near a river where we camped for two days.

"This is Nagchu Shabden Monastery," Father told us. We visited it early in the morning. There were many clay statues in the temples and the monks' assembly hall. There were about two hundred monks living there altogether, and it seemed to be a wealthy monastery. It was the first time we had seen a monastery since the day we left home. Father put some bowls on the ground near the monastery gates.

"I will sell each bowl for two silver coins," he announced. Monks came and bought all the bowls. They asked if we had any more. In the afternoon we sold twenty more bowls. The only one left over was a small one with a piece broken off the top. A young monk came and asked my father to sell it to him.

"You don't need to buy it. I'll give it to you," he said, but the young monk left a small coin anyway. Was it the case that that monastery didn't have enough bowls, or did the monks have a lot of money to spend?

The next day we set off on our journey again. We arrived at a big river where there was a water-powered mani wheel inside a small building.

"That's called 'the Old Wheel of Nagchu,'" Father said. All the pilgrims crowded around it. Then we came to a wide valley known as "the place where pilgrims leave their pack animals." We left our pack animals there: five yaks and a horse. We departed on our horse Julu's back with nothing more than a few clothes and some food. Most of the pilgrims did the same. At noon we arrived at Damchoktse Mountain, where a large incense altar was burning. We added incense. Father pointed out a large snowy mountain that reared up into the sky away to the west.

"I want you to look at that snow mountain," he emphasized to me and Japey. "It's called Nyenchen Tanglha." Many pilgrims were prostrating toward it. Even as a small child I had heard that Nyenchen Tanglha was a powerful mountain deity for all Tibetans. I felt so happy to see it at last. Then we set off on foot for Lhasa. There was no order of traveling, now, and everyone went at their own pace. We came to a big river with a bridge made out of leather and

Pilgrims from Golok eating a meal while on pilgrimage to Lhasa.
Bild 135 S 15 05 25. From the collection of the Federal Archives of Germany, Koblenz.
Photographer, Bruno Beger. Ahnenerbe Expedition, 1938–1939.

chains attached to boulders on either bank. You could barely call it a bridge. There were just chains to the left and right that you had to hold with both hands. The chains were connected by leather straps on which was laid a pole to walk on. The bridge was so difficult to cross that they said if you crossed it you would be able to cross the rocky roads of hell after you died. Only two boys were brave enough to cross it.

"So, are you brave enough to cross?" Father asked us.

"The man is crazy!" my aunt and many others said. "The children will fall into the river!"

"No problem!" Father asserted. "*My* sons won't fall." Then Japey and I began to cross the bridge. The rest of the pilgrims waded into the river. The bridge swayed precariously, but we knew that if we kept hold of the chains very tightly with our hands we would not fall off. We made it across safely.

Later we began to ascend a valley, and on the heights above we saw a large rock covered with juniper bushes with a small house in the center.

"Look up, boys," Father said. "That's Tagmar Sele Godtsang." Some monks were living on the mountain, and there were many statues. When we climbed to the roof of the temple and looked up, we could see a long gray piece of wood set into the rock.

"That is the merchant Norbu Sangpo's arrow," one of the monks told us. There was another long arrow hanging from one of the pillars of the temple.

"This arrow was carried here by an injured vulture," the monks said, "and this monastery was built on the nest that vulture made on this rocky mountain." Looking down from the rock temple made me feel giddy.

"Tonight we will camp in the pass," Father said at the end of the day. "Tomorrow before sunrise we will go to seek the golden roofs of the Jokhang." That night all the pilgrims camped in the Go La Pass.

The next day all the pilgrims, men and women, young and old, came to the Go Mountain to wait for sunrise.

"When the sun shines on the right side of Go Mountain," Father said, "the sun will also touch the Tsuglakhang in Lhasa. Then we'll go to the pass and look for the many-sized golden roofs of the Buddha that are the reward of karma and merit. Those with bad karma and little merit will not be able to reach them."

"The sunshine is here," one of the monks called out a little later. All the pilgrims ran over to the middle of the pass. When we got there, we saw the golden roofs of the monasteries and the cone-shaped golden roof of the Jokhang Temple shining in the sunlight. We prostrated and burned incense, and so did all the other pilgrims. People were yelling with happiness. I was gripped by an excitement and joy I could not explain, and sobbed uncontrollably.

"The Three Precious Jewels. . . . Oh, the precious stone of the Buddha that fulfills all wishes. I really made it here. I have really got to Lhasa now!" I cried out.

"The pointed golden roof we can see is the Tsuglhakang [Jokhang] in Lhasa. There is a lot of mist today, so we still cannot see the roof of the Potala, the Ramoche, and other smaller monasteries," said my father. Later we saw all these golden roofs. The Go La Pass was steep, and the way down was hard, zigzagging from side to side. When we were halfway down the mountain, the mist cleared, and we could see the whole of Lhasa nestled in a bend of the Kyichu River, which threaded its way between wide sandbanks. The Potala palace and Chakpori hill were high above the plain. When we reached Lhasa we camped near the river to the east of the city. Praise the Buddha! We finally got to Lhasa! We had longed day and night to get here, and now we had made it. For six months we had traveled through the clouds, over hundreds of mountains, across thousands of rivers. We had escaped many thieves and bandits, and now here we were in Lhasa, the Sun of Tsang.

That afternoon our high chief called a meeting. "Every day we are going to visit one large monastery," he announced. "The rest of the day you can do whatever you like. Do not fight and argue, and do not rob anyone. Beware of thieves, and always leave someone to guard your tents. And while in Lhasa, leave your guns in the chief's tent."

That night, my father gave me two silver coins.

"This is all your spending money while you are in Lhasa," he told me. "If you want to offer it in worship, or spend it on food, or whatever you like, it is up to you." They were the first silver coins I had ever owned, and I was ecstatic. I gave one coin to my aunt and kept one for myself. Then Father took Japey and me to the market near the city, where we met a friend of his. This man changed my silver coin into smaller coins that he had in his shop, pouring them into my hand. After that I had around fifty coins, called *sho*, of various denominations.

"I gave you some extra little coins as well," he said.

"Ah, oh, oh, I have so much money!" I thought, seething with excitement. "Tomorrow I will give some as offerings in the temples and buy some candy, too. And I will give two small coins to every child beggar." After I got home, Aunt Neney made me a bag and filled it full of *dongtse* and sho, to which Japey added another handful of dongtse for me until it was full to the brim. I fell asleep that night clutching the bag in my hand.

30

The Precious Jewel of the Buddha That Fulfills Our Wishes.
Hoping to Visit Again and Again.

That morning the Madey Chugama pilgrims arrived at the door of the Tsuglakhang Temple carrying long white silk scarves, and butter to add to the butter lamps. People also carried tea, cake, and other offerings. The door of the Jokhang Temple was still shut, so we lined up and waited outside. There were a lot of stray dogs around the temple entrance. There were also many barefooted beggars with torn clothes: their hands and feet were black, and their hair was black and matted. I felt a little frightened by them. Whenever the pilgrims threw away a leather bag that had contained butter, or dry meat, or tsampa, the beggars descended on it like dogs. Beggars and dogs fought over the leather bags, pulling them this way and that and tearing them into pieces. The beggars fought with the dogs as though they were dogs themselves. I could not explain the sadness this sight aroused in my mind. "Why does Lhasa have so many stray dogs and beggars?" I asked myself. We waited for the door to open. When it did, my father led me inside at the head of the pilgrims.

Making an offering of incense and tsampa in front of the Potala Palace, Lhasa.
Bild 135 S 15 46 07. From the collection of the Federal Archives of Germany, Koblenz.
Photographer, Bruno Beger. Ahnenerbe Expedition, 1938–1939.

We visited every temple and chapel, offering the scarves, prostrating and praying, and adding butter to fuel the butter lamps. When we reached the statue of the goddess Tara, there were many rats drinking water from the offering goblets in front of the statue and eating the barley offered by pilgrims. When we approached, they ran back into the statue's clothes. Father gave some white silver coins to the caretaker, and after visiting the statues of the minor deities, we entered the Buddha temple. After we had made three prostrations we approached the Buddha from the right. I placed three dongtse in front of the Buddha statue. Father held me up so I could touch the Buddha with my forehead. Immediately, a *dobdob* pulled us away. But I had already touched the statue, and I felt very happy. I thought, "When I looked up at him, the Buddha Rinpoche who can deeply understand all our prayers, joys, and sorrows smiled at me and looked at me cheerfully, laughing with joy. Now I would be content even to die." Once more I visited the Buddha, this time from the left side, and once again the dobdob pulled my forehead away from the statue. Then I went upstairs and visited the Macheg Lhamo Buddha and many other statues. Behind one of the statutes, the Ramachamo Buddha, I could see a little yellow goat with his head turned, looking back at us. When I had finished my visit the goat followed me to the temple doorway, but he stayed inside.

Later, father reappeared with a monk, smiling broadly.

"A doorkeeper I know helped me buy a *tedarlung* for a blood antler horn and some silver coins," he told us. He seemed very happy.

"Father, what's a tedarlung?" Japey asked. Father showed us a pill like an egg covered by yellow cloth.

"Here it is. It's a medicinal pill. As long as you do not expose it to the sky, it can protect life." After we got back home at the end of our pilgrimage, my father cut a piece off to give to our cousins and friends. He did it in the open air and at that time did not seem to care whether it was exposed to the sky or not. It was a black pill like a cockerel's egg, with five pieces of colored silk at its center.

After visiting the Tsuglakhang, we walked a little way north to visit the Mikyodorje Buddha in the Ramoche Temple in Lhasa.

"The Shakyamuni Buddha in the Jokhang was invited to Tibet from China by Songtsen Gampo's Chinese wife Gongjo," Father said. "But the Mikyodorje Buddha in the Ramoche Temple was invited to Tibet by Songtsen Gampo's Nepali wife." When we visited the Ramoche Buddha, we were able to take our time, and there were no dobdobs to pull us away. Again, I took out dongtses and put them in front of the statue of the Buddha. After visiting inside, we walked around outside the temple where there was a pile of small prayer wheels lying on the ground next to the path. The pilgrims ate their tea close to the temple's entrance, but we couldn't enjoy a relaxed meal because of all the beggars and dogs. Then we all went over to the Potala palace. The tall and magnificent Potala is built on top of a steep hill, and as I stared up at the palace I felt as though it would fall on my head. We also had to climb steep stairways at every temple inside the palace. The statues we visited were made of copper, silver, and gold. In some of the temples we were not allowed to wear shoes. One Buddha we visited was called the "Logeshara Buddha," which was the main statue inside the Potala. One of the doorkeeper monks held me up so that I could touch my forehead to a small box at the base of the statue. It made a sound like "Gog-cha" when I touched it.

"You touched Logeshara," the monk proclaimed. I put a few dongtse in front of the statue. Father had told me that I should always give two or three small dongtses to the three images of the Buddha, but not to all the other statues, otherwise my dongtses wouldn't last more than a day. I wanted to give coins to all of them, but I held back.

After visiting the Potala, we went to the Tibetan medical college on the rocky Chagpori hill.

"If you need to buy *dashel* you can buy it here today," Father told the pilgrims. They bought dashel, *jyado*, and many other pills. Then we took the path around the mountain and across the rock face. We visited the Lingkhor circumambulatory path where many statues had been carved into the rock. We stopped in front of them and prostrated. Ragged beggars were living on both sides of the path in torn white tents.

On one side, two beggars had died, their faces covered with rags. They smelled rotten. No one knew whether they had died of hunger, or illness, or for some other reason. A little farther on was a small shop that we walked around, window-shopping. Later we met a vendor selling warm sausages. Japey bought one and we shared it.

"You can't eat that," some of the pilgrims said. "It's dog meat." Whatever it was, it tasted delicious. While we were eating, Father and Neney came up to us.

"Father, is this dog meat?" I asked.

"Absolutely not, dear boy! Keep enjoying your meal." He bought some sausage for himself and Neney, and they both ate it.

We continued along the Lingkhor. When we came up to a large gate, I looked inside and saw some people whipping two men on their bare backs. They were standing against a wall with a yoke on their shoulders. They stood facing the wall, and their bodies were dark with bruises. I thought they would die from the beating. As we walked on, I could still hear the sound of the whip and the cries of the men.

"Those are the government's executioners," Father said. I felt sadness in my heart as we continued our circumambulation. There were many beggars, limping, lame, and without hands, some dumb and some blind. All of them were sitting beside the road, begging. The pilgrims gave them food, tea, and butter from their leather bags. I gave dongtses to two child beggars.

"The Three Precious Jewels bear witness! What should we do? I can't give to all of them," Neney said to me.

"All the lame, dumb, and blind beggars in the world are in Lhasa," Father said. "We definitely can't give something to all of them." While we were circumambulating, we saw some men shackled and with yokes on their necks begging by the path. The pilgrims gave a lot of food to them.

"Father, what happened to them?" I asked.

"These are all people whom the government sentenced to be punished," he replied. "Some have been blinded, and some have had hands or feet cut off. The government's executioners know all kinds of tortures: burning, skinning alive, and beheading. There are more punishments than the world knows." I did not see any of these punishments at the time, and only he who sees these things knows the true sadness of it. But even though I did not witness any of them, I remembered a saying I had heard often that went, "If you would know the sufferings of hell, go to Lhasa." I felt sad and uncertain. I thought, "This Lhasa is an honest, raw place. Here joy is intense and sadness is deep. The strong are too strong and can do whatever they want. The weak are too weak and have no protection. The rich are too rich, and their butter and meat rot uneaten. The poor are too poor and eat plants beside the road. But whatever happens, it is the will of the good-hearted Buddha. In life our joy and sorrow, our good and bad experiences are karma, the consequence of our previous life and lives."

31

An Audience with the Fourteenth Dalai Lama.
Visiting Sera and Drepung Monasteries.

One evening, the high chief announced that the Madey Chugama pilgrims would have an audience with the Fourteenth Dalai Lama the following day. We ate at daybreak and made our way to the Norbulingka, the Fourteenth Dalai Lama's Summer Palace. Pilgrims had been waiting in line since before daybreak, and we were in the middle. At dawn, the pilgrims entered two small temples nearest the gate. Inside the wall of the Norbulingka there was a park full of trees and the sounds of birdsong. Two officials stood guard at the temple doorways and beside the path. If you made a mistake, they beat you with the branch of a tree. Later, we approached the entrance to the Four-teenth Dalai Lama's chambers, as the first pilgrims left the audience chamber. Surely that day was an auspicious one, because at last I was going to meet the Fourteenth Dalai Lama. I had started feeling excited the day before. When we got near, my father gave me a *darkha*. I took three dongtses out of my bag, wrapped them in the darkha, and prepared to offer them.

"You cannot wear shoes," a monk said when we got to the doorway. We all took our shoes off and laid them beside the door. We walked up the stairs and entered a suite of rooms. Ahead was a very narrow doorway wide enough for only one person. I entered the small door alone. The Dalai Lama was sitting on a high throne on my left, smiling and holding a *dadar*, which he used to bestow blessings. He was looking straight at me, and I felt a bit scared. Father had stopped outside the door.

"Go up and see him," he said. I went up to the throne carrying the darkha and dongtse. The Fourteenth Dalai Lama watched me, smiling steadily. I ac-cidentally dropped the dongtse on the ground and then picked them up and put the darkha and dongtse offering on the throne. I could not see him well because his throne was so high. When I looked up, he was saying something and laughing, but I didn't understand what he said. An old monk in front of

Soldiers of the Tibetan army guarding the Dalai Lama's summer residence in Lhasa. Bild 135 S 13 13 33. From the collection of the Federal Archives of Germany, Koblenz. Photographer, Bruno Beger. Ahnenerbe Expedition, 1938–1939.

the throne held me up so I could touch foreheads with His Holiness. Then he bestowed his blessing on me with the dadar. He flicked my forehead with his forefinger and laughed again. It was a little painful, and my eyes filled with tears, but I felt so happy. Then the old monk put me back on the floor. A monk who had been pouring water into the vases used for water offerings gave me a ribbon. Father had already finished his blessing, and we went outside and put on our shoes.

"The Rinpoche flicked you with his finger, didn't he? You're lucky to have felt the blessing of his warm hand," Father said. I felt even happier. When we got to the wall outside the palace, they gave each of us a bowl of barley soup filled with balls of flour. The soup was called *zanto*. Someone said that the Dalai Lama had asked that it be given especially to the Madey Chugama pilgrims. The pilgrims chanted many manis while drinking the soup. Some prayed,

"Oh, Jalwa Yibzhen Norbu, we thank you deeply. Your compassion is not small." Others repeated in supplication, "May we meet Jalwa Tenzin Gyatso again and again!"

After visiting the Norbulingka, we walked along the river, across the sandy plain of Seri Shetang Tamo, and went to visit Sera Monastery. As we climbed the shallow slope up to the monastery, we saw its golden roofs glinting in the light.

After we entered, the pilgrims made a line as before, visited every temple, and paid their respects to the statues. One statue we visited had a horse's head, and we were told that it was the principal statue of Sera Monastery.

"This statue's name is Red Tamdrin," father told me, and he helped me to put my head in a small wooden space under the throne so that I could see it better. Then an old monk put black soot on my nose. I left three dongtses in front of that statue. Looking over to Japey, I saw that he too had soot on his nose. He told me that the black marks would remain there permanently. By then, all the children had marks on their noses. We visited many temples in Sera and saw a monastic assembly hall large enough to accommodate 6,600 monks.

People told us that at that time there were 3,800 monks in the hall. Our pilgrims handed over prayer request letters, *darkhas*, and money to the monks who were studying in the hall. Then we visited the monks' quarters and many temples. While we were waiting with the other pilgrims, I saw a small monkey tied to a pole. Children were playing games with it. I went over and gave it a little cheese, but it grabbed my sheepskin robe by the cuff and tore a piece off of it.

Then every pilgrim was given another bowl of zanto. "This is a gift from Sera Monastery to the Chugama pilgrims," an old monk said. "Thank you," we all said, and chanted manis.

Then the pilgrims went to the nearby monastic sky burial site. There were two dead bodies lying on a large, flat rock. We prayed and prostrated from a distance, as we weren't allowed to approach. Across this span we could see about fifty vultures eating the dead bodies, pulling them this way and that. Twice that many vultures, already sated with meat, perched on the mountain above the sky burial site. Later we went to the big stone, and, after prostrating and praying, we enacted a ritual: we lay down and pretended to be in our death throes and to die on the stone. Then we cut off some of our hair and nails and threw them onto the stone.[4] By the time we had finished at the sky burial site and returned home, evening had come.

The next day, before dawn, all the pilgrims went to visit Drepung Monastery. We got to the monastery at sunrise. I walked barefoot, and on the way my feet were punctured many times by thorns. Even pilgrims wearing shoes had their feet pricked. "In Lhasa, even a clean place cannot be cleaned of thorns," people said. That's really true. When we got close to the mountains, we looked up and saw Drepung Monastery. It really looked like its name, a "pile of rice" on the mountainside. It was huge and beautiful. One temple stood out, taller than the others, with a particularly gorgeous cone-shaped and gilded rooftop. When we reached the monastery, the pilgrims lined up again and went to visit every temple and statue: prostrating, praying, offering money, giving darkha, adding butter to butter lamps. From one large statue we cut a tiny piece of clay and ate it.

Later, Father showed me a very lovely statue. "This is the main statue of Drepung. It is called the Buddha Maitreya," he told me.

After visiting many temples, we came to the main assembly hall of the monastery, which we were told could seat 7,700 monks. There were many monks taking class there. The doorkeeper told us that at that time 3,300 monks were studying in the monastery. We prostrated as before, and pilgrims gave notes requesting prayers and left dedication offerings for the dead. After that we circumambulated the inside of the monastery. Then we walked down the mountainside and went to visit a small monastery that we could see on a ridge below and to the left of us. There were paintings of snakes in white, red, and yellow all over the walls and pillars of this temple.

"This is Nechung Monastery," Father told us. We visited the statue of Nechung in the Tsenkhang Temple and then went outside where pilgrims were burning incense on the altar near the outer wall of the monastery, and we also burned incense. After that, we walked back in the direction of Lhasa, stopping on the way to sit and eat on the grass. When we arrived, it was nearly dark.

4. To symbolize abandoning attachment to this life and their desire to return.

The ferry to Sera Monastery across the Tsangpo River, central Tibet.
Bild 135 S 15 07 37. From the collection of the Federal Archives of Germany, Koblenz.
Photographer, Bruno Beger. Ahnenerbe Expedition, 1938–1939.

32

Mountaintop Ganden. The White Stupa of Samye.

The high chief gave notice that on our last day in Lhasa we were going to visit Ganden Monastery. We prepared food and clothes for the journey. That morning, before daybreak, the pilgrims set off along the Kyichu River in the direction of Ganden. By noon we had reached the metal bridge at Pudo, where the first group of pilgrims was already sitting on the ground, cooking. After eating, we crossed the bridge and continued along the river, which led to a big valley. We walked to the other end, where around ten families were living in a tiny village. That night all the pilgrims stayed there, and I fell asleep early because I had walked far.

The next day, we slowly climbed the mountain. When we got to the top, most of the pilgrims were already there. We cleared the ridge and continued to the left. There was another ridge behind the first, and just below it we could see many gilded rooftops, both low and cone-shaped, gleaming in the sun.

Their brightness hurt my eyes, but I could see that it was a very big monastery. When they saw it, many of the pilgrims started prostrating.

"This is Ganden Monastery," Father told us. "It is known as 'Mountaintop Ganden.'" When we arrived in the monastery, the pilgrims made a line to visit the temples. One temple we visited had a big golden stupa studded with jewels, turquoise, and coral. "This is the 'Great Serdong of Ganden,'" Father said, "and it contains the remains of Tsongkhapa." I offered a darkha and placed three dongtses in front of the statue. We entered the monks' assembly hall, where we were told that it could accommodate 5,500 monks and that there were 2,800 monks studying there. As before, we made offerings for the deceased, prostrated, and left prayer request letters. Then we went on an interior circuit, visiting the remaining temples as we went. After we came out of the monastery, on its northern boundary, we found a group of monks feeding rice soup to the pilgrims. They said they were from our native land and were offering soup to all Chugama pilgrims. Later we circumambulated the mountain again, and on our path around the mountain we saw white inscriptions and reliefs of monks, dogs, birds, and many other interesting things carved into the dark stone.

Behind the mountain was the sky burial site, which not all the pilgrims were allowed to visit. However, my father went there with hair and nails that had belonged to my dead mother, uncle, and grandfather, and to others such as the woman killed by wolves on the journey. All these he left at the sky burial place.

Afterward, we arrived on the eastern side of the mountain, where we visited Tsongkhapa's meditation hermitage. That was a busy day, and it was dark before we got home. The pilgrims stayed inside the monastery for three days to circumambulate and make formal offerings for the pilgrimage. The Ganden Monastery officials and two groups of lamas fed our pilgrims. The Madey Chugama chiefdom's pilgrims were always friendly and well-behaved, and our leaders were worthy men who won us respect and honor from all the monasteries we visited.

And so the pilgrimage to Ganden Monastery ended, and the next day at dawn, we set out again. We walked down the great hollow of the mountain on the opposite side from the one we had ascended. At one point the slope turned to sand, and many of the pilgrims descended the mountain "riding" their walking sticks as though they were horses. My brother, Japey, and I took off our robes and slid and bounced in the sand with the other children. We were thrilled. Halfway down the mountain there were caves in the rock, and two of them were inhabited by meditating monks. Then, as the afternoon grew dark, the pilgrims made camp at the foot of the mountain.

The following morning the pilgrims continued down the valley and reached Tangshong on the Yarlung River at noon. As we walked on, we saw the golden roofs of a temple surrounded by trees and bushes, and all the pilgrims prostrated.

"That golden-topped one is Samye academy," Father told me. "Because it is located among these sandy mountainsides, we have the saying, 'Samye lives in the heart of sand.'" Sometime later we arrived in Samye itself. It was not a big monastery. An earth wall surrounded it, and there were many white stupas. We entered by the main gate, and the pilgrims went ahead to the academy. Then we visited the large temples and all the little ones. My father took the pilgrims to see the white stupas of Samye, the "white chicken" of Samye, and other religious sites. The famous "white chicken" was a chicken painted on a wall. After visiting the temples within the boundary wall, we walked up a hill called Samye Heypori. Samye really was all on sand—there was sand anywhere you walked. Heypori was not a large hill, but at the top was Padmasambavha's cave and an incense altar. We visited the cave and burned incense on the altar. Then we went to see Samye's sky burial site. It was in another sandy area near the mountain. On the site's flat rock we saw knives, axes, and many other tools. The pilgrims added knives and axes to the pile.

"After the people of the 'southern continent of the rose apple tree' die," Father explained, "their bodies are taken here. Every night, thousands of dead people's bodies are cut up. The knives and axes we leave here today will be blunt by morning, because during the night they'll be used to cut up thousands of dead bodies." The next day many of the pilgrims went to examine their own axes and knives that they had left there, and it was true: they were now worn down.

"If you can visit this place while you are alive," many pilgrims said, "your consciousness will not wander after your death."

After our visit to Samye, we crossed the river on a ferry and continued walking along the sandy banks of the Tsangpo River for many days. Most of the pilgrims were on foot and found it very hard to walk in the sand. It was a bit easier for Japey and me if we walked along the top of the sandbanks. When we felt too tired to keep going, Aunt Neney made us tsampa with cold water, and then we would start walking again.

After walking for ten days, we reached Tashilhunpo Monastery midday. The monastery was on a wide pasture with a high, craggy mountain at its end, and faced south. There were many temples with golden roofs, and we thought it looked very interesting. The first statue we visited at the monastery was called Jyawa Shamgon. It was three stories high. All the pilgrims prostrated, gave darkhas, and added butter to the lamps. I gave a darkha and placed three small coins in front of the statue. Then we visited many other temples. That day in the assembly hall of the monastery there were 2,300 monks studying.

We gave prayer request notes, we made prostrations, and we offered *ngoden*. After we left the monastery and circumambulated the boundary wall, a group of lamas blessed all the pilgrims with holy water. The lamas gave us barley wine and told us that the monastery had offered the Chugama people an official invitation to stay. After staying in the district of Tsang for four or five days, we headed back in the direction of Lhasa. On the way, we passed a huge white stupa on the side of a hill. "That is the Gyantse Palkhor stupa," Father told us.

The next day we crossed a big plain and kept moving toward Lhasa. I don't know how many days we spent on the road, but one day we arrived back at Lhasa in the afternoon.

33

Celebrating Losar (Tibetan New Year) in Lhasa and Saving a Prisoner's Life.

When we got to Lhasa, all the pilgrims went their own way, visiting holy places and browsing in the shops. We went to the market in the Barkhor, where there was cheese, sausages, butter, sugar shaped like horses' hoofs, tsampa, and much else. The temples were crowded with people because of Losar, the Tibetan New Year. The officials and dobdobs beat or fined whichever pilgrims fell into their hands.[5] One day in the Jokhang Temple a dobdob hit one of the old men in our party with a key and made his head bleed. The old man's son hit the dobdob on the head with a chaggor and toppled him. Some other dobdobs and monks beat the old man's son, throwing him to the ground. Then their family's son-in-law and all of the pilgrims from our group attacked the monks with knives and chaggors and whatever they had in their hands. Two or three of the dobdobs dropped to the ground.

"Amdo people are criminals," snarled the other monks watching this fight. No one lost face, however, and after our high chief came and broke up the fight, everyone stopped arguing and went on their way. For a few days after that our pilgrims were forbidden to enter the Jokhang Temple.

That night was the Lhasa New Year's Eve, and after sunset every family was invited to the *medzagad* "exploding fire teapot" ceremony. We did not know how many explosions there would be, but it was said that each blowup

---

5. During Tibetan New Year the secular authorities handed over the policing of the city to the monastic police (the dobdobs).

was a good omen. All day things were happening: at noon, as we came out of the Ramoche Temple, we saw a procession with some Lhasa aristocrats on horseback. The local people bowed to them, letting their arms hang down loose. After the horsemen came some people riding on the necks of other people. It was the first time I had seen humans riding humans in that way. The monks studying in the Jokhang Temple had finished their class, and the market and all the streets and grassy areas were crowded with monks with bowls held high and sheepskin bags in their hands. How wonderful it was. Of course this was to be expected, as we were in the homeland and center of religion. There were so many monks! People said that there were monks from Sera, Drepung, and Ganden in Lhasa to receive teachings, but the vast numbers surprised us. That night all the pilgrims visited the Jokhang Temple because the high chief had sent a message to say that we would be leaving the following day. When it was almost dark, my father bought a gun and a hundred rounds of ammunition.

"This is called an Indian *motsa*," he said. Everyone looked at it. "I paid eight branches of dried antlers for it."

The next day was the day of our return to our homeland, so the pilgrims went to Tabzhi Lhamo hill to burn incense on the altar there. On the way back we passed the Chinese ambassador's compound, where there were many big red balls attached to the tops of the doors. It was Chinese New Year. When we got close to our camp, we saw our fellow pilgrims milling around waving guns and knives and yelling. Ten Tibetan soldiers were escorting a young man in handcuffs, surrounded by the agitated crowd. Our people were arguing with the soldiers.

"If you don't let that man go, you won't move another step today," one of our people shouted.

"We are bringing him back to our homeland," another person bellowed.

"Since you Amdo men are so brave," the officer commanding the Tibetan soldiers said, "we could let you walk away with this murderer and watch the results. But that is not going to happen. Official prisoners cannot be set free. You do understand that, don't you? The army will stop you from taking him away and will butcher you if you try." They said many belligerent things.

Around one hundred horsemen from Chugama then disarmed the ten Tibetan soldiers and took the man away from them. The prisoner was taken before our high chief, and the Tibetan soldiers were tied up with leather thongs and forced to join the pilgrims on the road out of Lhasa. At noon, when all the pilgrims stopped for a meal, the high chief gave the Tibetan soldiers their guns, unloaded, and sent them back to Lhasa with thirty silver coins in their chief officer's hand.

"Thank you! Thank you!" the officer said many times, and bowed, before taking his empty guns and his troops back home. For several days after that the pilgrims' armed escort stayed at the rear of the caravan for fear that the Tibetan army would pursue us. A few days later we reached the valley where we had left our livestock and camped there while we prepared for our journey home. No soldiers came, and no messages arrived, so we took the prisoner to our high chief's native land. After that, I never heard of him again.

The pilgrims made good time on the return journey. The livestock walked fast and seemed less awkward to drive than on the way out. Both they and the pilgrims seemed to be missing their native land! We walked swiftly and were full of happiness. On the way, my father killed some Tibetan gazelles and antelopes for us to eat on the journey.

One day we looked into the valley below and saw a large herd of wild animals with brightly colored horns.

"The ones with circular horns are male argali sheep," Father said, "and the ones with pleated horns are the females." There must have been four hundred in the herd. Until then we had only seen them from a distance, and they just looked like creatures with big heads. That day we saw them close up, and they were large and beautiful animals.

In the night we awoke to a lot of commotion: dogs barking, people yelling, and gunfire from the direction of the pilgrims above us. Father went out with his gun.

"Don't go. We don't know what's going on!" Aunt pleaded with him. We saw Uncle Mgontse running past our tent with ten other men.

"It may be the Tibetan army," Father said. "If it's the official army we won't stand a chance, so we won't fight with them. We'll escape up the mountain while Mgontse's men hold them off." He sent a group of armed men up the mountain, along with forty of our horsemen. We could still hear shooting in the distance.

"Durkho!" I heard a man shouting. "Should we join them on the mountain?"

"There haven't been that many shots," Father said, "and we've got enough armed men to handle a small conflict. We'll stay here until daybreak." When dawn came, we could still hear the gunfire. My father led our armed men toward it, and a little later a burst of shots erupted in the distance, and we saw ten horsemen speeding away toward the mountain on the opposite side of the river. More shots rang out, and horsemen plunged to the ground. One of them stood up and began to run away. His horse had been killed right under him. By the time the sun was fully risen, our men had returned. Two had been shot, and my father's horse had been grazed on its rear. The wound bled for many days, but the horse was able to walk.

"It wasn't the official soldiers," Father let us know, "just some thieves from Nyamtso. We surprised them this morning when they attacked the high chief.

We shot them as they were running away, and they lost their loot. Two companions of the high chief were injured, and four of our livestock killed. But we killed three of them, injured two, and captured a few of their boys. Six of their horses were injured or killed. Most of that happened after I got there." This was just one of the many stories we heard him tell about his battles with bandits. It was the only time we were attacked by raiders on our way back from Lhasa. We got home safely without meeting any other thieves.

34

Disaster Strikes Us after Our Return Home.

As the pilgrims returned to Golok, we split into two groups because there were two roads, an upper road and a lower road, and the pilgrims had decided that half the group should return on each one. Our high chief left it to us to decide which road to take. A few days later, my father put me on the back of his horse, so that we could go hunting together. He shot a gazelle.

"Father, tomorrow Aunt is going home," Japey said that afternoon when we got back to our campsite. I was devastated. For a whole year, whenever troubles had befallen us, through happiness and sadness, Aunt had looked after us as though she were our real mother. I had never known what it was like to have a mother, and since Aunt had arrived at our home, I felt as though I had one. Now we suddenly had to go our separate ways as if that wasn't important. The suffering in my heart was hard to bear, and I cried.

"Father, where is Aunt Neney going?" I asked.

"If Aunt finds an encampment of her chiefdom's people tomorrow," Father replied, "she will go with them to her own home."

"Lovely Aunt," I begged her, "you can stay at our home! You don't have to go, do you?" Aunt held me in her arms, and tears fell from her eyes.

"Nukho," she told me, "Aunt has to go and look after her parents. Later she will come and visit both of you." She tried to comfort me all night, but I just became more and more unhappy. Father gave her a red sash, some cloth for making robes, some candy, and other things that we had bought in Lhasa. That night I slept, as usual, with Aunt in her bed.

"Dear Nukho, you mustn't cry," she told me as I curled up against her for the last time, "tomorrow Aunt needs to leave." The next day, the pilgrims came to a group of families living at the foot of a mountain. Aunt's own family was among them, and she went to them, carrying all her things on her back. Before she left, she held Japey and me and wept.

A monastery in Amdo, northeastern Tibet.
123441-245416. Photographer, Joseph Rock, 1924.
© President and Fellows of Harvard College, Arnold Arboretum Archives.

"Aunt will come to visit you, and you will come to Aunt's family. Under-stand?" she said. Then she walked away without looking back. She just left. None of us imagined that we would never meet again. My aunt will never leave my heart.

I felt unhappy for many days after Aunt left. Most of the pilgrims had re-turned to their own families already. At that time the Chugama people were living in Sogpo, and by the time we reached the monastery there, only our family and four other families were still traveling together. At last we reached the Machu River ferry where we had begun our journey a year before. We had set out in the Tiger month and it was in the Tiger month that we returned. In all the places we had visited, we never found a place as pleasant as our own home. When we entered our own monastery, we saw friends and people we knew and felt completely contented. Father and I visited many families and gave them gifts, such as beads and candies from Lhasa. A few days later, fa-ther made a parasol with peacock feathers he had bought in Lhasa and gave it to the monastery. He also gave them a copy of the Kathang Dennga and other scripture books he had bought in Lhasa. That was the first time in the entire history of Chugama Monastery that it had possessed a peacock feather parasol. From that time onward it was to be used in procession on the six-teenth day of the Tibetan New Year, when the statue of Maitreya Buddha was processed around the monastery. It became famous, and everyone called it the "Naktsang family's peacock parasol." Uncle Jakho was especially pleased.

"That's a fantastic gift," he told my father. "Over one hundred families went on pilgrimage, but none of them returned with anything as good as that to give to the monastery!"

Ten days after we had arrived, my father brought me to the monastery to "take the thread," so that I could take my monastic vows in front of Alak Merdo. I became a real monk and started studying scriptures with teacher Thogmed. A few weeks later, my father went to Ngawa, and a week later at dusk he returned home. While the three of us, father and sons, were having a meal, some monks from the monastery came to see us. They led father outside and told him something.

"You two stay here," he returned to tell us. "Father has something to do." And he left with the monks. Japey and I went to bed.

The following morning class began in the monastery. A group of monks were reciting and memorizing scriptures on the steps leading up to the class-room door. Suddenly they stopped and craned their necks toward the gate.

"What's happening?" one monk said to another. "It looks like the Naktsang man under arrest." When I heard that, a sound like "zing" went off in my head. I looked toward the gate, and there was my father in handcuffs being pulled forward by three monks. My heart was full of anger, and my eyes full of tears. I could not see my father's face clearly. Then father raised his hand-cuffed wrists.

"Four hundred monks of Madey Chugama!" he shouted. "Look at me to-day! I am a son of the Naktsang clan who has thought of nothing but this monastery and its monks since I was a boy, more so even than my own life. I am no longer rich, but I brought a peacock feather umbrella and other things for the monastery from Lhasa, rather than spending the money on my sons, or on my own food. However, today the head of monastic discipline here, Wasang, made an accusation against me: he says I rode a horse past him last night, through the monastery, while fully armed. Never since the foundation of the monastery of Madey Chugama has it been acceptable to handcuff and arrest people." He raised his hands again and said, "Look, people of Madey Chugama and monks! This monastery will not prosper, because today the bald-headed Wasang did this. Do the consequences of karma not apply to high-level Gelug monks? This monastery is repaying my good deeds with evil." He said a lot more things like this. Then the monks took him into the assembly hall. They led my father to the end of one of the monks' benches.

"Naktsang Durkho," the head of discipline Wasang announced, "you have denigrated the monastery and religious laws with your insulting speech. For that your punishment is five hundred strokes of the whip, and a fine of two yaks to be given to the monastery's kitchen tomorrow morning."

"Bald-headed Wasang," my father replied, "you may be the head of discipline, but I am not in breach of religious law—it is you! Since I was born, this monastery has never arrested anyone and put handcuffs on them. You may do whatever you want today, but the karmic consequences are yours. If I can't bear a thousand strokes of the whip, may my Naktsang family's sash be the sash of a dog." The monks sat silently. Some of them removed my father's handcuffs and took off his sheepskin robe. They made him lie on the robe, his neck level with the line of their benches. After a while, two monks entered with willow branches and stood on either side of my father. They took turns striking my father's bottom with the branches. That day four monks altogether beat my father alternately. When they first lashed his bottom, some dust rose from it, but later it became bloody and red. The monks continued to hit him, changing from one hand to the other. His bottom began to bleed all over, and the monks who were beating him got his blood on their hands and clothes. They removed their plaids,[6] and wrapped them around their wrists, continuing to whip him as before. My father never moved and just lay still. Some of the monks who were beating my father got tired and sat down, with sweat pouring from their faces.

"How can these men be monks if they have no compassion?" I thought to myself. "It seems they do not know they are beating a person—it's as if he were a stone. Would they even have the heart to do this to a horse?" I had no idea what to do but just watched. The noise of the beating resounded through the monks' assembly hall with a "sher-tsug, sher-tsug" sound. The other monks kept silent with darkened and lowered faces. The sound of the whip held my attention like a black hook.

35

Gracious Wasang, the Head of Discipline.
One Thousand Five Hundred Lashes.

A person was arrested, handcuffed, and taken to the Madey Chugama Tashi Chulong Monastery assembly hall, where he was whipped across the monks' benches, a thing that had never happened before.

6. Loose upper garment worn over the tunic.

"The head of discipline Wasang has breached the laws of religion," some said.

"This will be the end of religious teaching in Tashi Chulong Monastery!" others said. However, that day, the misfortune only fell on the heads of the father and the sons. The monastery's fate was yet to come. At the end of the benches, all four monks were still beating my father one after the other with the willow branches. Blood kept flowing whenever the whip fell. My father bit his robe and made no sound from beginning to end.

"We have administered 1,500 strokes," the monks said at last, and they stopped the beating. Each monk had used three willow wands together, so 500 strokes counted as 1,500. Then my father bellowed:

"Right, bald-headed Wasang, if you're still alive beat me more! You have no compassion, no shame, and no legality. Why don't you kill me in front of these four hundred monks? It will ease your dead feelings." It was silent in the assembly hall. Then, I could no longer control my feelings about the pitiless way the monks had whipped my father, and I burst into tears.

"Don't cry, you baby devil," Wasang said, coming over to me. He hit me on the head with his wooden whip. I saw stars, and then I didn't remember anything else. People told me later that Japey ran over to Wasang and scratched his face, leaving a red line. Wasang kicked Japey to the ground with his boot, and started to hit him with the whip. But a monk called Monlam stood up and grabbed Wasang's whip.

"Even if you have to beat the father," he said, "there's no reason to beat the son. If you don't stop, I will make a dead body of you, and you won't get up again." Monlam carried me out of the hall.

Uncle Jakho also went up to Wasang.

"You worthless man," he told him, "have you been bitten by a mad dog? This is the assembly hall here, not your home. Beating children! Do you want dead bodies on our hands?" Then he went out, too. Wasang stood and watched without saying a word. Japey told me about it all later.

Japey, Jakho, and Monlam were holding me when I came around after Zodpa the water carrier poured water on my head.

"Something must be done to stop Wasang," Jakho said.

"Wasang, may your dead head turn to blood!" Zodpa shouted. "If you're a normal man, then I'm a dead one!" They washed the blood off my face, then took a piece of sheepskin from Jakho's shirt and put it on the wound.

"Brother, where's our father?" I asked Japey.

"Some monks of Mgontse's clan carried him to our home," he let me know. "Even after he had been beaten 1,500 times, father kept saying insulting things to Wasang, but Wasang didn't answer. The monks said it was because Monlam had spoken sternly to Wasang. Father couldn't stand up, so Mgontse's monks got a yak hair carpet to put him on and carried him home."

When we got home, ten monks from Mgontse's clan were chanting ritual prayers. Father was lying on his bed with his head up, drinking tea. He was talking to the monks and laughing, so I thought he must be getting better. I was worried that he would die from the 1,500 strokes, and when I got to him I cried a little and hugged him around his neck.

"Don't cry, my son" he told me, "because a brave boy's life will know a lot of sadness. This is a small thing. If you are a brave boy you won't cry." I stopped crying. "What's wrong with your head?" Father asked.

"Wasang beat me with his whip," I told him.

Father said, "I'll send that bald-headed Wasang to hell. If I let him live after I recover, then I'm not a human being."

"Don't say such things," Uncle Jakho put in. "Just forget it. He's still head of discipline in this monastery."

"If that weren't true," Monlam said, "I'd have knocked him down today."

"The bigger the argument, the worse it will be for the chief and Alak. I think it would be better just to leave it," Uncle Jakho said.

The next day the monastery slaughtered our two male yaks as an offering to the kitchen. Zodpa brought the two heads, one leg, and both the hides back to our home. Father gave him one of the heads. That night, Wasang sent three monks to our home to ask my father to give them his gun. My father shook with rage when he heard that, but he still couldn't get out of bed.

"Tell bald-headed Wasang that he can do whatever he wants," Father said to the monks. "If the leaders of the monastery want to come and get my gun, I'll spill their blood. You can tell them the Naktsang old man isn't dead yet. If anyone wants my gun, then let them come. I'm not playacting. I'll show them what I can really do. Jabey, bring me my gun and bullets." Jabey gave father his gun and ammunition belt.

"We can't decide for Wasang. We'll go talk to him now," Jakho said.

"You had better not come back with a message," Father told them. "If Wasang wants the gun, he better come and get it himself. I am always the lucky one in a fight, and if I stop fighting, it will be a sign that the Naktsang family is finished." He loaded his gun. Jakho went back to the monastery with the three monks. Monlam and the other monks continued to chant their ritual.

"I don't want to be a monk anymore," I told my father.

"That's fine, my dear boy," Father said. "You and your brother will no longer attend classes in the monastery. You can't be a monk under Wasang's authority after this. When father is better, we will go far away. We definitely won't stay here under the bald-headed Wasang. We three will find a good life wherever we go." Whether it was because of what Uncle Jakho told him or not, from then on we heard nothing from Wasang about taking the gun. After a month, father was better and could walk again. Soon after that he went to Ngawa, but Japey and I stayed behind. Japey didn't attend monastery classes anymore, but read books at home. I stopped wearing my monk's habit and, as before, did housework, fetched water, collected firewood, and other things. My dream of being a good monk was killed by Wasang's whip. My monk's karma lasted for only three weeks in this life.

And after that I thought, "Meeting the head of discipline on horseback while carrying a gun doesn't seem to merit such a harsh punishment!"

36

Meeting the Tenth Panchen Lama (Amitabha) at Labrang Monastery.

That summer our father took us to Labrang Monastery on pilgrimage. On our way we visited Uncle Mgontse's family, and then we went on to Labrang together. After a journey of seven days we arrived at the monastery. I thought, "I remember everything they told me. Labrang Monastery is home to three thousand monks. It is in the bend of a mountain that looks like an elephant walking, and lies on the right bank of the Sangchu River. It has many temples with golden rooftops, representations of the Buddha in pictures and statues, and an image of Gungtang Jampeyang that offers deliverance when one looks at it. I'm glad that the karma of my previous life has given me the chance to see this place!"

When we got to Labrang we stayed in the Gungtang guesthouse. One day my father took Japey and me to an audience with Alak Gungtang. When we came before him, he recognized my father, because when we first got there we had dined in his chambers. He was about twenty years old, and his face was wreathed in smiles.

"Oh, yes, here they come," he said to my father. "Are these boys both yours?"

"They are," my father answered.

"It's such a tragedy that their mother died," Alak said.

"Yes," my father replied, "but now they are getting older and must rely on your mercy. Even when I am an old man, please do not forget them."

"Yes, yes, I understand," Alak told him. "In the future they can come to me with any problems they may have. The elder one is a monk, and the younger is called Nukho, right?" He fed us all cake, bread, and many other things. Then we went back to the monastery. When we passed the outer wall, we met two

A gathering of monks in the courtyard of a monastery, Amdo.
123360-243890. Photographer, Joseph Rock, 1924.
© President and Fellows of Harvard College, Arnold Arboretum Archives.

very old monks leading a child monk. Father stopped and prostrated, then started a conversation with the adults.

The child monk pulled my ear. "How old are you?" he asked me.

"I'm eight years old," I replied.

"Yes, I'm the same as you," he said. "I'm a marmot-year eight-year-old." Then he walked away, but as he left he patted me on the head twice with his hands. I realized that he was a high reincarnation of a lama called "Jamyang Shadpa the Protector." At that time he was too young to spend much time giving audiences. It was our karma to meet him there. He pulled my ear and blessed me twice on my head, too! My father had noticed.

"He pulled your ear didn't he?" he said. "That's good! That's very good!"

"Tomorrow His Holiness the Panchen Lama is coming," people began saying a few days after our pilgrimage arrived at Labrang. One morning we looked over to the road that wound through the forests on the other side of the valley from the monastery. All the monks and lamas of the monastery in their yellow and gold ceremonial robes and headdresses were awaiting his arrival. Suddenly, many cars appeared in the distance.

"His Holiness is in the third car," the occupants of the leading car announced when it arrived. The first car contained a two-way radio, which was why it was in front. Then the other cars arrived, and we could clearly see a gold-robed figure in the third car. He drove into the courtyard of the monastic assembly hall, where that day he gave an empowerment to tens of thousands of people who were waiting inside the monastery.

When we tried to get into the monastery, it was already too late to enter by the main gate—too many people were pressed together inside. Uncle Mgontse, Japey, and I went with Father around the back of the monastery wall where there was a small gate. It was being guarded by two Chinese soldiers, who would not let us in. But while we were there, some monks came through the gate with their religious equipment. My father took me in his arms and Japey by the hand, joining the crowd of monks, and slipped through the gate with us. Uncle Mgontse and five others followed. The Chinese soldiers kicked at us and struck out with their guns as we passed but couldn't stop us. Some other soldiers came and sat us down close to the front, near His Holiness's throne. My father's head was bleeding a little after being hit by one of the soldiers at the gate, and a monk servant gave him a piece of cloth to wipe away the blood. When the Panchen Lama had finished giving his empowerment, he gave an audience for the lamas and the people sitting near the front of the crowd. The Chinese soldiers close to us pushed us into the line for the audience. As we got near His Holiness's throne, devotees had to approach one by one. When I was close to the throne, holding out my darkha, I saw that the throne was very high, and a lot of silver money to honor him had already been placed in front of it. I tried to approach the throne but slipped on the coins. I looked up at His Holiness's face, and he smiled back at me. In his hand he held a dadar arrow, which he used in his empowerment and to bestow blessings. One of the Chinese soldiers pushed my back to get me closer to the throne. His Holiness reached out and struck me on the head with the point of the dadar, which made a sound like "tag, tag." My face was covered in tears because of the pain. As I left, a monk was giving a commemorative red ribbon to each person and distributing *wum chu* blessed water. Another monk was passing out large pieces of fried bread tied together with yak hair string to the devotees. We went outside, and when we reached the circumambulation path around the monastery, there were many old men and women out there.

"Please, give me a piece of your offering bread," they asked me. I pinched off a little and gave some to each of them. So many people wanted a piece that I used up one of the bread chunks almost immediately.

A view of the Yellow River in Golok, Amdo, northern Tibet, with
Ragya Monastery in the foreground. 123221-243843. Photographer, Joseph Rock, 1924.
© President and Fellows of Harvard College, Arnold Arboretum Archives.

37

Return to Chugama.

One night we went to the market to watch a movie that contained many
scenes of soldiers. Many People's Liberation Army (PLA) soldiers were quar-
tered in Labrang, and after we had seen the movie we saw many soldiers
marching in line down the street.

"They are like the soldiers in the movie," people said. I thought that too.

"No, they aren't," my father said. "That movie was Chinese magic—a fairy
tale."

Our pilgrimage to Labrang ended, and we headed home. The morning we
left, the three of us went to the market to buy food. Labrang used to be very
famous for its bread and fruit, and we thought it would make a good gift for
our cousins and friends when we got home. Father bought one box of bread
and two leather bags of fruit. He weighed the fruit on the scales from the fruit
shop and put it in our bags. But Japey and I ate as much as we could, first, and
the Chinese shopkeeper packed as much as would fit into our pockets. We

also bought a bunch of vermicelli and half a bag of tsampa. Then we started our journey

— RETURNING TO THE GRASSLAND —

We had been at Labrang for about a month. For part of that time we had been on pilgrimage to Labrang Monastery and had met many lamas and reincarnate *tulkus*. We had met the Panchen Lama, Jamyang Zhedpa, Gungtang Jampeyang, Alak Tag, and many others. After seven days traveling we reached our home district. At first we stayed with the Meshel family for a few days, then with Uncle Mgotag's clan. Uncle Mgotag was very kind to us, and sister Tugpatso, brother Getag, Japey, and I went often to the river and played games.

"Hey, Durkho!" Aunt Rigdron said. "Don't take my boy Nukho away again. My family can look after him!"

"I'm going to take him away now," Father replied. "But next year we might go to Lhasa again, and you would be together then."

After that we stayed with Uncle Norta's family for a few days.

"Leave Nukho, and we'll send him to you next summer," Aunt Damkho said when the time came for us to leave.

"I'll take him this year," my father said. "Next year we may go back to Lhasa. It would be good if the two boys could be together in a monastery there."

"This is sad!" Aunt Damkho said. "I'm sure we won't meet again for a long time."

We headed in the direction of Chugama Monastery.

After two days traveling, we reached the ferry on the Machu River where we could cross over to Chugama Monastery. After the ferryman Lochu had taken us across, we rode up to the monastery. As before, we stayed in Uncle Jakho's house, and the following day Japey went to class in the monastery. Wasang had been replaced as the head of discipline, and the new holder of the office was called Jangjug.

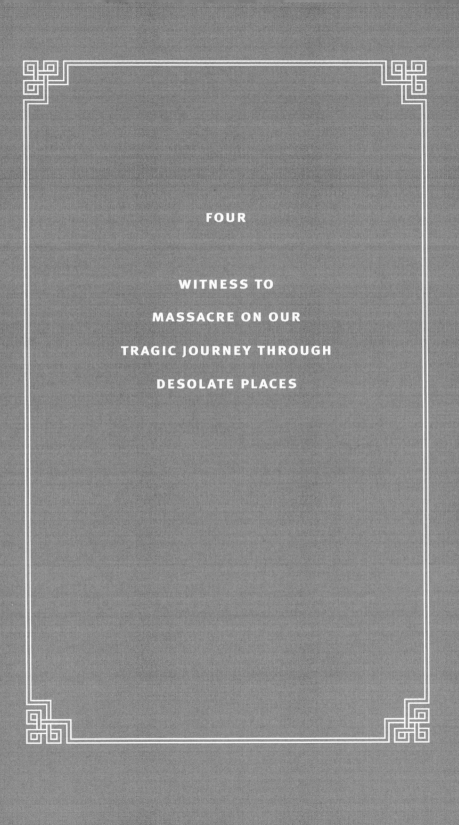

FOUR

WITNESS TO

MASSACRE ON OUR

TRAGIC JOURNEY THROUGH

DESOLATE PLACES

38

First Signs of Danger. Drafted to the Madey Chugama Army.

In those days no one had good news to tell.

"A Chinese army or some other evil thing will arrive soon," a man called Wyiga from Golok said. "I was talking to a Mongolian from Sogpo who told me about it. He said that during the day they kill people, and at night they kill dogs. If you surrender, they will cut off your head, and if you run away to the mountains, they cut off your legs. I heard they are the Ma Chinese." He said many things like that, but Father didn't respond. In the afternoon the monk Chukho visited us.

"Durkho, the Chinese are coming," he said. "They will throw the old people into an insect's hole, force the children to drink yogurt until their stomachs are full to bursting point, and then throw them off a roof so that they explode."

"That's not true," Father said. "We saw many Chinese troops in Labrang, didn't we? Were they like that? Although, I suppose if they are the Ma Chinese it might be possible." This kind of talk made me unhappy.

"The Liberation Army made a bridge of wet leather over the Machu River by magic in a single night," Uncle Mgontse told us. "The Datsen chiefdom has already been completely eradicated by the Chinese troops. A thousand Chinese troops have camped in Dromda, and if Amchok Jarig's army cannot stop them, our chiefdom will be destroyed like Datsen was." We were more and more frightened every day. Everyone was afraid but had no idea what to do apart from pray!

"The Three Precious Jewels bear witness!" Uncle Jakho said. "Changing times are surely coming. This year we have seen a comet and a *tin garu* cloud in the western sky. We know this isn't good."

"There's going to be a war, I'm sure of it," my father put in. "A tin garu is the sign of a big war to come. In the past it foretold the war of Red and White Russia. Bad times are coming, and even if the monastery carries out a Powa offering, they can't stop it."

"Don't say such stupid things," Jakho scoffed.

"I didn't say anything stupid," Father replied. "The last time the monastery drove away an evil spirit, its head fell off before it left. I heard that it set fire to part of Alak Tagrang's clothing, too. If these aren't evil omens, what are they?"

"By the Three Precious Jewels," Uncle Jakho said, "we don't know what's going to happen in the future, but don't we have to try to avoid war now? There's nothing our chiefdom's army can do against the Chinese troops. It would be a disaster for the chiefdom, and all the clans and families, to fight against them." We worried and argued about it endlessly. Everyone, young or old, was talking about the "time of revolution" and the "time of great changes," or sometimes they called it the "age of revolution." They spoke of little else. It was hard for me to express my fears, but questions kept forming in my mind: "What is a 'time of revolution'?" "What is the reason for these changes?" "Why does everyone seem to be so frightened of it?" "If the 'time of revolution' comes, what misfortunes will strike us?" These questions unsettled me. There were so many questions for which I couldn't find answers. Once I asked my father, "Father, if the 'time of revolution' comes, where will we live?"

"We could stay in the monastery," he said.

"If the monastery is destroyed by the 'time of revolution,' then where will we live?"

"Son, don't say such unlucky things, and make my tea," Father replied. As I waited for the water to boil, I thought, "Everyone seems sure that this 'time of revolution' will come, but they don't know how large the changes will be. If the changes are good for some, will they be bad for others? If it makes the rich poor and the poor rich, then the best people may have a shorter life, and bad people be raised to high honor and position. If the Chinese troops force this change on the Tibetans, then that's the result of bad karma. Tibet will have to live through bad times. The bad news is coming in bit by bit, but so far there is no clear answer to these questions. Now we can say whatever we want to, but when the bad times come, everyone who speaks their mind will be punished. Will Karma keep some people from suffering?" Father went out later, and Jabey returned from his classes.

"Today the head of discipline Jangjug told us," he said, "that the Chinese army will arrive at the monastery soon and that the men and boys of Madey Chugama have already joined the chiefdom's army. The lamas and chiefs have ordered that all the boys and men should leave the monastery now and go with the army. Anyone who stays will be acting against the ruling of the monastery."

"When Father gets back, what will he do?" I asked.

"Father is still out somewhere," he told me. "I left a message with Aunt Tamkho to tell him to come back to the monastery at night, when he won't be seen." Then Uncle Jakho arrived.

"It's happened," he said. "The Chugama chiefdom's army and the Chinese army have started fighting already. Norta and all of his sons have joined the fighting—they've gone to their deaths. I see that your father isn't here. Has he gone to join the army?"

"Do you have to join the army?" I asked.

"Normally monks don't have to," Uncle Jakho said, "but if the enemies of Buddhism try to destroy the monastery, they will find that monks can fight. The Three Precious Jewels bear witness it won't come to that, though."

That night I had a nightmare. Thousands of armed horsemen, neither Chinese nor Tibetan, were galloping across the grassland on a dark and misty evening. The sound of gunfire filled the air, and people fell like trees. I had no place to stand or hide and ran behind my father, crying. I could not run properly because my feet were paralyzed. I called, "Father!" but he ran ahead, his face bleeding, without stopping for me. I yelled again and cried, "Father!" and heard a voice saying, "Nukho! Why are you shouting?" It was my brother, Jabey, punching me, waking me up. My heart was thumping. Then there was a knock on our gate.

"Father's home!" Jabey and I shouted, and ran outside. Father was on foot without horse or gun. When he neared the house he said, "Are there any guests here?"

"No guests," Jabey said. "We are alone." The three of us entered the house together. "Father, did you join the army?" Jabey asked.

"How could I go and leave you two alone?" Father answered.

"If the monastery knew this they would punish you again," Jabey said.

"The monastery is in no position to punish anyone," replied my father. "It can't even defend itself. Nukho, tomorrow I want you to ask Uncle Jakho to come here."

"If you don't go, it will be bad for you," I told my father.

"It's fine," Father said. "Call your uncle here. I will stay inside the house. Don't tell anyone that I am here." The next day I went to fetch Uncle Jakho.

"Are you crazy?" he asked my father. "If you don't go to the army, how will you deal with the chiefs when they come back from fighting? And if the monastery finds out, it'll be bad for you, too."

"My sons are too young to join the army," Father said. "So I must stay and look after them. Everyone in our chiefdom went to the army as the chiefs ordered. Men over fifteen and under sixty have been sent to Sogpo. Our army has already driven out the Chinese land surveyors and killed at least one hundred soldiers. But a few days ago all the lamas and chiefs in Tsu were arrested secretly by the Chinese. All the monasteries in the Achong Lhade chiefdom have been destroyed. I heard that about five hundred Chinese troops are marching to attack us, and they'll probably be here tomorrow. If that happens, I'll have no choice but to surrender, but I will not leave my sons unless I am forced to."

This was shocking to hear. Jakho said that the monastery had already prepared darkhas for the arrival of the Chinese troops because they were planning to surrender.

"It was decided yesterday in the monastery that the monks would not resist the Chinese army. You should hide your guns in case the Chinese troops see them and it causes problems. This is truly terrible. Fill your mouth with ashes! These really are times of great changes." Despite this, we hoped that after the surrender we could live comfortably. These were empty wishes.

"Father, you should hide at home," I said. "If anyone from the monastery comes here, I won't open the door."

"This is all going to happen tomorrow, and the monastery is too busy to come here," he replied. "And you can't stop the Chinese army by refusing to open the door. Anyway, everything may go well. Nothing may happen to the chiefdoms and monasteries, or even to us. It is our karma whether we have anywhere to hide or not." For the next few days I felt fearful about the arrival of the Chinese troops and worried about the monastery finding out that my father had not joined the Madey Chugama army. Then I thought, "What reason do I have to be afraid? Jabey and my father are both with me." My father was fearless and left the house during the curfew, always returning before dawn. I had no idea what he was doing or where he went.

39

The Misfortunes That Followed the Occupation of the Monastery. Troubles Limitless as the Sky.

It had rained during the night, and in the morning the grass was soft and clean, the dew sparkling in the strong sun! White, yellow, and red autumn flowers spread bountifully over the misty Tashi Chulong grassland in front of the monastery. The flowers turned to the sun and filled the air with their fragrance. The birds and insects living their lives of happiness and sadness in the sunshine made a cheerful noise.

I was making breakfast as usual, and said to father, "Father, it's time for your breakfast."

"Yes, my boy," Father replied. "Did Aunt Gorto bring any butter and cheese yet?"

"She brought it yesterday," I said. "She brought some milk too, so I made milk tea." Suddenly Jabey rushed in and shouted, "Father, the Chinese troops have reached the river! There is no class today, and all the monks have been ordered to line up and welcome them." Father stood up.

"So the monastery will surrender," he said. "That won't do them any good."

"If they surrender, will they have their heads cut off?" I asked.

"They won't get their heads cut off, but they'll be punished or beaten in some way," Father replied.

"The head of discipline, Jyangjug, told us that if we surrender, then they won't destroy the monastery, but if we don't, they will kill people, destroy the monastery, and take everything away," said Japey.

"What a pity. Tibetans are really very naive," Father said. "I heard that Labrang Monastery has already been destroyed. If they hadn't wanted to destroy this monastery, then they wouldn't have come. I'm sure they won't leave our monastery as a stronghold behind their lines."

"Eat quickly," Jabey said to me. "We're going to see the Chinese troops."

"Jabey, is this the Chinese army from Labrang we saw last year when we went to the monastery," I asked, "the one they call the Liberation Army?"

"No, the Liberation Army is Jalwa[1] Chairman Mao's army," my brother explained. "This is the evil Chinese Red Army."

"Will the troops take us away?" I asked.

"Even though the Chinese army doesn't attack children," Father warned, "don't get too close." Jabey and I went out. We could see a lot of people looking down toward the Machu River from the top of Jazor hill beside Chulong Valley. The people who lived in the monastery and the dewa seemed to be running up and down without any reason. When we got to the top of the hill, we could see a lot of Chinese troops wearing dark yellow uniforms, ready to cross the river.

"I heard Lochu wouldn't ferry them across the river," someone said.

"I heard they are going to swim across," said another. They passed around rumors and kept watching.

"Hey, everyone," an old man said, "we shouldn't stay here because the Chinese troops will think we are soldiers, occupying the hill. They might fire at us!" Most people walked down to the foot of the hill, but Jabey and I stayed

---

1. Jalwa means chief or king, or possibly leader in this context.

where we were, watching. Then the troops across the Machu fired a couple of shots, and all the soldiers jumped into the river and walked across with their arms tied to each other. When they got out the other side, their uniforms were colored dark from the water. All the monks were standing in a long line waiting for them on the road that led to the monastery.

"Most of the Chinese troops have already crossed," a messenger came to tell us, "and the ferryman, Lochu, has been arrested. Six Chinese soldiers drowned, and the others have brought their bodies with them." After they heard these words, most of the people who were watching ran away and hid on the mountain. We were a little scared but thought we'd wait until we had seen the Chinese troops from a bit closer. The monks and lamas were standing and holding out darkhas.

"They're coming now!" someone shouted from far away. About one hundred soldiers were marching in formation along the edge of the forest from the Machu River toward the monastery. They sang a song as they marched, and carried their rifles on their shoulders. It was fascinating! Most of the soldiers' uniforms were still wet. Suddenly Jabey recognized their uniforms.

"It's Mao Zhuxi's Liberation Army!" he called out. "There's nothing to be afraid of." I had seen the Liberation Army many times before, when we were staying at Labrang Monastery. They had given us beans and candy, and smiled at us as they marched past. Because of that, I had no fear of walking near the soldiers. When the troops arrived at the line of monks, all of them were given darkhas. They applauded in return and handed the darkhas back to the tulkus and lamas. The last Chinese soldiers were still coming up from the river—people said that there were around three hundred altogether. The lamas and tulkus welcomed them to the monastery warmly. We waited to see the last of them arrive.

After the Chinese entered the monastery, they billeted in the monastery's chapel of protective deities, Alak Tag's house, and other monks' quarters. They put a lot of metal radio masts on top of the houses. That evening they held a meeting in the winter *chura* with all the monks and people from the dewa. Jabey and I went, too. The chura plaza was full, and Chinese troops stood guard around everyone with loaded guns. A senior Chinese army officer gave a speech.

"Thank you to the monastery for your welcome today," his translator said. "No one needs to be afraid. The Chinese and Tibetan people are one family. We will be leaving in five or six days." He said many soothing things, but then his tone suddenly changed. "Starting today, no one, monk or layman, is allowed to be out of doors during the hours of darkness when our troops will be patrolling the monastery. If you do so and the soldiers shoot you, it is your responsibility. Tomorrow we will have a meeting in the summer chura. All monks and laymen must attend. If anyone does not do so, they will be arrested." After that, I was frightened. I couldn't explain exactly what I was afraid of, but I thought that his welcoming words had just been a trick.

Next morning the entire monastery was surrounded by troops with guns. The smiling faces they had worn the previous day when they received their darkhas were replaced by scowls. They looked angrily at everyone as they walked up and down. That day a monk called Chage went around the monastery with an announcement.

"The Chinese army commander has called all the monks to a meeting in the monastery assembly hall," he shouted. "All monks to the assembly hall!"

"Did you hear any other news?" asked a monk named Ngotse.

"No other news," Chage declared, then dropped his voice to a whisper. "Things are going badly. The head of discipline and the principal lamas and tulkus have been under arrest since yesterday. I heard they are going to arrest more people today. We'll find out at the assembly hall meeting, anyway."

"Would it be all right if I don't go to the meeting?" the monk asked Chage.

"I'm sure it wouldn't be all right," Chage said. After he had gone, I thought, "Is this the 'time of revolution'? Yesterday the Chinese commander thanked us for our welcome and said that we were all one family, Chinese and Tibetans. Today they have arrested the head of discipline. This isn't the real Liberation Army. This must really be what they call the 'Chinese Evil Red Army.'" My mind was full of questions, but I couldn't find the answers.

I followed the monks to the main door of the assembly hall. A group of soldiers stopped me from going in, and when the translator arrived he said, "They have orders not to let children into the assembly hall." I stayed nearby. Inside the hall the monks were sitting in groups with their *khamtsen* study groups. Nobody spoke—they sat in sullen silence. Later a Chinese officer arrived to make a speech.

"You are permitted to speak but to do nothing else," he said via the translator. "You are going to discuss whether you need the monastery any longer. The Chinese commander is going to speak now. If you do not say anything, you will show your unhappiness, and if you are unhappy, you will show that you intend to resist. So if you are not a rebel you must speak." Then two of the Chinese soldiers led in the head of discipline Jangjug. He was in handcuffs, and they took him into the Lhakang Temple. He was wearing nothing but his monk's skirt.

"So this is how they repay our welcome," a monk called Tsechu said. "If we tell them what they want to hear, they will destroy the monastery, and if not they will arrest us, and maybe worse."

"They might as well go ahead and do whatever they want to," Lama Denche said. "If they want to destroy the monastery, they will destroy it, whatever we say."

"This isn't what you are supposed to be talking about," the translator, who had returned, said. "Today they are asking you if you need the monastery any longer or not, aren't they?."

"Of course we need the monastery," Lama Tsechu said. "You are a Tibetan, so you must know that, but you can see that there is no safe way we can decide that we need it."

"The Chinese are just being stupid," Lama Sherab said. "How can you ask monks if they need their monastery? They want to destroy it, and they are just trying to find an excuse." The translator left without responding. I was standing in the doorway and could hear what they were saying. I thought, "What a pity! This 'time of revolution' has brought misfortune as limitless as the sky over the monastery. Who can say anything good about this?"

40

Intimidated by the Military Occupation into Destroying the Monastery Ourselves.

The monks were still sitting in the assembly hall, discussing whether they would have to close their own monastery. Then the Chinese officer returned.

"The other *khamtsens* have decided that this monastery is not necessary," he said through the translator. "What is your decision? You must decide." A monk called Tsengon got to his feet, angry.

"Put ashes on your mouth," he said forcefully. "Who said they didn't need the monastery? Tell us who said that!" I couldn't hear what the translator told the Chinese officer, but the officer was furious.

"If you can't sit down you can get out!" he told the translator to say. He waved his hands, and two soldiers came and dragged Tsengon away. Tsengon turned his head on the way out.

"Now you can do what you want, enemies of the *dharma*! I hope you die soon, enemies of the dharma!" he shouted.

"Now, does anyone else wish to leave?" the Chinese officer asked. "Or will you give me your opinion?"

"It is up to you now," called out some of the monks. "We aren't free to disagree with you."

"Now we're all in real danger," a monk named Kharge said. "The laypeople's lives and possessions are threatened, too. We'd better tell the Chinese we

Walled monastery in Amdo with surrounding settlement for laypeople.
123232-243822. Photographer, Joseph Rock, 1924.
© President and Fellows of Harvard College, Arnold Arboretum Archives.

don't need the monastery. As long as a group of us survive, we can restore the monastery someday."

"Now, you've all decided that the monastery is unnecessary, haven't you?" the Chinese officer said through the translator.

Some monks answered, "Yes," but most said, "Whatever you say."

A little while later most of the monks were gathered in front of the Chinese officer. He was full of smiles.

"The meeting today was an excellent one!" the translator relayed. "Because the majority, both monks and laypeople, have decided that they no longer need the monastery, we have agreed to their request to close it. Every monk at this meeting should help to remove all statues of gods, Buddhist scriptures, and any other religious objects. They will be sent to the county headquarters in Machu in a few days." Immediately, most of the monks stood up and began shouting.

"If the monastery's going to be torn apart, you can do it!" some shouted. "We won't do it for you!" "You're not tricking us into destroying our own monastery!" "You can do this yourselves. We are leaving." They argued noisily. Suddenly Chinese troops appeared as if from nowhere and surrounded the assembly hall inside and out, loading their guns as they took up position. A number appeared behind the skylight of the assembly hall with machine guns at the ready, aimed toward the monks. Suddenly two gunshots rang out, making a sound like "Pag-sher, pag-sher!" I looked over to where the Chinese commander was standing with a smoking pistol pointing toward the ceiling.

"Right!" he said through the translator. "Everybody sit down! You have agreed that you don't need the monastery, whether you consent to dismantle it yourselves or not. Anyone who wants to disagree, please stand up." The monks sat on the ground with bent heads, afraid of bullets and violence. Then some troops came forward, shoved the monks who were sitting at the front of the hall toward the high altar, and forced them to throw the statues, the Kangyur and Tengyur scripture book, and the three statues of the Buddha to the ground. The monks inside the assembly hall were crying out and yelling, and so were people outside, who had been attracted by the noise to come and witness what was happening. Some elderly people in the doorway began to prostrate toward the assembly hall.

A detachment of troops arrived and drove the bystanders away from the door. Some of the older people told them they could not walk and were made to sit on the ground. I sat in the doorway and watched. The older monks were kept under guard on one side of the hall, while others threw down the statues of the Buddha, the offerings, and other sacred things. The big statues that stood on the high altar fell to the floor with a loud crash, filling the room with a cloud of dust. A monk called Khachig tied a leather rope around the neck of the Yama statue in the Lhakang chapel and pulled it to the ground with a loud "Chap!" Many people were praying, murmuring, "The Three Precious Jewels bear witness!" I was extremely frightened and thought, "How brave these monks are to pull down the statue of Yama, the Lord of Death. Aren't they frightened of his anger and the evil he can do to them?" Later Khachig and others dragged Yama's plaster statue out of the Lhakang Temple and threw it into the assembly hall. I thought, "This is strange. Normally we are forbidden even to raise our voices above a whisper near Yama, but even though he's been dragged through the dust, nothing has happened. Where have all those ferocious protective deities gone? This really is a 'time of revolution.' Maybe the beneficial gods and the wrathful gods can't do good or evil anymore." I felt unlucky. I had never seen a temple or a religious institute being created, and I had never thought carefully about gods, or religion and temples, but during that day of destruction I had seen every statue thrown down from every altar, seen every religious scripture torn from the bookcases and thrown to the ground. Many monks, propelled by fear, were playing an energetic part in the destruction. Chuge threw down a Kangyur.

"Hawo!" he shouted, weeping fiercely. "Why have I suffered this pain? I pray that these crazy Chinese don't get what they want!" Some Chinese soldiers dragged him out of the hall like a dead dog. The monks near the altar were running around in terror, and Chinese troops rushed to the front of the assembly hall shouting things that no one could understand. Suddenly, one of the soldiers had blood pouring from his head, and two of his comrades picked him up and took him outside. Four monks near the altar were handcuffed and taken outside. Later we learned what had happened. One of the monks near the altar had thrown a statue at a Chinese soldier, which had struck him on the head. The troops didn't see which monk was responsible, so they arrested four who were close by.

The broken statues and scriptures were taken to the center of the assembly hall and piled there.

The monks were still pulling the statues down, while soldiers watched from a distance. This "time of revolution" had unleashed a cruelty that we were unable to oppose. As the old saying goes, "Even reinforced by anger, what can weakness do?" Before the troops came, the chiefs and the monks hadn't believed that any harm would come to the monastery, so they had given the order not to offer any opposition to the Chinese. The previous day, the monks had lined up and given darkhas to the troops. All that brought them were empty words like, "Thank you for your welcome," and the real outcome had been the complete destruction of the monastery. Many such thoughts came into my head while I was walking around the assembly hall near the pile of broken statues and scriptures. Then my eye was caught by what looked like a deity at my feet. It was a picture book that had been used by a religion teacher. I glanced over my shoulder and saw that the Chinese troops guarding the objects were not looking, so I quickly picked up the book and slipped it into my robe. I slowly made my way out of the assembly hall with what I hoped was an innocent look on my face.

When I got to the door, one of the guards looked at me and said something to his companion, grinning. I didn't understand what he had said, and I was worried that he might have seen me take the picture book. I thought, "No, that can't be right. If he had seen me taking the book, he wouldn't be smiling." Then another soldier arrived and, without saying anything, punched me hard in the face. He took the book out of my robe and started to beat me over the head with it. Another soldier intervened and stopped him from hitting me. Tears of hopelessness fell from my eyes. Then an older soldier came over and pulled me out of the assembly hall by the ear. I thought, "This is not the courteous Liberation Army that I saw in Labrang. These must be the evil Red Chinese troops that Jabey talked about." I walked down the stairs from the monastic assembly hall, and when I got to the bottom I looked back. Two large photographs of Mao Zedong and Zhou Enlai had been fixed to the pillars on either side of the entryway. I thought, "So this is the Liberation Army we saw before, but they are different, now—bad and cruel. I definitely don't understand what has happened."

41

All the Chiefdoms and Monasteries on the Opposite Bank
of the Machu River Are Defeated and Abolished.

At home, I told my father exactly what I had seen and heard in the monks' assembly hall.

"Did the monks destroy everything themselves?" asked my father.

"Everyone who did it was a monk," I said. "In the temple of the local gods the Yama statue was dragged down by Khachig. He put a rope around its neck and pulled it over."

"Were Uncle Jakho and Jabey there?" Father asked.

"Uncle Jakho wasn't there, and Jabey went to Aunt Gorto's house and still hasn't come back. What are we going to do now that the monastery is destroyed?"

"I don't know what we are going to do. It's terrible. This misfortune is all because of our chiefs." Someone knocked on the door. It was a monk named Tenzin.

"Nukho, is your father here?" he asked.

"Father hasn't got back yet," I told him.

"Don't lie," he said. "He and I came back together a few days ago."

"I was joking," I said. "He's in here."

"Hello, Tenzin, how are you?" Father said, opening a window. "Come in quickly." Tenzin entered.

"Nothing good can come of this," he sighed. "In three days all the dewa households have to move from the monastery to the other side of the Machu River. Our clanspeople have moved there already." I wanted to listen to what they were saying, but Father said, "Nukho, go and give the last of the flour to Aunt Gorto." I had to leave the house, and I thought, "They're discussing something that I'm not allowed to hear." I went out of the main gate and bolted it behind me. When I arrived at the dewa, it was as though it was disappearing back into the mountain before my eyes. Men and women, their possessions on their backs, were driving their yaks and sheep downhill. They led their crying children down toward the river. Dogs trotted in and out of the crowd, some completely unchecked, snarling and barking. Horses neighed, sheep bleated, and yaks grunted to add to the cacaphony and chaos. I heard gunshots from the direction of the woods and saw dogs lying on the ground, howling. The scene filled me with sorrow. When I arrived at Gorto's house, I handed her the flour.

"My dear boy, sit down," she said, "and Aunt will give you some yogurt.

Those Chinese are going to push us across the Machu River, starting tomorrow. After that I really don't know what will become of us." An old woman was sitting near the stove.

"It's all so sad," she said. "May the evil Chinese people have their mouths stuffed with ash. They will throw us like insects into a hole. It's my bad karma that I couldn't die when the monastery was in a healthy state. Now I'm going to die in Chinese hands."

"Don't say such silly things," Gorto said. "The Chinese have old people too. They won't throw us in holes. But the rumor is that they will take all the children far away—wouldn't that be a nightmare?"

"Aunt," I asked, "is it true that they make children eat yogurt until they can't eat any more, and then throw them down so that they explode? Is that true?"

"I don't think that's true," Aunt said. "Why would they want to kill you? But I heard that they take children to school and change their brains in some way." She said many things about that. After a while Jabey and Brother Datag arrived.

"Mother, the upper end of the dewa has already been forced across the Machu River by the Chinese," Datag said. "Many of their possessions were carried away in the current when they were crossing. The yaks, horses, and sheep were driven across the river in a mixed herd."

"When will our clan move out?" the old woman asked.

"Tomorrow morning," Datag told her. "The day after tomorrow the monks have to move out of the monastery."

"Oh, that's terrible!" she said. "Even after destroying their own monastery the monks have been arrested! What a pity that they didn't join the army when they had the chance." Jabey and I left and walked up to the monastery. Below us we could see the Machu River with women and men hurrying toward it. Old people were crying, and possessions were piled up beside the river with their owners waiting around them. The Chinese troops stood at the edge of the forest looking on. Here and there lay the dead bodies of dogs. The Chinese waved at us to move on and stop staring. We walked up through the forest toward the monastery. Suddenly we heard a voice whispering from the shadows under the trees, "Jabey, Nukho!" I walked a little farther into the forest. It was the ferryman Lochu. He said, "Nukho, is your father at home?"

"Yes, Uncle, he is," I replied. "Didn't the Chinese troops arrest you?"

"Yes, but yesterday they arrested so many other people that I got the chance to escape. Tell your father I'm coming to see him tonight. Now, both of you go. Don't walk this way—the dogs will bite you." He moved back into the darkness of the forest. When I got home, my father and the monk Monlam were still talking.

"When times are as bad as this," my father was saying, "each man must make his own personal decision. Divinations and things like that aren't any use in times like these. We can't tell what's going to happen, good or bad. You will have to decide for yourself whether to go or to stay."

"That's right," Monlam agreed. "It's our own decision, and we just don't know what will happen after we leave. Even the oracles and diviners have no monastery to shelter them anymore."

"Uncle Monlam," I said, "it's getting dark. You should go now. The Chinese troops will arrest you if you break the nighttime curfew."

"I will my little one," he assured me. "If Uncle wears his black hat as a disguise, there'll be no problem. The Chinese troops won't be able to see him then." As he was leaving he said, "Durkho, don't go outside. It would be terrible if they caught you, so stay here."

I tried to sleep but couldn't tell if I was dreaming or not. My mind was choked with images of families on the move. As their yaks, horses, sheep, children, and old people crowded down to the river I could hear, "Now have you seen the time of revolution? Now have you seen the time of revolution?" More images invaded my mind—the statues and scriptures on the altar, falling down on top of me. And I heard the chant "Now did you see the time of revolution? Now did you see the time of revolution?" over and over again, until I was awoken by the door opening. Some people had come into our house and were muttering to my father, talking fast. I could see the ferryman Lochu in the dim light, but I could not identify the other two, except that they were dressed as monks. I pretended to go back to sleep and tried to make out their conversation. I could hear bits of it, "The Chinese troops . . . the monastery's horses . . . a small group . . . Lhasa . . . India," but I couldn't hear a complete sentence. I don't remember falling asleep. Then Japey called me.

"Nukho," he said, "get up and eat something. Father said that we must go to Uncle's house."

"Why are we going there?" I asked.

"Father wants us to borrow two bridles," Jabey replied.

"Why do we need to borrow bridles?" I asked. "We don't have any horses."

"Lazy boy! Get up quickly or I'm going on my own." We went out and met Uncle Jakho on the monastery road.

"Where are you two going?" he asked.

"Father told us to go and borrow some bridles," Jabey replied.

"Come back to the house," he said. "I've got the bridles already."

"You're crazy!" Jakho told my father when we got home. "Whatever happens to Madey Chugama will happen to you whether you run away or not. Don't you understand there's nowhere you can escape to? But you're going to take the boys somewhere far away, aren't you?" Then Father closed the door so that we couldn't hear what they were saying. Later Tenzin arrived and went inside. I thought, "They are planning to go somewhere." Their discussion lasted until after midday. When father came out he asked us, "Did you hear what we were saying?"

"No, we didn't," I replied. "Father, where are we going?"

"The day after tomorrow all the monks have to cross to the far side of the river, and after that the Chinese troops will demolish all the houses," Father said. "We have to leave before they start doing that."

"Father," Japey said, "now that the monastery has been destroyed we have nowhere to live. You need to take us wherever you are going."

"I didn't obey the orders of the lamas and chiefs and join the army because of you two—you are all I have left in the world. From now on, whether we live or die, we will do it together."

"Father, is there anywhere we can go where the Chinese troops can't find you?" my brother asked. Father thought for a little while, and then said, "I don't know yet exactly where we will go, but when the others get here we will leave the monastery—it might be tonight or tomorrow night." Stunned, my mind shut down. I fell into a daydream.

42

Night Came after the Wretched Day.
Wandering Away from Our Native Land.

While Father, Jabey, and I were talking nervously about where we would go and where we would stay, Aunt Gorto called from the gate, saying, "Tell Jabey to come here."

I went out and said, "Aunt, come inside."

"Oh no, Nukho," she told me, "there's no time to come to your home. Our clan has got to go over the river. Take this butter and cheese to your father. He is at home, isn't he?"

"Thanks, Aunt," I said. "Yes, father's at home."

"Tell your father to get out of here quick. Yesterday the Chinese were asking about him. All the monks have to move to the far side of the river. After that, he'll have no place to hide!"

"I'll tell him, Aunt," I promised.

"Well, my dear," she said, "we'll meet again." Then she left. I looked over the wall, down at the monastery. The Chinese troops had surrounded the monastery walls and the dewa beyond them and were searching everyone who went in and out. I hurried home to tell my father about what Aunt Gorto had said and what the Chinese troops were doing.

"I've been thinking about going on pilgrimage to Lhasa," Father said. "What do you think?"

"But the Chinese soldiers would never let us go!" Jabey replied.

"Well, it's one idea," said father. "When the monastery and chiefdom are destroyed, where else will there be to go other than Lhasa?"

"Should we escape to the mountains secretly and hide there from the Chinese?" Jabey asked.

"We won't be alone," father said. "Some others will come with us. If we can get clear of the monastery this evening, we'll be all right!" I felt a jolt of fear and thought, "If the Chinese are surrounding the monastery and the dewa day and night, how can we get away to the mountains?"

"Father, if we escape to the mountains," I said, "the Chinese troops will kill us, and we won't get to Lhasa. It would be better if we didn't run away."

"They won't kill us," Father stated. "We'll be going in company—the others will help us avoid them. When we get to Lhasa, we will stay for a few years, and after that the Chinese troops will have left and we can come back."

"We have no choice but to go into the mountains," Jabey said. "If we don't, father will be arrested. It's much better to try to go to Lhasa." My brother and father packed food, clothes, cooking utensils, and other things. I sat near the stove and daydreamed. This really was a "time of revolution" if we were being forced to leave our native land and wander far away. Despite what they said, I felt that nothing good could come of this, but I had no other idea of what we could do.

That afternoon as I was coming back from fetching water, I saw the Chinese troops stop a group of people and search them. After they had taken away their knives, ammunition belts, and so on, they made them sit on the ground. Nearby some old women were weeping. I was afraid to watch, and ran home with the water. At the gate I met the monk Khangge, who whispered, "Hey, Nukho, tell your father that the soldiers are searching all the houses. Got that?" Then he went away. As I was walking home, I wondered how he had known that my father was around. When I got there, my father, Jabey, and the monk Tenzin were having a meal and talking. I told them Khangge's message.

"There's no doubt about it," Tenzin said. "I'm leaving now, but I will arrange the horse. Don't worry. And don't let them catch you." He left.

It was nearly dark when someone knocked on our gate. It was different from the way our neighbors knocked, so we were a bit scared. Father sped into the inner room. I went out and when I opened the gate saw five armed Chinese soldiers standing there. I thought, "They know Father is here! He won't be able to escape to the mountains. He'll be arrested!" I opened the door for the soldiers, but they didn't come inside. They just cuffed me around the head and tweaked my ear, asking me things I couldn't understand. Then the monk Chage, the translator, and someone who looked like a Chinese officer arrived. The translator asked, "Boy, how many people are there in your house? Do you have any guests?"

"There's only Jabey and me," I said. "No guests."

"There are only the father and two sons in this family," the monk Chage told the others. "The father has run away from the chiefdom, and we don't know where he is. There are only these two little children in the house.

"Stay inside your house," the translator told me. "If you go out at night the troops will kill you. Do you understand?" Then he went away. My heart was thumping, but I didn't go back inside yet. I just stood there watching them go from house to house, knocking on every door. Then I locked the gate and went back in. Father was standing in the corner with his gun trained on the door.

"What did the Chinese soldiers say?" Jabey asked.

"I told them we had no guests, and one of them said that if we go out at night they will kill us," I said. "Chage told them that Father had run away from the chiefdom and we don't know where he is."

Father said, "I know why they're questioning people. Last night ten of their horses were stolen, and the radio mast they installed on top of Alak's rooms was smashed with a stone."

"Who was brave enough to do that?" I asked.

"It must have been monks who smashed the radio mast," Father replied.

After dinner my father told Jabey and me to go to bed, but he stayed up drinking tea. I fell asleep. Later in the evening I was awoken by the sound of knocking on the outside of our rear wall. "Dug! Dug!" I raised my head and looked up. Jabey was in the house, but I couldn't see father. There was more banging on the back wall: "Dug! Dug!" I was terrified and blurted out, "Where's father?" and burst into tears.

"Don't cry," Jabey said. "Father's right outside. Our companions are here and ready to go."

"I won't go!" I said fiercely. "The Chinese troops waiting around the monastery are going to kill us!" Someone entered the house, but in the darkness I couldn't see who it was. Then he moved into the light of the butter lamp, and I could see that it was the ferryman Lochu.

"Nukho, brave boy, get up! It's time to go," he whispered. I got up without thinking and walked outside. I gasped, startled. There were many horses, already saddled, with a few monks holding them. Our yard gate was closed behind them. The stirrups were tied to the saddles to prevent them making noise. There was a moon that night, but its light was sometimes obscured by clouds. Then everyone came very quietly into the house and drank tea and ate tsampa in silence. I made out Lochu's son Kelsang, Uncle Jakho, and a few others. "The Three Precious Jewels bear witness! The moon is bright right now. Let's wait a little while! If we don't, we'll be caught. We'll go when we can't wait any longer," said Tenzin.

"We should wait," Father agreed. "People can go ahead if they want, but I'm going to wait." There was another knock on the wall. "They're here now." When the gate opened, two monks came in with some more horses.

"The Chinese patrols are all around the monastery," a monk said. "They can see us easily."

"Don't wait any longer," Jakho said. "I'm going to keep an eye on the soldiers for you, and the others will join you at the top of Chulong Valley. Now go! Hurry!" He opened the gate and we went through, but I was shivering with fear. Everyone crept along quietly until we got to the Kangyur prayer wheel house. Suddenly a horse grunted and we fell silently to the ground, waiting for any sign that the Chinese had seen us. We watched them walk around the monastery, shining their torches this way and that. Sometimes the light fell on us or our horses, but we weren't spotted. We crept along the foot of a bank very slowly. We joined up with two monks leading horses, but I couldn't see who they were because I was at the back of the line. Then we moved along the side of the monastery. The moon shifted in and out of the clouds. We could hear the soldiers saying things we couldn't understand, and we pressed on. I thought, "Gungtang Jampeyang, bear witness! The Chinese are going to see us!" I followed the others, leading my horse by its rein. Jabey walked beside me. We walked for short stretches, stopping to listen every few meters. It was a silent and terrifying evening. I could hardly feel my own feet stepping on the earth, and all I could hear was people and horses breathing. It seemed as though I was in a strange world, inhabited by silent creatures. The only way to escape was to leave my native land and wander far away.

43

Twelve Monks and Laymen Thrown Together
by the Karma of Their Previous Lives.

We kept on walking under the moonlight, farther and farther around the monastery. All of a sudden we heard the sound of a woman screaming from the direction of the dewa. We pressed ahead even more urgently, our fear increased by the fear in the scream.

"That's bad," the monk Tenzin said. "Maybe it's my mother. I have to go back and check. I won't be long. I'll catch up with you." He turned back and rode his horse into the darkness. Later the woman stopped screaming, but Tenzin hadn't returned. We waited for him, but he still didn't come.

"We can't wait any longer," Father said. "We'd better go." After a short ride we arrived at Chulong Valley, where we joined the road. We sent a scout ahead to see if there were any troops in the area. He returned and said, "It's very quiet, although there are a lot of spotlights shining around the monastery. If we go by the road they won't be able to see us."

Tenzin caught up with us.

"We need to go quickly," he said. "The Chinese troops have moved from the dewa into the monastery." Before he had finished speaking, gunshots rang out from the houses above the monastery. Dogs started barking.

"That can't be good," Father said. "Yes, we should take our horses up to the road and ride on that. We will wait at Youda grassland. If anyone gets separated, meet us beneath Youda Mountain. Right, let's go quickly." He put me on the back of his horse and headed for the road. We galloped along at top speed. Everyone else was galloping with us, the pounding of the horses' hoofs and the panting of their breath filling the air with noise. We rode hard for a long time, but when we heard nothing from the troops, we slowed down.

"Maybe Dragpa and the ones with him haven't been able to get out," Tenzin said. "Could we wait for them for a while?"

"You go ahead with the children," Father replied. "I'm going to wait here for them until daybreak. If they don't come, I'll follow you then." We went on ahead. A little while later, gunshots rang out from the direction of the monastery, and the Chinese troops started sweeping the mountain to the right of the monastery with their spotlights. I thought, "Maybe the Chinese are following Dragpa and the stragglers. What will happen to my father now that we've left him behind?" As we rode on, we heard the sound of horses' hooves behind us. We took off as fast as we could because we thought it must be the Chinese soldiers.

"Slow down, it's us!" my father yelled after a few minutes.

"It's father!" I shouted, recognizing his voice. "Father and the others are here!" The people in front of us slowed down.

"A dog is chasing us," the monk Tenzin said. "That's not good—shall I shoot it?"

"No, don't kill it for no reason," another monk said. "If they hear gunfire it might lead the Chinese to us." A few minutes later I heard a gunshot and a dog barking and whining. I knew what had happened. We rode on.

"Did the troops shoot at you?" Tenzin asked.

"I don't know who fired the first shot," a monk replied. "When the troops came back from the dewa and surrounded the monastery, they shone torches in our direction, so we hid behind the mani wheel house until they had gone. After that, we started to circle past the monastery toward the road. We heard gunshots from the right-hand side of the monastery and saw torches scanning the mountain, so maybe they spotted us. We just rode on, anyway."

At daybreak we passed Youdra Mountain. We hid in the forest beside the river that ran behind the mountain. In the daylight I recognized all the people who had come from different places to be with us the night before. The first one was the ferryman Lochu, a fifty-year-old layman. Lochu's son Kelsang was a monk of about fifteen. Uncle Monlam was a monk aged twenty-five. Monlam's nephew Khangtrul was a monk of about eighteen, and the four of them had left with us from our house. Uncle Tenzin was a monk of thirty-three, and his nephew Lekho was a monk of nineteen. We had met them under the monastery and then come on together. Uncle Dragpa was a monk of thirty-two, and his nephew Tsekho was a monk of sixteen. His cousin Dongtrug (a monk) was fifteen, and these three had been the last to arrive. In addition to these monks, my father, Durkho, was a layman of forty-seven, my brother, Jabey, was a monk of fourteen, and I was a boy of ten.

Altogether, there were twelve of us, monks and laymen. Whether because of the cruelty of the Chinese or the karma of our previous lives, the previous night we had experienced fear and terror. We had escaped from Madey Chugama Tashi Chulong Monastery to the mountains, on our way to Lhasa. Whether as a result of our good or bad karma, we had taken the decision to journey to distant lands together.

The four older people took the eight younger ones under their protection as though they were their own children. We had all firmly decided to enter the Yeshe degree course at the monasteries in Tsang or Lhasa. We left our own native land behind and headed for Lhasa without regret.

We felt we could escape the sadness of the "time of revolution." Maybe this would be the beginning of happiness, or maybe the decision itself would make us happy. But we also knew we could be wrong—it could all be the start of more difficulties in this "time of revolution." Whatever the future held, the only road we could follow was the one that lay ahead—there was no turning back. That morning we rested in the woods behind Youdra Mountain and cooked our meal. Father and Lochu went up the mountainside to stand guard. After eating, everyone fell asleep. Two of the monastery's stallions arrived, although I had no idea how they found us. They followed us day and night, and whatever we did, we could not drive them away.

"We must keep to this schedule for two or three nights," Father announced as sunset approached, "because the Chinese troops have occupied this chiefdom already." We pressed on through the night, under the moonlight. Once we got into trouble in a small stream whose bed was so muddy that, once you rode into it, it was very difficult to get out of. Uncle Monlam got through, and so did we, but when Jabey tried to cross, his horse's back legs sank into the mud and it reared up.

"Brother, hold on tight or you'll fall into the stream!" I shouted.

"Japey, hang on to his mane!" Father called. "Don't fall off!"

"I'm not letting go," my brother said calmly. "No one else come this way, because the mud is very deep." He whipped his horse, and it had to jump five or six times before it finally struggled up on to the bank. After it was safely on land, the horse staggered and trembled.

"Japey is very strong," Lochu said, impressed. "What would we have done if he was badly hurt!"

Later, dogs ran up to us while we rode.

"That's not good," Father said. "There must be tent families around here." Through the gloom, it was just barely possible to see tents in the distance with butter lamps lit inside them.

"Keep going in this direction," Father said. "Lochu and Molam, lead the way. Tenzin and I will follow behind you. If we come across any Chinese troops, Lochu must go on with the children while we deal with them." We pushed on until we had left the tents behind. Before midnight, we reached another large encampment with a big fire at its center. We had no way to avoid it and still continue ahead. My father and Uncle Tenzin took their guns off their backs and rode toward the camp's people. A woman came forward.

"Don't shoot," she said. "We are droma diggers." Father went over and spoke to a group of women. Later he came back and said, "We can go now. These women are from the Khangsar chiefdom, which has been destroyed by the Chinese." When we came into the light of the fire, some of the women stood up and prostrated, praying.

At daybreak we arrived at another encampment. The air was thick with smoke, and the ground was strewn with broken black yak hair tents, wooden boxes, butter, cheese, and tools. Dogs wandered through where the people used to live. Tenzin picked up some of the butter and cheese to take with us.

"We can't stay in this area any longer," Lochu said. "The Chinese haven't been gone for long. There are some dead people at the bottom of that cliff over there." We kept moving. That was the first time I had seen a family crushed by the Chinese. However, I did not see any corpses.

Launching a traditional Tibetan boat into the river.
Bild 135 BB 081 12. From the collection of the Federal Archives of Germany, Koblenz.
Photographer, Bruno Beger. Ahnenerbe Expedition, 1938–1939.

--- 44 ---

Thankful That We Worked Together with One Mind.
Crossing the Machu.

For the next few days we rode day and night, stopping for a short time and hiding when it seemed necessary. It was a tough journey. If we met people on the road, they would gallop away up the mountain as soon as they saw us. Sometimes we did the same if we saw people coming toward us. As the saying goes, "It takes a bear to scare a bear." There was no time for me to be afraid, and every day my agitation subsided a little. When the other riders ran away, I fled, too, and when they stopped, I stopped. I thought, "Whatever happens to us, as long as I don't fall off my horse, I'll be fine!"

One day we started on our way after midnight. When dawn came, we reached the entrance to a valley and looked down. Beside the river we could see many white tents and horses.

"This isn't good," Father said. "Horsemen with tents like these—this has to be the Chinese army."

"I'm going to have a closer look," Tenzin said. He rode forward with his gun in his hand.

"Stop!" Father said. "It's already daylight. Whether this is the Chinese or not, we can't turn back. Let's go into that small valley that branches off of this one and bypass them that way. They won't be able to see us there."

"That's right," Lochu said. "It's better if we don't let them see us, whoever they are." We rode on past a small hollow in the flank of the valley. We looked down from the rim, where we could see the tents better. It didn't seem to be Chinese troops. There were around thirty horses, and we could see monks walking among them. We couldn't see clearly who it was, and we just continued on our course. When we reached the end of the valley, we could see a wide river.

"That's the Machu River!" everyone shouted.

"We must try our best to get across," Father said. "After we do that, we can relax a little." When we got close to the river, we saw the water was the characteristic dark yellow of autumn. The Machu was wider here than it was in our native land and had a rougher surface. Everyone stared at it. No one had any idea how to cross it.

"It scares me how wide it is," Dragpa said. "I have no idea how we will do this. The older ones might be able to swim with the horses, but what about the children?"

"Even the adults couldn't swim this," Lochu said. "Maybe if we had some wood . . . but where are we going to find wood here?"

"Hey, everybody!" Father interjected. "If we ride along this river, we will get to the border of the Kangsar chiefdom. We should look for a family or hamlet there, and maybe there will be wood near the homes." We rode on next to the river. After a bend in the river, we saw a few houses ahead. We could see that they were some families' winter houses, but they hadn't arrived yet. Three Precious Jewels bear witness! That meant we could take as much wood as we wanted to. Jabey and I cooked, while everyone else hauled logs down to the river to make a raft. When the afternoon shadows got close to the houses, we were ready to put all our baggage on the raft.

"Durkho, Tenzin, and I will drag the raft behind our horses," Lochu said. "The younger children should sit in the middle of the raft, and the others can dangle in the water and hang on to the side of the raft. We can tie the other horses behind." Everyone followed these directions. Jabey, Dongtrug, Kelsang, and I sat in the middle of the raft, and the others held on to the sides. Lochu, Tenzin, and Father waded into the turbulent river, with the horses dragging the raft behind them with leather ropes. It floated on the water as the horses swam ahead. Everyone began to shout with excitement as we moved across. But when we got to the center of the river, the three horses that had been tied up behind the raft panicked and turned back. Uncle Monlam pulled them back toward the raft. Then the ropes that had held Tenzin's and Lochu's horses to the boat all broke. Only my father's horse was left, and it couldn't drag the boat forward on its own. Then the people, the raft, and the horses began to float down the middle of the river, without making any headway toward the other side. Tenzin left his horse and tried to swim up to the raft.

"Stay where you are!" Father shouted. "I can do it. The river is too cold for swimming. Stay there!" However, Tenzin continued to swim behind the raft. It drifted down the river, with only my father's horse trying to pull it toward the other side. Tenzin still hadn't made it to the raft. Then, Uncle Monlam managed to drag one of the horses from the rear to the front of the raft. It began to help the other horse haul the raft forward, and as they pulled together, it slowly began to cross the river. Another monk, Khangdrug, brought two horses up from the rear of the raft and then went to help Tenzin, who was still in the middle of the river, riding one horse and leading another. Finally, gradually, the raft made it to the far bank. Later, Tenzin said that he was lucky that Khangdrug had come to his rescue because he couldn't really swim and would surely have died. After we had loaded the horses, we rode up a side valley and camped there. Some of us pitched the tents while others began cooking. My father was so cold he couldn't speak. He just lay under his robe, shaking and numb with cold. Tenzin was shivering too, but not as badly. Lochu piled many extra robes on my father and made ginger tea for him, but my father found it hard to drink because his mouth was trembling so much.

"Our precious one is getting better," Lochu said. "It's a good sign that he's shivering, and he's not going to die. If he couldn't shiver, he would die of cold because of his liver—he's old."

Everyone had an anecdote to relate about that crossing of the Machu River and how we were able to make it across safely because we worked together. The small valley where we camped was rich in both grass and water. Later that day we killed a wild yak and roasted sausages that we made from its intestines. For several days everyone had ample food to eat, and the horses had plenty of grass. We felt at ease. The people and horses could take an enjoyable break.

Once, when Tsekho went to fetch the horses, he came back and said, "Hey everyone—I saw some horsemen driving pack animals lower in the valley. They're coming this way. Could they be Chinese?" Everyone got up fast and looked down the gorge. A drover with pack animals was already nearby.

"He's not Chinese," Monlam said. "He is wearing a golden hat. He looks like a lama with a monk-servant."

"We don't know who he is yet," Father said to Tenzin. "Don't shoot. Let him come closer." The drover didn't see us hiding near the road. Then my father and Tenzin stood up and aimed their guns at him.

"Where are you from?" The drover stood silently, dumb with fear and amazement. Then all of us stood and went toward him. I looked carefully at the man. He wasn't a lama, just an ordinary layman wearing a lama's golden hat. When he was calm enough to answer our questions, he said, "Our Khangsar Monastery was destroyed by the Chinese troops. We are taking some things from the monastery to the Chinese army camp. The monastery is completely empty now. The lay followers of the monastery have been driven to the other side of the Machu by the troops." He and his companions gave all the golden hats they were wearing to our monks, and some silver coins too.

"When you get to Lhasa," they said, "please say some prayers for us, and give this as an offering for the dead." Uncle Monlam took the money.

"If we get to Lhasa, we will certainly dedicate this offering to Jowo Rinpoche. You may be sure of that." When we told them we were from Chugama Monastery, it made them happier.

"We were given some packets of Chinese food," one of them said. "You can take some if you like."

"Thank you very much, but we don't need any at the moment," Father said. "If we take it, you won't be able to account for it to the Chinese tomorrow." After that we went our separate ways.

Later that day I mused on many things. These people told us that they had heard Chugama Monastery was destroyed because the Chugama people killed many Chinese. But their monastery had also been gutted, and their people driven across the Machu. It had not only been Chugama. Probably the Chinese troops had defeated all the clans and chiefs, and forced the local people to dismantle their own monasteries. The drovers told us that they would take the three Buddha statues they were carrying to a local government office, and then the statues would be brought to the county headquarters.

45

The Misfortunes of the "Time of Revolution."
Chiefdoms and Monasteries Destroyed.

We rode on. From a hollow on the sunny side of a high mountain, we could see a monastery in the distance with golden rooftops and medallions shining in the sun.

"That's probably Khangsar Monastery," someone said. We approached the monastery by a road that led up to it from below. We could see a few burned-out houses above the monastery, some of them still smoking. The ceremo-

Approaching a monastery while ascending a valley.
122649-243499. Photographer, Joseph Rock, 1924.
© President and Fellows of Harvard College, Arnold Arboretum Archives.

nial flagpole wrapped in prayer flags had been burned all the way to the top. There was smoke flowing across the monastery, but it was impossible to see the source. Red monks' robes were strewn across the road. The mani wheels had been torn from their niches, and most of the golden medallions on the temples and assembly halls had been ripped down. Many little mani wheels lay on the ceremonial *kora* that circled the monastery, and religious scriptures lay in the dirt. When the mani wheels were thrown down, the sacred pages they held had fallen out onto the ground. Only the sound of a few dogs barking in the distance broke the heavy silence. No human voices could be heard. Smoke drifted everywhere through the monastery, and the sight made me sad and fearful.

"This is terrible," Dragpa said. "Chinese troops did this. The Three Precious Jewels bear witness! Many people must have died here."

"Compared to this, our monastery is intact," Uncle Monlam said. "The people here must have died or been driven out when their monastery was torn apart."

"Fill their mouths with ashes!" Lochu said. "Our monastery must have had this treatment by now." We rode on and came to a wide pasture on the mountain above the monastery. There was a huge tent there, with some people sitting outside it making a fire. They walked over to greet us and took off their hats.

They told us that the enormous tent was the monastery's meeting or preaching tent. Inside, the monastery's possessions were all piled up together. There were stacks of scriptures, statues of local deities, drums, brass horns, other musical instruments, gold medallions, statues of animals, mani wheels, and many other objects. The people said they were their guardians. I thought, "This monastery was so rich, but now it has been torn apart. Not just Chugama Monastery—everywhere must be like this."

"Father, Uncle Monlam," I asked, "if we get to Lhasa, will we find that Ganden Monastery and the others have been ruined too? If they have been, where will we go then?" Father said nothing.

"How can he think such terrible thoughts? It's blasphemous," Monlam said, but before he had finished, Tenzin broke in.

"I am sorry to say this, but his questions are reasonable," he said. "Who knows what has happened in Lhasa? The Chinese troops occupied it last year."

"I really think the worst might be true," my father said. "Who can tell where the Chinese troops have reached? It is like a wildfire—once it has broken out, it can't always be stopped! And if everywhere is like this, it's going to be hard to get to Lhasa anyway, without being captured. But for now, whether for good or ill, we have to keep going. Until this old man dies, he is going to try to take you to Lhasa."

"Oh, yes," Dragpa said. "The Three Precious Jewels bear witness. We have no idea what's going to happen, but if we have good karma, then we will succeed." We all rode on, with these thoughts playing nervously in our minds. A few days later we arrived in Golok and could see Amnye Machen snow mountain in the distance. On the way there we met many travelers.

"Don't go this way," they told us, "the Chinese soldiers are there. Don't go that way. You will run into Chinese troops." However, we traveled for many days without seeing any sign of Chinese soldiers. We rode on despite what the people said. Every day, as dawn broke, we would find some corner or small valley to hide in during the hours of daylight. One day we rode on past dawn. We saw wild yaks, horses, and herds of sheep being chased by wolves. As we went on, we saw a pack of dogs on top of a mountain. Some of them were eating the flesh of dead yaks and sheep, and others were just howling and barking with their muzzles pointing toward the sky. When I heard this noise, I felt my whole body gripped with fear. Many vultures and other birds circled in the sky. "A kakaka . . . this doesn't look good," I thought. "What's happened here? Do these sheep and yaks and horses have no owners? There shouldn't be dogs wandering wild everywhere. Something must have happened." Everyone rode on warily. A little later we came to the end of the pasture. May the Protector bear witness! Possessions were scattered all over the mountains and the grassland. We could see about ten black and white tents, most of which had fallen over. Dead bodies were everywhere—humans, livestock, every place had its corpse.

"Fill their mouths with ashes!" Tenzin said. "This is another clan that was attacked by the Chinese, isn't it?" The monks dismounted and chanted prayers over some bodies closest to the road. In front of one of the fallen tents, a dog was tethered. It looked close to death from starvation.

"Son of a great father," Dragpa said to Lochu, "would you untie that dog?" Jabey and Lochu went over to the tent and uprooted the wooden peg to which the dog had been tied.

"Let's get out of here quickly," Father said. "We'd better not hang around in this place." The monks remounted their horses, and we set off again. On our way we saw packages of a family's butter and cheese that had been scattered over the grass.

"Hey, Durkho!" Tenzin said, "Let's take some dried meat and butter to eat on the journey." Before my father could say anything, Monlam broke in.

"They say cloudy weather is for a horse's stomach and sunny weather for a dog's stomach. When people have had so much sadness in their lives, how can you think of taking things from beside their dead bodies? We have enough food to eat. We shouldn't be grabbing anything else." No one else spoke, and we rode on without another word. I thought, "That was extremely sad. Whose clan is this? Did they resist the Chinese troops, or did the army just slaughter them without hesitating? When the rider dies, the horse also falls. No one was left to deal with the corpses, and the crows fed on their eyes. No one was left to protect the clan's possessions, and its wealth was tossed all over the pasture. No one remained to herd the livestock, and they became food for the wolves. Anyone with compassion in their heart would feel pity, and anyone with love in their heart would feel love." I followed along without knowing whether it was mainly fear or sadness that I was feeling, maybe because this was the first time I had seen such a slaughter of livestock and people.

"That was truly terrible," my father said. "This clan was exterminated like the Datsen chiefdom in Sogpo. Look at this place. It's in the chiefdom of the Golok Khanggen. They are fierce in Golok and must have fought against them."

"These corpses don't smell," Tenzin said. "They must have been killed only days ago." We left the bodies of the destroyed clan behind and headed for a steep mountain. In the distance, we could see vultures crowding around a corpse. Most of the vultures had finished eating and were sitting in a line on a mountain ridge.

"What a tragedy!" said Monlam. "Many years ago a singer sang of the 'time

of revolution: The mountains and the pastures full of bodies and bones /
The gluttonous vultures vomiting meat / The wild wolf sated.' The song has
become real for this clan now." I thought to myself, "Our old life was full of
prosperity like the yogurt-making time. We could never have foreseen troubles like this. And no matter how fast we run away, our troubles will catch up
with us sooner or later. Even our time of death is determined by the karma of
our previous life—we can't affect that. It was pitiful to see those dead bodies
without anyone to care for them. I hope I never see such terrible destruction
again." I thought many dark things like that on the journey.

For several days, we followed the main road without any difficulty and
had no frightening or dangerous experiences. But the sights we had seen, the
dead bodies, the destroyed monasteries, the abandoned livestock, were always
before our eyes, whether we were awake or dreaming.

"This was true cruelty and nothing but evil," Father said. "They say that
before the Chinese came to the grassland it was a place where we were like
horses who could gallop fast and free. After they came, we became like a herd
of goats and had to surrender."

"That is clearly true," Tenzin said. "Our monastery surrendered and gave
darkhas to welcome the soldiers. The Chinese said, 'thank you,' but by the
next day they had destroyed the monastery. This is like when leather boots get
wet and little by little squeeze tighter and tighter." I thought, "Our laypeople
and monks were living in the yogurt-making time, so why was it all suddenly
destroyed for no reason?" I asked these things repeatedly in my mind but
could not find a clear answer.

46

Slipping Past the Chinese Army's Camp.
Face-to-Face with the Local Chiefdom's Army.

We kept following the main road as we had before. However, I kept revisiting
what I had seen again and again. I couldn't eat because of the thoughts that
played in my mind, and I couldn't sleep at night, either. So many living beings
had lost their lives for no reason at all. My fear had gone, and my tears didn't
fall anymore. I thought: "May the innocent children receive compassion, and
especially may the mothers who tried to flee with their children, but were
unable to escape death, receive compassion."

We kept going until midday, when we met two women who told us about
the massacre.

Those people were pilgrims from Amdo on their way home from Lhasa," one of them said. "We heard that Mongolian troops fighting with the Chinese killed them." She continued, "You should stay off this road or you will meet the Chinese army at Gyemdo [Darlag]. That area is full of troops these days." We broke our journey, lit a fire, and cooked a meal.

"Let's ride through the night," my father said that afternoon. "If we can't get beyond the area of Gyemdo by daybreak, we're in trouble, because it's on a wide plain, and we'll be spotted easily. If we ride quickly we'll be through by first light." Our progress was rapid now because each of us had a horse. There was a little moonlight before midnight, which made our traveling easier. Sometimes dogs barked from the tents on the mountainside, and sometimes people shouted at us.

Once we heard a loud roar up ahead. The horses bolted with fear, and my father and Lochu sped ahead. Lochu and Lekho fell off, but our horses were not as scared as theirs and stayed steady. Then we heard two gunshots and another roar, and the riders in front dismounted. "No need to worry," said Jabey. "It's only a bear." We rode on. Later the ones at the front told us that a large bear had stood up just ahead of them and roared thunderously. Father fired at it but only wounded it. Lochu fell off his horse again, but then the bear made a hasty retreat.

We rode on until we came to a wide road near a mountain. We followed it until we heard a loud noise in front of us.

"It might be an airplane," Tenzin said.

"It can't be," Dragpa replied. "Airplanes don't fly at night."

"It might be a truck or a car," said my father, "in which case we're safe because it can't follow us off the road." We rode on, but the noise became louder and seemed to get closer. "This isn't good. This is a road for cars, isn't it?" Father said. "Let's get over the river!"

Before he had finished speaking, a powerful light filled the sky, and the noise, now clearly ahead of us, became even louder. We wheeled around and fled, but the light seemed to follow us. Apparently, our pursuers could see all the people and horses escaping very clearly. We heard the sound of staccato gunfire, "Pag-shar, pag-shar!" and saw earth thrown up by bullets that landed between us.

"Get off the road!" Father shouted. I was a little afraid then, with the bullets flying past my ears with a "Zer! Zer!" sound. We rode around the back of a mountain until we couldn't see the lights shining any more. By that time we had all split up. Dongtrug, Kelsang, Jabey, and I were together, but we didn't know where the others had got to. Down below, we saw ten trucks moving slowly away. When they were quite a distance from us, we called out to each other, and before long we were back together. Father and Tenzin hadn't scattered far like the rest of us. They were right above the road, lying down with their horses, watching. A little before daybreak, we passed the Chinese army camp at Gyemdo. When we got up the mountain on the far side, it was becoming light, and we looked back toward Gyemdo. The plain was full of Chinese troops, tents, and horses, but we had made it: we were safely past the famous Chinese army camp at Gyemdo.

We rested for three days at the end of a small valley, and the monks chanted prayers for our safe journey, while father and Lochu burned incense. It seemed to help me forget the suffering of the past few days. I had become used to riding night and day without fear or tiredness. By that time we had been traveling for about a month since we left Madey Chugama. Night or day, I never once fell off my horse. The monks called me "frog on horseback" because of the way I clung to my horse. I assumed that I wouldn't fall off, so I never did. Also, I never believed that the Chinese troops would kill me if they caught me, but I did fear that if I fell off my horse I would be left behind in a wild and lonely place. That fear was so strong in my mind, especially at night, that it kept me from falling off as we galloped over the rocky terrain.

The following day we started our journey again. We reached a small valley where we could see smoke ahead of us.

"We will go and check," Father said. "Follow us slowly." Father and Uncle Monlam went ahead. When we caught up with them, they were trying to light a fire to make tea. "A wild ass was killed here this morning," Father said. The ass's head and some of the hide were still there, as well as a bone from which someone had gnawed most of the meat. Someone had been here recently. We revived the smoldering fire so that we could cook.

Afterward, we rode on until we came to a narrow valley full of rocks. The leading riders, my father, Khangtrul, and the others, dismounted and waved to us not to approach. Everyone dismounted except for me, and we waited. After Tenzin got off his horse he ran ahead. I wondered what was going on with my heart. Fear seemed to be attacking it. I could hear some people ahead of us shouting to each other.

"Hey! Don't be afraid! We're going to Lhasa," Tenzin called in the direction of these voices. "Almost all of us are just monks and children. There's nothing to be afraid of," and things like that. We led our horses on until six men emerged from the rocks high up on our left and began to climb down. They were carrying guns. By the look of their big sheepskin robes, they were Golok people. When they came close, they took off their hats. A group of them sat with my father, most of them still carrying their guns. Up ahead I could see that they had pack yaks with wild asses' meat on them.

"We are from the Golok Matod chiefdom's army, and we're hunting wild asses for meat." They said that they hadn't shot at us after realizing that most of us were monks. They approached the monks, and some of them offered them silver coins. A few of them made dedication offerings to the monks and put prayer request letters in their hands.

"If the Chinese are searching for us it's bad for you, isn't it? So hadn't we better surrender to them together?" my father asked them.

"These days it does not make sense for monks and lamas to surrender to the Chinese," an old man said. "All the monks and lamas in our area who they wanted to arrest have already been arrested. Anyone they decided to kill they have beaten to death already. You precious ones leave now. We will be all right around here among our own people."

"Thank you. We wish you success in everything you do," our monks replied. After this exchange of courtesies, we went our separate ways.

"What a lovely old man he was to let us keep going like that," Lochu said, "but I'm afraid that when they get back to their native land they will become victims of the Chinese. Maybe they should get away from that area."

"They will be fine because Golok people look after each other," father said.

"It's interesting that the Chinese put so many guns in the hands of Tibetans around here," Dragpa said. "Aren't they afraid that they will turn against them?"

"These people must have surrendered to the Chinese," Father said.

"Our chiefdom surrendered too," Dragpa replied, "but instead of giving us guns, the Chinese arrested everyone." I thought, "Whether the local army is stronger than the Chinese or not, they were good to us. I hope these good-hearted old men don't meet with any misfortune. Since we left our native land these were the first people we met who had guns but who had the grace to avoid using them to kill people. That is a precious virtue indeed!"

47

Yaks and Sheep Abandoned without Herdsmen or Shepherds. No One to Tend the Wounded.

That day the sky was dark. In the morning the rain turned to sleet.

"We're in Achong chiefdom now, and in this area sleet often falls in the autumn," Father said. As we rode on we saw some saddled horses grazing on the mountainside above the road. One of the horses was dragging a saddle under its belly.

"Look," Tenzin said, "those horses don't seem to have owners. Should we bring them with us?"

Armed warriors on horseback in a typical highland valley.
122738-243523. Photographer, Joseph Rock, 1924.
© President and Fellows of Harvard College, Arnold Arboretum Archives.

"Be careful!" Lochu said. "There may be an owner around somewhere." Later Tenzin returned with the three saddled horses. These horses were very strong, so we exchanged them for our weaker ones. We gave two to Monlam and Lekho to ride, and substituted one for a packhorse. We set the weaker horses free on the mountain and rode on. Beside the road we saw ten more horses and about a hundred yaks grazing by the river.

"There are a lot of horses and yaks wandering around," someone said. "It's strange that nobody is taking care of them." A little farther on, we saw even more untended yaks, sheep, and horses roaming the grassland.

"Well, that's bad," Father said. "This is another area that must have been attacked by Chinese troops. That's the only possible reason for all of these loose herds."

"That must be right," Dragpa said. "Probably a lot of families had gathered their livestock here, and the Chinese let them loose. I've never seen so many sheep in my life!" We rode around the other side of the mountain. Packs of dogs were wandering through the grassland feeding on the bodies of dead sheep. In a fold of the mountainside lay the carcasses of about a hundred sheep that had been killed by wolves. We kept following the river.

"Hey, how about keeping these abandoned animals and living here for a few years?" Lochu said.

"Don't say such stupid things," Monlam replied. "Their owners have been killed, and their clans wiped out—we can't take advantage of that. In any case, there's nowhere to stay."

"Has anywhere been spared from these Chinese devils?" Dragpa said.

"My guess is it's just the same in Lhasa," Father said. "The Tibetan government doesn't have a large army, and there is no possibility it could stand up to the Chinese forces." We felt unhappy as we continued our journey. We came across more flocks of sheep without shepherds as we rode up the road. Tenzin, Khangtrul, and Tsekho drove those sheep with us. I thought, "Soon we will come across another chiefdom that has been wiped out." The strange thing was that we traveled for a whole day without seeing a single shepherd or herdsman. There was no sign of human life at all, apart from a few stray domestic dogs. I thought, "This is strange! If everyone has been killed, why are there no dead bodies? If they are alive, why can't we see anyone?"

That night we camped near a river close to where about a thousand sheep were grazing.

"Tomorrow we're going to take a rest here," Lochu said. "In the morning we need to slaughter some sheep, or else we'll have no meat for our journey."

"We can't stay long in this area," Father said. "We need to go on ahead as soon as we have butchered the sheep. There is a concealed valley ahead where we can hide for a few days." Snow fell heavily that night. In the morning we slaughtered three sheep and then continued on. When we had got a long way ahead, I looked back. Most of the sheep were still huddled together, as though sleeping. The yaks above the snow line on the mountain were walking out of the blue mist toward the sheep. Although it looked like a rich family's pastures, actually it was a desert, inhabited only by ownerless livestock.

We stayed in a small valley for three days and then continued our journey early the following morning. Later the sleet and the wind came, sometimes snowing, sometimes raining. My ragged sheepskin robe was full of holes, and the wind came in from all directions. The younger monks were shaking with cold, too. Once, a horseman approached us from the other side of the river, leading two horses. Lochu and Tenzin rode over to meet him. The rest of us stopped to make a fire. After a few minutes, Tenzin and Lochu returned.

"This chiefdom has been wiped out," Lochu announced, "and the people forced into a commune. They said the Mongolians fighting with the Chinese devastated this area. They arrested or killed everyone they saw. Nobody was allowed to surrender to the Mongolian troops, they told us. No one is left alive around here, or travels this way, and we should not follow the main road."

"If they capture me now," Tenzin said, "I do not fear it more than a horse's hair. But I can't be happy even if we escape, because of the devastation I've seen across the lands of these chiefdoms."

"Our only chance," Dragpa said, "is to keep going toward Lhasa."

"The Three Precious Jewels bear witness!" Lochu affirmed. "We have left our native land and are wandering in the wilderness because we wanted to send these children to a religious school. Whatever happens to us in the end, we must focus on reaching Lhasa."

"These days we won't have sweet dreams any more, and we can never relax," Father said. "But we have nothing to be ashamed of, even if we are killed because of our karma from a previous life. We have upheld our honor. We came together as monks and laypeople and tried to achieve something." Everybody said many things like this, and they made me feel unhappy.

"Father, I have been having a lot of bad dreams, too," I said. Actually, I had dreamed that my father and I had been shot by the Chinese and had blood pouring from our heads. The previous night I dreamed that our family was wiped out by the Chinese, and only Jabey and I were left. We fled to a wild place far away, and then the dream ended. It was hard to let myself fall asleep at night because I was afraid of more nightmares. I didn't dare tell any of them what happened in my dreams.

We continued our journey. Suddenly the leading riders, Khangtrul and Lekho, stopped.

"There are people on the ground up ahead," they called back to us. When we got there, we saw a group of old men and women, most of them wounded and lying on the ground. They told us they could not walk. There were some children with them.

"This is tragic," Lochu said. "This is yet another clan that has been destroyed by the Chinese, isn't it?" Father, Lochu, and Tenzin tended their injuries by putting sheep hide on them. Father tied up an old man's leg wound.

"This will be fine," he said. "The bleeding has stopped. You're not going to die." They treated all the injured people, and the monks gave them goat meat and tsampa. A little girl aged six had been shot twice in the arm, but her bones weren't broken. Japey and I made tsampa and fed it to her. She cried and said her parents had already been killed. My eyes filled with tears, and I could not control my feelings.

"We are from Dzachuka," one of the old men told us, "the Dzamira tulku's chiefdom. The tulku is still alive, but many of our people have been killed. Most of our chiefdom fled after fighting a battle with the Chinese. We are all that remains after the defeat. But there are more of us, more wounded people, higher up the mountain. They have no food to eat—please help them." We climbed until we found ten people sitting under a bank, boiling water in a cracked pot. As we approached, they got up and prostrated. Most of them were women. Father and Lochu took food from one of our packhorses, and the monks distributed it to these wounded people. Father and Lochu looked after their wounds.

"Most of our clan ran after we lost to the Chinese," one of them said. "If you meet them, please tell them we are here. We're going to die in this wilderness," and she began to weep. We saw some yaks roaming the mountaintop, and Father and Lochu went to round them up. There were five two-year-old female calves and five male yaks. Father and Lochu slaughtered two of the male yaks, and Tenzin brought over one of the old men from the first group.

"Look after these yaks carefully and eat this meat," Tenzin told him. "Then you won't die of hunger. Someone will come for you." He gave him much advice, but we left with grief weighing on our hearts. I thought to myself, "It's better to die in your own native land than to run far away and end up like this." We went on ahead.

48

Raiding the Caravan and Seizing Guns.
Compelled to Stand and Fight.

For the next few days, my mind was filled with thoughts of the wounded girl whose parents had been killed. It was tragic that they had thought they could get to Lhasa and never imagined that such misfortune would befall them on the way. But after her parents died she was abandoned in this desolate place, and we were going on the same route for the same reason and with the same goal. So far we had been fortunate enough to avoid her fate, but as the days went by it seemed less and less likely that we would make it to Lhasa. In my heart I thought, "If we are all slaughtered, today is too early but tomorrow is too late. Do we have any way to escape where no one has escaped before?" Escape seemed almost impossible.

We rode to the top of a sandy hill. Suddenly, the leading riders all dismounted and lay on the ground. Everyone except me followed their lead.

"It must be the Chinese troops," Khangtrul said. "Get off your horse." I just stayed stubbornly on my horse at the rear of our column. On the grassland near the river ahead hundreds of troops were riding in line, although our view was obscured by the swirling cloud of red dust that blew across the plain.

"This must be the road to Lhasa," Father said.

"I feel so frustrated," Tenzin muttered. "I would like to kill them all."

"We can't wait around here," Father said. "Go back to the river and cook something for everyone. I'm going to watch from a safe place."

"Is it safe to cook?" Lochu said.

"Of course, no problem," Father replied. "There's a strong wind. They won't smell the smoke." We descended the slope to the river and cooked a big meal. Tenzin took meat and tea up to father. At noon they waved us forward, and we traveled on. That night we pitched our tent in a beautiful pastureland beside a river, but then Dongtrug and Kelsang suddenly ran up to us yelling, "It's the Chinese! More soldiers!" Everyone sprang to their feet.

"Stay there," Lochu said. "We'll deal with it!" He ran to his horse with his gun at the ready. My father and Tenzin mounted their horses and joined him.

"Yes, stay here," Father said. "If we don't make it back and you have to surrender, look after these children well! But you will be fine." The three of them rode away. I walked to the top of a nearby bank and watched them.

"Nukho, don't stand up there! Get down!" one of the monks called. But what I saw made me feel a little less afraid, and I stayed where I was. All I could see was a caravan with a few yaks loaded with packs and no soldiers. My father and the others dismounted and concealed themselves behind a low mound in the path of the caravan, resting their guns on top of it. The drovers clearly hadn't seen our people because they just kept going directly toward the hiding place. When they got to the mound a shot rang out, and one of the riders, who was wearing blue Western-style clothes, fell to the ground. Some of the riders bringing up the rear rolled off their horses, afraid, but they quickly jumped up again with their hands in the air. Then my father and the others stood up and approached them. When I looked back, I saw that the other monks were still hiding. I waved for them to get up, and they came over to where I was standing. Then Uncle Monlam, Dragpa, and Khangtrul rode over to join my father and the others. When they returned to our tent, Father and Tenzin each had new rifles with a plentiful supply of bullets, and Lochu had another new type of gun I had never seen before. They gave their old guns to the drovers, after they had removed the bullets and took a large amount of the caravan's rice, flour, and bread, before sending them on their way.

"If you and Durkho hadn't stopped me," Tenzin told Lochu, "I would have killed both of those soldiers."

"If you had killed two Chinese, then other Chinese would have killed five Tibetans tomorrow," Father said. "By sparing Chinese lives, those Tibetan drovers have been saved from death." Later, they told many stories about how they had raided the Chinese troops' supply caravan. Tenzin was very happy that they had killed a Chinese soldier and gotten three new guns and a lot of ammunition. After the raid, we set off before daybreak and rode as fast as we could for a night and a day. Once, while we were ascending a wide valley, my father allowed me to ride behind him on his horse because I had a headache. That was the first time I had not ridden by myself since we left our house. Ordinarily, I rode in the middle of the horsemen with my brother, Jabey. I was never allowed in the front or the rear. However, that day I rode with my father, so I felt very happy. When we got near the head of the valley, the way became rocky and narrow. Tenzin rode first, and after him my father and I together. Suddenly two dogs ran down the mountainside toward us. Lochu jumped down from his horse and picked up a stone. At just that moment, Tenzin's voice rang out.

"Chinese soldiers!" Tenzin shouted, and he pulled the gun from his back. The sound of heavy gunfire filled the air, "Pag-shar! Pag-shar!" There was a loud sound from close by, and a vibration shook my body. Father and I fell off our horse. I thought, "Father's been shot," but when I lifted my head I could see my father running up the mountain carrying his gun. Lochu was running with him, and Tenzin was firing back at the Chinese troops from behind a rock. The other monks were rushing around. I stood up to catch Father's and Lochu's horses and then hid behind a big rock. Lochu came down to us.

"Dragpa, take the others back to the lower part of the valley," he said, "and wait for us there. There are more Chinese than there are of us, and we can't hold them here." Dragpa mounted Tenzin's horse and pulled me up behind him, and we galloped back through the river to the bottom of the valley. We got to a place where, although we couldn't see what was happening, we could hear the sound of the battle. I mounted my own horse. My headache was gone—fear must have cured it.

"We can't go any farther," Dragpa said, "or we'll lose contact with them."

"We need to go on!" Monlam said. "If they can't get away then there's nothing more to say, but if they do get away they'll find us wherever we are. We're leading horses and they won't have to, so they'll be faster than us." We rode on until we couldn't hear gunshots any longer. Then everyone stopped and looked back uneasily. We were all thinking the same thing: "Something must have happened to them."

"They're coming!" someone said. I turned around and saw the three of them racing toward us with Chinese troops in pursuit and firing at them.

"Come on, everyone!" Monlam yelled. "Ride up the mountain on our left. We'll hide in the rocks at the top." When we reached the peak of the mountain, my father and the other two had already made it to the foot of the slope and were out of sight of the Chinese cavalry. The three of them climbed to the top, and we watched ten soldiers galloping down the valley firing their weapons. Tenzin, Lochu, and my father dismounted and rested their guns on the rocks, waiting for the Chinese to get within range. Tenzin had injured his left arm and was bleeding. Father dressed the wound.

"Son of a great father!" Tenzin said. "This is a perfect place to lie in wait, no doubt about that."

"Let them get a bit closer," Father said. "If we can shoot some of them down, the others will run away." We watched from behind a boulder close by. The Chinese rode closer, and we could hear bullets whistling overhead as they fired at us from their galloping horses. Then we heard the clap of my father's gun, and the first of the Chinese soldiers fell from his horse, which turned and raced away. The others kept on coming. Tenzin and Lochu fired, and the next soldier and his horse fell over. Then my father brought another one crashing to the ground with his horse. Most of the Chinese horsemen escaped down the valley. A few of them got off their horses and, lying flat, fired at us. One soldier with a bloody face charged at us from the right. My father fired, and the man's body fell from the saddle and pitched down the mountain. Tenzin and Lochu also hit their targets, and two more bodies went down. The remaining troops fled, and we stopped hearing shots from their side, although we could hear the faint crackle of gunfire in the distance.

"It's getting dark now," Father said. "Let's go. They won't follow us now." We climbed down the rocks on the far side of the mountain, leading our horses, still hearing the far-off sound of the Chinese guns.

49

Another Battle with the Chinese Troops in Kharri Dzagen Valley.

We rode far away from the valley where we had fought with the Chinese troops and hid in another one for a few days. In the distance we could see Ngoring Lake. The day we left, we rode away at dawn.

"Tonight I hope we will reach the Wujud chiefdom in Kharri Valley," Father said. "I have friends in that chiefdom, so everything should go well there." That night we stayed near a mountain called Kharri Tsadi Marlab. We found a perfect hiding place out of sight of the main road, but from which we could see everything up and down the valley, and camped there for two days. The second morning Jabey and Dongtrug went to collect firewood. When they got back they told us, "There are a lot of tents farther up the valley." We walked up the side of the mountain and looked. It was true. Many white canvas and black yak hair tents were pitched on a pasture in the valley, and there were a lot of livestock too.

"We don't know who it is," Father said, "so don't let the horses walk up the bank in front of our camp, and don't make too much smoke. If we stay behind the bank, they can't see us. And if any yak herders come this way during the day, we can question them." Later that day a group of horsemen left the other camp with pack yaks.

"They are Chinese," Lekho said. "The riders in the middle of the caravan are all Chinese soldiers."

"The first group are Tibetans with guns," Khangtrul added.

"So this area is controlled by the Chinese, too." Tenzin said fiercely.

"Fill their mouths with ash!" Uncle Monlam exclaimed.

"If the Wujud chiefdom is under Chinese control," Father said, "then the seven fords of the Drichu River must be under their control too. If that's true, it makes it well-nigh impossible to get to Lhasa. We are going to have to think of some secret route because we definitely can't fight our way through against the Chinese army." Later I climbed the bank to have a better look. Some sheep were nearby, and two women shepherds sat on the ground near them.

"There are two shepherds just over there," I told my father.

"Just wait here," Father said to the others, "I'm going to ask them something." He walked a long way around to the shepherds, creeping between the rocks. He talked to them for quite a while. Then he came back the long way again, still skulking. He said, "They are from the Wujud chiefdom, part of the Dodtsang and Ngotsang clans. Their chief has surrendered to the Chinese, and they have been forced into a commune. The white tents all belong to the Chinese government. They say their monks have been arrested." Tenzin came over with an elderly man who was holding a cloth bag full of bullets.

"This man offered me a gun that he has hidden on the mountain over there," Tenzin said, "but I told him all we needed was ammunition."

"Our clan has been totally wiped out," the old man said. "We can't let the Chinese find that we still have guns or bullets, but they might be useful for you. I only have these bullets right now, but if you decide you need a gun, I'll bring you mine tonight. Our chiefdom's weaponry was almost all confiscated by Chinese soldiers. Our chief surrendered to the Chinese, and our clan's lamas, monks, and laypeople have been arrested. They tricked them into it. Now the Chinese troops are everywhere in this area. A huge group of them are at Jachensumdo, where the three valleys meet. All of the pilgrim caravans bound for Lhasa have been attacked and broken up at the seven fords of the Drichu. You will find it very difficult to get past them." He gave us much hard and dispiriting information, but Tenzin and the others weren't unhappy. They had their bullets, and they were in good spirits.

"Now that we have some bullets, son of a great father, your shooting will lead us to success," Tenzin said to my father. "If we die, it is our karma, but we need to kill some of them in return. If we don't, we'll never be free of the Chinese."

The following day we came to a place with many small hills. We were riding along a sandy road when we heard a gunshot from behind us.

"It's Chinese troops!" someone called out. We galloped onto the grassland, but the gunshots intensified. Bullets peppered the ground around us, spraying dust and sand into the air.

"Tenzin!" Father shouted. "Make for the top of that hill! If we can't find the right place to make a stand, we're as good as captured!" The Chinese troops were making a tremendous noise firing at us, but luckily their aim was faulty and none of our people or horses were hit. When we reached the summit of one of the hillocks, we could see around twenty Chinese soldiers heading our way, shooting at us rapidly from horseback as they rode up the slope.

"You younger ones take cover," Father said. "Tenzin and Lochu, take up position on the other flank of the hill. This is a good place. We might be able to stop them here." He rested his gun in front of him and waited for the troops to get closer. Jabey, Khangtrul, and I sat behind my father. The others held the horses behind Tenzin's position.

"Durkho, you son of a great father," Lochu said, "we know you are a good shot. Don't suddenly start making mistakes with your new rifle today." When the Chinese soldiers reached the hill, Tenzin shot the first one, and rider and horse both hit the ground, kicking up a great cloud of dust. A shot rang out from my father, and another of the leading riders fell from his horse. Two of the horsemen farther back also dropped, but the others came on.

"Over there!" Father shouted. "The one on the white horse!" Immediately a shot rang out, and a white horse and rider fell in a cloud of yellowish dust. Another of the leading riders was brought down, but it was not clear whether by Tenzin or Lochu. Then the remaining Chinese soldiers wheeled around and fled toward the hills behind them. Tenzin came up to my father.

"You chose a good place to make a stand, that's for sure," he said.

"It would have been better if we'd used fewer bullets," Father said. "Now they have taken cover. Let's see if we are good long-range marksmen." Suddenly one of their soldiers broke cover at the top of our hillock and shot at us with a machine gun. Tenzin and the others fell back. Some other Chinese troops joined the machine gunner.

"Tenzin! Come over here!" Father shouted. "This needs both of us!" They fired, and the machine gun misfired with a strange noise when its operator was hit.

"You got him! You got him!" Lochu shouted. He ran over to us.

"Father, Chinese troops behind us. Look!" Jabey shouted. Four horsemen were galloping toward us around the side of a small hill.

"The black horse's rider first!" Father shouted. A shot rang out, and the soldier was flung off his horse, tumbling through the air. Tenzin and Lochu accounted for two more horses and their riders, and the fourth turned and ran. Then another soldier broke cover at the top of the hill where the machine gun still stood, apparently undamaged.

"Another one over there," Lochu said, but before he could finish, Father's gun fired again. The soldier toppled, then rolled down the hill.

"Tenzin, don't let that hilltop out of your sight for a moment," Father said. "Don't let anyone near that machine gun!"

"Om mani padme hum!" Monlam said. "Today we have taken many lives."

"Everyone, how is the ammunition?" Father asked.

"I have sixteen bullets." Tenzin replied.

"I still have around twenty," Lochu said.

"Conserve your ammunition," Father said. "The Chinese army has plenty more troops, and we won't be able to stop anyone without bullets." As afternoon approached, huge shadows fell across the mountainside in front of us. Suddenly, another detachment of troops appeared from the edge of the pasture. We could make out around thirty of them.

"We need to get away to the tallest mountain we can find," Lochu said, "otherwise we're done for."

"We'll be fine," my father replied. "It won't be as hard as you think." He handed me some meat and ate some himself.

Then he hitched his gun around from his back. "This really is the Chinese army, not some small patrol. Don't let them get too close." The Chinese galloped toward us.

"The three of us target the nearest riders," Father ordered. Our guns fired, and two horsemen and one horse dropped. They fired a few more volleys, and two or three more soldiers went down with their horses. Then most of the other horsemen fled to cover. The bodies of horses and people lay below us. Then troops appeared at the top of the hill opposite us, and their machine gun opened up again. The bullets ricocheted off the rocks around us, sending sparks flying through the air, bright in the gathering gloom. No troops were riding toward us any more.

"When darkness falls," Father mused, "the Chinese troops never come anywhere near us." He still sat with his guns at the ready, though. After sunset, we turned away from the hill and rode across the river and up the mountain.

50

Eventually Overpowered by Superior Numbers, Defeat, and Death.

We reached safety on the mountain that night.

"We killed some Chinese soldiers today," Father said, "so the army will try to intercept us." We rode across the mountain all that night. At daybreak we arrived at a broad river. As the sun rose, we lit a fire and cooked on hot stones. Then we sat down to eat.

"Up ahead I saw some yak drovers," Lochu told us. He and Tenzin went to find them, carrying their guns. They came across three horsemen driving four yaks with empty saddles and invited them to eat with us.

"We are from Chumar," they said. "The Chinese troops are everywhere there. Don't go that way. You'd be caught." They continued on their way, and we continued on ours. At noon, we came to a big sandy valley.

"Chinese soldiers—coming this way!" Lekho shouted.

"There are dozens of them heading straight for us!" Tenzin yelled. "We wouldn't have a hope of stopping them."

"We'll fight them if we're cornered," Father said, "but not until then. For now, let's ride up this small valley." We entered a side valley and climbed the mountain from there. Near the crest we concealed ourselves in a hollow and waited. Beneath us we could see about a hundred troops crossing the river, but they didn't see us hiding. Then we rode to the top of the mountain.

"This valley is called Ngamri Khog," my father said when we could look down from the peak. "That high mountain to the right is called Ngamri Chongshog. We'll head down and cross that river. From there we'll ride up a valley called Chumar Godmalong. We should get to the Chumar River to-night." We descended the mountain until we arrived at a corner of the valley where someone had left rocks inscribed with scriptures and prayers.

"What a lovely valley this is," Dragpa said. "Why don't we stay here for tonight?"

"The horses and all of us are tired after the last three days. Let's make camp early today," Uncle Monlam said.

"Durkho, should we stay here?" Tenzin asked.

"Whatever you say," Father said. "But I think it would be better to pass the Chumar River tonight. This valley is narrow, and if Chinese troops find us here, we are done for." The majority wanted to stay where we were, so we pitched our tents near the valley's entrance. Some of us cooked, and others unsaddled the horses. Father tethered his dark brown horse near the entrance to our tent. Lochu and Tenzin also left their horses tied up. Some of the monks fell asleep under a cliff, and Lekho and Khangtrul went down the mountain-side on lookout. Father fell asleep in the tent with his gun by his side. I was cooking a sausage over the fire when I heard a gunshot in the distance, and dust drifted across the fire in front of me. Everyone started rushing around.

"Chinese troops!" they were shouting. Father ran out of the tent holding his gun. Tenzin rushed up behind him.

"Where are they?" Tenzin shouted. Father pointed to the west. When they heard the shooting, all the untied horses had run away.

"I'm going to round up the horses," Tenzin said. He ran over toward them.

"Not yet!" father said. "Don't run off until you're certain where the enemy is." Tenzin either did not hear or did not pay attention. When he reached the horses, he mounted one of them and rode downhill yelling. Bullets rained down from the mountainside, and he and his horse fell.

"Hawo! This is terrible!" the monks shouted. From the left flank of the valley came another volley of shots from the Chinese.

"Hawo! May their heads turn into blood," Father said, aiming his gun toward them. One of the soldiers stood up and threw a hand grenade, but my father shot him, and he slumped. Then a huge explosion made the earth shake, but no one was injured. Lekho and Khangtrul were running up the side of the valley toward us, with the Chinese troops shooting at them from the mountainside above.

"Hey! You two!" Father shouted to them. "Take cover!" They kept on running toward us, and Lekho fell with blood spurting from a bullet wound. Khangtrul ran back to Lekho, but before he could reach him he was shot too. Then Tenzin opened up on the Chinese troops from under a cliff. Two of them rolled down the mountain, their yellow uniforms standing out against the gloom.

"Hawo! Fill their mouths with blood!" Tenzin yelled. He ran back up the mountain.

"Not that way!" Lochu shouted. "There are soldiers there! Over here!" Tenzin ran over to where we were. The Chinese had killed his horse, but he had not been harmed. Then he and Lochu trained their guns on the western side of the valley and fired at the troops there. Soldiers stood up and ran away. I was still hiding.

"Nukho! Come up here," Jabey said. The others had taken cover under a cliff. I ran over to them. Then I heard a rushing noise in my ears and dropped to the ground with sparks in front of my eyes. When I recovered consciousness, my father was holding me in his arms.

"Sweet boy, how are you?" he asked me. I didn't know what had happened. My head was bleeding. "My dear boy, there's no problem," my father said. "Your head was grazed by a bullet, that's all." He turned to the others and said, "We can't stand against them here; it's the wrong place. Tenzin and Lochu, you need to hold them off while the young monks wait under the cliff. I'm going to try to get around the other side of the mountain. If I can't get away after I ambush them, it would be better to surrender. The older people will be arrested, but it won't be too hard for the younger ones. If any adults are spared, we must look after these children." He ran over to his horse and galloped away. More troops had arrived at the mountaintop where Tenzin had shot the other two before, and they fired at my father, while Tenzin and Lochu fired back at them. Father turned his horse and charged straight toward them, shooting as he went. Two of the troops tumbled down the mountain, but it was impossible to tell who had shot them. A soldier lying on the mountaintop fired toward my father, who was crouching in the saddle as he rode up the slope. His gun fell from his hands, and he slid from the horse, holding on to the saddle as he fell. The horse broke free and ran back to us, neighing. One of the soldiers walked down to where my father was lying. All of us watched openmouthed, not knowing what to do.

"Come on! Shoot them, shoot them!" Uncle Monlam said. Nobody fired.

"There's no ammunition left," Tenzin said, and threw his gun to the ground. The soldier pointed his gun at my father. Before he could shoot, I heard a gunshot, quieter than usual, and saw smoke close to my father. The soldier bounced away down the far side of the mountain. Then I ran to my father without any fear. The troops fired at me but missed. Then Jabey and the others ran after me. When we got to my father, he was holding a pistol in his right hand, and his stomach with his left. Tenzin and Monlam sat Father up.

"Hey, Durkho. Are you badly hurt?" they said. They both started crying.

"My gun! Get my gun!" Father said. Tenzin grabbed my father's gun and fired toward the troops on the western side of the valley. Then Lochu went over to the bodies of the dead soldiers and brought back about ten bullets, which he loaded into his gun, and fired at the others. Lochu kept firing, but it was too dark to see whether he had hit anyone. Monlam and Tenzin held my father in silence. When the firing had died down, my father spoke to Tenzin slowly, in a low voice.

"Go and see what's happened to Lekho and Khangtrul. I am sorry to say I don't think there's much hope for either of them."

"It's over for those two. Nothing to see, they must be dead already," replied Tenzin.

I thought, "This is the end of the 'time of revolution.' The greatest disasters which that time could have brought have already befallen us. Our group is broken up, my father has been wounded, and it looks as though he may die. Our karma has placed us in the jaws of the Chinese army, and they are going to kill us." So I sat beside my father while the sun sank behind the mountain. I felt indifferent to the gunshots far away, to whoever was shooting, and whoever the target was. My sadness was too deep for tears, and I just sat watching my father.

51

Karma Prevents Our Pilgrimage to Lhasa.
My Dear Father Departs This Life.

Lochu was still firing at the Chinese soldiers from higher up the mountainside, and Tenzin and Monlam were holding my father. Father's face became grayer and grayer. I thought, "This is a desolate place. The fear we suffered night after night has all been for nothing. What more could have happened to us, even if we had stayed in our own chiefdom? Now Father is going to die, and we're not going to make it to Lhasa. This must be what they call karma." I thought these things as I sat beside my father. Then he spoke.

"The Canadian pistol," he said, "no bullets left," and handed it to Tenzin. Tenzin gave the pistol to me, and I put it in my robe.

"A brave man should pray to the Three Precious Jewels," said Tenzin. "The son of a great father should take courage!"

"There were some mani stones up there, weren't there?" Father said. "Can you lay me down there?" They picked my father up and took him over to the pile of mani stones. As they carried him, blood poured from the back of his robe. The bullet had struck the silver *dolen* of my father's dagger and ricocheted into the right side of his chest, piercing his back and exiting his robe under his shoulder blade.

"Is there anything we can do to heal the wound?" Monlam said.

"Thank you," Father replied, "but there's nothing you can do." Then Chinese troops called from the mountaintop.

"Surrender, or we'll kill you!" they shouted. Tenzin and Lochu loosed off their guns toward the voices, and the troops opened up a hail of machine gun bullets.

"Tenzin, monks," my father said, "there's nothing I can do anymore. Don't try to resist any longer. You've got to surrender. If you continue fighting, the Chinese will kill you all, children as well as older people, and it would be the greatest tragedy if they killed the children. Even if we can't send them to a religious school, we might be able to save their lives."

"Of course, I understand," Tenzin told him. "Don't worry! Even if we can't do that, we'll save their lives."

"The Chinese will ask you who your chief is," Father said. "Tell them it was me, then they'll be easier on you. In my robe there is a piece of tedarlung. Please give it to me!" Monlam took the bloody cloth package out of father's robe and put it into his hands. He gave him a sacred medicinal pill from the packet. My father said, "You eat the rest of it—I don't want the Chinese getting their hands on it." Uncle cut it up and gave each of us a piece to eat.

"Father, how are you?" Jabey asked. He was crying.

"Who is that crying?" Father said. "Japey, you mustn't cry. Did you never hear it said that a man never cries when he is sad? Dear boy, don't cry!"

"Father, when I grow up, I will take revenge for you," Japey insisted. "Don't worry."

"Darling boy, you are a monk," Father said. "You mustn't think like this. After I am dead, you need to take good care of Nukho. You must be his father and mother now. When you return to our native land, if you find that everything has been destroyed, just put yourself under the protection of Alak Gungtang. He will take care of you both."

"Don't worry, Father, I will take care of Nukho," Japey answered.

"When I grow up, I will take revenge myself!" I said to my father.

"There's no reason to take revenge on my account," Father told me. "The Chinese troops have destroyed and killed in many Tibetan areas. It is said that in the 'time of revolution' there will be no enemy to take revenge on, and nowhere to take revenge. You have seen many people die—not only your father—on this journey, haven't you? Today Lekho and Khangtrul were killed. Anyway, do as your brother tells you. Your father failed to take you to Lhasa, and will leave you in this desolate place, but everything will be all right. As long as they live, Tenzin and the others will look after you both. And no matter what I say, it's the protection of the Three Precious Jewels that will save your lives." When he finished speaking, my father closed his eyes. Lochu came over.

"I can't see the Chinese soldiers any more. How are you, my brother Durkho!" he said. He held up my father's head and wept.

"There's nothing we can do for him now," Tenzin said. "When Durkho's breath is gone we must surrender. We have killed many Chinese troops, and the others won't spare our lives. But if we surrender, it won't be too bad for the children." My father coughed weakly, twice, and blood came out of his mouth.

"Durkho, son of a great father," Monlam said, "don't be afraid. You must pray!" Monlam started crying.

"Be calm, my brother," Tenzin said. "We will look after your boys. In the past few days you have killed many Chinese soldiers, so you have already avenged your own death. Now stay calm." He began to cry, and nearly everyone in our company was sniffing or weeping too. My father raised his head a little.

"Tenzin, son of a great father," he whispered, "don't cry. Karma has brought us to the place where we must part. You are trapped in the teeth of the Chinese troops now. You must find some way out and save the children."

"I see no way to escape," Tenzin said, "but we will find a way out for the children. There's no need for you to worry. I am very grateful to you and apologize for burdening you with this suffering." Father searched for Jabey with his eyes.

"My son," he said, "you're not crying, are you?"

"Father, neither of us is crying," I answered.

"No," Father said. "You shouldn't cry. In this world your father killed many people. When we were fighting the Ma family's armies, I killed many of their troops. These days I have been killing soldiers of the Chinese Red Army, but tonight the Chinese paid me in kind for all my killing. But at least the karmic consequences have come about in this lifetime, so I'm not afraid anymore. I'm just going to pray to Alak. . . ." My father's voice became weaker, and after that we couldn't hear what he said, even though everyone listened in compete silence. Then the monks began to chant prayers for the dead while Tenzin gently laid my father on the mani stones. Jabey didn't cry, and neither did I. I thought, "It's true what Father said, that 'There are so many dead bodies in this world every day, and it is always the same for everyone.' We are all subject to the laws of karma."

As the stars grew brighter in the sky, my father's breath left his body, and he slowly departed, leaving my brother and me behind. He left for the realms of peace, never to return to this world. Tenzin and the other monks removed my father's robe and began to make arrangements for the funeral. The Chinese troops fired two flares into the sky but didn't shoot at us. While I waited, I prayed from the bottom of my heart: "Three Precious Jewels bear witness! The father and the sons are to be separated in this wilderness, one going to death, while the others remain alive. We have left our native land far behind, and intended to reach great Lhasa. The white clouds were above our heads, and we strode across the black earth. Today we have reached this place where father and sons gave up their freedom to the metal bullets of the cruel Chinese. My dear father's red blood has spilt in the valley of the mani, Dza Ngamri Chongshog Gomgo. This small valley of mani stones, where my father's skull rests for the last time, is ready for my father's sky burial. This great suffering has taken away my hope, and despair has dried my tears. My father's consciousness drifted away, desiring to reach the *Sukhavati* paradise of the Buddha Amitabha in the West, of the precious protector, the Dalai Lama. Hear us, precious Protector! All of Tibet is suffering! Listen and remember! The rabbit that the eagle kills calls to the sky, but the sky gives no answer. Beneath him is the earth and his small hole. I am weak in this remote place, but even though I have suffered intensely, my mind only thinks of you, and my mind can only find refuge in you! I take refuge in simple trust in the Precious Protector, the Dalai Lama. My kind father's red heart has stopped. The enemy has stopped his heart. He has no lama at his head, no monks chanting prayers over his body, no liberating meaning of sacred rituals or prayers of dedication. Gracious root lama, do not let his soul feel fear. Let it not feel the wind's cold nor wander in strange realms. Do not let it be reborn into a bad life. Please keep these things in your mind and show this consciousness the way to liberation. You are the refuge for our future lives—do not forget us. Throughout Tibet, many thousands of people cannot perform the rituals for the dead, and many souls are now seeking their path to liberation. Precious Protector Dalai Lama—*do not avert your gaze!*"

Again I prayed: "Father, I pray you will reach the Sukhavati paradise of the Buddha Amitabha. On the red path of the intermediate state between birth and death, may you feel calm. Do not regret that the correct rituals were not performed, or that no one could dispose of your dead body the right way. Until I die, I will follow my father like a true son. I will go up to Lhasa, I will pray and practice my religion diligently. Wherever you are, give an ear to my words. One day your conscousness will be freed, and I will chant om mani padme hum all my life for you, my dear father."

I sat by myself and thought for a long time. I don't know how long. I reflected again that the suffering of the "time of revolution" had spread across the entire country. It had not only destroyed the lives of this father and these sons, but the refuge of the monasteries had been destroyed, and nobody could hide from the "time of revolution." There was nowhere left to escape to. I knew that, and now everything was finished, regrets or no regrets.

Later I came to know that the day of our destruction was the ninth day of September 1958 by the Western calendar.

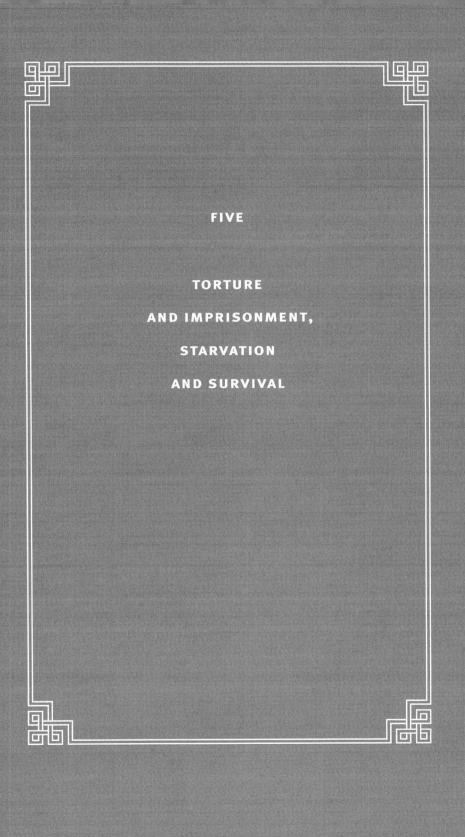

FIVE

TORTURE

AND IMPRISONMENT,

STARVATION

AND SURVIVAL

The Evening of Terror. Arrest and Relief.

Father breathed his last. I had seen so many frightening things, and had seen so many injured people on our journey, that I had no more tears left. Jabey sat beside me, and he didn't cry either. After a while, Tenzin broke the silence.

"You two go over there under the cliff and chant some dedicatory prayers, while Lochu and I take the bodies of the monks to the marsh." The younger monks went over to the cliff, and Jabey and I went with them. It was midnight, and I could still hear Chinese guns firing in the darkness. I thought, "When daybreak comes, the Chinese soldiers will shoot us. Three Precious Jewels bear witness! Who's going to be the next to die?"

"What shall we do with the guns?" Lochu asked Tenzin. "Throw away the ammunition?"

"At the moment I'm thinking about surrendering at daybreak," Tenzin said. "Apart from that I have no idea what to do. If we are forced to surrender, it's our karma. And if the Chinese ask who our chief was, remember what the boys' father said last night. He was the chief. If we don't tell them that, we have no hope, and the older ones will have no chance of escaping. Let's destroy the guns and hide them in the stream." Lochu and Tenzin broke the guns on a rock and threw them into the water. Then we went back to our hiding places. After midnight the moon rose, but it was cloudy, and we couldn't see clearly. Our hiding place was about one hundred paces from our tent. A group of Chinese soldiers walked down from the western side of the valley and stood around our tent, saying things we couldn't understand. We were watching them when suddenly a nearby voice said in Tibetan, "You! Hand over your guns and surrender. If you do, things will go easier for you." No one answered. Many troops were walking down the mountain—they surrounded our tent. We could hear them loading their guns, but they hadn't spotted us. The Tibetan said again, "Listen! You've got to surrender. If you don't, we're going to kill you." Then Tenzin stood up.

"We're over here!" he called out. "Don't shoot! We surrender." The troops took up firing positions and pointed their guns at us. Tenzin walked toward them and said again, "Don't shoot us! We'll surrender." We followed him down the slope.

"Put down your guns! Put the guns down!" one of the Tibetans said.

"We are just monks and children." Tenzin replied. "We haven't got any guns."

"Sit on the ground and raise your hands to the sky!" We sat down and raised our hands. Troops surrounded us, including several armed Tibetans.

"You father's dead body eaters! Put your hands up properly!" one of them said. He started kicking the ones sitting in front, but a Chinese soldier told him to stop. After dawn, soldiers took Lochu to one side and said to take off his sash so they could check the inside of his robe. Then they let him sit down again. Two Tibetans checked the monks one by one. They took off their sashes and tore their red religious ribbons from around their necks. One of the Tibetans removed a small knife from under Tenzin's robe and hit him on the head with it.

"You eater of your father's dead body!" he shouted. "What is a monk doing carrying a knife?" Suddenly I remembered that I still had the Canadian pistol in my robe. "What can I do?" I wondered. "If I drop it on the ground, they will see it. If not, when they check me they will find it and beat me. Will they let me get away with it because I am young? I will have to pretend I don't know anything about it." After they had checked Jabey, they told me to stand up. One of the Tibetans took me by the ear and pulled me away. When I took off my robe, the pistol fell to the ground.

"This eater of his father's dead body was hiding a gun," the Tibetan said. He yanked me by the ear over to the head Chinese officer and spoke words to him that I didn't understand. The officer took the pistol in his hand and looked at me. Through the translator he asked, "Whose pistol is this?"

"My father's," I answered.

"Who is your father?" he asked.

"You have killed my father already," I replied. I looked up at the mountain, which was bathed in sunshine. Many vultures were gathering on the mountaintop. The Chinese officer just stroked my face gently and investigated the wound on my head. He spoke a few words of Chinese, and a young soldier came up and helped me tie the sash on my robe. A Chinese woman with a first aid box dressed my wound and wiped my face. Then they took me to their living quarters and gave me some bread.

When I returned, Jabey said, "Look toward the mountain. There are some

Chinese dead bodies over there." I could see six Chinese corpses lying on some marshy land near the mountain, covered in white cloths. At the doorway of the tent there were a couple of Chinese soldiers with bandaged head wounds. I thought, "Judging by their behavior so far, they probably won't kill the older people. Now I'm not worried anymore. Even though we have been arrested, there's no reason to be afraid." I saw additional troops dressed in yellow uniforms riding over the mountain and thought, "Most of the Chinese troops have arrived today. Yesterday there were only a few." The Chinese soldiers cooked their meal, then let us cook ours. There was a patrol in the distance, but it wasn't looking for us. While we were eating it seemed as if they had forgotten we were there. Many of their weapons were lying unattended near the tent.

"It's so frustrating," Tenzin said. "I'd like to get my hands on some of those weapons. I'd fight them, even if we died in the attempt."

"Stop thinking about that—you'd only bring more suffering to the children," Monlam told him. Later that day, many more Chinese wearing blue uniforms, and the Tibetans fighting on their side, arrived. It amazed me to see so many troops in the valley. It was as full as the sheath of a knife. I estimated that there were at least two thousand there. The Chinese officer brought some Tibetans and some of the blue-uniformed troops over to us. He made a long speech, pointing at the mountain and other places. He stroked my head, while he gestured at the mountain. I guessed that he was talking about yesterday's battle. Then our two Chinese guards left and were replaced by two Tibetans. A military bugle sounded, and the troops swiftly formed ranks and rode away. Only the two Tibetans were left guarding us. Later some Chinese and Tibetans came, tied up all of our companions—except for Jabey, Dongtrug, and me—and put them on horseback. The three of us were given horses of our own and told to follow them.

"If you lot are thinking about escaping, you'll have to be very quick," one of the Tibetans said. "If you aren't, we'll shoot you." As we rode across the face of the mountain, I looked back. High on the desolate mountain I could see a mass of vultures eating my father's dead body. There were none on Lekho's and Khangtrul's bodies, but the marshy pasture around them was stained red with their blood. My eyes were full of tears of sadness and compassion, but I didn't cry. I could see the tears rolling down Jabey's face, but his pain was silent. We just continued on our way, leaving our father's body in that bleak place, far from his native land.

Dust flew around us, whipped up by a wind that grew stronger as the day went by. The escort left Jabey and me a long way behind, but no one paid us any attention. Had we been older, we could have escaped easily, but we never thought of running away. We were more worried about getting lost, and so we urged our horses to catch up with the others. That night we reached an encampment. The soldiers took Jabey, Dongtrug, Kelsang, and me into a tent and told the family to give us food. There was a young woman and an old woman in the tent who poured tea and gave us tsampa and yogurt.

"They should be ashamed for arresting such a small child," the old woman said. "Those Chinese should be killed."

"Mother, are you insane?" the younger woman asked. "If the Chinese hear you, you'll be arrested, too! Yes, my little brothers. Eat and drink."

"I'm not afraid!" the old woman said. "Everyone else has been taken away. I don't care if I'm arrested or not." She said many things that the Chinese would have been very unhappy to hear. I thought, "So this chiefdom has been attacked and destroyed." One of the Tibetans arrived with a gun and took Dongtrug and Kelsang away. The young woman looked at my robe, torn in the front and the back.

"Are you cold?" she asked.

"Not very cold," I said.

"How can you not be cold when it's ripped open back and front?" she asked. She brought a needle and woolen thread and mended my robe. My eyes filled with tears, and I wept uncontrollably as Jabey and I continued our meal.

53

Ferociously Tortured by the Chinese Army.

Jabey and I weren't done eating when one of the local soldiers came and took us away. Outside, we walked toward a huge Chinese tent that had been pitched nearby. Before we entered the tent, I could hear someone shouting in Tibetan.

"You father's dead body eaters! Refugees! Chinese killers! So, you want to kill some Chinese now. You are going to kill the Chinese now, are you?" There was the sound of whips cracking. I thought, "Now we are all going to be whipped. Jabey and I are going to be whipped, too." Inside the tent, Lochu, Tenzin, Monlam, and Dragpa were lying on the ground, tied up with ropes. Their upper bodies were bare, and their hands were fastened behind their backs. The ropes were almost invisible because they had cut so deeply into their flesh. Lochu was lying down, and his head was bleeding. Sometimes he shouted with pain, "Ara! Ara!" Blood was running from Tenzin's nose, and his face was covered in bruises. Uncle Monlam's face was bleeding, and his eyes were invisible beneath bruises. Beyond them, Tsekho was also tied up, but his face was less bruised than the others, and farther away Kelsang and Dongtrug were sitting on the ground with their heads lowered. A short Chinese soldier in a yellow uniform was using a whip and a wooden staff to beat them, one after the other. The other torturers were all local Tibetans. As I sat there I thought, "Even our own people, fellow Tibetans, treat us like this. Our people didn't kill their fathers or do anything terrible to them. They are beating this monk and this old man so brutally for no reason at all. The hand that can do this is a very harsh one." Another Tibetan came and hit Jabey over the head with a stick.

"Just sit there," he said. Jabey sat beside Dongtrug. The Tibetan hit me on the head with a "kag" sound. He said, "Little refugee, sit down," and struck me again. Then he smashed us all on the head with his stick one at a time and went over to Lochu. He pulled him up.

"You father's dead body eater, who is your chief?" he asked.

"You all told me it was me, so let it be me," Lochu replied, "and you can do whatever you want with me. You are a Tibetan, aren't you? Aren't you ashamed of beating this old man?" Before he had even finished, the Chinese and Tibetans ran over and started beating him again.

"Stop hurting that old man!" Tenzin shouted. "Our chief is already dead!"

"Father's dead body eater!" one of the Tibetans said. "If you don't shut your mouth I can easily do that for you." He started beating Tenzin.

"Fill your mouth with blood!" Tenzin shouted. "If you want to eat your father's dead body, you should eat it, since you love the Chinese so much. If you are a really brave man, why don't you just kill me now? You're attacking that old man because you just want to kill someone, don't you?" He shouted many things like that.

"Worthy monk," Dragpa said, "don't waste your breath on him."

"It doesn't make a difference if we talk or not," Monlam said, "because these are devils with their mouths stuffed with ash. Listen, if we killed some Chinese, they weren't your parents! If we had done that, you would have had a reason for all this: it would have been the pain in your heart that forced you to kill me. You people should melt the blood that is frozen in your hearts. If you don't feel some compassion, you cannot be really Tibetan." Then the beating got even worse. The Chinese and Tibetans picked up Tenzin and Monlam and dragged them to the tent door, as an eagle drags a rabbit. Then they tied them upright again. Their hands were pulled up their backs toward their necks. The ropes were still so tight, they could not be seen inside their flesh.

"You two father's dead body eaters!" the Tibetan said. "Pretending to be brave men, are you?" Then he smashed the stick into their mouths and broke their teeth. Uncle Monlam seemed to be unconscious. Tenzin continued to berate them, but a little later he blacked out, too. You could see that he and

Monlam were still alive because their bodies moved when they breathed. The torturers rested for a while and then ran over to Lochu.

"Hey, old man!" the Tibetan said. "You saw everything, right? If you don't want to die, tell the truth. Who is your chief? If you don't tell us, we will send you to hell before you die!"

"I told you already. The chief's dead," Lochu said.

"That man was nothing more than a worn-out robe," the torturer replied. "He didn't even have a pistol. Were you the chief, you eater of both your parents' bodies? You need to tell us the truth." He whipped him across his head.

"Drown your dead head in blood!" Lochu yelled. "You shit-eaters! If you want to eat your parents' dead bodies, you have them already. So, yes, I'm the chief. So what do you want to do? Kill everyone?" The Tibetans and Chinese beat the old man nearly to death after they heard that. Kelsang jumped up and tried to stop one of the Tibetans.

"Your dead head turn into blood!" he shouted. "If you want to kill someone, then kill me! Do you have even the tiniest bit of compassion for that poor old man? You despicable dog! Kill me now!" Tsekho stood up and held on to Kelsang. A Chinese man struck Kelsang's head with his whip until he bled. When the Tibetan joined in, beating Kelsang, Dragpa stood up and tried to stop him.

"Don't beat children!" he shouted. "If your heart is in pain, you can beat me." The Tibetan man whipped Dragpa a few times. Then two Tibetans carrying guns entered the tent.

"What happened?" they sneered. "Is this pathetic one fighting back?"

"No," Dragpa said. "When the son protests because his father is beaten, is that fighting back?" Then one of the gunmen asked Tsekho, Dongtrug, and Jabey in turn who their chief had been.

"The chief was my father," Jabey said. After he had beaten everyone around the head with his whip two or three times, the gunman came to me.

"Did you see that?" he asked. "People who don't tell the truth are going to be beaten to death."

"Yes, I did," I replied.

"Who was the chief?"

"My father was the chief," I answered. "The Chinese troops have killed him already."

"It wasn't your father," he said. He pointed toward Lochu with his whip, saying, "Is it the old man?"

"That old man is a ferryman, not the chief," I told him. "The chief was my father." He pointed to Tenzin.

"Was it him?" he asked.

"He's a monk. He's not the chief," I said.

"You little father's corpse-eating refugee!" he shouted. "This one's a devil." He pulled my ear, and Jabey stood up and tried to protect my head with his arms.

"If you want to eat a father's dead body, you can eat it," he said, "but don't beat children." The man attacked Jabey, beating him until the Chinese man stopped him.

"If you want to eat your father's dead body, then go ahead!" I shrieked. "Your face is turning into a devil's."

"Hey, even this kid is fighting back!" he said. He raised his whip to hit me.

"Your face is turning into a devil's. Beat me! Beat me now!" I yelled. But a Tibetan standing next to him stopped him, looked me in the eye, and said a lot of things in Chinese. Then all the Tibetan and Chinese torturers left the tent. Two women came into the tent, bringing tsampa and tea. Dragpa, Tsekho, and Kelsang went over to Lochu, Tenzin, and Monlam and sat them up, loosening their bonds. They could not use their hands after being tied up so long, so the women mixed the tsampa for them. Dragpa, Tsekho, and Kelsang helped them to eat. When the light began to fail, some Tibetans and Chinese came in and tied them up again. They put black yak hair carpets on the ground and told us to sleep there. I could not sleep at all, and the beatings I had seen filled my mind. I thought, "If Father hadn't been killed, they would have beaten him to death today anyway."

"Aren't you asleep?" Jabey said.

"I miss our father," I answered. "They would have beaten him to death today. I'm glad he was shot dead instead of that."

"It would have been even worse for him," Jabey said. "They beat them enough today, but what would they have done to Father if they had found out that he was the chief and had killed so many Chinese soldiers? The Chinese commander said that the man on the mountaintop who killed all those Chinese troops must be the chief. And he had a pistol, too. Imagine what they would have done to him if he had fallen into their hands. It was better to be shot dead. And if Father had got away, we would have worried ourselves sick about him, and he would have been horribly worried about us. It is for the best that he did not live to suffer what happened today. But now we have nobody left to worry about except for each other." I totally agreed with him.

"Death would have come to him sooner or later anyway," I said. "It is better that we did not have to see him suffer. If you and I were separated, we would worry about each other, but now we can relax. If I don't die of anger, I'll survive, because I don't think the Chinese will kill me. If it's my karma, I will find a way out of here."

"When our father died without much suffering, it eased my fears—let us pray for the same when we are both adults and our time comes to die." Jabey had changed his mind since yesterday. Having witnessed the torture, he wasn't so concerned about his own safety anymore.

"We'll both be fine now. When we're grown up, we will return to our native land," he told me. We lay there trying to comfort each other. I don't remember when I fell asleep.

54

Sticking with Our Companions. Sent to Prison.

Dawn broke, and the sun rose. Two women brought tea and tsampa. I recognized one of them as the woman who had mended my robe the day before. She took Jabey, Dongtrug, and me out of the Chinese tent and into the tent where we had eaten the previous evening. We ate tsampa and yogurt.

"It's so sad that their father was killed by the Chinese," the woman said. "What will become of them now?" She began to cry. There were some other women in the tent with us, and tears were falling from their eyes, too. The woman said, "You two boys are invited to stay in our home. Is that all right with you? My father and husband and many others were arrested by the Chinese. Only my mother and I are left now. You could live with us just like my own sons."

"We don't want to stay here because we are returning to our native land with our companions."

"The Chinese army isn't going to set your companions free," she replied. "If you live with us, then when you are grown up you can return to your native land."

"We won't stay here," Jabey said. "We will go with our companions wherever they go." But I thought to myself, "Three Precious Jewels bear witness! What a good heart this woman has. If we didn't have our companions with us, we would definitely stay with her family. It is very hard for her that her father, husband, and clansmen have been arrested." The woman made more tsampa and pressed it into our bowls, telling us that we could eat it on our journey. Then a Tibetan soldier came and took the three of us to where the horses were tethered. Two Chinese and more Tibetan troops arrived. They put Tenzin and the other older ones on horseback with their hands tied behind their backs, and Dongtrug, Kelsang, and Tsekho were told to lead them, with Jabey leading my horse. When the strong wind blew snow into the air, we almost became separated, but eventually we arrived at a large encampment. People came out of their tents to see us and especially clustered around Jabey and me.

"They have arrested a little child!" they exclaimed. "These are all young monks!" "They must have been refugees on their way to Lhasa." Everybody said something like that. I realized that most of the people around us were children, old men, and old women.

"What a pity!" an old man said. "No, these are not refugees. They are monks who were on pilgrimage to Lhasa, but now they have nothing." We youngest ones were taken into a large tent, and our older companions somewhere else. There were three big copper pots on a huge hearth in the center of that tent. A woman gave us soup, and another woman made tsampa for us in a big copper ladle and put it into our robes. A man with a long mustache came in.

"Why are they here?" he asked. "They are both children." Then he stroked my head and said, "How sad. These must be the two whose father was killed. What is your name?"

"My name is Nukho," I replied.

"How old are you?" he asked.

"I'm ten," I said.

"Then you two can stay here," he told us. "I am a teacher, and I have a school here. My students are all children whose parents have been arrested. They eat here, and the Chinese officials have already agreed that you can stay."

"I don't want to stay in this school," I said. "We are going back to our native land with our companions."

"We don't want to stay at school either," the others said. "We want to go to our native land together."

"Your companions have killed many Chinese soldiers," the teacher said, "and they will not be let out of prison. If you stay at school here, you won't have to live in prison. It will be better for you."

"If they have to go to prison," Dongtrug said, "we will go with them."

"It would be good to stay here," Kelsang said, "but it could be that they are just trying to trick us into staying here while they take our companions away." The woman saw that we were worried.

"It's still snowing," she told us. "They won't leave without you. Just eat your meal." We ignored this and went outside to look around. It was snowing. We looked down the hill and saw the Chinese and Tibetan horses tied up in the yak pen.

"Where are our companions?" Kelsang asked a child.

"They are under guard in the Chinese tent," the child replied.

"Yes," the teacher said, "they're not going any farther today." That night we slept in the tent with the enormous hearth.

The next day we had our breakfast and got ready to leave, but then the teacher and some girl students appeared.

"Children, you aren't allowed to travel with your friends today," they said. "You need to stay with us." A Tibetan soldier arrived carrying a gun.

"Yes, you lot!" he said. "You can't go with us, you'll have to stay in the school. Otherwise, you'd have to go to prison."

"That's fine. Prison is no problem," Jabey said. "We don't want to stay in the school. We'll stick with our own people."

"No, my little man," the Tibetan soldier said. "You're staying here."

"I won't stay here," I said. "I want to go to my native land with my own people." Later on a Chinese man came, and they had a long conversation. Then the soldiers took us away and we traveled with them as usual. I thought, "We're going to prison today and we'll all become prisoners, but whatever happens, we are nine people together, and alive, and not separated. My only sadness is that three of us are dead." Later I thought, "They are no longer suffering and have found peace. That's the difference between us, just two days since karma separated us by death."

At midnight, we arrived on a pasture where some black yak hair tents and some white tents were pitched. After we dismounted, armed Tibetans escorted us to the door of a big tent where they untied everyone's ropes before leading us in. Inside the tent it was so dark we couldn't see. We could feel that there were a lot of people sleeping on the ground, so we found a clear space and lay down to sleep, resting against each other's bodies for warmth. In my mind I heard the words "Today you have become a prisoner." I remembered the teacher's words, "Your companions have killed many Chinese troops, and they will not be let out of prison." Then I thought, "Are that woman's father, husband, and clan members here?" I could not sleep because of the thoughts that filled my head, and I could hear Chinese people talking behind the tent. In the morning when the sun came out, I had a big surprise. There were about a hundred people sleeping, lying down in every direction. Later they opened the tent door and ordered us outside. I had not been able to see clearly the night before, but in the daylight I could see that there were about ten tents divided into groups—four of them were being used to hold prisoners. Beyond these were the tents housing the Chinese troops. There were about fifty Chinese soldiers in uniform, and some official workers and translators. After the prisoners had used the latrine, they were told to sit on the ground with their robes untied. There were about 60 female prisoners and 150 male. Some of the men were monks, and some wore lamas' yellow jackets. Looking carefully at them, I guessed that they were Alaks. The Chinese troops surrounded us, holding guns. Later they escorted all the female prisoners into one tent. The women's robes were still untied.

"I hope these Chinese people die of the plague—they are devils," one of the men near us snarled. "They have arrested nearly all of our clan—lamas, monks, and laymen—and almost all of the women, too!"

"Our clan didn't surrender to the Chinese right away," another said, "so after we surrendered they sent us here."

"We're really done for now," another man said. "We have no horses to ride, no guns to fight with, and the Chinese can do whatever they want with us. And if they kill us, there's no one to take revenge."

"Did your chiefdom resist the Chinese army?" Tenzin asked.

"We fought with dead people's bodies,"[1] an old man replied. "The chief of the Wujud surrendered right away to the Chinese and gave them all our bullets and guns."

"The chiefs are paid one hundred Chinese white silver coins a month," another man said. "They're happy enough, but after those chiefs surrendered, they tricked everyone in our area into being arrested. Our chiefdom was very strong before the surrender, and if we'd fought with the Chinese, we might have won. Whatever the outcome, we shouldn't have just given up." Tears rolled down his cheeks. I thought, "This really is tragic. The Wujud chiefdom used to be very strong, and on pilgrimage to Lhasa we had called them the 'Wujud enemy.' Now they have no strong and brave men left. All of their people are in prison, telling each other sad stories. Above all, this chiefdom didn't even fight against the Chinese. They surrendered immediately, so then why were they all arrested later?" That was really difficult to understand.

55

My Fellow Prisoner Lama Wula and Kindhearted Ragshe Jadog.

The prisoners were telling each other stories about the families they had left behind. Tenzin and Lochu told them about when we ran into Chinese troops, fought with them, and killed them. I felt a bit hungry, so I took a piece of tsampa from inside my robe and gave a little to Jabey.

"I've still got some," he said. "You eat it, but don't eat too much." I went ahead and ate it.

"What a wonderful smell," the people around me said. "It smells like tsampa! Who's got tsampa?"

"Little boy, please give me a little," an old man with white hair said, holding out his hand. It made me feel uncomfortable, but I took a mouthful-sized piece of tsampa out of my bowl and put it into his hand.

"You kind boy!" he said. "May you have a long life! I am an old man, and

---

1. Meaning that no one fought.

I have been here for about twenty days, but I haven't had so much as a sniff of tsampa all that time. It's making me feel giddy!" He kneaded the tsampa in his hand and touched it on his neck and head. He broke off a piece and gave it to another old man near him, saying, "Hey, put some on your neck and back. It will stop you from feeling angry and giving yourself a disease of the heart." He still had a bit left, so he held it in his hand and sniffed it occasionally. I thought, "It's sad that they don't want to eat it because it's too precious." I wanted to give him a bit more, but then there wouldn't have been enough for me. That night Jabey also gave a mouthful of tsampa to the old man. The man said, "May you have a long life! Now I don't need anymore. It's more important for you two to have some." He did the same as before and showed it to the people around him, touching their mouths and faces with it.

"Thank you so much!" a man sitting nearby said. "It makes you feel wonderful when you smell it, even if you don't eat it. That feeling is enough."

At noon the prisoners were all ordered out of the tent and told to sit down outside. Among them were two or three wearing yellow lamas' jackets. Tenzin asked one of his fellow prisoners who they were.

"That's Ganden Wula," he explained. "The old one beside him is called Sera Lama."

"Do you think it would be all right to approach him and ask him to offer dedication prayers with us?" Tenzin asked.

"Definitely," the old man said. "Let's go—I'll take you over and introduce you to him. Ganden Wula is respected by the Chinese. He'll be able to chant rituals—they'll let him." Tenzin, Monlam, Dragpa, and some others went over to Wola, and the Chinese guards didn't say anything. Later, Tenzin waved for us to join them, and Jabey and I went over.

"How young these two are!" His Holiness said. "Now, you boys mustn't worry. I have already made the dedication prayers for the arrival of death."

"Thank you, Alak," Jabey and I said, and we added many other formal courtesies.

"Alak," Tenzin said, "our adult companions are not going to be released from prison. You are well respected by the Chinese. We would like to place the two boys under Your Holiness's protection. Please don't forget to look after them."

"I don't have all that much respect from the Chinese," His Holiness said, "but I can take them with me when I leave in a few days. I will look after them and send them to school. If in the future you are released, you may come retrieve them from me. Don't worry about them."

We told him how grateful we were. "Well, that is a good outcome," Tenzin said. "Now we can go to our deaths without fear. You two follow Alak, and you won't go hungry." Jabey and I were relieved, too!

Suddenly the female prisoners started yelling, "Come and eat!" Everyone ran over to get soup from the pot, selfishly shoving each other out of the way. Each person ladeled the soup into his own bowl. I couldn't use my bowl because it still had a little tsampa in it, and the soup was soon all gone. Uncle Monlam and Jabey gave me some of their soup. Then an old man who was lame in one leg called me over to the cooking pot.

"Hey, child! Come here!" the old man shouted. I looked at Jabey.

"Go on, it's fine," he said. When I got over to the man, he poured some soup out of his big metal bowl into mine.

"Well, that was a black sadness! The soup was all finished by those greedy people, and my little boy didn't get any," he said. "Hey! You can help me cook from now on, can't you? Then I'll bring you food to eat."

"I'll be glad to help you cook," I said. "Thank you, Uncle!"

"I'm sad to see you in here." he said. "You are from somewhere in Golok aren't you? My name is Ragshe Jadog, and I'm one of the Chinese army's servants. Starting today, you are my servants, and you'll get your share of food." I took the soup over to Jabey and Monlam.

"This meat smells terrible! What kind of meat is it?" Lochu said.

"It does smell bad . . . it's pink," Tenzin said. "It must be wild ass meat." We drank the soup anyway.

Every morning and afternoon I helped the man make soup and tea for the prisoners. Sometimes Jabey and I collected firewood, and sometimes we helped Ragshe Jadog cut wolf meat into pieces.

"You two have some of the wolf meat," he would say each time. "Cook it over the embers, then eat it." But the wolf meat was so disgusting that I couldn't make myself eat it, except sometimes a few flakes of the dried meat from around the edges. The old man let Jabey and me wander wherever we pleased. At the morning and evening mealtimes, Jadog always kept back one big metal pail of soup for me.

One day he gave some cooked meat to Jabey and me and said, "It's so sad! My youngest son is the same age as you. I am going to die in prison, and I won't be able to see the faces of my people again before I die. Maybe you will meet them. Remember me to them—my name is Ragshe Jadog." His eyes were full of tears.

"Uncle," I questioned him, "why were you arrested?"

"They accused me of not liking the Chinese," he said.

"Did you ever kill any Chinese?" I asked.

"No, how could I? They took my gun away," he replied. Then he looked around carefully and murmured, "You wait and see. In two or three days I may be able to escape, after I have killed the Chinese guard."

Just then, Ganden Wula was sitting near the doorway of the tent. He waved me over, and I stood in front of him. He gave me a bowl of yogurt. I ate half of it and put the other half in my robe.

"Why did you do that?" His Holiness asked.

"I want to give the rest to Jabey," I said. His Holiness refilled my bowl.

Beside him was a man with no legs and long, matted black hair, singing songs as he wove cloth. He called to me: "Hey, little boy, come here! I'll help you mend your robe." I went over to him and took off my robe. "If your robe is full of holes like this," he said, "you will die of cold in the winter." He mended all the holes in my robe, front and back.

"Thank you very much, Uncle," I said. He touched his forehead onto mine.

"Shame on them!" he said. "How could these Chinese devils kill the father and, as if that wasn't enough, make prisoners of the children?" I thought to myself, "This is really harsh. Even if the Chinese think they need to arrest people who flee from them, like us, why arrest someone like this man with no legs who was sitting at home doing nothing?" I walked away with the sound of his weaving and his songs in my ears. Later I found that his name was Kherey Montsey. I can still hear his songs and see him moving along with his hands on the ground. I can't remember how many days I was a prisoner in the tent. The prisoners drank wolf soup with noodles and had very little meat or bones to eat. We were not beaten or physically attacked, and we lived quietly and calmly without anyone dying or becoming seriously ill. But every day many new male and female prisoners arrived.

"Most of the prisoners are from wealthy families," people said. I asked about my father's sworn friends among the Wujud chiefdom, Hordug Laglo the fingerless man, Kebang Chusem, and others.

"They were arrested a long time ago and taken to the county headquarters," people who knew them told me.

As long as my brother and I were together, I felt that I had nothing to worry about. Every day I collected firewood and helped Ragshe Jadog to make a fire and cook meals. We ate the meat he gave us and stayed near him.

One morning a large number of Chinese troops arrived. After breakfast the prisoners' hands were tied behind their backs, and they were roped together in groups of thirty, male and female prisoners separately. Kelsang and Dongtrug walked behind without their hands tied, but they were roped together by one wrist. I was put on a small black stallion with a yak saddle, and Jabey walked ahead on the lead rein. Among the prisoners I could see Ganden Wula, Sera Lama, and some other monks with their hands bound behind their backs. An officer came and spoke to us through a translator.

"Today you are all going to Chumarleb county headquarters," he informed us. "There you will study for two months. If you obey the rules, you have no reason to be afraid. After you have finished studying, you may return to your own native lands. No harm will come to you on the way to headquarters, but if anyone tries to escape, they will be killed."

About three hundred prisoners walked on foot through the dust and wind that morning to Chumarleb county headquarters. Sixty or so armed Chinese soldiers escorted them at the front, middle, and rear of the column. I thought, "I'm sad that Ragshe Jadog could not escape by killing that Chinese guard." Even though Ganden Wula was supposedly respected by the Chinese, that day he was roped up and driven with the others, his hands tied behind him.

56

A Torturer Faces the Consequences. A Terrible Lynching.

Through the red dust the prisoners walked, their heads bowed, roped together in lines of six. The Chinese troops and their Tibetan servants led the packhorses because the wind made it too cold to ride. Sometimes Jabey and I dismounted and led our horses for the same reason, but if the prisoners and their escorts walked very fast, we couldn't walk fast enough to keep up. At noon we reached an encampment where another group of prisoners had already finished their meal and were ready to go. A young man came over.

"You two, don't get left behind, all right?" he said. "If you do, the wolves will eat you." He led us into a black yak hair tent and gave us some food. The man told an old woman, "Mother, those monks who the Chinese hunted down in our area were the companions of these boys."

"What a pity," the old woman said. "I remember that! Are these the two boys whose father was killed?"

"Yes," he said. "They didn't let them stay in Wayan School, and now they are sending them to the county prison."

"May these Chinese die young!" the old woman snapped. "Why would they imprison children?"

When we finished our meal and left the tent, the Chinese troops and prisoners were already far away in the distance.

"Really," the old woman said to the young man, "you should help these boys to catch up with the others. Take them on the yak." The young man mounted the yak, put Jabey on the yak's rump, and led my horse. I thought, "What a lovely young man this is. Even though life is difficult for him and his family, they still want to take care of us." At the foot of a small hill we caught up with the main party.

"Don't get left behind! Hurry up!" the young man said.

"Which chiefdom do you belong to?" Jabey asked.

"I'm from Wayan chiefdom," he said. "My name is Tagpa!" And he turned his yak away toward home.

"Thank you so much!" we both shouted, then headed for the Chinese troops and their column of prisoners. That night we stopped again beside an encampment of families, all of us under guard beneath a black cliff near the river. Kelsang, Dongtrug, Jabey, and I went to herd the horses.

"It's so frustrating," Kelsang said. "We could escape from here if we stole some horses."

"You dead body!" Dongtrug said. "Where would you escape to? It is better to be with our companions, dead or alive." At sunset we went back to the encampment. All the prisoners and the local people were gathered in a large crowd, and Tenzin, Lochu, and Monlam were among them. We went over to sit with them, but they were roped together, with a lot of soldiers surrounding them, and there was no room. A little later the Chinese officer made a speech through a translator.

"Prisoners!" he said. "You have no need to be afraid. If you don't try to escape and you do as you are told, you will see your native lands again," which was exactly what he had said the day before.

"These hell-bound people," Lochu said. "They are just afraid that we would cause trouble if we knew what's really going to happen to us. How do we know we're going to be set free?"

"There's nothing we can do for now," Tenzin said. "We just have to go wherever they drive us."

"We're going to call out some names," the translator said. "If your name is called, you are to go into the cloth tent. If your name isn't called this time, you will go there tomorrow." He called out, "Lama Wula, Sera Lama, Ragshe Jadog, Thubjam, and Hordug, stand up and come over here." I thought, "That must be my father's sworn friend Hordug Laglo."

"Who is that Hordug?" I asked an old man beside me.

"He's the robber Hordug Laglo," he replied.

"Then do you know Keba Chusem?" I asked again. The old man looked at me curiously.

"Chusem was arrested by the Chinese and shot by a firing squad when he got to county headquarters. Why did you ask? Did you know him?"

"Well, I'd heard the name," I said.

"Whatever they say," another old man beside me muttered, "it doesn't make any difference that the Chinese supposedly respect Wula, Sera Lama, and the others. That's why Dubjyam and Jadog have been released."

"The worst of it," another said, "is that we know they're lying to us. We're never going to be released." He kept saying things like that. I thought, "Now

Ragshe Jadog doesn't need to kill a Chinese guard to escape. Luckily he's going to be let out."

"You two boys remember Ganden Wula, don't you?" Tenzin asked. "Be sure to find him after you are set free and follow his advice. He'll look after you." Two other soldiers drove a line of bound prisoners past us.

"Hey, Tenzin, Lochu, look at that prisoner at the end," Uncle Monlam said. "That's the one who beat us so badly after we were first taken prisoner."

"Yes, that's him," Kelsang said. "That hell-bound man! You watch what I do to him. I'll pay him back." Two soldiers escorted the prisoners past us, and suddenly someone knocked the torturer on the head with a rock and felled him. "You father's dead body eaters!" he snarled. "Who threw that rock?" After he turned away, I could see that his head was bleeding. When he saw us sitting there, he stared at us with a black look on his face and said, "Someone hit me with a stone." Nobody said anything.

Then Tenzin spoke up. "Keep your father's dead body," he whispered. "If you say another word, you'll be dead before you know it." The man sat on the ground, a line of blood trickling from the wound on his head.

"Three Precious Jewels bear witness!" Monlam hissed at him. "This is your reward. Now the torturer and the tortured will die in prison together." I was worried when I heard this because I knew the one who had hit him with the stone was Kelsang. Before that I hadn't thought he was going to die.

When the sun set, the prisoners were all driven into a corner of the cliff. They told Jabey, Dongtrug, Kelsang, and me to guard the horses and the Chinese baggage.

"Brother Kelsang," I asked, "did you hit that man with the stone?

"Yes, I did," he said. "How did you know?"

"Because everyone else's hands were tied except for Dongtrug's, yours, and mine," I answered. "We were the only two behind him, so if it wasn't you, then who was it?"

"I'm just sorry I didn't hit him harder," he said. "I'm going to kill him next time." Just then a young man carrying a gun came up to us.

"Hey, you Chugama people!" he said. "What's on your minds?" He sat down.

"Which chiefdom are you from?" Kelsang said.

"I'm from Amdo-Tsongunbo [Kokonor]," he said. "My name is Jigmed Dorjee. Is it all right for me to join you?"

"Are you a Chinese official worker?" Kelsang said.

"Definitely not! I'm just a servant working for the Chinese," he answered. "I recognize you from that day you refused to stay in the school. When you get to Chumarleb, though, there will be a school for you. You children have nothing to worry about."

"Brother Jigmed," Jabey asked him, "those people who arrived yesterday—where were they from?"

"You knew one of them, didn't you?" he said. "I know you hit him with a stone. I wouldn't do that again if I were you. The Chinese would not like it. Children aren't supposed to know anything." I fell asleep before he finished talking.

At dawn the next day it was snowing heavily. Later, two Tibetan soldiers came and put saddles on the horses.

"When are we going?" Kelsang asked.

"Last night the soldiers who were billeted in the family tents had their horses stolen," one of them said, "so maybe we won't be leaving today." Later more and more people came into the encampment, and we waited for a long time but didn't receive any orders for departure. Then a woman came and took the four of us into a tent. There were some Chinese soldiers sitting inside, but they immediately left.

"There's a meeting today. You're not allowed to go to it," the woman said. "I've got to go, but you're supposed to sit here."

"Why can't we go to the meeting?" Jabey asked. "What's going to happen?" She seemed terrified and at first made no reply.

Then she said, "I've heard that they're going to beat Ganden Wula, Sera Lama, and the other high lamas to death." I was staggered by this and couldn't believe that it was true. No one said anything, and we just continued eating in silence. She went out. Later we heard a lot of yelling coming from a nearby tent. We went out and looked. Chinese troops had surrounded the crowd of Tibetan nomads from the encampment where we were staying. One of the Tibetans was shouting, "Today . . . today . . . ," but we couldn't hear anything else. Then one of the Chinese soldiers brought Ganden Wula and five others out of the tent. They moved through the crowd with difficulty because people were jammed so close together. A Chinese person shouted something, and those near him turned to Ganden Wula and the others and started to pull them this way and that, the way a vulture does to a dead body. Some tried to pull them up, while others punched and kicked them to the ground, screaming, yelling, and jumping on top of them with their boots, as though they were doing a traditional Tibetan dance. We could see all this from on top of the cliff. After a few minutes, some Chinese soldiers went over and stopped the beating. None of those beaten could stand up, and they lay still as though already dead. Lama Wula's clothes had all been torn off, and he was covering his groin with his hands.

Whether from terror, or grief, or amazement, I was numb, thunderstruck. Though I saw it all clearly, I could not believe the evidence of my own eyes. Thoughts raced through my mind, like, "A mouth filled with ash! What was this for? If Father hadn't been killed, is this what would have happened to him? What law justified this killing?"

57

The Emptiness of Betrayal. A Savage Murder.

The old saying is true. "As floodwaters cannot stop rushing, people cannot hold back their passions." A woman made a speech, and then everyone ran forward again, yelling. They punched, stamped on, and kicked Ganden Wula and the others. They thrashed them like leather and tore them to pieces like stems of ginger. Then the Chinese and local troops ran forward again and stopped the beating. Our companion of last night, Jigmed, came to us and said, "Let's go over there where we can see." We went closer. There were many people standing in a circle around the bodies. Sera Lama's upper body was naked, and he had been thrown to the ground, his body bent and broken. He was dead. Then one of the Chinese people shouted something.

"You cannot just kill without a reason," the translator announced. "First you need to state what someone's faults are and why they deserve to die. After you've done that, you can beat them." A woman with wild matted hair put her foot on Sera Lama's head.

"Maybe this exploiter is already dead," she shouted. "Since he ate people's flesh and drank their blood, today we should destroy him and root him out." She stamped on Sera Lama's head with her boot.

"We're going to beat these flesh-eating wolves today, aren't we?" a man called to the crowd.

"We will beat them!" the crowd shouted back.

"Today they are going to pay for flesh with flesh and blood with blood, aren't they?" shouted the man.

"Yes, we will make them pay for it, pay us back! We're going to destroy them!" they yelled, and everyone surged forward, dancing and jumping on top of the bodies. The Chinese man spoke again, but the crowd wasn't listening any more, just beating and tearing at the bodies. I thought, "They are already dead. What a savage, unfeeling place this must be to produce people who would attack their chief lama. Is there anywhere else in the world where they kill like this? This chiefdom will surely suffer consequences for what they have done."

"They are all dead now. They're dragging the bodies away," Dongtrug said. People were pulling the bodies toward a cliff. The rest of the crowd followed them, yelling and shouting. They dumped the bodies over the edge of the cliff, down onto the rocks in the river below. They lay there in a heap. The crowd began to return to the meeting place, still yelling things. Jabey pointed to the pile of bodies.

"One of them is still alive," he said. We saw Ragshe Jadog's head and feet move.

"The precious jewel Ragshe Jadog's still alive!" someone said. Then a woman from the crowd who was still at the edge of the cliff screamed, "Ragshe Jadog isn't dead yet!" The crowd scrambled down the cliff and started stamping and dancing again, attacking Ragshe Jadog like vultures eating the flesh of a dead body at a sky burial. The sound was very loud. I thought, "What bad karma this man had. When he came to, he should have pretended to be dead. Why did he raise his head up at that moment? Ragshe Jadog, my friend in this chiefdom, a kind old man who gave me food—they have killed him for sure." The fact that impressed me most was that everybody had told me how much the Chinese respected Lama Ganden Wula, but today he had been beaten to death. Not only had he not been able to look after my brother and me; he had not even been able to save his own life. The Three Precious Jewels bear witness! We must all die, but to die the way these people did is like going to hell while still alive. It was a terrible way to die. All of us have a different death according to our karma, and this is something we cannot choose or alter. My father died from bullet wounds, and that seemed like a good way to die. Now I realized why the woman told us we could not go to the meeting place this morning. I hoped my eyes would never see something like that again.

But I continued to observe the scene. The crowd had left, and the heap of bodies, blackened by bruises, lay at the bottom of the cliff. Some children stood at the top of the cliff, throwing stones at the bodies, and dogs circled hungrily.

"This is a terrible, cruel clan—they killed those people so viciously," Kelsang said when we got inside the tent.

"It wasn't this clan's fault," Dongtrug said. "The Chinese troops forced them to do it!" I asked, "Dongtrug, do you think people in our native land are doing things like this?" He said, "It's very possible." I thought, "In that case it's better to be far away. If our chiefdom was told to kill our own head lama and chief by beating them to death, I could not bear to see that." Then a woman came with our food. She talked a lot about what had happened that day. That night, I dreamed over and over about the beating, and I could hardly sleep.

The sun rose on another day. The prisoners all went to the door of the tent and were given food.

"Yesterday they only gave us breakfast," Tsekho said. "May the faces of those people turn to blood! We are faint from hunger." After our meal I led my horse to the foot of the cliff. Dogs and crows were feeding on the bodies of those slaughtered so savagely the day before. "I thought, "How sad it is that these people have no one to care for their bodies. If our own lamas and our own chief are being eaten by dogs in their own land, then how can manis be chanted? How can the religion be practiced there?" Then Jabey ran over.

"Nukho," he shouted "it's time to go!" When I got back to the doorway of the tent, I heard shouting and saw soldiers running in that direction. Although I couldn't be sure, it looked as though some prisoners had been fighting and then soldiers broke it up. We found out later what had happened: Tenzin attacked the man who had arrived yesterday. Tsekho came over to us.

"Tenzin finished off that man," he said. "He smashed him in the forehead with a bowl and the man fell down. When he tried to get up, Tenzin hit him again and cut his eyebrow. No one knew the real reason Tenzin did it, and the soldiers just said, 'Stop fighting you two.' The man's head was covered in blood, but the troops paid no attention." We were all very happy when we heard that. I thought, "That's giving him what he deserves."

The prisoners trudged on through the snow. There were many rivers and streams, large and small, to cross that day, most of them frozen already. Dongtrug, Jabey, Kelsang, and I journeyed together and weren't under guard, so we walked slowly behind the others. Lochu, Tenzin, and three others were lashed together in the last group. Sometimes we were able to talk to them as they walked. Once we heard some gunshots from the direction of the leading group of prisoners and saw the middle group, who were all women, sit down on the ground. Chinese soldiers ran toward the front. They told us to stay where we were and sit down, too. There were more shots, and more troops running past, and the soldiers came back and tied all the prisoners together with ropes. They even took Kelsang and Dongtrug away and tied them together, but they left Jabey and me alone. Then the translator shouted to all the prisoners, "Keep moving on peacefully. If you try to escape or resist, we will kill you." The prisoners stood up and kept walking. A little ways on, we reached two soldiers sitting on a high bank next to the road. One soldier was lying there dead, with a white cloth covering him, and nearby another soldier was dressing the head wound of a third one. On the other side of the road, farther down the slope, two prisoners' bodies sprawled, and higher up the mountain was the corpse of another. That must have been why we heard so many gunshots. I thought, "Those poor prisoners. They were crazy to think that they could escape on foot with so many soldiers nearby. Maybe a devil deceived their hearts." That night we stayed near another encampment of families. Before sunset the prisoners were given something to eat.

"The people who tried to escape today didn't come from our chiefdom," an old man told us. "They were from Golok. They had knives hidden inside their robes and used them to cut their ropes and attack the Chinese guards. They managed to kill two of them and seize their guns. They shot at the other Chinese soldiers but missed, and then the soldiers killed them. Some of them were old men; it's sad that they couldn't get away." When I heard that, I thought, "What brave people the Goloks are. How did they think of that plan? What a pity they didn't win their fight against the Chinese. Now there are dead bodies without anyone to care for them—more dead bodies to be eaten by dogs and wolves. The law of karma is unpredictable and very hard. Whatever we do, karma calls us to death when we must die, and nothing can avoid it. However, those people who died today died well compared with those who were so cruelly murdered by their own clansmen. Their souls cannot have found peace. At least those who died today had the satisfaction of killing two soldiers and wounding another."

58

The Old Man Is Sent to the Sukhavati Paradise of the Buddha Amitabha. We Are Thrown into a Hole.

It was the sixteenth of November 1958. We assembled after breakfast that morning. One of the Chinese officers addressed us through a translator.

"Today we will arrive at Chumar county headquarters," he told us. "Everybody should walk calmly and steadily. If anyone tries to escape or resist, we will kill them." The prisoners were roped together again. When we reached a high mountain pass, one young woman, another woman, and an old man lagged behind. It looked as though the young woman was sick or in pain. She would walk for a short distance and then sit on the ground. When she got near Jabey and me, we were not riding our horse because it was so cold.

"Nukho," Jabey asked, "shall we let the sick woman ride your horse for a while? Would that be all right?" I led my horse up to the woman.

"Aunt, this is my horse," I said. "You can ride it if you like."

"Oh, I couldn't do that," she said. "I wish you a long life!"

"It's OK," I replied. "The Chinese soldiers lent this horse to me." I gave my horse's reins to her.

The sick woman rode the horse, her friend led it, and we walked along together. Later we heard a noise from the prisoners at the back of the column. When we got there, an old man was sitting on the ground. Since the prisoners were all roped together, if one of them couldn't walk, all of them had to stop. Two soldiers came and kicked the old man, shouting at him to go on.

"You can kill me now!" the old man said. "I can't keep walking, even to save my life." The soldiers kicked him again and beat him with the butts of their rifles. The old man stood up and said something we couldn't hear. A little later he sat down again.

"You'd better kill me," he said. "I can't walk at all." He lay down on the ground. The Chinese troops untied him and led him away from the other prisoners, who kept walking. We watched them for a while, but then they said something in Chinese and waved at us to keep going. We had not walked far before we heard a single gunshot from behind us. I looked back but couldn't see anything. A Chinese soldier came and took the sick woman's friend away and tied her to the other prisoners. The sick woman rode my horse, and I led it. A little while later, the two soldiers who had beaten the old man showed up again, but there was no sign of the old man himself. It was obvious what had happened. I thought to myself, "One bullet, and he's gone to the Sukhavati paradise of the Buddha Amitabha. Again, there is no one to care for the body. It has just been abandoned back there."

At noon the prisoners came to a big river. We were told to stop near a wall of carved mani stones called "Wuchen Dokha." Two local Tibetan soldiers arrived soon thereafter with the body of a dead Chinese soldier on a horse. They stopped the horse so that they could tie the body on more securely. They gave me the bridle to hold, and I stood there while they worked.

"Uncle, did you see an old man coming from back there?" I asked one of them, when I thought no one could overhear us. He looked around nervously.

"You idiot baby devil!" he said. "Shut up, or the Chinese troops will hear you. They killed him." Then he went away.

"My lovely baby boy," the sick woman said, "don't mention that again, or the Chinese will beat you." We stayed by the river, with nothing to eat, until darkness fell. When the moon rose, the prisoners at the head set off, and we followed. Ahead of us, some Chinese soldiers were standing in a group, discussing something. Suddenly the translator shouted, "Come on! You've got to walk faster! Faster! Come on!" The moon was very bright. We kept going, with me riding and Jabey leading my horse. The sick woman and another woman walked behind us. The sick woman came up to me.

"Little boy, are you hungry?" she asked.

"Not much," I answered. She put something long in my hand.

"Eat this, OK?" she said.

"Thank you, Aunt."

"Hush," she said, squeezing my hand. Later I had a stealthy look at what she'd handed me. It was a small dried sausage about the length of a hand. I gave half to Jabey, and we ate it. It was a bit salty but really delicious.

Later there was an announcement in Tibetan.

"When we get to the county town, you're not allowed to speak." We walked on until we reached a town consisting of many white tents and houses. The prisoners were directed down the middle of the road, and we walked between rows of white houses that stood out clearly in the bright moonlight. Even though there were many prisoners, we were very quiet. We could hear nothing but the sound of our own footsteps. Then we walked through a tall gate with high walls on either side. Since the prisoners were tied together in rows of six, it was difficult to squeeze through the gate, and people had to shove against each other to get in. Soldiers ran over and beat the prisoners with the butts of their rifles, driving them cruelly through the gate. Jabey and I were crushed in line between Monlam and Tenzin. After we made it through the gate, there was a tall wall in front of us. In the moonlight I could see guards walking around on top of the wall carrying torches, which they played over the heads of the prisoners. As people arrived, their robes were untied, and our sashes, belts, and bootlaces were taken away. The prisoners returned to their places with untied, flapping robes and boots. I watched carefully. The troops were taking the prisoners forward line by line, but when they approached the center of the wall they seemed to disappear.

Another group went forward, but when it reached the center of the wall, it too disappeared! In the distance I could see the wall clearly in the moonlight, but as soon as the prisoners got there they completely vanished. Soldiers came over, cut thirty more prisoners away from the main column, and took them over to the wall. Among them were Jabey and Monlam, with me following a bit behind.

"Jabey," I called out, and caught up with him. A Chinese soldier grabbed my ear and pulled me back.

"It's all right. I'll look after you, Nukho," Tenzin muttered from just behind me. Jabey and Monlam were driven ahead, away from us. I fixed my eyes on them, but when their group reached the wall, they disappeared, just like the others. No matter how hard I stared, I could not see any of the prisoners up there. The troops drove another thirty forward. This time I was part of the group. When we reached the middle of the wall, a Chinese soldier pulled a trapdoor up from the ground. It covered a deep hole. A terrible smell rose from the darkness. Soldiers ordered the prisoners to jump down into the darkness, and I could hear them landing on the ground at the bottom. From inside the hole I could hear people crying in pain, "Ara . . . ara . . ." I got to the hole.

"Hey, you!" a soldier, who spoke Tibetan, shouted to someone. "Help me with this one." Then he grabbed me by the waist and pointed me down into the opening.

"How terrible, it's a child!" someone said from below, and he reached his arms up to carry me down into the hole. The stink of unwashed bodies, urine, and feces was so strong that it was difficult to breathe. People already there were sleeping noisily. We had arrived last, so there was nowhere to sleep or even to stand comfortably. We kept treading on people's heads, and they would cry out, "Ara . . . stop . . . That hurt me!" That happened again and again as we tried to find a place where we could rest. I thought to myself, "Now we are in Chumarleb county prison, but this isn't a prison. It's a storage hole for people."

That night I couldn't sleep at all. The noises of people sleep-talking, snoring, farting, and grinding their teeth filled my ears. The nauseating smell filled my nose. I thought, "What kind of place is this? There are so many people down here! What the old people in Madey Chugama feared about the insects' hole that they'd be thrown into by the Chinese has come true, except the Chinese have mixed prisoners and children in with the old people, and thrown us all into the hole. How many insects are here in this hole? What do they eat? And what happened to Jabey? Will I find him again?" The press of bodies meant that it was very hot in the hole, and sweat poured down my face. Sometimes I came close to fainting—instead, I retched. Inside the hole there was no day or night. Looking up, I could see a tiny light, and I guessed that must be the trapdoor, but the light wasn't strong enough to see anything at all at the bottom of this pit, or have any idea how many people were there. Eventually the trapdoor opened, and I could see across the hole for the first time. It was not wide, perhaps wide enough to allow eight or nine people to sit side by side, but long enough to allow maybe 50 people to sit in the same way. There were about 360 prisoners jammed in there, and in the center there were three wooden pails for the prisoners to defecate and urinate in. Some people had defecated inside the pails, but others had missed the target. A Chinese man lowered a metal ladder through the trapdoor opening and walked down a few steps before calling out each person's name. When he called their names, the prisoners had to shout out their number, which was printed on a white cloth pinned to their breasts. Most people did not know enough Chinese to say the numbers.

"I'm here," they said.

"This man is dead," others called. That morning in our hole there were two dead people among the prisoners.

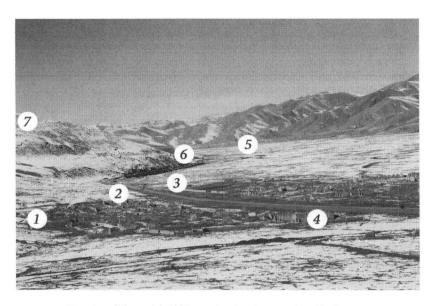

Remains of Chumarleb Old Town, showing sites mentioned in the text.
Key: 1. Underground jail; 2. House where Nulo and Japey stayed after release;
3. Army barracks; 4. Government school; 5. First site of "Joyful Home";
6. Second site of "Joyful Home"; 7. Grazing commune.
Courtesy of the C. V. Starr East Asian Library, Columbia University in the City of New York.

59

Prisoner 3299. Meeting a Friend from My Native Land.

The Chinese man was still calling out prisoners' names from the ladder. One of the prisoners next to us understood Chinese and helped nearby prisoners to read out the numbers in Chinese when their names were called. After everyone's names were called, the pails containing the prisoners' feces and urine were taken out of the hole. Some people were ordered to leave the hole, and we were told to lift the dead bodies out. Finally, two Chinese people and a translator climbed down into the hole and lined up the newly arrived prisoners from last night. Each of us had a white cloth with red numbers pinned to our chest, and we were ordered out of the hole one by one. When I got into the open air, I was surprised to see that the yard was filled with hundreds of prisoners. Some of them were lining up, ready to leave the yard, and some of them were sitting inside the wall. There were many Chinese soldiers walking around on top of the wall. We were ordered out of the west door, which was close to a steep mountainside. There was a latrine dug out of the earth at the foot of the slope. Men and women formed two lines. As soon as we squatted over the latrine pit, the Chinese civilians who were monitoring the prisoners at the latrine and the Chinese guards farther off started throwing stones and earth at us with all their might, so we had no time to defecate or urinate but stood up quickly and hurried back. We lined up and went back through the wall. When I arrived at the gate, I saw Jabey and Monlam on their way out.

"Brother! Brother Jabey!" I shouted. He laughed and looked my way. Then Tenzin pushed me in the back.

"Run over to your brother," he said. I almost reached him, but a guard grabbed my ear and pulled me back, saying indecipherable things in Chinese. Monlam said, "It's all right. Stay with Tenzin. You two will meet up soon."

I went into the hole with Tenzin without any idea if or when we would meet the others again. The two dead bodies were still lying near the entrance of the trapdoor. Looking around, I could see other holes, and they seemed to have dead bodies lying close to them too, but I wasn't close enough to see them clearly. There was a rumor that these people had killed themselves.

Later the prisoners were fed. Each prisoner was given two steamed bread rolls and a bowl of rice soup. I could not eat all of it and gave one of the rolls to Tenzin. Looking around, it seemed that the older people had not had enough to eat. It was good food compared with what we'd been given in the black yak hair tent. Then the trapdoor slammed shut loudly. All the prisoners began talking. They talked about their lost happiness and about death. They spoke of the parents, husbands, wives, and children left behind in their native land. They could not stop talking about their grief.

Tenzin and I were sitting beside the young man who understood Chinese.

"I used to work for the Chinese," he said. "Then they accused us of planning to rebel against them, and five of our workers were arrested. The Chinese have given me a twenty-year sentence, so I'll probably die in prison. My name is Damba Tsering from the Chumar Ratsang chiefdom. My mother and sister are both living in Chumarleb, near the Chinese barracks."

That afternoon, near sunset, the trapdoor opened again, and we came out of the hole again to go to the latrine. I saw Jabey in the line. He waved to me. A little farther on, our lines came closer together, and I ran over to him. He took steamed bread from his robe and gave it to me.

"Every prisoner was given two bread rolls this morning," I told him.

"The man who gave us our bread was a Tibetan, and he gave me three rolls," he said. The guard who had caught me that morning was still there, and he made me go back and stand next to Tenzin. They threw stones and turf at us again while we were in the latrine. By the time we got back to the hole, it was already dark. They gave two bowls of flour soup to each prisoner. People had different kinds of bowls and so got different amounts. Tenzin had a big metal bowl, and if they filled it with soup twice, that was more than enough for him, and he would share it with those on either side of him. I had a little wooden bowl, so that even two bowls of soup were not enough for me. Most of the prisoners' bowls were small. After soup time, it seemed as if they hadn't gotten enough to fill their bellies. As darkness fell, we stacked our bowls in the center of the hole, and the smell of urine and feces intensified. That ended my first day as a prisoner in Chumarleb county prison. I will never forget it, and it still often comes to my mind.

The next day at dawn the trapdoor opened and a Chinese man climbed down the ladder to do the roll call. Most of the prisoners said, "Yes, I'm here," but a few of them said nothing. I thought, "More people have died."

"Nukho," the Chinese man called, and Danba Tserang read out the numbers on my chest in Chinese. I have never forgotten those numbers. "San qian, er bai, jiu shi jiu!" was ringing in my ears all the time. Sometimes I tried to read out my numbers myself, "San qian, er bai, jiu shi jiu!" but the Chinese man just laughed at me. Later we went to the latrine, and then we were fed. That day, two Tibetans came to give us food.

"I can't believe it! Are you Dragpa?" Tenzin said to one of them.

"Keep it down," the man said and waved Tenzin closer.

"Tsampa from Monlam and Jabey!" he said. "All of your people are fine. Take it, you two," and he gave us some steamed bread and a small bag of tsampa.

"Jabey and this one are the Naktsang old man's sons," Tenzin whispered to him. "The old man's dead. Their future depends on you. Great father's son, I leave them to your care. Please look after these boys." Dragpa was called away and left through the trapdoor.

"Nukho," Tenzin said, "don't forget this man. He is a monk, and Alak Gungtang's trusted servant. He will definitely take care of you both." From then on Dragpa brought us food every morning and afternoon: tsampa and four or five pieces of bread. We never went hungry.

One time the Chinese door guard, who was a prisoner too, hit me and pulled my ears painfully as we returned from the latrine. Danpa Tserang argued with him in Chinese, and the guard slapped him. Danpa Tserang swung at the man but unfortunately missed. Then Tenzin punched the man in the nose, and he dropped. Danpa ran at him and kicked him several times.

"Kill that man!" the men and women by the wall shouted. "Give him what's coming to him!" "Kick him to hell!"

"Eat your father's corpse! That's not enough for him!" an old man standing near us yelled as he kicked the guard in the face. The man's nose and mouth were pouring blood.

He was crying, and yelling, "Ayo! Ayo!" Some Chinese soldiers came and drove us back behind the wall, but no one else protected him. Not long after we were back inside the hole, five soldiers with guns at the ready climbed down. The translator was with them.

"Sit down in your places," he said. "If anyone moves, you'll be shot dead." When the soldiers got to Tenzin and Danba, they didn't say a word but attacked them with the butts of their rifles. Blood trickled from a wound on Tenzin's head. Danpa Tserang pointed to me and spoke to them in Chinese.

"Did the guard beat you?" the translator asked me.

"Yes, he punched me and pulled my ears," I answered. "Everybody saw it!" The troops handcuffed Tenzin and Danpa, then left. Another soldier, who looked like an officer, led me out of the hole ungently. But then he said something to me, stroking my hair.

"Go through that little door over there" the translator said, "and sit down in the kitchen." As I walked across to the door, I looked back, but the soldier waved me on. I opened the small door, my mind filled with questions like, "Why is it only me that's been let out? What will happen after I go through this door? If they let me free tonight, where will I go by myself? Where could I stay? Maybe this was a trick and they won't let me come back." I kept on walking.

60

A Terrible Beating and an Inhuman Killing.

I looked back from the door, but the Chinese soldier had already gone. There wasn't a soul to be seen in the prison yard. All the thousands of prisoners were in their underground holes. I passed through the door and entered a walled courtyard. An old man was there.

"Hey, Dragpa, your little cousin is here," he said. Dragpa came out of a small room.

"Hey there, Nukho, what's going on?" he said. "Who let you out?"

"A Chinese officer sent me here."

"Come in, sit down, and drink some tea." He gave me tea, and as I drank it I looked around the room. Dragpa set a stack of steamed bread on a yak hair cloth. Then he turned back to the fire and kept on cooking. Dragpa was the prison cook now. He asked me how things were, and I told him exactly what had just happened. He said, "You children should be OK, but I'm not sure whether the older ones are going to be released or not." While we were talking, a Tibetan man working for the Chinese government, called Norbu, arrived with Jabey.

"Hey, Dragpa," he said, "you are responsible for these boys from now on. I've spoken to Secretary Li about it already. You should take them out of the hole in the morning, keep them here during the day, and return them to the hole at night." Then he asked my name and a few other things about me, stroking my hair the entire the time. "Listen to Dragpa, OK?" Norbu said. "Don't be afraid—you'll be out after a few days. During the day you can play games near the wall and sit in the sunshine, but don't leave the main gate." Then he left.

Before his arrest, Uncle Dragpa had been Alak Gungtang's agent. When the "time of revolution" began, Dragpa was on his way to Lhasa, but he was arrested in Chumarleb by the Chinese. In prison he and his friends—Sherab, Lundrub, and Zodpa—all cooked for the prisoners. From that day on, either Sherab or Dragpa would take us to the kitchen after morning latrine time, and we stayed in the kitchen or went to the wall and played games. We had tea to drink and plenty of bread to eat. Sometimes we stayed with Dragpa and the others to eat and talk, or to help them make the fire and clean out the ashes. There were many sacks of tsampa in a corner of the wall that was protected from the sun. There was also cheese, butter, and even brown sugar piled in the corner.

"Prisoners brought those to eat on their journey, but after they were arrested it was all brought here," Dragpa said. "You can eat whatever you like." In other sacks we saw a lot of jewelry: amber and turquoise necklaces, coral, black and white striped agate [dzi], silver chased belts, and other silver and jewelry as well. They said it had all been taken away from prisoners after they were arrested. Jabey and I played near the wall day after day but were always returned to the hole at night. We could eat what we wanted and play whatever games we liked but were still not happy because we were still prisoners and had to sleep in the hole. As you know, that hole was a terrible place. No description could do justice to it. It was a living death. But we brothers had warm clothes and plenty of food, so we couldn't be too unhappy. Sometimes we kneaded tsampa and butter together and took it to Monlam and Tenzin when we went down into the hole at night.

Every day, after latrine time, I watched the prisoners carefully from the kitchen door. There were nine holes in the yard, and each hole contained about four hundred prisoners.

"There are 2,300 male prisoners," Dragpa said, "and 1,600 females." Cooks always know exactly how many prisoners there are. The women's heads had been shaved, and when they went to the latrine their robes were untied and disheveled. But they looked as though they came from wealthy families, because most of them wore robes made from lambskin with otter fur trim. The youngest were about twenty, but the oldest were very old and needed help walking. Many of them had wounds on their feet and heads. Each morning the bodies of those who had died as a result of the Chinese soldiers' cruelty were carried out of the main gate. Two prisoners used to tie their arms and ankles to a pole and carry the bodies, hanging beneath the pole, to a mass grave outside the wall. That day there were two women's bodies among them—you could tell by looking at their robes.

"Their own karma," Dragpa said, "causes five or six prisoners to die every day. If they die quietly, there is no need for regret, but some of the women prisoners are killed for no reason other than the cruelty of the Chinese. They are really to be pitied!"

"It isn't just the women," Lundrub said. "When Sherab and I went to give the prisoners their food yesterday, there was a man's body lying near one of the trapdoors. His face, chest, belly, and genitals had been seared by hot metal. They must have tortured him to death."

"This morning," Zodpa said, "when we went to the hole with the food, we saw a young woman's body lying on the ground. Her breasts and genitals had been burned, too. Her friend told us that last night she was raped and beaten by some of the Chinese and then tortured with hot metal, but she was still alive. The Chinese told them that if they didn't tell anyone what had happened, they could go back to the hole. The older woman promised not to tell anyone, and they let her go after beating her a little. But then the young woman lit into the Chinese, calling them many bad names. She told them that if she got out of prison, she would come and find them, and then they would see what she 'could do to Chinese devils.'" This morning she was lying dead near the trapdoor. She didn't just die in the night, the Chinese murdered her." At latrine time, Jabey and I sometimes saw our companions Dongtrug, Kelsang, Tsekho, Lekho, and Lochu, and we waved to each other. All of us were still safe then.

Once, when we were having a meal in the kitchen, Zodpa the cook rushed in.

"Aka! Aka! This is terrible—they just killed two women on their way to the latrine!" he said.

"Why were they killed?" Dragpa asked. "Any reason?"

"It all started when one of the women seemed to go crazy down around the latrines," Zodpa said. "She started running around wildly and shouting like a mad thing, and most of the other women ran away from her, scared. The soldiers and prison guards attacked her and another woman with metal poles and the butts of their rifles, but I heard that it was De Shan who killed one of them." We went over to the main gate where the bodies of two women were lying. Sonam Norbu, one of the workers, came over.

"Come on, you people, what are you staring at them for? Let's go inside," he said. We went into the kitchen.

"What happened to them?" Dragpa asked.

"I haven't a clue," Sonam Norbu replied, "but I heard that some of the women were causing trouble and attacked the troops with rocks. The soldiers killed two women. Terrible."

"No, I saw what happened," Zodpa said. "One of the killers was De Shan."

"The dead body eater!" Sonam Norbu exclaimed. "He's a prisoner—going around killing people! He'll see what I do to him when I get the chance." Sonam Norbu looked at me.

"Hey little man," he asked, "does it make you afraid living here?"

"I'm not afraid," I said.

"Are you afraid when you're in the hole, my man?"

"No, I'm not," I said.

"Phew! What a boy this is. So brave! You won't be here long, you'll see. The only thing that's stopping them letting you go is that there's no school in this county. If it wasn't for that, they'd let you out."

"Will they let our other companions go?" I asked.

"Well, they'll let the children out soon," he said, "but as for the older ones, I couldn't say." Then, after talking for a long time about the women who had been murdered, he finished his meal and left. When the afternoon darkened and came near sunset, Dragpa took us back to the hole. Again, I gave a big piece of tsampa mixed with butter to Tenzin.

"You can't let them see you bringing in tsampa," he said while he was eating it. "They're not giving us much food these days. Everyone's close to starvation."

"No one can see—there's only Jabey and me at the tsampa-making place," I told him. "Uncle Dragpa said it's no problem if we take it."

I tried to sleep, but the burned breasts and genitals of the women prisoners kept coming into my mind. Eventually I did fall asleep, but a nightmare in which I saw the dead bodies of prisoners, their arms and legs dangling, tore me out of my sleep. In the pitch dark the smell of feces and urine was as disgusting as always, and the noise of farting, grinding teeth, and voices calling out . . . was it ever going to stop? The pain! So much pain! There was no hope for more sleep that night. I raised my head and stared into the darkness.

We Survive a Famine. We Are Released from Prison.

The next morning we rose for roll call, but again, a few people failed to answer.

"They're dead," somebody called out. When we went to the latrine, two of our fellow prisoners didn't follow us because during the night they had died of dysentery. Diarrhea from the dysentery went all over the people who had to lift their bodies out of the hole. When I got into the open air, I walked over to the kitchen as usual. Every hole had some dead bodies around it. When I arrived at the kitchen, the cooks were preparing tsampa soup. There wasn't enough flour left to make bread anymore, so the afternoon bread ration had been replaced by flour soup, and the morning meal was tsampa soup.

"What will happen if we go on like this?" Dragpa asked the chief of the kitchen. "The prisoners will die of hunger."

"We don't know yet what's going to happen," the chief said, "but everything should be fine when we get new supplies of flour. Until then, just do your best." That night I made tsampa and took it to Tenzin as usual. The prisoners got less food every day.

"Those corpse-eating people are going to starve us," someone shouted.

"If we'd known they would treat us like this, we would never have surrendered," many prisoners said. "We would have fought against them, but there's nothing we can do now because the high chief has already surrendered our chiefdom. He received all sorts of respect from the Chinese, but now we are all going to die together, him along with us."

"All the men in our chiefdom are going to die—there will only be women left," others said.

"No—as many women have died here as men. The women will be exterminated also," someone else said. People burst out with their feelings of despair.

My thoughts were easier that day, so I fell asleep in the hole. I awoke to hear a commotion among the prisoners at the other end.

"Hey, you people, what's happening?" Danba Tserang called out.

"Two people have died over here," an old man shouted back, "one right after the other, and another one will be dead soon."

"We should call the Chinese to come down here," a voice called. "If it's a serious disease, everyone in this hole will die!" The people near the trapdoor started shouting at the top of their voices. After a long delay, a Chinese man raised the trapdoor. Danba Tserang and the guard talked briefly in Chinese, and then Danba turned around and spoke to us in Tibetan.

"He says we should take the bodies outside." The ladder was lowered. Tenzin, Danba, and some others lifted the bodies out of the trapdoor.

"There's another one dead over here," someone said. They removed that body, as well. Everyone was very frightened. I thought, "Maybe these are the first of many deaths, because three people have died in a very short time, and people say two more are going to die soon. If it goes on like this, everyone in this hole will be dead by morning, but I'm not afraid of that. Why should I fear death and worry about myself when three hundred of my fellow prisoners are going to die? But if I die, it will cause suffering to Japey. In any case, the Three Precious Jewels have our fate in their hands." I was thinking these things when a Chinese man wearing white clothes climbed down the ladder, accompanied by six soldiers carrying guns. The one in the white clothes was a doctor, and he gave medicine to the sick prisoners. Before he left, he announced something in Chinese.

"Everyone close your eyes," the translator said. "I'm going to spray some medicine liquid over you." The doctor sprayed liquid over everyone in the hole, which filled the air with vapor. Then he and the troops climbed out the trapdoor and closed it behind them. Everyone started coughing, and our eyes and mouths watered. My eyes stung, and my robe was wet with fallen tears.

"Someone else just died over here," one man called.

"Those evil father's dead body eating Chinese have sprayed poison on us," another said. "We're all going to die!" Everyone was terrified and stood up, shouting in fear.

"The Chinese have sprayed us with poison, so calling them for help is useless," an old man said, but everyone shouted and screamed anyway. The trapdoor opened slightly,

"Shut up down there! What's wrong with you?" a voice yelled.

"The Chinese sprayed us with poison, and one of us has died already," a prisoner said. "The rest of us are going to die too!"

"Don't lie, you eaters of your fathers' dead bodies!" the voice from behind the trapdoor shouted, furious. "That liquid wasn't poison, it was medicine. I swear you'd all be dead if they hadn't given you some. They've done it in all the holes. If you want, I'll open the door for a while to let the fumes out." I recognized the voice. It was Sonam Norbu, the government worker. Then he said, "Hey, you lot, help the little boy who is in your hole get out of the trapdoor."

"Thank you, you're a kind man," Tenzin said, handing me up to Sonam Norbu, who lifted me onto the ground.

"Hey, boy!" Sonam Norbu said. "Why are your clothes so wet?"

"The doctor sprayed water on me."

"Boy, that wasn't water," Sonam Norbu told me. "It was just a medicinal liquid that makes things clean." He shouted into the trapdoor again. "You people have nothing to be afraid of. Go to sleep." He turned to me and said, "We're going to the kitchen, all right?" He led me across the courtyard and into the kitchen, where a lot of Tibetan and Chinese people were sitting. Dragpa poured tea for Sonam Norbu and me and gave me a handful of cheese. I listened to their conversation. It seemed as though 130 people had died in the past ten days from hunger, cold, despair, and dysentery.

"The county leaders are coming with some doctors to inspect the prison today," Sonam Norbu said.

"They should keep the two young boys out of the hole because of the dysentery," Dragpa said. "Do you have any idea if they might allow that?" Sonam Norbu stroked my head.

"All right," he said. "I'll talk to the secretary about that tomorrow, but tonight you'd better let them sleep here, OK?" I thought, "This is a Chinese official worker, but he's a kindhearted man despite that." We slept in the kitchen that night, but the next day there wasn't any news, so Japey and I stayed in the kitchen all day. That night, sleeping in the hole with Tenzin, I began to dream. Tenzin's voice snapped me out of it.

"Boy! Get up! Get up!" he said. I looked up—the trapdoor was opening, and sunshine was streaming in. I could hear Dragpa calling me, and Tenzin lifted me into Dragpa's arms. I followed him across the yard, and to my surprise we didn't go to the kitchen but toward the main gate. I realized that something strange had happened—he had called for me. Normally I just went to the kitchen myself after we had all been to the latrine. I thought, "Where are we going?" but I just followed him without asking any questions. Standing at the main gate were two Chinese and Tibetan official workers talking to each other. Sonam Norbu and I walked up to them, and they led me over to a Chinese man wearing white trousers, a cigarette hanging from his lips. The man brushed the dust from my clothes with his hand and spoke to Sonam Norbu in Chinese.

"Today you are leaving prison and going to Ratsang School," Sonam Norbu told me.

"I don't want to go to school," I stated. "I want to stay here with Japey and my companions."

"Japey is going with you," he said.

"We are going to wait for our companions," I insisted, "and then go to our native land together." The Chinese and Tibetan workers smiled, and then the Chinese man who had spoken to me said something else, and Sonam Norbu translated.

"You must both go to school. If you learn how to read and write, when you are grown up you can return to your native land."

"Nukho," Dragpa said, "you should say yes to this. First go to school, and then we can all go back to our native land together." The Chinese man took the white cloth with the red number off my chest, cutting a small piece of my sheepskin robe off with it. Then he threw my number, 3299, on the ground, still attached to the piece of sheepskin. I went to my brother, who had arrived during all this, and held his hand. The man cut off Japey's number, 3289, and threw it on the ground, too. Sonam Norbu started giving us many arguments about why we needed to go to school.

"We don't want to go to school," Japey emphasized. "We need to wait for our companions here, and then travel home to our native land together."

After a long discussion, Sonam Norbu said, "Then both of you should leave the prison today and live for a little while in the next town. Wait there for a few days. Then, if your companions are released, they'll find you, and you can go with them to your native land."

"All right, we agree to that," Jabey said.

"We'll meet again in the future," Dragpa said, giving us a small bag of tsampa. Then the government officials led us out the main gate of the prison.

62

Living in the Town. Waiting for Our Companions.

As we left the main gate, Dragpa said, "Have a safe journey. Japey, look after your brother well. I plan to come and find you when I get out."

"Good luck, Uncle Dragpa," we both said, "and we hope everything goes well with you."

"Uncle Dragpa," I said, "please tell Tenzin and the others where we have gone—we'll wait for them in the town." The metal prison gates swung closed behind us, slamming loudly, leaving Dragpa and the others inside the wall. We were delighted to be out of the prison, but when we thought about our companions still in the hole, it hurt and made us sad. We were prisoners of Chumarleb jail no longer. We had really left the prison at last. I thought, "Is this the result of karma from our previous lives, or is it just one part of these evil days, the 'time of revolution'?"

When I was ten years old, I left my own native land, Lhade, to travel to Lhasa with my father. We tried for forty-eight days to reach Lhasa, but in the end we couldn't. After I was separated from my father, I stayed in Chumarleb prison for eighteen days: eighteen nights and eighteen days. I could survive the daytimes easily, but the nights were a kind of hell. In my body I felt hunger, thirst, and cold, and my mind trembled in terror and fear of cruelty. Lamas and the Three Precious Jewels! I have seen people in what is called a "living hell" with my own eyes. I pray for His Holiness the Dalai Lama to free all living beings from this kind of suffering.

The Tibetan and Chinese workers took us to a very nice house. Sonam Norbu kept saying that we should go to school, but Jabey and I persisted in telling him that we would wait for our people in the town.

"Well, children these days are so difficult," he said irritably. "I suppose if they won't listen to us, they can do as they please." We waited in the house, and later a Tibetan official worker named Karma Tashi, wearing a sword inside his robe, appeared. Sonam Norbu handed us over to him.

"Come on!" Karma Tashi said. "How am I supposed to look after children this young? Where are they going to stay?"

"Listen to me," Sonam Norbu told him. "There are vacant earth houses opposite the army barracks where some mothers from Golok are living. You could leave them there."

"What about food?" Karma Tashi asked.

"I'll bring some tsampa from the prison, but otherwise you'll have to sort it out," Sonam Norbu said.

"How about clothes?" asked Karma Tashi.

"Son of a great father, you'll manage somehow," said Sonam Norbu.

"All right," said Karma Tashi. "I'll think of something." Later that day, Sonam Norbu brought a sack full of tsampa and cheese. He handed it to us, saying, "Here's some food, but there's no butter for it just yet."

"Right, you little boys, let's go," Karma Tashi said, and we followed him, carrying the tsampa bag. We walked through the gate of the wall surrounding the official workers' compound. As I looked back, I could see the Chinese guards patrolling the top of the prison wall. "It's so terrible," I thought. "My companions are still in that underground hell hole. Will they ever get out?" Karma Tashi led us through the door of a big shop.

"You two should really go to school, where they'll give you enough to eat and clothes to wear," he said.

"We are going to wait in the town for our companions," Jabey said.

"Wait for me here, and don't wander off," Karma Tashi said. "I'll be back soon." He returned after a while with half a bag of barley and said, "Fine—I'm not going to take you to the school. Just follow me." We walked to a barracks, where many troops were living, on the edge of town. There were some small earth-walled houses opposite the barracks. He opened the door to one of them, and we went in. Inside there were some robes and woolen clothes. There was a fireplace, a cooking pot, and other cooking utensils. There was some firewood, and a small grain mill for making flour and tsampa.

"Some Golok people used to live here," he said, "and you'll stay here from now on. I'll come and see you in a few days." After he had gone, we cleaned the little house thoroughly, and then I went to fetch water. When I got back, Jabey had already lit the fire. We boiled the water and ate tsampa. That was such a happy day for us. Not only had we been released from prison, but we had been given a small house free of charge! It was a great place for us to wait for our companions.

That night two women who lived next door came to see us. They asked us many questions, but we didn't tell them who we really were or why we were living in the house.

"If our people come back tomorrow," one of the women warned us, "you two won't be able to live in this house—they'll need to stay here." Neither of us paid much attention. After our evening meal, we went to sleep early, lying against the inside of the threshold. Our sleep felt wonderful that night. The dreadful smells of the prison hole, the sounds of teeth grinding, snoring, everyone's voices, and the fear and trembling in our hearts were all gone. We slept peacefully until the sun rose.

When it was light, I went out to have a look around. On the grass, soldiers were marching in ranks and doing other military exercises. Some people were slaughtering and butchering two yaks near the gate of the barracks. The small intestines, the heads, feet, lungs, and livers just lay abandoned on the ground. I went back and told Jabey.

"Walk over there slowly and look around carefully," he said. "See if they'll let you take anything. I'll watch you from over here." I ambled over to the place where the soldiers had slaughtered the yaks. I picked up a liver that was lying on the ground, but a Chinese soldier spotted me and gave chase. I ran around the corner, but he caught me and led me back by my ear. However, when we got to the yak carcasses, he cut off a big piece of meat and put it in my robe. He also tied the yak's head and feet together with a rope and put them on my back. Then he smiled at me and waved me away.

"Thank you," I told him, giving him the thumbs-up sign, and he and his friends said something to each other and laughed. On the way home I retrieved the liver I had dropped, too! Brother Jabey came running up to help me carry everything. We got back to our little house in high spirits. We cooked the liver and some of the other meat right away. We cut out the tongue, but we didn't have a knife good enough to split the head, so we left it just outside the door with the feet. Later, when I went outside, the head and feet had disappeared! We realized the two Golok women must have taken it all, but we didn't say anything to them because we thought they must have been hungry.

That afternoon, Jabey and I walked up the mountain behind the army barracks to collect firewood. On the way back we picked up a yak's stomach that had been left near the slaughtering place. After we had been home for a short time, two soldiers came to our door, saying something that we didn't understand. I thought, "It must be about us taking the yak's stomach." A soldier took Jabey by the hand and started to lead him away. I thought the man must be arresting him, so I tried to pull him back. The soldiers laughed and held my hand too.

"I think it will be OK," Jabey said. "Let's go." The troops led us past the guard at the gate of the barracks and into one of the buildings inside the wall. The soldier who had given me the meat that morning was sitting there, and he gave us some candy. He seemed to be the commander of this detachment of troops. Later a translator arrived.

"Don't be afraid," he said. "This soldier wants to tell you that if you herd their yaks he will pay you four yuan a day, starting tomorrow. But he will only need you for five or six days."

"We can start tomorrow morning!" Jabey said. The Chinese soldier put a letter in Jabey's hand and spoke through the translator.

"If you have this letter," he said, "you'll be allowed into the barracks tomorrow morning at sunrise. When the sun has risen completely, come inside the gate and drive the yaks away. In the early afternoon herd the yaks back inside the wall. As I said, your pay will be four yuan a day." The Chinese commander took us back through the main door, laughing and holding my ear. We were on top of the world as we walked back home.

"Jabey," I said, "you can herd the yaks tomorrow. I will cook the tea, grind barley, and have tsampa ready for when you come back." We had a lot of cheerful things to say to each other.

The next day Jabey went to herd the army's yaks. There were twenty-two male yaks in the herd, and that afternoon he drove them back inside the wall of the barracks. I stayed at home making tsampa. The troops killed two yaks every day, so every day I collected the yaks' heads, feet, stomachs, and other meat. When Japey got home, I had tea, yaks' head meat, tongue, and other food ready for us to eat. Every afternoon Jabey would return home with food from the barracks, such as cooked rice and bread, as well as the four paper yuan. During that time we had work, and we were getting paid. In our house there was meat, tsampa, bread, rice, and a lot of other food to eat. For me, that life was the definition of happiness.

— 63 —

Went to Ratsang School. Staying in the "Joyful Home."

One morning two of the Golok women came to see us.

"Hello, little boy," one of them said. "We have no food to eat. Could you please give us the yaks' head and feet?"

"No," I told her, "but if you need food, you can go to the place where the troops slaughter their yaks. They have plenty of food to give away there."

"We can't go there," they said. "The soldiers will bother us. Please give us some of yours. We are so hungry." I gave them the head, hoofs, and a little liver.

"Oh, thank you," the elder woman said. "Could you bring us some food tomorrow as well, please?" The next day I brought them the head, feet, lungs, and some other things. I did that for about ten days. By then Jabey only had three yaks to herd, but the troops still gave us four yuan, bread, and other food every afternoon. Sometimes Jabey and I went together to buy tea, salt, candy, and more. Our lives were very fortunate!

One day when I went to the shop, a Chinese woman took my hand and led me away with her. When we got to her house, there was a pile of clay with a puddle of water in the middle. She put a metal spade in my hand and mimed shaping the earth with her hands. I realized what she meant and helped her make the clay into a stove. When I had finished, she gave me two yuan, some candy, and three steamed bread rolls. That was my first salary. When I got back to our house, Jabey had made supper, and I felt very content. Jabey was happy too. We spent eighteen wonderful days together like that. The troops sometimes just had a few yaks to herd, but sometimes there were as many as ten. The troops slaughtered yaks every day, and I would go and collect some meat. Those eighteen days flew by. Every three or four days we went to the prison gate to check whether our companions had been released yet, but we saw nothing except the dead bodies of prisoners being carried up the mountain. I thought, "Oh, no! Maybe some of them have died already."

Before dawn one day, Karma Tashi came to our door. That day, we learned later, was the twentieth of December 1958.

"Right, you two, get up quickly," he said. "They've told us you've got to leave today."

"Where are we going?" Jabey asked.

"You can't stay here anymore. You've got to go to Ratsang School. The school has come to collect you. Put your bowls in your robes, but other than that you won't need anything else. When you get to the school, you'll have whatever food you want to eat." We sat down to eat our breakfast and waited.

"Jabey," I asked, "should we give our food to the Golok women?"

"Go and call them," he said. I brought them over, and Jabey and I gave them our tsampa and meat, and all the other food we had.

"Thank you very much!" the women said. "Where are you going?"

"We have to go to school," I said. Sometime later, an old woman arrived, driving five pack yaks. We tied our possessions onto the yaks and sat behind them. We rode along until we came to a river and crossed it. There were about one hundred black yak hair tents pitched on the banks of the river beside the road. We rode along the center of the road with many children and old people looking at us from the entrances of the tents on either side. Farther on we came to a place where there was a very big tent. Children crowded around us, asking us things, and some people came to help us unpack our bags. A tall young man led us into the tent and gave us food. He asked us our names, ages, and where we were from. He asked why we had come there and many other things in great detail. Jabey answered very carefully too.

"I'm a teacher," the man said. "My name is Tserang Dorje." At first, we were surprised that we could understand every word he said so clearly. When he heard that we were from Golok, he was very happy.

"I'm from Golok, too," he said. "Our native land is the same! Now you should stay here at the school, enjoy yourself, and when I go to the town I will check whether your companions have been released yet. If you have any problems, just let me know, and I will help you. Everything will be fine. Thanks to our leader, Mao Zedong, we have enough to eat and drink. Now stay here, and this will be your joyful home." A student called Kunchong took us to the sleeping tent. It was huge, and there were thirty children sleeping around the edges. Jabey and I were given places to sleep beside each other near the tent door. Then Kunchong took us to the classroom tent. It was an enormous black yak hair tent that formerly had been the property of their chiefdom's monastery. There were about three hundred children in the tent, noisily reciting the Tibetan alphabet, "Ga ka gha nga . . ."

"This is group one, and there are two other groups: two and three. This is called the 'Joyful Home.' The three groups together total about a thousand students, and most of the children's parents have been arrested. They have no one to look after them. They are orphans. There are also six hundred old women and men here whose families have been arrested, too, so they are destitute, and the government is feeding them all." At lunchtime a woman melted three big chunks of butter in the kitchen, mixed in barley flour and cheese, and made beautiful tsampa. She gave a big piece of tsampa to each of the children, but they weren't hungry, and many of them wasted it, leaving it around everywhere to be spoiled. I thought, "What bad orphans these are, wasting this delicious buttery tsampa." Jabey and I had already known hardship, so if we didn't want to eat our food, we would save it carefully for later. I stored my food in a gazelle-hide bag and also put in some of the tsampa that students had discarded on the ground. There was meat soup for dinner that evening and plenty of food every day. I thought, "Where do they get so much food that everyone can eat as much as they like and still have food left over? This is truly a 'Joyful Home,' if old people can be fed this well. In this place the old people have not been dumped into an insect's hole, and the children have not been stuffed with yogurt and thrown down from the roofs of the houses. Everyone is living very happily here. If we had known that earlier, we would not have tried so hard to avoid this school. The only bad thing is that this chiefdom's families have been arrested and pushed into those holes." While I was walking around thinking about all this, I came to the entrance of a big tent and looked inside. I was astonished to see endless leather bags of butter, sacks of dried cheese, barley, tsampa, and much else, stacked up on all four sides of the tent.

"Aunt, where did they get so much butter and cheese?" I asked a woman beside me.

"This was all taken from the families of rich people," she replied. "There's another tent full of meat farther up the hill."

"Oh, the Three Precious Jewels bear witness! These orphans and destitute old people have fine lives here. They get as much food as they want and have no work to do. It is definitely a 'Joyful Home' when old people are fed and children are educated. How wonderful it is to see a place like this in these hard times!"

Every afternoon after tea the teacher Tserang Dorje organized a traditional Tibetan circle dance. One day Tserang Dorje addressed all the students.

"Children!" he said. "Today we, the proletariat, have political power and happiness. We owe this to our leader, Mao Zedong. You must remember that and study as hard as you can." He said many things of that nature. I thought, "Precious lama! Wouldn't the people from this chiefdom who have been arrested feel content if they knew that their children and old people were living as happily as this? Even if they died in prison, it would ease their cares if they knew about this place. Jabey and I must have been granted happiness here as the result of our karma." However, sometimes I doubted my conclusions. The whole country was suffering as a result of the "time of revolution," so why was there happiness only in this one chiefdom? I thought, "Is it real? Will this good fortune last? After the Chinese army has arrested or killed all of the parents and others, will it care for the children and old people who have been left behind as nicely as this?" I brooded about this. My bag was crammed with buttery, kneaded tsampa, but I didn't need it. I took it up the mountain and hid it in a cave.

Tibetan schoolchildren in traditional robes.
Bild 135 S 10 03 04. From the collection of the Federal Archives of Germany, Koblenz.
Photographer, Bruno Beger. Ahnenerbe Expedition, 1938–1939.

64

Told about Our Deep-Rooted Superstition. No Fear of a Bully.

That night, when we went to bed, I told Jabey about hiding the tsampa on the mountain.

"Well done," he said. "We don't need it yet."

When I got up the next day, thick snow lay on the ground. I swept a path through the snow from our tent entrance. Later on, all the students rounded up the stray dogs in the area by holding out tsampa as bait, and then tying them up. After that, they took them to the cliff and stoned them to death. Then they gathered the mother dogs and puppies living near the mountain and stoned them to death too.

"Hey, little orphans," a woman said to them, "why are you killing those dogs? If you do things like that, you'll never be rewarded with a successful life." She scolded them fervently for a long time. Listening to her dialect, I could tell she came from Golok. The following morning, some students came over to Jabey and me. One of them was a boy called "Broken Nose Dabla."

"Those Golok boys didn't join in and kill dogs with the rest of us," Broken Nose Dabla said. "We won't give them any food this afternoon. But now let's go kill some dogs." He tried to drag us with them, but we refused to go. One of the teachers was carrying a gun—he walked over to the mountain to shoot dogs. Many of the group two and three students ran over to watch. At noon, everyone finished killing dogs and returned to the tent.

"Today the 'Joyful Home' killed one hundred dogs!" a boy called Wannor Kunchong stood up to announce. After lunch, the students, including Jabey and me, assembled outside the tent.

"Today we must start the 'time of revolution'!" Broken Nose Dabla said. "Everyone take off the protective amulet and threads you have around your necks and put them over here." In the middle of the group of students we could see a heap of religious scriptures. Nearly everyone, young and old, removed their protective amulet and ribbons and put them on the pile, but students went up to some old people and tore them off their necks by force.

"These wretched children will pay for this one day!" an old man named Chunnor said. "This morning they slaughtered dogs, and now they are burning precious scriptures and protective amulets! Are they trying to bring death upon us? They will never be free of this shame."

"Let's go into the tent," said Jabey. We went into our sleeping tent and sat down. The smoke from the burning scriptures, amulets, and ribbons drifted in and made my nose burn. Then Broken Nose Dabla appeared with a group behind him.

"Why didn't you watch us burn the protective amulets?" he asked.

"We don't have any protective amulets," Jabey said.

"Well, you'd better watch the religious scriptures burn; otherwise we'll know that you are against the 'time of revolution.'" He and the students with him yanked us out of the tent and over to where the scriptures were being set on fire.

"These Golok boys didn't want to attend the burning of the scriptures. We should beat them, don't you think?" Dabla shouted to the crowd.

"Yes, let's beat them!" the children shouted back. Then Kunchong came over with the teacher, Tserang Dorje.

"What are you doing?" Tserang Dorje asked the crowd. "What have the Golok boys done?" He came and stood next to us.

"These two are deeply religious and superstitious," Dabla said. "They walked away from where we were burning the protective amulets, and this morning they didn't even go and kill the dogs."

"Whether they were there or not, it is not your problem," replied Tserang

Dorje. "What responsibility do you have for that? Now, everybody go back to your tents. And Dabla, you'd better stop with this." He told them all to be on their way. Then Tserang Dorje took us over to the kitchen. Wuglo the cook was there.

"I told Kunchong to call you, otherwise they would have beaten these two," she told Tserang Dorje.

"You don't need to be afraid of that devil," Tserang Dorje told us. "If he tries to do anything bad to you, just come and tell Kunchong, Wuglo, or me, and we will deal with him." I thought, "We are so lucky to have a kindhearted man like this looking after us in this desolate place. And Kunchong, Wuglo, and others are so good to us, too!"

The next day most of the children caught colds.

"It's because you burned the protective amulets and scriptures yesterday," an old woman told them. I thought, "Can that be true? The people who destroyed the monastery didn't even get a headache. How can these children have caught colds as the result of a relatively small thing like burning religious scriptures?"

"Broken Nose Dabla and Tsejab despise and bully us," Jabey said one morning soon after. "Let's show them what we can do." I put a long piece of stone inside my robe and followed my brother, but I couldn't see what he had put inside his own robe. Dabla and his friends were playing a game near the doorway of their tent. He was fifteen, one year older than Jabey, but they were about the same height. We walked up to him.

"So, you Golok bastards, what are you doing here?" Dabla said. "Have you come to eat shit, you little beggars?" He turned to his friends and said, "They've done a shit in their robes. We'd better scold them." They said many nasty things like that. Dabla gripped Jabey's chest and wouldn't let go. I was standing behind Dabla and saw Jabey reach into his robe to extract a long piece of metal, which he swung hard into Dabla's ear. I took the stone out of my robe and hit Dabla hard on the back of the head, drawing blood. He turned his head toward me, blood dripping down his neck. Jabey swung the metal into Dabla's head again, and he fell to the ground. Then Dabla panicked, first crawling and then staggering to his feet in an attempt to run away, blood pouring from his nose.

"The Golok boys are killing people," children shouted, and they ran away. Jabey grabbed Tsejab, a twelve-year-old boy who was one of Dabla's friends, and hit him hard on the ear with the metal. I ran toward Tsejab and scratched his face with my fingernails, drawing blood. Then Jabey punched him in the face and he ran away, crying. The other students were yelling.

"That's what Broken Nosed Dabla deserved," some of them shouted. Then Wuglo the cook arrived and took us away.

"What happened?" she asked.

"Dabla and his gang were always bullying us, so we showed them what would happen if they didn't stop," Jabey said. The next day the teacher came up to us secretly and whispered, "Well done. That will do someone like him good." Louder, he told us, "From now on, no more fighting. Do you understand?" We all laughed. From then on, no one tried to bully us, or even to say a bad word to us. Most of the students really liked Jabey and started calling him "Brother." They made him leader of the tent and chief food distributor. After that day, we had respect.

The next day was Chinese New Year, and snow fell heavily in the early morning. We got up early and swept it away. At noon they said that students from group three could go watch some dancers from the town. We went over, and there were many male and female dancers wearing lambskin robes trimmed with otter fur, and long-sleeved red and white shirts. They danced, sometimes in line and sometimes in a circle, and sang songs. It was the first time I had seen Tibetan dancing. They sang a song called "Dage Dalojid" while they danced. The performance lasted for a long and wonderful time.

Karma Tashi was with them, and we asked him how our companions were. "I'm not sure," he said, "but I'll find out when I get back to the town and tell you." He gave Jabey and me brown sugar, deep-fried bread, and other food. Later that afternoon Tserang Dorje took Jabey and me into the tent to meet some guests. A young man there stroked my head kindly and gave me meat and yogurt.

"This is my friend Chuga," Tserang Dorje said. "He's one of the Ngangchen king's clan, and now he is an official worker in the 'Joyful Home.'" We ate and drank with him, then returned to our tents.

That night the students danced and sang songs ourselves. The old people stood around watching us, and we played happily. It was the first time I had celebrated Chinese New Year. At one point the new official, Chuga, came up to me.

"You, Golok boy, come here," he said. He put a cloth packet in my hand. "Take this and share it with your brother, but don't let anyone else see you."

"Thank you, Uncle Chuga," I answered. I took it into the sleeping tent. Luckily, most of the students hadn't returned yet. I peeked inside the cloth and saw a piece of meat and some Chinese bread. Jabey and I ate most of it, and I gave some to two little children, a boy and girl who slept beside me.

"It's New Year, so we should enjoy ourselves," I told them. "This is our special New Year food!"

"Brother Nukho, who gave you this?" the boy asked me.

"Found it on the mountain," I said. So we celebrated New Year with bread, meat, and much happiness!

65

The Agony of Ice and Cold on the Outside,
Sickness and Hunger on the Inside.

The children who slept beside me seemed so happy when we had finished our New Year food. The boy was eight, and the girl only five years old. Because they were brother and sister, they were allowed to sleep in the same tent, but neither of them knew their parents' names.

"These two were found with some captured refugees," Tserang Dorje told me, "and the soldiers sent them here, but we've no idea where they're from." Jabey and I made sure they had enough food, helped them make up their bed at night, and generally took care of them. We felt a lot of love and pity for those children, whose lives had been so much like my brother's and mine. The worst thing was that they didn't know their parents' names, which was terrible luck, but at least our karma meant that we were able to live in the same tent together.

Three months after New Year, the food in the "Joyful Home" became sparser and of poorer quality. At first the cooks had put half a pot of butter in with the tsampa, but the butter grew less and less, and the cheese grew more and more. It didn't taste as good, and there wasn't enough for all of us to satisfy our hunger. The evening soup contained no meat, and when some old women came to the school to beg for food, they were told we didn't even have enough for ourselves. The students had a little tsampa, but that couldn't prevent the pain in their stomachs. The old people and the children all suffered the same hunger pangs, but no one had any idea what to do about it. Like blind people, we held out our hands for whatever was put into them. What food would fill the blind person's bowl? The kitchen was helpless.

"There's no need to worry about food," Tserang Dorje said one day. "We'll be able to get flour and rice from town very soon." The old people looked worse than we did, and I heard that they had been eating nothing but hard, dry cheese. In those days of shortage, many children and old people fell sick. Some of them caught colds, and some developed dysentery. We started calling it "the Month of Severe Famine." The weather was extremely cold, the food sparser and sparser, the disease more and more serious.

One day the cook Wuglo said to the teachers, "You and the official workers have to find food from somewhere, or all my children are going to die of hunger."

"I'm going to Chumarleb tomorrow to get food," Tserang Dorje reassured her. A few days later he and Chuga returned from the town carrying food, but it was a pathetic sight. All they had was four sacks of wheat flour and two sacks of beans. This was all there was for four hundred children and old people. Everyone, young and old, watched this food arrive with a mixture of sadness and fear. Tserang Dorje's face was unhappy too. As he looked around at all of us, his expression became more and more troubled, and with good reason—he was wondering what would happen to these four hundred people if he could not get enough food.

The next day I went to Tserang Dorje's tent to help fetch water. He and Chuga were sitting miserably inside their tent. The authorities had told them that there was no barley or livestock left over for the "Joyful Home," and they would have to find food themselves.

"How can four hundred people feed themselves?" Tserang Dorje had retorted. How could he and Chuga not be worried? People were wandering around crying of hunger. I thought, "What is going to happen in a few days when we finish the cheese and beans? We're going to die of starvation. And there are so many people sick, and getting sicker." When disease had first broken out, doctors came from Chumarleb to examine the sick and dispense medicine, but now no doctors came, even when we asked for them. However, no one had yet said that they would prefer to die fast of disease than waste away slowly from hunger.

There were fifteen children in our tent, and even though some of them were complaining of hunger, they were all still healthy. I thought, "They don't know what hunger is yet. In a few days, when we have finished the cheese and beans, we will feel real hunger, but the worst agony will be starving to death." All over the "Joyful Home" people pointed out, "There hasn't been a single grain of barley from the town!" but I did not share my thoughts with anyone. The winter weather attacked us from the outside with ice and sharp winds, and sickness and famine attacked us from the inside. At noon that day I told Jabey secretly what I knew: the authorities were not going to send food.

"We will have to see what happens," he told me. "Some groups may survive, and we may make it through with them. But we must think: How we can find food?"

That afternoon for supper there was nothing but bean soup without cheese. I thought, "So, the cheese is finished already. How long can we survive on two sacks of beans?" But later Tserang Dorje told the cook, "There's no need to be afraid anymore. Tomorrow each group will have a yak to kill." I told the good news to Jabey. He seemed very calm.

"It's going to be all right, as long as we don't get sick," he told me. "We're still a long way from dying of hunger. If things get bad again, I think we'll be able to find ways to feed ourselves." Jabey's confidence made me feel that I had nothing to fear, and my spirits rose. That night I dreamed of filling my belly with meat and tsampa!

I rose early in the morning. I hadn't slept soundly because I was so excited about eating meat the next day. Outside, a fierce wind was full of buffeting snow, so we didn't leave our tent. The sun had already been up for many hours before the kitchen announced that the food was ready to eat. Jabey went into the kitchen and came out with a pot full of meat cooked with blood and liver, which he gave to the children. They ate, competing to see who would be the first to finish. I hadn't heard so much noise in the eating tent since the food shortage had become really serious. When Jabey poured soup for me, he made sure that a piece of liver ended up in my bowl. I took out the liver and shared it with a little boy who was sitting beside me. One of the children said, "Jabey didn't share the soup out fairly. He gave a big piece of meat to Nukho."

"All right, if you think you can do a better job than me, you can pour the soup yourself. I'm sure I'm no expert," Jabey responded, carefully placing the pot on the table in front of the child who had complained. There was silence. No one was pouring the soup, and no one was taking any either.

"Let's pour the soup," said the one who had complained. "But what do we do if there's not enough for everybody?"

"You eater of your father's dark blue dead body!" said a child called Wugpa. "What's so terrible about giving him one little piece of liver?!" The boy who had complained hung his head and started to cry. He looked up at Jabey.

"Dear brother Jabey, please divide up the soup," he pleaded. "Don't listen to what any of us say." Jabey ladled out the rest of the soup and went to the kitchen to get some more. For six days after that, we had meat soup to eat every day, and our hunger receded, but when the meat ran out, we went back to eating half a bowl of bean soup each, enough to keep us alive. Then one day a detachment of Chinese troops arrived carrying ten bags of dried maize and broad beans on their horses. They dropped them in the doorway of the kitchen.

It turned out that our teacher, Tserang Dorje, had gone to the army camp and found us food there. Everyone's spirits were better because they knew they would have enough food to eat for a while. The following morning a yak was killed for each group, and we had meat soup to drink again.

A few days later, Chuga brought some Chinese and Tibetan officials to the "Joyful Home," and they gave us even more food: eight sacks of wheat flour.

"Children, don't worry," they announced, grinning. "We would never let you starve." The old and the young started to lose their fear of hunger. Every afternoon, after the midday meal was over, children danced and played games the way they used to do. Tserang Dorje and Chuga were smiling again. If everyone had some food to eat, they felt at peace.

One afternoon they called the entire school together. "Tomorrow we are going to move," they announced. "We are going across the river to Horda Valley. Early in the morning, pack up your clothes and carry them across the river over the ice. We'll eat after we get there." The next day they began to dismantle the tents before we had even gotten up.

66

We Finally Run Out of Food and Famine Strikes.
Death Despite Eating Leather and Hide.

We awoke to the sound of tents being taken down and started packing. Then we moved the entire school, tents and all, across the river. Jabey carried a quilt and two carpets, and I carried two small bowls, a big food bowl, and some other things, including one of the robes of the children who slept beside me. The little children and I went over the frozen river together toward the new campsite. Our new encampment was in the lower reaches of a valley near Chumarleb. We could see the houses of the town in the distance.

When we arrived at our new site, there were Chinese soldiers guarding it. That's when I realized that the people who had helped us move our camp were prisoners. I quietly asked about our companions, but no one among the hundred or so prisoners said they knew them. In the afternoon they formed a line, and the Chinese troops escorted them away. Our tent was pitched on a high shelf above the river, but the layout of the tents was the same as in the previous camp. There wasn't much food that day, and it was difficult to sleep in the night because wind blew under the skirts of our tent. The following morning Jabey and I went down to the river and brought back stones to weigh down the cloth. We arranged them all around the edge of the tent and covered them with earth. Then we poured water on the dirt, and it froze solid so that the skirt of the tent could not move.

For a little while after we moved camp, we had maize and beans to eat, but later all we had to eat was a watery flour soup. Even though our meals were so poor, no one had yet died of hunger. Sometimes the soup contained tiny pieces of dried lung. If we were very lucky, our bowl would contain one of these lung pieces, but if not, there was only flavored water, without nutrients or taste. Three Precious Jewels! Our bodies were weak, and we felt sleepy and had no desire to get up. If we walked around, our heads felt heavy and dizzy and we were very unsteady. Some children stopped talking and fell over whenever they tried to walk. Although there were children crying from hunger, the old people had it even worse. I thought, "Now we're going to die. We are stuck in this wild, empty, freezing place with only stones and earth, and no one out of all the children and old people has any income. The old are too old to look after us, and the young too young to take care of themselves—one by one we will starve." The teachers and official workers drifted away one by one, their numbers dwindling day by day. We had nothing to do but look at each other and await death.

One morning, Jabey said, "Come on! Today we're going to Chumarleb." We set off in the early morning. It wasn't far—we could see it from our encampment—but we almost didn't make it. We felt so hungry and weak we could hardly walk, and we sat down often to take a rest or drink some water from a hole in the ice of the frozen river. The first thing we did in town was go to the shop. Jabey paid five yuan for some biscuits, brown sugar candy, and peanuts. They almost filled our bag, but this was the only food the shop had to sell. On the way back, we passed the place where the Chinese troops tethered their horses and saw that there were a lot of broad beans on the ground. We gathered them all up until we had almost a horse's nose bag full of beans. Near the wall of the barracks, an old Chinese soldier was cooking bread on a metal griddle over a fire. We watched him for a while, and then the soldier waved us over. I walked over to him, and he put a big piece of bread in my robe. The delicious smell ravished my nose.

I said, "Thank you" and showed him my thumb. He smiled at me and said lots of things in Chinese that I couldn't understand. Then Jabey and I returned to our campsite. I was so excited about all the food we'd found in the town I could hardly keep from breaking into a run and falling over.

"Don't tell anyone about our trip to Chumarleb," Jabey warned when we got near our tent. "We won't go into our tent until after dark or they'll steal our food." We hid under the riverbank nearby. When it got dark, we went inside the tent. Most of the children were sleeping, but some of them were missing. Where had they gone? We hid our food under the bed, and I stealthily gave the little girl and boy some biscuits. A little later Wugpa showed up.

"Hey, you two, where did you go today?" he asked. "Two people died of hunger today, one young and one old." Jabey gave him a handful of dried broad beans, and I gave three each to the boy and girl.

"Where did you boys get broad beans?" said Wugpa in a slow, reverent voice.

"We found them," my brother replied. Later Tserang Dorje came to the door of the tent and called Jabey. He and Wugpa went out. They returned after a long time.

"One of the girls in our group starved to death. We were helping take her body away," Jabey told me.

"Did she die of famine?" I asked.

"Yes," Jabey said, "and another one will be dead soon."

That night I couldn't sleep for a long time. I thought, "Now the deaths have started, and there are a lot more to come." Finally I fell asleep.

The next morning Jabey and I stayed in bed, and at noon we didn't go to drink soup. It was only water anyway, and whether we drank it or not made no difference. We sat on our bed eating candy and beans. Jabey was deep in thought.

"I've worked it out," he said suddenly. "We should eat one biscuit, a little brown sugar, three peanuts, and ten broad beans each day. If we get hungry it won't be a problem—we can lick salt." From that day on we ate like this:

· In the morning a little brown sugar, one biscuit, and three broad beans
· At noon, three peanuts
· In the afternoon, seven broad beans

We stuck very strictly to the numbers Jabey had worked out, and he never gave me a single extra bean, peanut, or biscuit. Whenever I wanted salt between meals, he would give me some to lick. We got hungrier and hungrier, but apart from avoiding death, we had no plan. The sick child in our tent died the following day, and a teacher ordered us to dispose of the body. That day three old and young people died in the group tents. By that time we were getting used to it, and no one paid any attention when they were told that people had died.

— THE LEATHER EATERS —

"Brother Jabey, let's go to group three's tent!" Wugpa said one day. "Their group is eating leather and sheepskin. If we don't go quickly there'll be none left!" We ran over, but by the time we got there, many people were running away clutching their piece of sheepskin. Inside the tent, most of the leather and sheepskin had already been taken, but we pushed our way into the crowd to see if anything was left. Jabey came out with two pieces of sheepskin, and I got a piece of leather. When we got back into our own tent, Jabey shared his sheepskin with the other children. We taught them to eat leather and sheepskin by shaving off the hair and then cooking it over the fire. A few days later we had finished off the leather bags, all the sheepskins, and even the leather thongs that held up the tent. The tents swayed and leaned farther over each day! Some people took the leather bindings off the yak saddles and ate them and even ate their own boots. People were forced to eat whatever they could find—and could swallow—to save their lives.

One day I was walking through the third tent when I saw a boy snatch a strip of dried leather away from a shaven-headed old man who had been chewing it.

"These little devils are going to starve me to death," said the old man, and he started crying. He couldn't chase the boy and get his leather back, so I ran after the child for him, out of pity. The boy was dizzy with hunger and soon fell over, so I easily caught up with him and took the leather out of his hand.

"Brother, please, I beg you . . . give me a piece of that leather. I haven't been able to find any food to eat for four days. I'm going to die of hunger soon," gasped the boy, and he held up his thumb. I thought, "What a pitiful child this is," so I tore the leather into two pieces and gave one of them to him. Then I took the rest of it back to the old man.

"Oh, you wonderful boy," he said, "thank you very much!" Then he started chewing the leather again. Tears filled my eyes as I watched these desperate people. That night I told Jabey what had happened.

"Kindness and compassion are useless now," he said. "Yesterday three children died. Even the teachers who took the bodies away were staggering from hunger while they did it, and soon there won't be anyone left to look after the dead bodies."

The following day Jabey and I went to see the old man to bring him some beans, but he was already dead, still holding the leather in his hands. On our way back to the tent we saw two little girls lying on the ground, too weak from hunger to walk. Jabey gave each of them four beans, but they were so close to death that it was absolutely certain four beans could not save their lives.

67

Wealthier Children Die More Quickly.
Poor Children Like Me Dispose of the Bodies.

One day Jabey and I went to Chumarleb again. We went by the store, but the only food they were selling was brown sugar. We circled around to the back of the shop to look through the piles of trash. On the wall of a house nearby there were seven small fish hanging out to dry, and Jabey went over to grab them. Some Chinese people were walking down the road, but they didn't pay any attention to us. We put the fish in our bag and walked to the edge of the Chinese soldiers' camp where they usually tethered their horses. They must have moved their horses inside the barracks because we couldn't see them anywhere. But there were tents near the barrack wall, and outside the entrance to the farthest tent was a stack with bags of maize. We couldn't see anyone around.

"Go fill a nose bag with maize. Be careful!" Jabey hissed. I crept around the tents and returned with the nose bag full of maize. A guard on top of the barrack wall saw me but didn't say anything. We left Chumarleb and returned to our tent after dark.

That day, one of the children from our tent had died. Kunchong and some others arrived to dispose of the body and dragged it to the far side of the river. The following morning another child died in our tent. The teachers ordered two of the older children to take the dead body away.

"We're too weak with hunger—we can't do it," they complained, but they managed to drag the body to the bank of the river anyway. From there Jabey and I pulled it into a small ravine on the opposite side of the river where the other bodies had been taken.

Later that day, Jabey and I passed two women toasting the leather bindings of a yak saddle on a fire and eating them. Jabey gave them some salt.

"You kind little boy—may you live a long life," they told him and gave me a piece of the toasted leather. "Six or seven people die every day in our tent," one of the women said. "So many people dead, and soon we will be dead too." As we walked toward our tent, I suddenly remembered the food I had hidden when we first came to the "Joyful Home."

I told Jabey, excited, "When we were camped on the other side of the river, I hid a sack of tsampa in a cave, because we had so much food at the time that I couldn't eat it. Do you think it might still be there?"

"Can you remember exactly where you hid it?" he asked.

"I think I'd know if we went there," I replied. "It was in a cave."

"Let's go look," he said. We walked across the ice and back to the former campsite. I recognized the cave on the mountainside overlooking the site, and we went inside to look. It wasn't long before we found it. I had hidden it before the Chinese New Year celebrations. Since then, the bag had gotten water-logged and then froze together with the stones and earth around it. After we melted it, the tsampa was delicious, and Jabey and I were ecstatic. We had an entire gazelle-skin bag full of tsampa with butter, cheese, and sugar, and we would not die of starvation for a long time yet. We returned to our tent after dark. Everyone except the little brother and sister had gone to sleep, but they were awake and waiting for us. I told them to cover their heads with their robes so that I could give them a small piece of tsampa secretly.

When the sun rose the following morning, we were the only children with the energy to get out of bed. There was nothing to eat, and it was cold even inside the tent—going outside only made us feel colder. But Jabey and I went to the kitchen and asked Wuglo for a teapot full of hot water. We took the pot to a sunny place by the bank of the river and ate the tsampa we'd hidden in our robes with a little salt. Around noon we went back to the tent. Later, Wugpa came to see us.

"Hey," he said, "the boy sleeping beside me, Dorjap, died last night. They have already taken his body away." At bedtime that night a girl was crying with a stomachache. At midnight she stopped making noise, and in the morning she was dead, but no one came to remove her body, so it lay untouched for two days. Then Jabey, Wugpa, and I took it across the river. Almost all the children in our tent were very young, but Wugpa was thirteen, two years younger than my brother, Jabey, and strong enough to help with the bodies.

Many of the children at the school were from wealthy families, with comfortable homes, and had never experienced cold and hunger. They didn't know how to look after themselves, and even if you put a piece of leather or sheepskin in their hands, they didn't know how to eat it. They had no idea how to feed themselves, other than waiting to see what the kitchen provided, so their hunger was especially acute, and they died more easily than the rest of us. Even a small problem could kill them. Over the past ten days around two hundred children in the three groups had died, all the sons or daughters of rich families. The old people were at their limit also and died easily. Around one hundred of them had died too, all from wealthy families.

The following morning, more old people in the second sleeping tent had died, but the teachers told us that there was no longer anyone available to remove the bodies. A large group of children was peering in the entrance of a small tent nearby, and Jabey and I went over to have a look. Two old women without anyone to look after them were lying dead in the tent. The children told us that no one was allowed to go inside this tent. Five or six days later I went to look again. The dead bodies were still there, and it was clear no one was coming for them. I took out my pocketknife and cut all the guy ropes so that the tent fell down on top of the bodies. "You did right," Jabey said when I told him. "That tent will rot away in the summer."

Later, we saw a crowd of people standing near the kitchen door. We asked the cook, Wuglo, what had happened. "A big bowl of dog fat has been stolen," she told us, "and we have no fat to put in the soup. That thief will have an unhappy life!" It was the first time we had heard that they were using dog fat in the kitchen. Tserang Dorje was there too.

"Just forget it," he said. "I can understand why they stole it. We're all nearly dead from hunger." At noon Jabey and I went to the kitchen and drank watery soup. It smelled of tsampa, and there was oil floating on it, which must have been the remaining dog fat. The old people and children who were still alive tried to keep going from that one bowl of soup a day. That night I heard two children whimpering in the night—they said that their stomachs hurt. Jabey tried to help them, but it was useless, and after midnight they fell silent. I thought to myself, "How terrible. They must have died." I was right, because the next morning they were both dead, with swollen faces and a lot of oily vomit on their pillows. They were the ones who had stolen and eaten the dog fat. Jabey and I went to Tserang Dorje's tent and told him about it.

"Sons of a great father," he said. "Can you find any way to get their bodies out of there? I'm so sick I can't even walk." I went to find Kunchong, but there was a crowd of people staring into his tent. Two more children were lying dead on the floor of the tent with bloated faces and a pool of vomit nearby. People were talking about them.

"These are the ones who stole that dog fat," they said. "It's very sad! They ate so much that they died." I couldn't find Kunchong, so I kept on walking. At a third tent entrance another crowd of children and old people was standing, and beyond them another three children who had died in the same way. "The Three Precious Jewels bear witness!" I thought to myself. "How could a single bowl of dog fat kill seven children so quickly? They didn't die of hunger, exactly, they died because they ate too much too quickly."

"What a pity these children didn't know that overeating when you have been hungry a long time can kill you," said one old woman. It was such a horribly sad, ugly thing, and there was still nobody to dispose of the corpses. The teachers told us that the people sleeping in the tent where any children died were responsible for taking their bodies away. When I got back to our tent, there was nobody inside, just two children in the entrance who were giddy with hunger and couldn't possibly help me move bodies. I didn't know what to do, so I tied a rope around the neck of the younger child's body and dragged it out of the tent. I pulled it to the cliff and pushed it over the edge. Then I went back and hauled another one to the same place in the same way. The bodies of these young children were light and easy to drag. Then I walked down to the foot of the cliff and dragged the bodies into the ravine opposite the river. I had never been afraid of dead bodies. When I was very young, my father had helped cut up the corpses at the sky burial ceremonies in Chugama Monastery and had taken us along with him so that we could cook him a meal while he was working. Since then, dead bodies didn't scare me. But that day was the first time I tended to dead bodies that had nobody else to take care of them. I was very pleased with what I had done!

68

Pitching My Own Small Black Yak Hair Tent.
Killing and Eating Pikas.

"Jabey," Wugpa said at bedtime that evening, "I need to move to the second tent because my grandmother is close to death. If she dies, I'll come back." By that time, a group of children from our tent had already died, and the others could hardly walk and were certain to die very soon. In those days I looked death in the face every day. Just the day before, five people in the "Joyful Home," both young and old, had died, and that day another six had gone. They had been hungry for so long that no amount of water soup could save them. The next day, two children died in our tent. We had to report the deaths to the school, and then I put a rope around the neck of each corpse and dragged it to the small valley opposite the river. Every tent was losing people. They said that in one of the groups 270 people had died. Now that we'd lost two more children from our tent, only the little girl, Jabey, and I were left. When the little girl's brother died, she didn't know what had happened.

"Brother, get up," she called to him that morning, but he was already dead. I tricked her into going to the kitchen while I took his body away. She came back at noon.

"Nulo," she asked me, "where is my brother?"

"Your brother's gone away with one of his friends," I said. "He won't be back for a few days, but I'll look after you until then." She didn't know what had really happened and just believed me, but I felt so sad that I couldn't keep from crying. Starting that day, Jabey and I gave her an equal share of our food, but in a week she was dead. Hers was the last dead body I removed from the tent.

I thought, "Jabey and I are the last ones left in this tent." All the other children had died from cold and hunger in the past two months. Every day they woke with the fear that they would find one of their friends had died in the night. Every day they drank their one bowl of watery flour soup or watery tsampa soup, overcoming dizziness to make their way to the kitchen, trying to stay alive. Their hunger went on for a long time until, one by one, they set out on the long road that leads to the intermediate state between death and rebirth.

My own hunger increased every day. I was walking less steadily as light-headedness took hold, and the ringing in my ears grew louder and louder. My body lost energy, and I fell asleep very easily. The other children had died after long spells of sleepiness, and I was feeling sleepier and sleepier all the time. I felt that death could not be far away. Such thoughts filled my head all the time. One day Jabey came to me.

"Go to Tserang Dorje and ask him if we can set up a small tent," he said. I found Tserang Dorje lying on his bed in his tent. When I walked in, he raised his head from the pillow.

"Oh, that's great," he said. "Is Jabey still alive?"

"Jabey's in the tent. We're still alive."

"I'm so happy," he said. "Come over here." He got out of bed and gave me a handful of cheese from under the mattress. While I was eating it I said to him, "Teacher, the rest of the children in our tent are all dead. There's only Jabey and me left, which means the tent's much too big for us, and we aren't comfortable sleeping there. Can we put up a small one?"

"I only have cheese left to eat. You two be brave boys and try to stay alive. You can do whatever you like with the tent." He handed me another handful of cheese and said, "This is for Jabey. Do you have any food?"

"We have some candy, broad beans, and a little salt," I replied.

Yes, yes . . . you are both sons of a great father. You'll find a way to stay alive, won't you?" At that moment I thought, "If Tserang Dorje has no food, won't he starve?" I walked back to our tent and told Jabey what was on my mind.

"Tserang Dorje has no food to eat," I said. "Will he die of hunger?"

"Tserang Dorje's an adult," he replied. "They are different from children. Even if they have no food, they won't starve to death." The big tent was too difficult for us to dismantle, so Jabey cut all the ropes with his knife, and it fell down in two pieces. We cut out a square of tent cloth from the middle of one of the pieces, collected three tent poles, and tied them to the cloth. Using stones to weigh down the skirts of the tent, we pitched it close to the river.

From that time on we had our own little tent. We used a spare piece of tent cloth and the dead people's clothes to make our tent comfortable, and we cleaned the riverbank of trash. We made a fireplace in the tent, took a few cooking pots from the other tents, and the cook Wuglo gave us some cloth bags. We had everything a real family needs. That first afternoon while we were looking for flat stones in the Serwu River, we found a two-year-old yak's hindquarters in an ice hole in the river. It looked as though its forequarters had already been eaten by dogs, but there were bones and skin left, and a little meat on the bones. We were overjoyed about finding that yak and felt the fear of hunger ebbing away. We dug the yak's flesh, bones, and small intestines out of the ice very carefully. We shaved the hair from the hide and cooked it in small pieces. I found tea leaves on the ground behind the school kitchen and boiled them in water. The tea smelled delicious. We still had some broad beans, candies, maize, salt, and a handful of cheese left in our food supply, so we definitely weren't going to die of hunger for at least a month. Smoke drifted out of our tent morning and afternoon, but there was no fire in any of the other tents. Except for the school's, ours was the only working kitchen. Every morning some children who were close to death from starvation came to our tent entrance. Jabey and I gave them a little meat soup and a mouthful of cooked leather each. They never missed a morning. One day a group of adults came to our tent asking for food, too. Jabey and I gave them two or three mouthfuls of meat soup, and five each of the dried maize and broad beans, which made them very happy.

The school kitchen was about one hundred paces away. The cook Wuglo had a daughter of about five years who often came to visit us, and she called me "Brother Nulo." I always played games with her. Sometimes she secretly gave me tsampa with cheese.

"Go and beg more tsampa from your mother," I would tell her. The tsampa she brought was already fully prepared, and we'd eat it together. One day Wuglo came to see us.

"You're teaching my daughter bad habits," she said, but she gave me another bowl of tsampa with cheese anyway. I thought, "That's strange, isn't it? The others have nothing but water to drink, but the cook has enough tsampa to share with other people." Nevertheless, I was grateful that the cook was happy enough about my friendship with her daughter to give us food.

At that time Jabey and I never went to the school kitchen to drink soup, so we told the cook to give our share to two girls who came regularly to our tent door. We were never hungry anymore and could share our food with the children who came to see us. "There are pikas and field mice living around the river," Jabey pointed out one day. "I killed one with a stone trap today. I left the trap at the entrance to its burrow, so let's go there tomorrow and see if we have caught any more." Starting then, we butchered the pikas and cooked them every day. Even though they were small, they were very delicious. I put their heads, lungs, liver, and intestines into the soup pot and cooked the meat separately. Then I burned off the fur and put pieces of skin in the soup. When starving children came to our tent, I gave some of them the pikas' heads, and some got lungs or liver in their soup bowls. When these children drank the meat soup, sweat poured down their faces because they needed the food so badly. Every afternoon Jabey set more traps, and the next morning he would go to inspect them. He returned each time with pikas that he said were already dead when he found them. Every day I made soup with the pikas' heads, intestines, lungs, and livers and gave it out to the children. I thought, "If we can keep on killing pikas like this, these children definitely won't die of starvation."

A group of fuel collectors meeting on the surface of a frozen river.
123068-243707. Photographer, Joseph Rock, 1924.
© President and Fellows of Harvard College, Arnold Arboretum Archives.

69

Eating Horses and Dogs. Dying of Starvation.

One morning, Jabey and I went back to Chumarleb. Jabey still had about twenty yuan from his days herding yaks for the army, so we went to the shop and spent four yuan on two and a half kilos of candy and some black tea and salt. It was all the food they had for sale. On the way home we stopped at the place where the army tethered their horses and gathered half a sack of black broad beans. Farther along the road there was a dead horse, but two adults and a child were already cutting off the meat. We sat down to watch, and a man who looked like an official worker came over to us.

"Do you two need any horse meat?"

"Yes please, we do need some," Jabey affirmed. The man cut off a piece of chest meat and gave it to Jabey, with another large piece to me.

"Thank you very much!" we said. It was good, fatty meat. Then Chuga arrived with some more officials. It seemed as though the two men knew each other. While they were talking, the official cut off one of the fore fetlocks and gave it to Chuga. Then Chuga walked back with us. On our way, Chuga brought us into a warehouse and let us take away three bowls of flour.

"Don't tell anyone about this, right?" he told us.

"Don't worry, we understand. Thanks very much."

While we were getting the flour, he was talking about us to some other officials in the warehouse. "These Golok boys must be devils, otherwise I swear they'd be dead already," Chuga said.

"I hear that you two really need food, but I haven't got anything to give you today, so take this and buy some brown sugar with it," one of the workers said, handing us two Chinese banknotes.

"Thank you very much for your kindness," Jabey and I both said.

When we got back to our tent, we had fat horse meat and flour, so we made dumplings and ate them. Wugpa came by.

"I think my grandmother's going to die of hunger," Wugpa told us, as he sat eating dumplings and drinking tea. Jabey gave him five pika carcasses and a small piece of horse meat.

"Thank you, dear brother," he said before he left, taking the food with him. "Now I'm sure she will survive a few more days, at least."

"Come back soon, and we will think what's best to do. Maybe we can help her survive," Jabey told him.

"Yes, my dear brother," he replied. "I'm going to go now so I can give her the food as quickly as possible. She hasn't eaten for three days, and she can hardly even speak." He left the tent.

The following morning Wugpa came to see us again, carrying a bag full of yak dung fuel for the fire.

"Last night I made meat soup for my grandmother, and this morning she drank some more of it. She was able to sit up today, so I don't think she's going to die." We were so happy when we heard that.

A few days later I was fetching water and had just climbed back up the bank when Chuga waved me toward the entrance to the official workers' tent. When I was near enough to hear he shouted, "Hey, Golok boy! Bring me some of your salt." I went back to our tent to get salt. When I entered the official workers' tent, I saw Tserang Dorje there. I gave the salt to Chuga.

"All right, my lovely little brother. I'm going to buy salt tomorrow, so I'll give it back to you then," he said.

"No, we don't need any," I said. "We still have some that we bought."

"How did you buy it?" asked Tserang Dorje.

"When Jabey was herding yaks for the Chinese soldiers, they paid him, and we still have some money," I said.

"They have been to Chumarleb many times to buy tea, salt, sugar, and other things," said Chuga.

"You did well," said Tserang Dorje. "No one can deny it—Golok people are unique!" They salted the meat they were boiling and told me I could go after

I had eaten some of it. I told them I didn't want any and tried to leave, but Tserang Dorje wouldn't let me. He packed some leg meat in a cloth bag and insisted I take it before they let me go.

"Take this with you," he said in a low voice, "but don't let anyone else see."

"Thank you very much, teacher," I replied. When I got back to our tent, I handed the packet to my brother.

"This is dog meat," he said, opening it. Even so, it was good, fat meat. That month we had plenty to eat and never felt hungry. There was dried yak meat, horse meat, dog meat, beans, and Chinese wheat flour. We could eat as much as we wanted and still have enough left over to give other children meat soup with pika heads and flesh. That was just enough to prevent them from dying of hunger.

One day Jabey and I were collecting firewood on the far bank of the river. On our way back we stopped at the pika traps and removed six dead ones. When we went down to the river, we saw two children breaking apart a bone and eating the marrow. The remains of a human leg were near them.

"That's horrible," said Jabey. "They're eating raw human flesh, and they don't even realize it." He went over to them and said, "Would you like some pika meat?"

"Yes," they said. Jabey gave some to each of them. We went back to our tent without saying a word. When we looked back, we could see the children were still chewing the leg meat, their heads bowed.

That evening, we were sitting in our tent after supper when Wugpa came in.

"I've been told that the old people in the second tent are eating human meat," he said. I thought, "I'm sure that's true. When people are starving to death, they will eat whatever they can find. Children who don't know any better and have no other way to stay alive shouldn't be blamed, as long as they don't do it when the famine is over."

A few days later some students went to Tserang Dorje and made an accusation: "Those two Golok boys should be ashamed. They are stealing food and eating it."

"It's none of your business," Tserang Dorje snapped back. "And where would they find anything to steal? We're all dying of hunger. If you can find any food to steal, please go ahead. I won't object."

One day I was cooking pika meat on a hot stone when Tserang Dorje came into the tent, asking, "What's that delicious smell? Is that what you are eating today?" I stood up to let him by, to sit on Jabey's bed.

"Teacher, would you like some pika meat?" I asked him.

"How did you two kill all of these pikas?" he asked.

"Jabey set traps to kill them," I explained. Tserang Dorje took some pika meat and cooked it. "I'm going to tell some of the older students to start hunting pikas tomorrow," he said. "This meat could save us from death." I tried to give him more meat, but he said, "That was really delicious. I won't eat any more now. You need it yourselves."

"We have plenty more," I said, "and Jabey will bring a lot back later on." I raised the lid of our cooking pot to show him all the pika carcasses inside. He took another one and began eating it. "Does Uncle Chuga eat pika meat?" I asked.

"Whether he does ordinarily or not, he would be happy to eat it now, I'm sure." I packed three cooked pikas into the cloth bag Tserang Dorje had used for the dog meat and handed it to him.

"This is for Chuga," I said.

"Great," he said and headed out with the bag of meat in his hand.

"If you ever get hungry, come and eat with us," I said.

"Well, if you don't mind, we would really appreciate that," he replied. Jabey and I were overjoyed that Tserang Dorje had come to our tent for a meal. After his visit I sometimes saw the older students hunting for pikas, but I don't think they killed many because at least two more people, old or young, died every day. During that time we would greet each other, "Hey, not dead yet?"

Toward dusk Wugpa came to see us. "Brother Jabey," he said, "there's a yak that hasn't moved from the end of the valley since this morning. It might be sick. Should we go after dark to see?" When we looked out our door, the yak was still on the side of the mountain.

"We'll go at midnight," Jabey said.

"Can I come with you?" I asked. They agreed. At midnight the three of us set off for the mountain with a rope and knives. Wugpa and Jabey each carried a bag. At first we followed the riverbed, and when we began to climb the mountain, the moon came out. The yak was still there, but when it heard our voices it moved away. We crept closer and saw that it was a blind riding yak dragging a five- or six-meter-long rope attached to its nose.

"The Three Precious Jewels sent us this!" exclaimed Wugpa as he led it down the mountain by the nose. I thought, "This is really strange . . . a blind yak with a rope through its nose . . . almost as if it was waiting for us. Of course, the Three Precious Jewels have given it to us to prevent us from dying of hunger, but it's a pity the yak has to die." I followed Jabey, Wugpa, and the yak down the mountain until we reached the river.

70

Lost Yak Meat, Bitten by a Dog,
and Caught Stealing Sheep by the Shepherd.

After we got back to the river with the blind yak, I held it by the nose, and they tied its front legs together. Then they tried to push it over, but they couldn't. I put my finger in the yak's nose to make it jump, but it never even moved.

"If we can't push it over, would it work to tie up its mouth and suffocate it while it's standing up?" they asked each other, and not knowing what else to do, they went ahead and did it. The yak didn't move and just stood quietly. Then suddenly it bucked a few times and fell over. When it was dead, we butchered it, cut off the meat, and put all the meat into bags. I was in charge of the leg meat. By the time we started back for our tent, dawn was beginning to break, and when we arrived opposite tent three, it was fully light. Jabey and Wugpa were moving slowly because the meat in their bags was heavy. I was afraid we would be seen, so I said, "Hurry up, because if they see us, they will take the meat." I ran ahead. When I got near our tent, I looked back and saw the two of them had only gotten as far as tent two. I stuck my bag of meat inside our tent and watched them from behind the cloth of the tent's entrance. They were struggling and stopped for a rest. Some people were walking around on top of a nearby bank but didn't notice them. Then suddenly some children standing near the kitchen door of tent one saw them pass by the foot of the bank.

"Look," they shouted, "Jabey and Wugpa have been out stealing." They yelled for the rest of the children to come out. The teachers, cook, and students came to the kitchen door to take a look, and some of the students ran up to see what was in the bags.

"It's meat, stolen meat!" they called out.

"Hey, you two, bring that meat into the kitchen," said the teachers. There was nothing else they could do, so Japey and Wugpa carried it into the kitchen. Later they returned to our tent with black looks on their faces. The kitchen had taken most of the meat but gave them two pieces of meat, three pieces of liver, and three bowls of tsampa and cheese as their reward. We divided that between us, and Wugpa took his share away with him.

"Come back here after dark," I told him at the door.

"All right, see you later," he said. Jabey and I cooked the meat and drank the soup with tsampa in it, and then I went to the kitchen to get our share of the soup the cooks had made with *our* meat. Wuglo poured the soup into my pot.

"The two of them get an extra-good portion of soup," she said. "We wouldn't have had any meat soup without them." She put plenty of meat into the pot and added a bowl of tsampa and cheese as well.

"Even though they took the meat away, at least this soup will last three or four days," Jabey said when I showed up with the pot.

"I made it back to our tent with my meat," I told him. "It's still here." My brother was overjoyed when he heard that.

After dark, Wugpa returned. When he had eaten his meat and drunk his soup, I reported the news, "I wasn't carrying as much meat as you were, but nobody saw me get back to the tent, so I've still got it."

"It's too bad that we didn't take a bit less—you could have stashed more of it away before they stopped us," he remarked sadly. Again we divided the meat into three parts. Even though I had only been carrying meat from the yak's leg, it was enough to last us a while. Wugpa returned home with his share.

The next day I thought, "Maybe if I go back to where we killed that yak yesterday, there'll still be some meat left." I hid two knives in my robe and started up the mountain. When I got to the dead yak, I saw that two dogs were gnawing at its leg bones. I threw stones at them to drive them away, but another five dogs, which I hadn't seen because they were concealed by a bank, ran at me. They surrounded me and attacked, biting and pulling me to the ground. I managed to get up and threw rocks at them, but it didn't do any good, and they pulled me down again. I noticed that the dogs didn't bite when I was on the ground, but only barked and snapped, so I lay flat for a while. When they moved away, I got up and ran. The dogs chased after me and bit me again, but I managed to stab the biggest dog in the nose with my dagger as it bit my left hand, and it ran away howling. Another dog bit me, but I stabbed him under the foreleg, and he retreated. My dagger was stuck in him and pulled out of my hand as he ran off—I couldn't get it back. Four dogs were still stalking me, and one of them bit my leg, pulling me to the ground again. As before, I lay still on the grass while the dogs barked, dripping their saliva on my face. Then the dogs went away again. I saw that there were lots of stones nearby in the riverbed. I ran toward them, and when I reached the river, I threw a rock at the dog closest to me and hit him. After that, the rest of the dogs turned back. I watched them leave, then headed for home. I definitely had no chance of getting the rest of the yak meat and had almost given my own flesh to those dogs instead!

When I got home, Brother Jabey was cooking, and I told him about the dogs. We checked my wounds and found that I had six large and small gashes on my left hand, and four wounds other places on my body, as well as many bruises and marks from the bites. We had no medicine, so I peed in my bowl, and Jabey washed the wounds with my urine. We also cut some of the sheepskin off my robe and put that on the wounds. While I healed from the bites, I lay on my bed for a few days. In about ten days, all the wounds were closed up.

Jabey was still trapping and killing pikas, and neither of us went hungry. Jabey and Wugpa went to Chumarleb, and when they returned, they said that there were a lot of Mongolian soldiers in the town. But they came home with a lot of cooked rice, square bread, maize, and other things the troops had left behind. So we had yak meat, pika meat, grain, and everything else we needed. That same day we were given some dried lamb to share. The lambs had died of hunger, and even though there was barely any meat on their bones, there were a few scraps between the ribs. Jabey and I didn't like the meat, so we cut it up and gave it to the children who came to our door for food. They thought it was wonderful!

One day Wugpa came by.

"Today we're going to steal lambs from the government's grazing commune," Jabey informed us.

"Right, let's do it, but do you really think we can catch those lambs?" said Wugpa.

"If we get it right, we can do it," Jabey said, "although if the shepherd sees us we might not have time to carry them away." They discussed strategies. The three of us took knives, ropes, and small sacks and set off toward the grazing land. We took the road toward Chumarleb and then walked up a mountain. Then we waited in a small valley for the sheep to arrive. It wasn't long before sheep started to come over the top of the mountain and head our way. They were grazing all around us, and Jabey got out a lasso and tried to catch one of them. He missed, and some of the sheep ran a short distance away. However, most of them stayed nearby, and there was no sign of a shepherd. Jabey and Wugpa crept around the edges of the flock and drove the sheep between them. Jabey managed to get his lasso around the neck of one of the sheep, and Wugpa helped him drag it into the little valley. It looked as if there were two or three thousand sheep on the grassland. I thought, "It's strange that there are thousands of sheep grazing up here, while down in the valley hundreds, maybe even thousands, of children and old people are dying of hunger. This must be how the Law of Karma affects each of us as individuals." I walked over to Jabey and Wugpa, who had just finished butchering the sheep. They were cutting up the meat and draining off the blood. Jabey gave me a piece of liver and said, "Go up to the top of the mountain and see if anyone's coming." I climbed up above the valley. I could see a drover with a pack yak approaching Jabey and Wugpa from below.

"Hey, you two, be quick! There's a man with a pack yak coming up the valley." There was a dog behind him that ran toward me, barking. Suddenly we heard shouting from higher up the mountain.

"Hey, you robber devils!" There were two men yelling at us. They loaded stones in slings and shot them in our direction. The sheep ran away. It was definitely the shepherds.

71

Feeding Ourselves. Killing a Calf.

We fled down the valley. I carried the sheep's head, and the others carried the rest of the meat. The last we saw of the shepherds, they were far off, still looking around the place where we'd slaughtered the sheep.

When we got back to the tent, I made a fire and cooked the sheep's breast. Jabey and Wugpa cut up rest of the meat and made sausages. After we had drunk our tea and eaten our meal, we divided the meat and sausages. Wugpa went home with his share, and Jabey and I mixed the leftover blood with flour and salt and cooked it in one of the lungs. It was really delicious.

The next day Jabey and I went across to the kitchen, where we met Tserang Dorje at the door.

"Nulo, how are you—are you ill?" he asked.

"No, we haven't caught anything," I told him. I thought, "I would like to give my kind teacher some of the meat, but I daren't take it to him. Would he come to our tent if I asked him?" I went and stood next to him.

"Hey, teacher, I've just finished cooking. Would you like to come to our tent?"

"I'm happy to come and be your guest," he said. He entered our tent, and I poured tea for him.

"You have tea?" he said, surprised.

"I bought it from Chumarleb," I told him.

"Do you have any money left?" he asked.

"We've still got a little."

"You two boys really are wise." I put some sausage in front of him, which I had already heated up.

"Have some more pika, teacher." He realized right away that the meat was not pika and gave me a searching look.

"You are a pair of little devils, aren't you?" he laughed. "Where on earth did this meat and sausage come from?" He ate a few mouthfuls and then said, "Well, I wish you two a long life, anyway. This sausage is delicious. You keep the rest. I'd just like a little more of that meat soup, please."

"Teacher, you can eat as much as you like. We have plenty more." Some children were hovering nearby, so I called them to our door, poured a little soup for each of them, and gave them a piece of sausage about the size of a thumb.

"Who are they?" asked Tserang Dorje.

"They are from tent number one, and there are nine of them. We give them a pika's head, or some meat, or leftover soup, so they come by often."

"Were Jabey and Wugpa angry when I took away their meat last time?"

"No," I said. "They didn't stay angry, because you took the meat that they were carrying, but you didn't take the meat I had."

"So you had meat, too?" he asked.

"I didn't have as much as them, so I got back to our tent before daylight."

"You are great boys. Keep searching for food for a bit longer. If we can survive another month or two, we will have a delivery of food from outside." Then he left. I was so glad that I had been able to feed my teacher again.

Later, I was sitting in my tent drinking tea. A girl's voice called to me from outside, "Brother Nulo, they're sharing out meat today. Are you going to get your share?" I walked outside and saw that it was a child called Sanji Dolma. We both went to the place between the tents where they were sharing out meat. In fact my name wasn't really "Nulo" as the children there all called me, but after I got to Ratsang School everyone called me that because that was how they pronounced my name in their dialect. There was a crowd in the center of the encampment. I walked to the front to have a look. Some wolf paws, and legs with the hide still on, were lying on a cloth—I couldn't tell who had brought them. When the person sharing it cut off the hide, the meat underneath was blue and rotten. Some old women and children were scooping up the stinking liquid that oozed from the meat with their hands and drinking it. I felt like vomiting because of the disgusting smell and I thought, "The Three Precious Jewels! Bear witness to what people will do if they are starving. And if they can drink this rotten meat liquid without getting sick or dying, they must be indestructible." Jabey and I were allotted the lower part of a wolf's leg, but I didn't take it inside our tent. I gave it away to one of the other children, instead. When I returned to our tent, Jabey wasn't back yet, so I went to collect firewood, carrying a bag. It was springtime, and the young grass beside the river was green tipped with red. I walked along the riverbank collecting wood. Down by the river there were two mother yaks with their calves, and some pack yaks eating grass. A newly born yak calf and a newborn bull and yak hybrid calf with a red hide were asleep on the ground in front of me. "How about killing a calf?" I thought. I looked around but couldn't see anyone. The two were sleeping at the foot of the bank, their ears twitching. I jumped on one of the calves and grabbed it around the neck, holding it to the ground. It struggled to its feet, knocking me over, and ran away, terrified. I stood up with a strange sound in my ears and walked off. A bit later I found the calves sleeping in the shade under the bank, where they were less bothered by biting insects. I walked to the top of the bank and studied them again. The red bull calf was a bit bigger than the yak, but I decided it was impossible to kill the hardier yak calf, so I thought I would try him. I jumped on the bull calf and pushed him down. He struggled, but I hung on. We fought all the way to the river, and I managed to get his head under the water. Soon he was dead. I pulled the dead body over to where my bag was lying, and shook the yak dung and firewood I'd collected out of my bag. Then I put the calf's body in the bag and disguised it with a thin layer of yak dung. I carried it home, but it was hard going. The calf was heavy. I took a rest on the way, staying underneath the banks of the river out of sight of our encampment. When I was opposite the third tent, I saw a woman walking through the river, singing a song. A little later she came up to me driving the two female yaks and the pack yaks.

"Hey, little boy," she said, "have you seen a red bull calf?"

"No, I haven't," I lied. She went over to the place beneath the bank where I had jumped on the bull calf and looked around. After a while she caught up with me while I was taking a rest at the foot of the bank because the bag was so heavy. She came up to me and asked, looking me straight in the eye, "Hey, did you really not see a red bull calf over there?"

"No, really."

"What are you carrying?"

"Yak dung. You can check if you don't believe me." She laughed, still looking me in the eye and then walked off, singing. My heart was thumping loudly. "Three Precious Jewels! She almost caught me." I sat down again for a rest. I could see the woman and some others driving pack yaks and female yaks down toward the end of the valley. A female yak broke away from the herd and ran back toward where I had killed the calf, grunting. I thought, "How sad the female yak is. Now I'm so sorry I killed her calf." There was nothing to be done about it, though—I had killed it already and was carrying its corpse on my back. Regret wouldn't help. When I got to the tent, Jabey wasn't there, so I butchered the calf and saved all the blood and meat very carefully. I cooked a little of the meat and waited for Jabey to arrive. Suddenly the official worker Chuga walked into our tent.

"Hey, you two Golok thieves! What are you doing?" he chuckled.

"Not much, just sitting and cooking meat," I replied.

"And where did you steal your meat this time?" he asked.

"We didn't steal it, we found it. Anyway, sit down, and I'll bring you some to eat." He looked at me very skeptically. I took the calf meat off the fire and gave him some.

"It's real meat," he said in amazement. "I thought you were going to give me pika meat again." When he had finished, he said, "Thanks, dear friend. That's enough for me. Even when we say we have nothing to eat, we really have some left, because you two always have food."

"We have more," I told him. "Fill yourself up. There's plenty."

After he'd eaten his fill, he reflected, "We will have food by the summer. But people benefit from suffering, you know. When the Red Army had nothing to eat, they ate their belts and boots, but they won in the end. So if we don't die of famine, our future will be bright." He said many things like that. When my brother got home, he told us that he had been to Chumarleb to buy tea and salt, and he'd brought half of a dried lamb carcass back with him, too.

"Sons of a great father! You really are brave boys. Even the adults are too weak by now to walk all the way to Chumarleb. They are in much worse condition than you two because they don't know how to trap pikas. They're going to starve while you are living like kings." After that, he left.

"Did Chuga give us this meat?" asked Jabey after he had gone.

"No, he didn't," I said. "I went to the river today and killed a bull." He burst out laughing. I told him what had happened, and he was delighted.

"Everything's going to be fine," he said. "Spring's coming." He packed one of the calf's legs, some tea, and some salt into a bag and handed it to me, saying, "Why don't you go to Wugpa's tent and give this to him?" I headed out.

72

Picking and Eating Plants. Eating Droma with Drippings.

When I arrived at Wugpa's tent with the bag of food, they told me he was sick, and I could see that he was lying in bed. There were two old women in the tent, but I didn't know which one was Wugpa's grandmother.

"Nulo, dear brother, come here and sit down," Wugpa said.

"Long life to you!" said one of the old women. "Is this the Golok boy? Without your help, we would have died of hunger a long time ago, but now we have nothing to eat again!" I gave her the tea, salt, and calf's meat. She said, "May you have a long life, you kind boy. Thank you very, very much,"

"This is the younger brother," Wugpa said.

"How lovely," said the old woman. "He is so strong and brave. You really will have a long life!"

"Dear friend, Wugpa," I said, "when you have nothing to eat, come to our home. We always have spare pika meat to give you."

"My friend, you are very kind," he said. I returned to our tent, thinking,

"It's good that those old women's lives will be saved for at least a few days by the calf's meat. I hope we can think of something else for them later."

The next morning, I went to fetch water, and the red-tipped green grass that grew along the water's edge every spring gave me an idea. I walked along the river's path until I saw a patch of wild vegetables called *jirelebmo*. I put down my water pot to pick it. There were other vegetables growing near the bank called *nelo* and *shagchu*. I picked a lot of them. I had eaten them in my native land, and I knew that they were delicious boiled in water or added to soup. I went down to the water to wash them. Then I saw some *drollo* plants growing in a bend of the riverbed and thought, "If there are drollo here, there must be droma nearby." I dug in the earth with a long, thin stone, and out came some big, white, hairy droma roots. I burrowed deeper and found that the earth was full of them. I thought, "This is really strange. There are people dying of starvation nearby, and right here under the bank there is so much droma growing. What a pity people from rich families don't know how to dig for droma." I went back to our tent, eating some of them on the way. After I had cooked the first batch, I returned with a small adze to get more. I dug for the rest of the morning and filled half a hat full of droma. Some of the larger ones were furry, but most of them were very nice. While I was away, Jabey made a vegetable soup with dried lamb and pika meat.

"Where were these plants growing?" he asked me when I got back.

"Over there at the foot of the bank," I replied. "And there's droma around here, too. There's lots of it in the bank and down by the river." Jabey was thrilled.

"It's strange how so many people have died of famine, and yet they never even tried to find droma. Why didn't they think of it?" he mused. That evening we cooked droma and pika meat together. I thought it was the most delicious meal we had eaten for a long time. The next day I spent all day digging droma, while Jabey went to check the pika traps. By noon I had dug a hatful of droma and was back in our tent. Jabey butchered a pika and removed its heart and lungs. Then we stuffed it with droma and grilled it on a flat stone—by the time the pika meat was cooked, the droma was ready too. The pika and the droma tasted wonderful together. We even named the dish. We called them "pika droma dumplings," and we made them every day for days.

"Let's go walk around the government grazing commune to see what we can find to eat," Jabey said one morning. We grabbed a sack and walked over. The first thing we found was a dried yak stomach they were using to store butter. Apart from that we found nothing except sheep bones scattered on the ground where some tents had stood.

"You should bring the bones," said Jabey. "There's marrow inside them if you break them open." I collected a bag full of sheep bones—some still had meat on them. When we got back to the tent, we smashed the bones and boiled them in water. We stirred the bones into the boiling water because we knew a lot of marrow would come out of the bones, and we remembered how delicious it had been when we drank it in our native land with tsampa and a little salt. The bone soup yielded about half a pot of marrow. We boiled the bone broth with tea. After we drank the "bone tea," sweat beaded on our faces and bodies. In the afternoon Japey poured out some bone tea for the children who came to our tent, and sweat poured from their heads and bodies, too. We made bone tea for many days, and whenever we drank it, it made us sweat heavily like that. We knew that was good for us. From that day on, we had droma and meat grease to eat whenever we needed it, as well as the pika dumplings. We didn't go hungry from then on.

One morning I was digging up droma near the river, when Tserang Dorje came to see me.

"Hey, Nulo, what are you doing?" he asked.

"I'm digging for droma," I explained.

"Don't tell lies, my boy. Surely there isn't really droma here?"

"There is, but only spring droma." Tserang Dorje came closer.

"You're right! It's hard to believe it's here, but it is," he said. "I'm going to tell the other children to come and dig some tomorrow. If they eat that, they certainly won't die of hunger." By that time, I had nearly a hat full. "Well," he said, "this is really good droma you've found. Let's go to my place, and I'll give you a little butter to eat with it." I followed him to his tent, and he hunted for the butter under his bedclothes and around the stove. "I'm sorry," he said after hunting for it unsuccessfully. "I hope you're not upset, but it looks like somebody's stolen it. I'll give you some of my cheese instead." He gave me two small bowls of cheese.

"Thank you, teacher," I said. "Please take the droma I dug today. We have plenty, and I can get some more tomorrow."

"No, no, I don't need it. It's much more important for you two. I'm coming to your tent to eat droma tomorrow, anyway!" I walked back to our tent. Later that day, the cook gave me a bowl of tsampa. The next day we cooked droma for Tserang Dorje and waited for him, but he never came.

Two days after that Tserang Dorje and Chuga came to our tent.

"Well, you two Golok thieves. What did you steal today?" they said.

"Today we stole droma," I replied. Jabey gave them some bone tea. We had made pika bone tea that day and mixed it with a little tsampa.

"I think this could help us build up our strength," said Chuga.

"This is just what you need if you are suffering from hunger," said Tserang Dorje. "Look at how the sweat is streaming out of us!"

"I have never seen boys as strong and brave as these two. They even make tea from bones. How did they think of that?" said Chuga. Jabey gave them droma and drippings, with a little tsampa sprinkled on top. They ate happily. "These two are a pair of devils. They even have tsampa and cheese!" Chuga was amazed. While we ate, Jabey told them about how we had come here from our native land, about the death of our father, how our companions had become prisoners, and other details of our story just as it had happened.

"I'm going to Chumarleb tomorrow," said Chuga. "I know Sonam Norbu, and I'll ask him about your companions." Before they left, they gave us a small bag full of cheese, and when we were standing outside the tent, Tserang Dorje gave six yuan to Jabey.

"Use it to buy something if you go to Chumarleb," he said.

"You are both very kind. Thank you so much," we said. We exchanged many affectionate parting words like this before they eventually went back to their tent.

— CONCERNED FOR OUR COMPANIONS —

Several days later Chuga came to see us.

"Sonam Norbu told me that the three youngest of your companions were released before Chinese New Year, but he doesn't know where they went after that. He said he didn't recognize the names of your elder companions." When we heard that, we felt happiness and sadness at the same time. Naturally we were relieved to hear that some of our companions had been released, but we were dispirited that we didn't know where they had gone. We were especially worried that the elder ones might be dead. My mind was full of thoughts like "If Dongtrug, Kelsang, and Tsekho were released a month after we arrived in the 'Joyful Home,' they have probably returned home already. We didn't die of hunger, so we could go there too." Even if our chiefdoms had been destroyed, I hoped that some of our cousins were left, and that Alak Gungtang was still there.

"They are going to build a school in Chumarleb this year," Tserang Dorje said one day, "and when it's ready I'll send you two there." I thought that we might be happy at a real school.

"We'll ask Dongtrug, Kelsang, and Tsekho about it when we find them," said Jabey. "They're still young, so they don't have to get back to our native land right away. We can see what this other school is like first." For a while we had been so beset by hunger that we didn't have time to think about our companions, but after we heard that they had been released, we could barely wait to see them again. However, we had no idea where they had gone, so we just had to wait for them, unsure what to do next.

73

The Girl's Life Is Saved. The Thief Loses His Life.

People were still dying of starvation in the "Joyful Home." Also, three children died from eating poisonous plants. In our group one tent, 260 children had died, and around 90 old men and women. Even more died in group two. The Three Precious Jewels knew that if we couldn't get more food for everyone, then many more people would die. I thought, "How hard it is for human beings to grow up, and how easy to die." People in the tents had begun to call the "Joyful Home" the "Dying of Famine Home" or the "Killing Old People Home." The Three Precious Jewels knew whether those not yet taken by death could survive or had even more suffering to endure.

One morning Jabey went to Wugpa's tent while I went to dig droma at the Sewo River, which was still partly covered in ice. There was some droma to dig, but it was hard going because the ground was frozen solid. While I was walking along the riverbank, I saw some white objects floating swiftly down the river toward me. When they got closer, I could see that they were the corpses of sheep, so I ran as quickly as I could to summon Jabey and Wugpa.

I shouted to Wugpa, who was outside his tent, and waved him over. Wugpa and Jabey ran to me, and we raced toward the river together while I told them about the dead sheep. When we got there, they pulled out four corpses, but many were still floating down the middle of the stream where the river was too deep for us to get to them. They put one sheep each on their shoulders, and took them back to our tent while I sat and guarded the other two on the riverbank. An old man came up to me.

"Where did you find those dead sheep?" he asked.

"They were in the river," I replied.

"Don't lie," he said. "How could they have been in the river? Dear little boy, would you give me one? I'm almost dead from hunger."

"I can't," I told him. "But there are more in the river." He walked along the water, but later he came back.

"Dear brother—son of a great father—please give me one. I give you my word that we are a group of old people, nearly dead from the famine." I didn't say anything, so he picked up one of the sheep. I thought, "It's a terrible thing to be near death from hunger."

"Long life and success with everything you do, my dear, kind little boy," the old man thanked me before he walked away with it. When Jabey and Wugpa got back, I explained what had happened.

"The old man said he was nearly dead from starvation," I told them. Wugpa called out to the old man.

"Hello there!" he shouted. The old man turned and stared at us without saying anything.

"Forget it," said Japey. "He's gone crazy from hunger." We carried the last dead sheep to our tent, so that day Japey and I had two sheep to butcher. All day we made sausages and cooked and stored away the meat. We made blood soup and gave a hand's length of sausage to each child who came to our tent. I thought, "We have so much food to eat now that those children who come to us for help surely won't die."

That evening Wugpa came by.

"Brother Japey, Jigjap and his friends are going to Chumarleb tonight to steal some horse feed from the army. Are you coming?" he asked.

"Maybe," Japey said, "but do you really think we'll find anything worth stealing? You don't need to go."

"I'll go. I don't have to steal anything with you—I can keep a lookout from a distance." They agreed that I could join them, and we set off. It was cloudy and pitch-dark. You could hardly see your hand in front of your face. When we got to the barracks in Chumarleb, we saw that the guards had flashlights, which they were shining to and fro all around the camp.

"Maybe we shouldn't do this," I said. "If the guards see us, they'll shoot."

"Yes, let's just go home," said Jabey. We turned back and were not far from our encampment when we heard gunshots from behind us, "Pag-shar! Pag-shar!" We turned and saw a mass of soldiers run out of the barracks, waving flashlights. The soldiers fired a few shots over our heads, but we didn't think they could have been shooting at us because it was pretty dark and far for them to have spotted us. We ran back to our tent as quickly as we could. It had begun to sleet while we were on our way back, so when we got to the tent, our clothes were sopping. We made a fire and sat down to eat.

"We came really close to getting in trouble tonight," said Wugpa.

"And the others were already stealing the horse feed when we got there," Jabey informed us.

That night it snowed heavily. At dawn, I left our tent. There were many soldiers walking around the tents, accompanied by Tserang Dorje and Chuga. I went back to our tent and told Jabey.

"They must be looking for the thieves," he said. "They'll see their footprints in the snow."

"Are our footprints still there?" I asked.

"No, they aren't," he said. "When we got to our tent, it was just sleeting. It only started to snow later." We made tea and sat inside drinking it. Tserang Dorje came to the doorway of our tent with a soldier.

"Hey, Jabey, did you two go out last night?" he asked.

"No," I spoke up, "we went to bed very early yesterday." They walked away. Later Wugpa came to our tent.

"Hello, you two. Two children in group two have been taken away by soldiers. Also, I heard Jigjab was shot and had to have his leg cut off, and one of his friends was killed by the army." I thought, "Three Precious Jewels! We almost got ourselves killed for a few beans last night."

"How did they know to arrest those two?" I asked.

"There were footprints in the snow because they got back after midnight when it was already snowing, so the soldiers just followed the prints to their tent and arrested them."

A few minutes later everyone was called to the kitchen door. Chuga was there with some soldiers, and he made a speech.

"Yesterday evening some children from group two went to steal bullets and guns and other items from the army barracks in Chumarleb. Two children have been arrested, another was killed last night, and one was badly wounded. The soldiers have released the two they arrested, because they are so young. But no child is allowed to go to Chumarleb!" We went back to our tent.

"They sure said some frightening things, didn't they?" said Wugpa when we got back. "Do you think those boys really intended to steal guns? I thought they were just going to get horse feed and beans."

"No. Those guards shot them just for trying to steal beans," said Japey. We ate some pika dumplings and some droma with dripping fat.

"Brother Japey," said Wugpa. "compared with our tent, every day in yours is New Year's Day—it really is! You have so many things to eat here."

"We still have dried meat from that yak we killed, and dried sheep meat, too. And we have droma and bone tea, lots of dried pika meat, cheese that Chuga gave us, and tsampa from Aunt Wuglo. It wouldn't last us for a year, but we won't die of hunger for a few months yet," I told him.

"We've had nothing to eat for a few days now," Wugpa told us. Japey gave him some dried yak meat and six or seven dried pika carcasses. "Thank you so much, my dear, kind brothers!" he said and went back to his tent.

"They have many mouths to feed over there—that won't last them more than a day or two," Jabey said.

It rained for the rest of the day, so I stayed inside. Later, I heard the sound of a child crying. I went to the tent door and looked out. The river had been rising all day because of the rain, and two children had gotten trapped between the channels. I waded across the shallower channel and realized that I knew the children: Sanji and his sister. She was lying on the ground, so stiff with cold that she was unable even to speak. I put her on my back and held

Sanji's hand. We got across the river with no problem, but she was too heavy for me to carry up the steep bank.

"Go call Wuglo the cook," I told Sanji. He ran off and a few minutes later reappeared with Wuglo and Tserang Dorje. It was still raining, and they took the drenched girl into the kitchen and gave her hot tea to drink. When she had warmed up a little she began to shiver, and after that she could talk again.

"If Nulo hadn't been there today, you both would have died in the river. Why did you go wandering off in such bad weather?" Wuglo scolded them. I was just happy that they were safe.

74

A Life-or-Death Decision. Meeting a Friend from Our Native Land.

One day I went to the kitchen for fire to light our stove, and Tserang Dorje and Wuglo were there.

"Starting tomorrow afternoon, all the children will have tsampa to eat, enough for all three groups, so I won't have to worry anymore," Tserang Dorje said. I returned to our tent and told Jabey. We were delighted, and that night I could barely sleep because of my excitement. I thought, "Everyone is going to survive! The suffering is over, and those children that made it this far are going to live."

The next morning it was snowing really hard. I made tea and swept snow away from our tent entrance. Wuglo gave me another tiny bowl of tsampa to reward me for helping Sanji and his sister the day before. I went home and cooked tsampa soup with pika meat, but I kept going outside to look around, thinking, "Is it true what they said about all that tsampa arriving today?" I could barely sit in my tent for a moment without jumping up and sticking my head out of the entrance to check. At noon a drum began to beat, and the announcement came, "Everyone to the kitchen!" Jabey and I went over carrying our bowls. The teachers were all there already, and the children were sitting in three circles, waiting to be given their share. Group two's teacher, Dogmed, brought out a medium-sized tub of tsampa with a small scoop.

"From now on, all fifty-three students in the three groups will have lunch here together. Anyone who does not come when they hear the drum won't get any food. Do you understand?"

"We understand, sir!" all the children shouted very loudly, and Dogmed started giving out tsampa. Each child got one scoop, although there was some unhappy muttering from the students because he shook the scoop each time to make the tsampa level, instead of heaped up into a mound. I thought there was no reason for him to level off the tsampa like that, but still: since the famine began, this was the first time we had been served tsampa, and each student got a whole scoopful. Most of the children fell asleep when they were finished eating.

"That makes sense," said Tserang Dorje. "They've been hungry for a long time."

I thought, "Three Precious Jewels! I hope no famine like this ever afflicts human beings again. It wasn't even half a year, just two or three months, and so many old people and children died in that short time.[2] Out of more than a thousand children and six hundred old people only fifty-three children and ten old people were left. Some of the children had been taken away by their relatives, but even a herd of livestock abandoned on a mountain will hardly suffer this much attrition. Now the dead had finished their dying, and it was useless to keep thinking about the manner of their deaths. They had no one to feed them before they died, no one to comfort them at the time of their deaths, no one to take care of their bodies after they died. What evil had they done in their previous lives to merit this? We must surely feel compassion for the elderly people whose end brought to a close the joys and sorrows of their lives, because it is clear their hearts were not at peace when their deaths came. But especially pity the innocent children. Their time in this world was short, and their lives were blighted by the arrest of all their parents and relatives, which they could not even understand. They had been sent to this place without parents or caregivers, to die an agonizing death from starvation. These misfortunes befell them for no reason." I always remembered what Tserang Dorje had said once in the kitchen, "The children in the 'Joyful Home' and the old people in the 'Old People's Home' have started to die. We can't eat the grass on the mountain, and we can't eat the stones in the river. We are in despair. It is better to die of starvation than to be as helpless as we are." I thought that he was right.

After that, the tsampa became more plentiful every day. Now each child was receiving half a bowl each. Ten days after these new supplies had arrived, the children were eating lunch when Chuga and Tserang Dorje came over.

"Thanks to Chairman Mao Zedong, we will have rice soup to drink, starting tomorrow," Tserang Dorje announced. Everyone clapped happily.

"Yes, Golok boys, the famine is over," Chuga told us. "You survived, so you

2. Estimates of total deaths among the Tibetan population resulting directly from the PLA invasion vary between 5 and 10 percent, roughly equivalent to the estimates for civilian casualties resulting from Hitler's invasion of the Soviet Union in 1941 and far higher, even at the lowest estimate, than losses resulting from the Japanese invasion of China.

will get to experience the happy times that are going to start now!" I looked at the beaming faces of our teachers Daglo and Tserang Dorje. I felt joyful, and I believed it: "Yes, this famine is really over."

The following morning the sun was shining, and many people were waiting at the entrance to the kitchen for their share of rice soup. I stood around too, and before long Wugpa arrived.

"Hello, my boy! So there really is cooked rice today," he said. When I got into the kitchen, it was filled with a delicious smell, but the big copper pot on the fireplace was making a noise sort of like "Wak! Wak!" I went back and told Jabey.

"Wait a bit longer," he said. "It's not ready to drink yet." We sat in our tent drinking tea and eating dry yak meat, and we gave tsampa tea and pika meat to the children waiting at the door. After that, I went to fetch water from the river. Down at the water there were two women driving six pack yaks, and behind them walked a young man, wearing a red sash knotted level with the seat of his trousers and carrying a gun fitted with an antelope-horn rest.

"Hi, boy! Where are you from?" he asked as he came level with me, although he didn't stop walking.

"I'm from group one tent," I reported.

"Is there anyone called Jabey or Nulo in your group tent?" he asked. I didn't reply but thought, "Who is this person? He knows our names." He asked again, "Is there a Jabey or a Nulo in your tents?"

"Why are you asking about them?" I questioned. He kept going, but then he called back, If you see them, tell them that Dongtrug, Kelsang, and the others are looking for them." When I heard those words "Dongtrug and Kelsang," I felt as happy as if I had met my own father! This man had to be one of my companions' friends.

"I'm Nulo," I said quickly. "Jabey's on the bank." The man stopped walking.

"What did you say your name is?"

"I'm Nulo. Jabey's up on the bank."

"Hey, girls. Bring those yaks over here." He jumped out of the riverbed and onto the bank. "Are you really Nulo?" he pressed.

"Yes, it's really me. Dongtrug, Tsekho, and Kelsang are three of our companions." He was very happy to hear this.

"My name is Lodru Rabten," he said. "Dongtrug, Tsekho, and Kelsang are working on the government grazing commune with us. Are you two well?"

"We're fine," I told him. "We're coming to see them! I'll just go get my brother." I ran up the bank.

When I got back to the tent and told Jabey, he was beside himself with excitement at the news.

"Let's go right now," he said. "We can put everything we need in our robes."

We ran out of our tent carrying our robes and bowls. I called to the children who waited at our door and told them they could have all the food in our tent, and if any of them wanted to sleep there, they were welcome. I saw Wuglo at the kitchen door.

"Aunt Wuglo, please tell our teacher that we are leaving because our companions came to pick us up," I told her.

"But you can't leave before you have drunk your rice soup," she said. "No thanks!" I told her.

"We wish you a long life, you two," said the children standing around. Calls of "Brother Nulo, have a long life!" rang in my ears until we were a long way off. When we got to the river, Lodru Rabten sat us behind the pack yaks' baggage, and we headed off in the direction of the government grazing commune.

75

Avoiding a Painful Death. Setting Off on the Road to Happiness.

We got to the commune that afternoon and visited the kitchen first for a meal. There was a cook there who they said used to be a monk. He was from the Khangsar chiefdom, and they called him the "monk-cook."

"These two shouldn't eat too much yet because they've been hungry for a long time. The food might kill them," he told Lodru Rabten. Outside in the livestock pen there were a lot of people who stared at us as we arrived.

"Their faces don't look as though they suffered that much," a man called Shagdor said.

"How lovely that these two young ones survived," said a woman named Zhimnog.

"People from Golok don't die as easily as the ones from around here," a woman called Zhirga said. I could tell by looking at their hats and robes that those people were all from Golok. Suddenly Kelsang and Tsekho rushed into the tent, flung their arms around our necks, and burst into tears.

"You two! You are still alive! That's fantastic!" they yelled. During and after dinner that evening, Jabey and I told the complete story of our life in the "Joyful Home" to Kelsang, Tsekho, and all the other people at the commune. The next day Dongtrug arrived, carrying a gun, and more tears of happiness fell.

"We were released from prison before Chinese New Year," he said, "and sent as a group to this grazing commune. We asked about you, but they wouldn't tell us anything about your whereabouts. Nor were we told whether

The author and his brother in Chinese clothing at their first government school.
Courtesy of the C. V. Starr East Asian Library, Columbia University in the City of New York.

the older ones were dead or alive or still in prison." Dongtrug was the government grazing land's messenger, so he was allowed to carry a gun. Kelsang and Tsekho were the commune's shepherds, and they told us that they had been the shepherds on duty on the day we stole sheep.

Kelsang said, "I knew that the sheep stealers were probably from the 'Joyful Home' because I heard that many people there were starving. So, all I told the yak drover who joined us was that we had been robbed by thieves with weaponry."

Three days later, Jabey, Kelsang, and Tsekho went off to herd sheep, and I stayed to herd calves for the Golok women—Zhirga, Zhimnog, and Kunzom—who were responsible for the milking yaks. Those three women looked after me and loved me as if I were their child. I called Zhirga and Zhimnog "Aunt," but I often called Kunzom "Mother" because she held me in her arms at night. Shagdor also called me his own son, helped me mend my clothes, and gave me a shirt. I will never forget the kindness and generosity of those Golok men and women until the day I die. And they made me very happy when they told me that after I had grown up, they would help me go to my native land. "Three Precious Jewels!" I thought. "How different this is from the 'Joyful Home.' And there are just a few people but a great deal of livestock, so we are definitely not going to die of starvation."

One day an old man named Wutse from the Nyamtso chiefdom asked me to help him make a fire down by the river. I blew the sparks into flames and helped him build a good fire for cooking. He boiled the meat in a pot, ate some himself, then gave me a little.

"Go on, eat some," he said.

"What kind of meat is this?" I asked.

"Why do you need to ask questions about the meat?" he burst out. "If you don't eat it, I will beat the shit out of you." After that I did eat a little, but that evening the "monk-cook" scolded Wutse.

"You don't ever get any smarter, do you? Even if you insist on eating marmot, why force the boy to eat it?" said the monk-cook.

"You devil marmot-eater! How could you make my son eat marmot? You want to make a dead body of him, don't you?" Aunt Zhirga snapped at him.

"It's fine, really it is," I intervened. "In the 'Joyful Home,' Japey and I ate every kind of meat except for human flesh. If it's meat, it can't be dirty."

"That's different," said the monk-cook. "Then you had to eat anything because you were starving, but now we have plentiful yak and sheep meat to eat, so there's no need to eat marmot."

One day Japey, Kelsang, and Tsekho came in from where they normally lived, in a camp far off on the sheep pastures. The leader of the commune, Cao Guo Yun, talked to them for a long time. Before they left that afternoon, they came to see me.

"We are going to school in Chumarleb tomorrow," said Japey. "Cao Guo Yun said that you are too young to go this year, but he will let you go next year." He passed along some other things I would need to know, and then the three of them left. That afternoon I went to see the monk-cook.

"I want to go to school with my brother. Please, could you help me tell Cao Guo Yun?" The monk-cook took me to Cao Guo Yun's place, and I asked him if I could go to school with Jabey.

"Only three can go this year," he said, "and you are too young, but I promise to let you go next year."

"Please, Cao Guo Yun, I really want to go to school with my brother. Let me go with him!" The monk-cook took my side, trying to persuade him. After a long time Cao Guo Yun had still not changed his mind.

"You really can't go yet. The other three are older than you, so they get priority. However, the next time I go to Chumarleb, I will talk to the school about this and ask permission to send you there at the end of the year." I was so relieved to hear that.

But after Jabey left, I no longer enjoyed life in the grassland commune. Every day I felt sadder and sadder. Ten days later, when Jabey and Kelsang came back to visit, they gave me some candy.

"We have leave for one day," Kelsang said, "and then we have to return to school."

"I'll come back to see you in another ten days," Jabey promised. Then I was left alone. I was absolutely sure that I could not survive that day, so I went to see Cao Guo Yun again.

"I really have to go to school," I insisted.

"The school has agreed that you can start in a few days' time," he told me. I was ecstatic and ran off to tell the monk-cook, Shagdor, Kunzom, and anyone else I could find!

"Of course, you should go to school," said the monk-cook. "If you know how to read and write a little, it will help you a lot in the future." Whenever people were talking to me, I thought about school—I longed day and night to go there. I kept remembering Cao Guo Yun's words: "I will send you to school in a few days' time." I was so excited that I couldn't sleep at night. When I did, I often dreamed that I had already arrived at the school, and I waited for that moment every day.

One day I was herding the calves down by the river when the monk-cook called me back to the kitchen door. When I got there, Cao Guo Yun and the cook were sitting, waiting for me.

"Nulo, you are going to school today. Is that all right?" Cao Guo Yun told me. I was elated.

"Yes!" I cried. "Thank you so much, Cao Guo Yun!" Then he gave me some adult boots to wear, and the monk-cook helped me tie up the laces. They helped me take off my robe and gave me a new blue shirt with a Chinese padded coat and a red cloth belt to wear over the top of it. Then they looked at me and laughed.

"Thank you very much, Cao Guo Yun," said the monk-cook. "This is a strange combination of clothes, but at least they are warm. So that's fine!" Then Cao Guo Yun lifted me onto his horse, and we set off for Chumarleb.

When we got to the gate of the school, Jabey and a mass of other students gathered around us. A teacher called Li Tseten came out, and Cao Guo Yun handed me over to him. Then he rode away. The date, they told me, was the thirtieth of December 1959, and from that day on I was a student at Chumarleb County School. They told me there were about one hundred students in the school. Our dormitory was an earth-walled building. "The Three Precious

Jewels bear witness!" I thought. "This is a very nice school." The teachers Li Tseten and Tso De cared for us like parents, and I had friends who were like brothers and sisters: Shuglo, Drodur, Ragkho, Tsega, Ragle, Ago, Kunsang, Deyang, Delo, and others. "Can this last?" I wondered. "When we first got to the 'Joyful Home' it was just as good as this, but within six months we had almost died of starvation. Will it change? Maybe because we are in a town, and not in the wilderness, we won't die of hunger. Whatever the Three Precious Jewels decide depends upon our karma. Can it really be true that we are on the road of happiness now? If so, it is all the more tragic for those children that died of starvation and have not been able to witness these joyful days with their own eyes. If my father could only see Jabey and me enjoying such happiness, he would be content.

Now we have grown up and are able to practice our religion and dedicate prayers to him. We are also certain that we will have the chance to return to our native land, and all our relatives will greet us.

"How wonderful that the Naktsang boys have returned to their native land alive," they will say. My dearest hope is that this day will come.

APPENDIX

Guide to Abridgment and Chapter Changes from Original

Prelude—from chapter 58 in original
  Amdo Tibetan publication
Chapter 1—from chapters 1 and 2
Chapter 2—from chapters 3 and 4
Chapter 3—from chapters 5 and 6
Chapter 4—from chapter 7
Chapter 5—from chapters 8 and 9
Chapter 6—from chapter 10
Chapter 7—from chapters 11 and 12
Original chapter 13 omitted entirely
Chapter 8—from chapters 14 and 15
Chapter 9—from chapter 16
Chapter 10—from chapter 17
Chapter 11—from parts of chapters 18
  and 19
Chapter 12—from chapter 20
Chapter 13—from chapters 21 and 22
Original chapter 23 omitted entirely
Chapter 14—from chapter 24
Chapter 15—from chapter 25
Chapter 16—from chapter 26
Original chapter 27 omitted entirely
Chapter 17—from chapter 28
Original chapter 29 omitted entirely
Chapter 18—from chapter 30
Chapter 19—from chapter 31
Chapter 20—from chapter 32
Chapter 21—from chapter 33

Chapter 22—from chapter 34
Chapter 23—from chapter 35
Chapter 24—from chapter 36
Chapter 25—from chapter 37
Chapter 26—from chapter 38
Chapter 27—from chapter 39
Chapter 28—from chapter 40
Chapter 29—from chapter 41
Chapter 30—from chapter 42
Chapter 31—from chapter 43
Chapter 32—from chapter 44
Chapter 33—from chapter 45
Chapter 34—from chapter 46
Chapter 35—from chapter 47
Chapter 36—from chapter 48
Chapter 37—from chapter 49
Chapter 38—from chapter 50
Chapter 39—from chapter 51
Chapter 40—from chapter 52
Chapter 41—from chapter 53
Chapter 42—from chapter 54
Chapter 43—from chapter 55
Chapter 44—from chapter 56
Chapter 45—from chapter 57
Chapter 46—from chapter 59
Chapter 47—from chapter 60
Chapter 48—from chapter 61
Chapter 49—from chapter 62

GLOSSARY

NOTE: WILEY ROMANIZED TIBETAN IN PARENTHESES.

Achong (*a skyung*). Chiefdom on the Yellow River, west of the author's home.

Akhu (*a khu*). Lit. "Uncle." Informal way of addressing a monk.

Alak (*a lags*). One of the principal reincarnated lamas of a monastery.

Amchod (*a mchod*). Wandering monk. A performer of Tantric ceremonies and exorcisms.

Amnye Machen Pomra (*a myes rma chen spom ra*). Sacred mountain in Amdo, permanently glaciated.

Ani (*a ne*). Informal way of addressing a nun.

Argali. Wild sheep.

Atarwatar (*a thar ba thar*). Dish made from placenta.

Bardo (*bar do*). Intermediate state. In Tibetan Buddhism, a period of limbo between the death and reincarnation of the consciousness.

Barkhor (*bar bskor*). Circumambulation route around Jokhang Temple in Lhasa. Central district of Lhasa surrounding the Jokhang Temple.

Chabri (*chab ril*). Wooden stiffener attached to a monk's skirt covered by a square cloth.

Chage (*khya dge*). Monk of Chugama Monastery.

Chaggor (*lcags skor*). Metal mace attached to a rope used as a weapon.

Chagpori (*lcags po ri*). Mountain in Lhasa opposite the Potala palace.

Changchub (*byang chub*). Future Buddha or bodhisattva.

Changtang (*byang thang*). Dry, desert wilderness in northern Tibet.

Chenrezig (*spyan ras gzigs*). Bodhisattva Avalokiteshvara.

Chodpa (*cho dpa*). Wandering monk. A performer of Tantric ceremonies and spells, including exorcisms.

Chokho Chugama (*khyo kho chu kha ma*). Chiefdom neighboring the author's home.

Chongjid (*chung skyid*). Author's childhood playmate.

Chorten (*mchod brtan*). Stupa.

Chujid (*chos skyid*). Author's father's former fiancée.

Chulong (*chos long*). Valley near the author's home.

Chumarleb (*chu dmar leb*). County in Qinghai Province.

Chumar Ratsang (*chu dmar ra tshang*). Chiefdom in which the "Joyful Home" was situated.

Chunnor (*chos nor*). Elderly man in the "Joyful Home."

Chura (*chos ra*). Debating courtyard in a monastery. The "dharma grove" in the monastery where monks studying theology meet to debate.

Dadar (*mda' dar*). Ceremonial wooden arrow decorated with colored strips of silk used by lamas to bestow blessings on pilgrims.

Damchoktse (*dam cog rtse*). Mountain near Lhasa.

Damzhung (*thang gzhung*). Valley near Lhasa.

Danba Tserang (*bstan pa tshe ring*). Fellow prisoner in Chumar town.

Darkha (*dar kha*). White scarf for religious offerings.

Dashel (*da shel*). Traditional Tibetan medicinal pill.

Datsen (*mda' tshan*). Mongolian chiefdom near the author's home.

Dewa (*sde ba*). Generic name for a settlement or village adjacent to a monastery.

Dewachen (*bde ba chen*). Heaven of Buddha Amitabha.

Dharma (*chos*). The teaching of the Buddha.

Do (*dos*). Place in a tent where family goods such as rice, butter, flour, and barley are stored.

Dobdob (*rdob rdob*). Ordained monastic security guards armed with staves; guardians of temples.

Dodtsang (*stod tshang*). Clan in Wujud chiefdom.

Dolen (*do len*). Inlaid hilt of a dagger, sometimes containing precious stones.

Dongtrug (*dung phrug*). Author's traveling companion on final journey.

Dongtse (*dung tse*). Tibetan coin.

Dorba (*rdor pa*). Author's playmate.

Dragpa, Akhu (*grags pa a khu*). Monk of Madey Chugama Monastery.

Drak, Alak (*brag a lags*). Senior monk of Chugama Monastery.

Drepung (*bras spungs*). Large monastery near Lhasa.

Dri (*dri*). Yak-cow hybrid.

Drichu (*dri chu*). Yangtze River. Drichu seven fords is the principal crossing point on the pilgrimage route from the east of the Tibetan plateau to Lhasa.

Drolma (*sgrol ma*). Goddess and common female name.

Droma (*gro ma*). Wild miniature sweet potatoes or potentilla bulbs.

Dromda (*brong mda'*). District of Amdo.

Drukmo (*brug mo*). Gesar's wife, a character in the Gesar epic.

Dukhar (*gdugs dkar*). Name of a bandit who attacked the author's caravan on the way to Lhasa.

Dungya kyi (*dung gyas 'khyil*). Right-turning conch shell, one of the "eight auspicious symbols" found in Buddhist, Jain, and Hindu religious cultures. Used as a wind instrument, its sound calls believers to awake and follow their religious vocation.

Durkho (*dur kho*). Author's father.

Dzachuka (*rdza chu kha*). District of Amdo to the south of the author's home.

Dzagpa (*rtsag pa*). Goatskin or sheepskin robe.

Dzamira (*rdza mi ra*). Chiefdom led by a reincarnated monk.

Dzi (*gzi*). Black and white striped or "shining" stone, made from agate, worn by Tibetans as an ornament and believed to possess protective powers, possibly related to the tradition of the "evil eye."

Dzo (*dzo*). Hybrid of yak and cattle.

Dzorge (*mdzo dge*). District to the southeast of the author's home.

Ganden (*dga' ldan*). Lit. "Heaven," a Buddhist paradise. A large monastery near Lhasa.

Ganden, Alak (*dga' ldan a lags*). Senior monk of Labrang Monastery, to which the author's family owes allegiance.

Gandenpa (*dga' ldan pa*). Reincarnated lama of Chugama Monastery.

Ganden Wula (*dga' ldan dbu bla*). Senior monk, leading lama, and throne-holder of his monastery, imprisoned with the author and beaten to death.

Ganlho (*kan lho*). Prefecture in southwest Gansu Province.

Geba Chusem (*ke 'ba' chos sems*). Friend of the author's father, met on the way to Lhasa.

Gelug Buddhism (*dge lugs*). One of the schools of Tibetan Buddhism, often described as "Yellow Hats."

Gendun (*dge 'dun*). Friend of the author's.

Geshe (*dge bshes*). Highest academic degree obtainable in a Gelug (Yellow Hat) monastery. *See* Yeshe.

Getag (*dge bkra*). Author's childhood playmate.

Gochen (*rko chen*). Clan of the author's chiefdom.

Gojara (*go khya ra*). Clan of the author's chiefdom.

Go La (*sgo la*). Mountain pass near Lhasa.

Golog/Golok (*mgo log*). Former tribal confederation; now a prefecture in Qinghai Province.

Gologpa (*mgo log pa*). Inhabitants of Golog.

Golog Wyiga (*mgo log sbas dga'*). Guide on journey to Lhasa.

Gongjo (*kong jo*). Chinese wife of King Songtsen Gampo.

Gonpo Tashi (*mgon po bkra shis*). Author's name at birth.

Gotsa (*mgo tsha*). Clan of the author's chiefdom.

Gungtang, Alak (*gung thang a lags*). Senior monk of Labrang Monastery. Senior monk of Madey Chugama Monastery.

Gungtang Denpi Wangchuk (*gung thang bstan pa'i dbang phug*). Senior monk of Labrang Monastery.

Gungtang Jamyang (*gung thang jam dbyangs*). Renowned lama in Labrang Monastery.

Gunne (*kun ne*). Author's childhood playmate.

Gusha (*ku sha*). Grass used in Buddhist ceremonies and in India generally for sacred rites.

Gyantse (*rgyal rtse*). Town near Lhasa.

Hepori (*he po ri*). Sacred mountain near Lhasa.

Hera (*he ra*). Felt robe.

Hordug Laglo (*hor sdug lag lo*). Friend of the author's father in Wujud chiefdom.

Horgurkar (*hor gur dkar*). Gurkar, king of Hor, a character in the Gesar epic; his family is featured in the Tibetan "King Gesar" epic poem—reputedly the world's longest—and, like Nulo's, suffered terrible hardships.

Jabey (*jam pe*). Author's brother.

Jachen Sumdo (*skya chen sum mdo*). Junction of three roads on the caravan route to Lhasa.

Jachur (*jas chur*). Sour cheese.

Jakho (*rgya khor*). Author's uncle. A monk at Chugama Monastery.

Jalwa Rinpoche (*rgyal ba rin po che*). Epithet of the Fourteenth Dalai Lama, Tenzin Gyatso.

Jalwa Tenzin Gyatso (*rgyal ba bstan 'dzin rgya mtsho*). Epithet of the Fourteenth Dalai Lama.

Jalwa Yibzhen Norbu (*rgyal ba yid bzhin nor bu*). Epithet of the Fourteenth Dalai Lama, Tenzin Gyatso.

Jampeyang (*jam pa'i dbyangs*). Bodhisattva Manjushri.

Jamyang Badma (*'jam dbyangs bad ma*). Author's brother.

Jamyang Shedpa (*jam dbyangs bzhad pa*). Senior monk of Labrang Monastery.

Jangjug (*jang 'jug*). Head of discipline at Chugama Monastery.

Jaring (*skya rengs*). Large lake in the eastern part of Golok.

Jazema (*rgya zi ma*). Needles.

Jazor (*rgya zor*). Hill above Chugama Monastery.

Jokhang (*jo khang*). Also Tsuglakhang. Large temple in the center of Lhasa, the central temple, or cathedral, of Lhasa and Tibet.

Jowo (Rinpoche) (*jo bo [rin po che]*). Large statue in Jokhang Temple.

Jowo Lokeshvara (*jo bo lo ki shwa ra*). Bodhisattva Avalokiteshvara.

Jowo Mikyodorje (*jo bo mi skyod rdo rje*). Jowo Akshobhya Buddha.

Jowo Yibzhen Norbu (*jo wo yid bzhin nor bu*). The Dalai Lama as an emanation, or avatar, of Avalokiteshvara.

Juchu (*rgyu chu*). Yangtze River (on the Tibetan plateau). *See* Drichu.

Julag (*rgyu lag*). Clan of the author's chiefdom.

Jyado (*brgya rdo*). Medicinal pill.

Kanjur (*bka' 'gyur*). Part of the Tibetan Buddhist canon of scriptures.

Karma Tashi (*skar ma bkra shis*). Government official in Chumarleb.

Kathang Dennga (*bKa'-thang sDe-lnga*). Sacred scripture particularly revered in the Nyingma school of Tibetan Buddhism. It contains a biography of the eighth-century Indian Buddhist missionary Padmasambhava, believed to have been written by one of his disciples, Namkhai Norbu.

Kelsang (*skal bzang*). One of the author's traveling companions.

Khamtsen (*khams tshan*). Organizational division of a monastery; a residential dormitory and study unit that contains monks from designated regions at different levels of study.

Khangen (*khang rgan*). Chiefdom near the author's home.

Khangsar (*khang gsar*). Chiefdom on the banks of the Yellow River in Amdo.

Khangtrul (*khang sbrul*). One of the author's traveling companions.

Kharri Dzagen (*mkhar ri rdza rgan*). Valley en route to Lhasa.

Kharri Ngulkar Drolma (*mkhar ri dngul dkar sgrol ma*). Mountain near the site of the author's father's death.

Khatag (*ka bdaks*). White scarf, traditionally made of silk, offered by Tibetan Buddhists to people, statues, and sacred sites as a sign of respect and good wishes.

Kherey Montsey (*khe re smon tshe*). Author's fellow prisoner.

Kochen (*rko chen*). Clan of the author's chiefdom.

Kora (*bskor ba*). Circumambulatory path around a monastery.

Kunchong (*kun chung*). Author's classmate at "Joyful Home."

Kunsang (*kun bzang*). Author's classmate.

Kyichu (*skyi chu*). River adjacent to Lhasa.

Kyiso (*kyi so*). Exclamation uttered in prayer analogous to alleluia in the Judeo-Christian traditions.

Labrang (*bla brang*). One of the largest monasteries of the Gelugpa order, on the extreme northeastern boundary of Tibet.

Lekho (*le kho*). Author's traveling companion.

Lhachen Dorje Yidra (*lha chen rdo rje yi sgra*). Mountain deity or god.

Lhade Karwo (*lha sde dkar bo*). Chiefdom to the north of the author's home.

Lhakhang (*lha khang*). Temple dedicated to local deities; lit. "God house."

Ling Gesar (*gling gi ge sar*). Legendary Tibetan king, subject of a long epic tale.

Lingkhor (*gling bskor*). Circumambulatory path around the Potala Palace in Lhasa, traditionally followed by pilgrims.

Lochu (*blo chos*). Author's traveling companion.

Logeshara, also Avalokitesvara or Chenrezig (*spyan ras gzigs*). Bodhisattva, or being, motivated by Buddhist beliefs, with the desire and supernatural ability to help others. The Dalai Lama is believed to be the incarnation of this Bodhisattva. The text uses a Tibetan approximation of the Sanskrit "Avalokiteshvara."

Losar (*lo gsar*). Tibetan New Year.

Lundrub (*klu sgrub*). Author's fellow prisoner.

Lungta (*rlung rta*). Sacred symbol in the form of a horse, also the small squares of paper printed with prayers and the image of a sacred horse, hence "lungta" or "wind horse."

Lutri Lumar (*lu khri lu dmar*). Area on the caravan route to Lhasa.

Machen Golu (*rma chen gos lu*). Mountain deity.

Machig Lhamo (*ma cig lha mo*). Deity.

Ma Chinese. Forces commanded by the Nationalist governor of Qinghai, Ma Bufang (1903–1975), who purported to exercise suzerainty over parts of Amdo.

Machu (*rma chu*). County in Gansu Province. Also Yellow River.

Madey Chugama (*rma sde chu kha ma*). Author's monastery and chiefdom.

Maitreya (*jam pa*). Buddha of the future.

Malon Me (*ma blon dme*). Neighboring chiefdom to Chugama, the lands of the chief, or king, of Ngawa, now Ngawa Prefecture, Sichuan Province.

Mani (abbreviation of om mani padme hum; mani stones) (*ma ni*). Prayer believed to be supremely efficacious and said to have been introduced by the eighth-century Buddhist missionary Padmasambhava (Guru Rinpoche). Can be found in prayer wheels, carved into stones, and painted.

Manrang, Akhu (*sman ring a khu*). Hermit who visited the author in infancy and attempted to heal him.

Markog (*mar lkog*). Container made from the stomach of a yak or sheep into which butter is packed and sewn tightly for storage or transport.

Medzagad (*me rdza dag*). Kind of firework, part of the Tibetan New Year celebrations held in Lhasa until the end of the government of the Dalai Lama, that was displayed in front of large crowds.

Memgon (*dme mgon*). Family related to the author.

Merab (*dme rab*). Author's childhood playmate.

Meshel Gejo (*rma shes dge rgyos*). Author's mother's clan.

Meshel Wachen (*dme shul sba chen*). Author's mother's chiefdom.

Monlam (*smon lam*). Author's traveling companion.

Motsa (*mo tsa*). Gun purchased by the author's father in Lhasa.

Nagchu (*nag chu*). District and river to the north of Lhasa on the caravan route.

Nagchu Shabten (*nag chu zhabs brten*). Monastery to the north of Lhasa.

Nagdeb (*nag rde*). Author's pet lamb.

Naktam (*a myes nags rtam*). Author's grandfather.

Naktsang Dradel (*nags tshang dgra 'dul*). Author's uncle.

Naktsang Durkho (*nags tshang 'dul kho*). Author's father.

Naktsang Nulo (*nags tshang nus blo*). Author.

Naktsang Tamkho (*nags tshang rtam kho*). Author's aunt.

Nangchen (*nang chen*). Senior monk's personal attendants and quarters. Also chiefdom in Kham (now Qinghai Province).

Nechung (*gnas chung*). Monastery in Lhasa; home of Tibetan national oracle.

Ngamri Chongshog Gomgo (*ngam r'i khyong shog rgo 'go*). Mountain near site of the author's father's death.

Ngawa (*rnga ba*). Prefecture in Amdo (now Sichuan Province).

Ngoden (*bsngo rten*). Offering dedicated to the dead.

Ngoring (*sngo ring*). Lake in Golok en route to Lhasa.

Ngulra Lharde (*dngos rwa lha sde*). Chiefdom near the author's home.

Norbu (*nor bu*). Government official in Chumarleb.

Norbulingka (*nor bu gling kha*). Summer residence of the dalai lamas.

Norbu Sangpo (*nor bu bzang po*). Legendary merchant.

Norjab (*nor skyabs*). Author's uncle.

Norta (*nor bkras*). Author's uncle.

Nuden Lobsang (*nus ldan blo bzang*). Epithet of the author.

Nukho (*nus kho*). Author's nickname.

Nyenchen Tanglha (*gnyan chen thang lha*). Mountain range near Lhasa.

Nyingma (*rnying ma*). Oldest school of Tibetan Buddhism.

Om mani padme hum (*om ma ni padme hum*). Tibetan mantra or prayer.

Orjen (*o rgyan*). Bandit from Nyamtso near Lhasa.

Panchen Lama (*pan chen bla ma*). Senior Tibetan lama of the Gelugpa (Yellow) school.

Phayul (*pha yul*). Native land; lit. "father home."

Phurbu (*phur ma*). Acquaintance from the author's journey to Lhasa.

Pika. Small "rock rabbits" the size of a large mouse.

Potala (*po ta la*). Dalai Lama's palace in Lhasa.

Powa (*'pho ba*). Empowerment. Tantric religious ceremony believed to confer supernatural benefits on the participants.

Prayer wheel (*mani korlo*). Handheld spinning cylinder containing prayers that are rendered efficacious with each turn.

Rabden (*rab brtan*). Worker on grazing commune.

Rabshung (*rab byung*). Cycle of sixty years in Tibetan calendar, used to describe years.

Rabten (*ra bstan*). One of the author's cousins and a childhood friend.

Ragkho (*rag kho*). Author's classmate in Chumarleb.

Ragle (*rag le*). Author's classmate in Chumarleb.

Ragshe Jadog (*rag shis ja thog*). Monk murdered by mob on journey to Chumarleb prison.

Ramda (*ra mda'*). Posse; pursuit by a group of mounted armed men.

Ramoche (*ra mo che*). Temple in Lhasa.

Ratsang (*ra tshang*). Site of "Joyful Home."

Rigdron (*ri sgron*). Author's aunt.

Rinchen Taso (*rin chen rta so*). Friend of the author's father.

Rine (*ri ne*). Author's nanny during Lhasa pilgrimage.

Rinpoche (*rin po che*). Senior lama.

Rose Apple Tree (*Jambudvipa*). One of the three continents that constitute the Earth according to Indian and Buddhist cosmology; named after the tree under which the Buddha first experienced meditative bliss.

Samsara. Buddhist term for the cycle of existence of which all sentient beings are a part.

Samten Gangsang (*bsam gtan khangs bzang*). Sacred mountain near Lhasa.

Samye (*bsam yas*). Monastery near Lhasa.

Sangha (*dge dun*). Community of Buddhist monks and nuns.

Segoyur (*sha mgo gyur*). Bearded vulture. Its solitary nature augurs family separation in Amdo folk culture.

Sept. In English, a subdivision of a clan, often used as a surname in Amdo. Tibetan *ris*.

Sera (*se ra*). Large monastery in Lhasa.

Seri Shetang Shamo (*ser ri bye thang khra mo*). Plain in front of Sera Monastery.

Seryim (*ser yim*). Solemn Buddhist oath referring to a revered scripture; lit. "by the Golden Prajnaparamita."

Sewo Jyachen Sumdo (*se bos sky chen sum mdo*). Ford across the Yangtze River on the caravan route to Lhasa.

Shagdor (*phyag rdor*). Resident of grazing commune.

Shegzod Migmar (*phyag mdzod mig dmar*). Chieftain of Wujud.

Sherab (*she rab*). Lama of Chugama Monastery.

Sho (*zho*). Tibetan coin in circulation in Lhasa.

Shotse (*zho tshe*). Tibetan coin in circulation in Lhasa.

Shugjid (*phyug skyid*). Childhood friend of the author's.

Shuglo (*phyug lo*). Author's classmate in Chumarleb.

Silema (*gsi lu ma*). Dancer at "Joyful Home."

Sogpo (*sog po*). Mongolian-inhabited area in Amdo adjacent to the Yellow River, abutting the chiefdom of Madey Chugama to the north.

Sonam Norbu (*bsod nams nor bu*). Prison guard in Chumarleb.

Songtsen Gampo (*srong btsan sgam po*). Tibetan king in seventh century CE.

Sukhavati. One of the Buddhist heavens. This one is believed to be the realm of the Buddha Amitabha.

Tabzhi Lhamo (*grwa bzhi lha mo*). Hill in Lhasa.

Tagmar Sele Godtsang (*brag dmar se le rgod tshang*). Monastery near Lhasa.

Tagrang, Alak (*stag ring a lags*). Senior monk of Chugama Monastery.

Tamdrin (*rta mdrin*). Wrathful horse-headed deity; Hayagriva.

Tamkho (*rtam kho*). Author's aunt.

Tashi Chulong (*bkra shis chos gling*). Alternative name for Chugama Monastery.

Tashilhunpo (*bkra shis lhun po*). Major Gelugpa (Yellow Hat) monastery in central Tibet.

Tawo Drala Tagtse (*skra bo'i dgra bla stag rtse*). Mountain on caravan route to Lhasa.

Tedarlung (*khri dar lung*). Consecrated medicinal pill.

Tenjur (*bstan 'gyur*). Part of the Tibetan Buddhist canon containing commentaries.

Thubjam (*thub rgyam*). Monk murdered by a mob after imprisonment.

Tin Garu (*sprin sga ri*). Cloud in the shape of a saddle, believed to be a bad omen.

Togmed (*thogs med*). Monk of Chugama Monastery.

Tolag (*tho log*). Former clan of Chugama chiefdom.

Torma (*tor ma*). Ritual offering made of *tsampa* and butter and shaped into sculptural or abstract form.

Tsagdom (*tsag sdom*). Freezing fog and wind.

Tsampa (*rtsam pa*). Flour made from ground roasted barley to which tea, sugar, butter, and cheese are added.

Tsang (*gtsang*). Region in Central Tibet centered on Zhigatse.

Tsangchu (*gtsang chu*). Tibetan river that becomes the Brahmaputra in India.

Tsechu (*tshe chos*). Monk from Chugama Monastery.

Tsejab (*tshe skyabs*). Classmate from "Joyful Home."

Tsekho (*tshe kho*). Author's aunt. His cousin and traveling companion has the same name.

Tse Lhamo (*tshe lha mo*). Dancer from "Joyful home."

Tsenkhang (*btsan khang*). Inner chapel in a temple or assembly hall.

Tsepel (*tshe dpal*). Childhood friend of author.

Tserang Dorje (*tshe ring rdo rje*). Teacher at "Joyful Home."

Tserangjid (*tshe ring skyid*). Author's mother.

Tsode (*tsho 'du*). Author's uncle in Ngawa.

Tsojid (*mtsho skyid*). Mother of author's childhood friend Gunne.

Tsolo (*mtsho lo*). Author's grandmother.

Tsongkhapa (*rje rin po che*). 1357–1419. Theologian, reformer, and founder of the Gelug (Yellow Hat) monastic order, whose leader is the Dalai Lama.

Tsongonbo (*mtso sngon po*). Qinghai lake, Lake Kokonor.

Tsu (*tsu*). Hezuo in Chinese, a town in the south of Gansu Province.

Tsuglakhang (*gtsug-lag-khang*). Also Jokhang. Large temple in the center of Lhasa; the central temple, or cathedral, of Lhasa and Tibet.

Tugpatso (*thug pa mtsho*). Author's childhood friend.

Tulku (*sprul sku*). Reincarnate lama.

Ü (*sbus*). Traditional Tibetan name for the province of central Tibet surrounding Lhasa, and the first area to be ruled by the administration of the Dalai Lamas.

Wannor Kunchong (*ban nor kun chung*). Author's classmate at "Joyful Home."

Wargen (*bar dgan*). Clan of Chugama chiefdom.

Warzhi (*bar zhi*). Clan of Chugama chiefdom.

Wasang (*pa sang*). Head of discipline of Chugama Monastery.

Wayin (*wa ban*). Amdo chiefdom.

Wuchen Dokha (*bo'u chen rdo kha*). Wall of carved mani stones on the caravan route to Lhasa.

Wuglo (*sbug lo*). Author's classmate at "Joyful Home."

Wugpa (*pug pa*). Author's classmate at "Joyful Home."

Wujud (*bu rgyud*). Chiefdom near Chugama.

Wum chu (*bum chu*). Water over which ten thousand prayers have been recited.

Yama. God of death and ruler of the hell realms in Hindu, Buddhist, and Jain mythology.

Yarlung Tsangpo (*yar klung gtsang bo*). River in central Tibet.

Yeshe (*dge bshes*). Title awarded by a monastery to a monk after successful completion of a prolonged period of religious study.

Yu Droma (*gyu sgron ma*). Dancer at "Joyful Home."

Zambuling (*dzam sbus gling*); Jambudvīpa in Sanskrit. The southernmost of the three continents that constitute the Earth according to traditional Buddhist and Indian cosmology.

Zanto (*zan do*). Soup given to pilgrims by monks.

Zhimnog (*zhes mnog*). Resident of grassland commune.

Zhirga (*zhes dga'*). Resident of grassland commune.

Zi (*gzi*). Black and white agate stone worn by Tibetans as an ornament and believed to provide protection to the wearer.

Zodpa (*bzod pa*). Chugama Monastery's water carrier.

INDEX

CPI Antony Rowe
Eastbourne, UK
October 08, 2014